The Herzl of Jewish Christianity

JOSEPH RABINOWITZ AND THE MESSIANIC MOVEMENT

KAI KJÆR-HANSEN

The Handsel Press Ltd
Edinburgh

Wm. B. Eerdmans Publishing Co.
Grand Rapids, Michigan

Originally published 1988 as
Josef Rabinowitsch og den messianske bevægelse
by Forlaget Okay-Bog, Århus, Denmark
Translated from the Danish by David Stoner
Additions to the revised Danish version translated by Birger Petterson

This edition published jointly 1995 by
The Handsel Press Ltd
The Stables, Carberry, EH21 8PY, Scotland,
and in the United States by
Wm. B. Eerdmans Publishing Co.
255 Jefferson Ave. S.E., Grand Rapids, Michigan 49503

British Library Cataloguing in Publication Data

A catalogue record for this publication is available from the British Library

ISBN 1 871828 37 6

Library of Congress Cataloging-in-Publication Data

Kjær-Hansen, Kai.
[Josef Rabinowitsch og den messianske bevægelse. English]
Joseph Rabinowitz and the Messianic movement; the Herzl of Jewish Christianity /
Kai Kjær-Hansen; [translated by Birger Petterson].
p.   cm.
Includes bibliographical references and index.
ISBN 0-8028-0859-X (pbk.)
1. Rabinowitz, Joseph, 1837-1899. 2. Converts from Judaism — Biography.
3. Jewish Christians — Moldava — Chisinau — History. 4. Missions to Jews —
History — 19th century. 5. Chisinau — Religion — 19th century.
I. Title.
BV2623.R33K53   1995
289.9 — dc20
[B]   94-40086
CIP

Typeset in 10.5 point Garamond

Printed in the United States of America

Joseph Rabinowitz on The Mount of Olives (see pages 19-20)

Fig 1

Fig 2

Fig 3

Fig 4

Fig 5

*Pages 39-40 have a detailed description
of the portraits of Joseph Rabinowitz*

*The interior and the exterior of Somerville Memorial Hall, which in 1890
became the place of worship for the Israelites of the New Covenant.
See the description on pages 143-149*

Samuel Wilkinson's drawing of Rabinowitz's tomb (see page 202)

Rachel Rabinowitz (Mrs Kinna) with her son (left), Mrs Rabinowitz (centre), and Sara Rabinowitz (right) outside their home in 1911 (see pages 207 and 211)

Nils Rosef, the Secretary of the Norwegian Israel Mission, visited Kishinev in 1935 and paid a visit to Joseph Rabinowitz's tomb (see page 228)

CONTENTS

Financial support for the research of this work was given by the Otto v. Harling-Stiftung, Germany. The English version has been published with support from participants in a seminar on Jewish evangelism in the summer of 1992, with Harvest Time Ministries, in Japan

INTRODUCTION

This book is about Joseph Rabinowitz, a Russian Jew, who in 1882 travelled to Palestine to look into the possibility of a Jewish settlement there. But he returned to Russia with a new-found faith: that Jesus was the Jews' brother and Messiah.

During the last fifteen years of the 19th century, Rabinowitz and the Messianic movement which he came to head became known to all who were then concerned with the topic of Jesus and Israel. Since his death in 1899 interest in him has waned in some of the circles which formerly backed him. Yet he has never been completely forgotten. He is usually included in accounts of recent Hebrew Christianity. But the portrayals of him are very sketchy. Nor are they particularly critical or independent.

But this "Herzl of Jewish Christianity", as he has been called,[1] still repays acquaintance. For the questions he struggled with as a Jew and a believer in Jesus have not yet found their ultimate solution. Today Jesus-believing Jews, whether they call themselves Hebrew Christians, Jewish believers or Messianic Jews, are wrestling with corresponding problems.[2] Some of these issues, which are of vital importance for the (small) portion of Israel which today believes in Jesus as the Messiah, may be defined by a historical account of Rabinowitz. The struggle for Rabinowitz, as it was fought in Gentile Christian circles, also has a message in a modern context. Provided, of course, that one is prepared to learn from history. An encounter with Rabinowitz sheds light upon some of the problems about which the early 'Christians' had to make up their minds. They were Jews. Jesus was too.

I have not attempted to trim the picture of Rabinowitz in such a way that one particular group of those who today are concerned with the question of Jesus and Israel might be better able to 'use' him than other groups. All in all, there is hardly anyone today who would be able to identify with everything that Rabinowitz stood for. Obviously, on a number of points he was conditioned by his time and place. In particular, the political circumstances to which he had to submit prevented his activities from developing as he wished. But it is fascinating to study his struggle for an independent Hebrew Christian congregation. In any case, his main views are challenging; to them we can relate.

This account is based on an independent study of the source material. I have tried to present it in a way that would not cause the ordinary reader any great difficulty. And for the sake of such readers I have not adopted a strictly chronological approach. This has entailed some repetitions and overlapping, which I hope will not prove irritating, but they make it easier to absorb the subject matter. The general reader may unhesitatingly omit the footnotes. In them there are only references to written sources for the benefit of those who may wish to make a detailed study or do further work on the topic. At the back of the book is a list of the complete names of some of the organizations which are mentioned. There, too, is an explanation why two dates are sometimes given for the same day.

In 1888 Rabinowitz said of himself: "I have two subjects with which I am absorbed - the one, the Lord Jesus Christ, and the other, Israel."[3]

When visiting London in 1889 he elaborated upon this view of his own position. He used a parable or illustration, something which Jews are less reluctant to do than the rest of us. And Rabinowitz was no exception. He said:

My position is to be compared with one who went out to the ocean in a ship and suffered shipwreck with all on board. Now all of those who are shipwrecked try to get some firm ground on which to save themselves. If one, after struggling for life, finds the rock, the moment he feels firm ground, being on the rock, he strives to shout to those still struggling in the sea. And if some are beyond the reach of his voice he will try to raise something - a stick or flag - to attract their attention and induce them to make for the rock.

Now that is my position. Russia is like the ocean, the Jews there are like shipwrecked people, and since, by God's mercy, my feet are on the Rock (which is Jesus) I have tried to do what that one I have spoken of tried to do; I am shouting and signalling to my shipwrecked people to flee to the Rock.[4]

How Rabinowitz himself reached the "rock", and how he "signalled" to his fellow Jews, will be main themes of this book. And to remain with the metaphor: it may also be of interest to clarify how Gentile Christian spectators joined in this "rescue action". Since it is now just a century ago that the Messianic movement was known by everyone concerned with the subject of Jesus and Israel, the time seems to be ripe for an exhaustive treatment of "the Herzl of Jewish Christianity", this interesting Jewish believer in Jesus, who also launched the expression "our brother Jesus".

Kai Kjær-Hansen   February 1994

Chapter 1

SOMETHING QUITE PHENOMENAL

A journey to Palestine made in 1882 was to become a turning-point for the Russian Jew Joseph Rabinowitz. When he returned to his home town of Kishinev, the capital of the province of Bessarabia in south-western Russia, he was a new man. At least, that is how he described it later.[1] On the Mount of Olives in Jerusalem he had made his matchless discovery: Jesus was Israel's king and Messiah, he was the brother of the Jews and thus the answer to the "Jewish question". Western observers paid particular heed to the expression "our brother Jesus" after Rabinowitz's first public stand as a Jewish believer in Jesus.[2] By W. Faber, the renowned German Professor Franz Delitzsch's collaborator, it was regarded as a "brilliant" expression.[3] More or less fairly it was taken by others to be the motto or watchword of the movement which Rabinowitz came to lead.[4]

Rabinowitz and his Christianity movement - or better the Messianic movement - rapidly attracted great attention. The Russian authorities were obliged to reach a decision about the movement, because of the applications they received from Rabinowitz. The Jewish press reacted caustically to his 'apostasy' and regarded him as a lunatic or a fool. But within the European missions to Israel of the time there was no lack of Christians who hailed him with high expectations. Great too were the quantities of words which were spent upon him and his movement in the various journals and periodicals of the missions to Israel. And knowledge of Rabinowitz and the Messianic movement spread rapidly.

Great expectations

Indicative of many people's expectation of the Messianic movement are the words of the Danish vicar of Finnerup, F. Gredsted in 1886: "The whole south Russian Christianity movement represents something quite phenomenal and deserves to be widely known."[5]

Later in 1886, A.S. Poulsen, the chairman of the Danish Israel Mission 1890-1921, published a booklet about the new movement. This maintained that it remained hidden in the counsels of God whether the movement would "bring about Israel's conversion as a people and thus become of world historical significance" or whether it would have only a passing effect, so that its significance would not go beyond being "a presage, a harbinger of what some time is to occur, according to the indubitable testimony of revelation".[6] According to A.S. Poulsen, it was certain that the movement was a "sign in church history" which had already had far-reaching effects: "about that there can be no controversy". In a lecture in 1888, A.S. Poulsen asserted that the goal at which Rabinowitz was aiming "is so consonant with the prophetic testimony of the Bible, and the way to it which he wishes to follow is so irreproachable that he ought to be able to count upon the love and prayers of all who share with him something of Paul's love for the nation of Israel."[7]

In January 1885 the magazine of the Norwegian Israel Mission wrote: "Throughout Christendom, wherever the cause of Israel is a heartfelt concern, our eyes have now been turning toward this remarkable movement. It evokes memories of the days of the early church."[8]

Such expressions were also used by, and largely inspired by, Franz Delitzsch, professor of Old Testament at Leipzig. He was the chairman of Der evangelisch-lutherische Centralverein für die Mission unter Israel (the Evangelical Lutheran Central Agency for Witness and Service to Jews and Christians) and also chairman of the Institutum Judaicum in Leipzig, a renowned training centre for the staff of missions to Israel. Not least, Delitzsch was noted for his translation of the New Testament into Hebrew in 1877. It would be no exaggeration to say that in the European Israel missions of the day Delitzsch was the figure who enjoyed the greatest international esteem.

In 1884, when Delitzsch published the first documents from the movement, he did indeed point out that his reason for doing so was their interest for ecclesiastical and religious history. He was placing them before his readers in an objective manner without critique and reflection, he said. As a scholar he took care to safeguard himself by claiming that he was quietly awaiting the development of the movement without pinning excessive hopes upon it. He added that the movement might have to pass through some fluctuations before it found its own level.[9]

But Delitzsch was too involved in mission to Israel for him to continue to view the movement with scholarly detachment. Other sources reveal that he quickly allowed himself to get involved. Even while continuing to safeguard himself and to enumerate points on which he disagreed, in 1885 he was looking upon Rabinowitz's works as documents of importance for church history. And not only that. The movement as such was a phenomenon of church history, a prelude to the conversion of all Israel, "a Pentecostal work of the Holy Spirit", at which he rejoiced. In Rabinowitz Delitzsch found a way of thought and a usage which had scarcely ever found expression on Jewish lips since sub-apostolic times. At Rabinowitz's home in Kishinev, a congregation had been formed, an "oasis" in which Jews professed Jesus as Messiah and loved his person. "The spring is here, the sun is breaking through, heaven is opening!" With these enthusiastic words Delitzsch concluded his address at the annual meeting on 2 June 1885. In it he had also asked the question whether Rabinowitz would prove equal to the task of being his nation's Reformer.[10]

In similar vein, Delitzsch does not stint his words in his foreword to Rabinowitz's autobiography: "Joseph Rabinowitz is a star in the firmament of his nation's history." And he adds: "May God preserve this star in his right course and in its right light."[11]

Delitzsch, who supported Rabinowitz until his death in 1890, merely posed the question whether Rabinowitz would prove equal to the task of being his nation's Reformer.[12] Others went further and presented Rabinowitz as actually being a Jewish Reformer.[13] The movement was described as "this Reformation" in for instance the Jewish Herald, the organ of the British Society.[14] The first documents were published in this paper under the heading "A Remarkable Christian Movement Among the Jews in South Russia". In a periodical published by another British missionary society, the Mildmay Mission, Rabinowitz was described as a "remarkable man who seems destined in God's providence to hold no unimportant part in the future of his nation.[15] A. Saphir, himself a Hebrew Christian and in England active from the outset in Rabinowitz's movement, described him as "a witness raised by God".[16] C.A. Schönberger, a missionary to the Jews in Vienna and one of Rabinowitz's spokesmen, said of him that he was "a chosen vessel, and powerful instrument in the hand of the Lord for the evangelization of the Jews of Russia".[17] In Basel, the clergyman F. Heman, who otherwise distanced himself from Rabinowitz on important points, said: "He is a preacher sent by God; it is said that since the time of the Apostle Paul, no one has understood how to preach so mightily to the Jewish people as Rabinowitz."[18] Samuel Wilkinson of the Mildmay Mission in 1897 compared Rabinowitz to the well-known revivalist preacher Spurgeon in his use of illustrations.[19]

The Swedish missionary to the Jews, P. Wolff, himself a Hebrew Christian, who knew Rabinowitz's work at first hand, wrote in 1896 from Kishinev: "Both the texts and the expressions in his preaching are unique, so anyone who has been a Christian from birth will find it hard to understand him. Even Swedish Jews will find it hard to understand him, but for Russian and Polish Jews he is a mighty preacher."[20] P. Gordon, also in Swedish ministry, wrote after meeting Rabinowitz in 1897 that he "appears to me to be an apostolic personality".[21] Already in December 1885 Dr Althausen wrote from St Petersburg something similar to Delitzsch: "In Rabinowitz the Lord has sent us an Apostle Paul and a Jewish Luther..."[22]

A. Venetianer, a Hungarian Hebrew Christian, who eagerly took Rabinowitz's side, was unstinting in his praise. In 1888 he wrote: "Rabinowitz is not a pastor! He is a Paul to us, first and foremost to the Jews, but also - we shall undoubtedly come to see - to the Greeks."[23] When A.J. Gordon, an

American clergyman, met Rabinowitz in America in 1893, he came to think of Isaiah or another of the prophets of the old covenant.[24]

And so we could go on quoting great words about Rabinowitz and the south Russian Messianic movement. Some would say that the words are too great and exaggerated, and in the fate of the movement after Rabinowitz's death in 1899 they will see confirmation of this. But this handful of great words will give an indication that Gredsted's characterization of the movement as "something quite phenomenal" accorded well with many people's perception of it.

Rabinowitz himself expressed his awareness of the importance of the ministry in which he was engaged (see the Introduction above).[25] But he refused to be called "teacher" and "Reformer".[26] In 1888 Rabinowitz had indeed been attacked for desiring to be a Reformer.[27] But G.A. Krüger, who made the movement known to French readers, rightly stressed that Rabinowitz did not give himself this title.[28] Rabinowitz was fond of designating himself the "brother" of the Jews.[29] To him, the true plight of Israel was that the Jews did not know Jesus as their brother and did not recognize him as their Messiah. It was therefore his main task to be a preacher to them.[30] This was clear right from his first public appearance, but because it later turned out that he was not given permission by the authorities to form an actual congregation, Rabinowitz the preacher did not find a competitor in Rabinowitz the pastor. W. Faber, Delitzsch's right-hand man particularly in this matter, in a report of 1895 directly cited his belief that more Jews had been influenced through Rabinowitz's preaching than through any other Hebrew Christian in the world.[31]

From his first public appearance until his death, Rabinowitz maintained the hope that other Jews along with him and through his proclamation might recognize Jesus as the Messiah without thereby giving up their Jewish identity.

In 1887 he is reported to have related the following at a meeting in London:

> There are many Christian ministers and others who do not believe in the conversion of the Jew. They think him so dead that he cannot be made to live again. This is a terrible mistake, which may be illustrated by the story of *A Soldier who was Written Down as Dead*.
>
> During the Russo-Turkish war, after one battle, two companies of soldiers went to pick up the wounded and the dead. In one place they picked up one hundred and fifty, and the serjeant wrote down, one hundred and fifty dead. The order was given that a grave should be dug, and the one hundred and fifty soldiers buried in it. Whilst they were putting in the dead bodies, it was found, that one was alive. He called out, "Have pity on me. I am not dead, I am alive." The serjeant

replied, "I am very sorry, I should like to save you, but, I have entered you on the the dead list, and you must be buried.

Even so is it with many theologians in their treatment of the Jews. They say, "The Jew is dead, he will never come back to his God or his land, and therefore he must be buried." In their sense of the term the Jew is not dead, he is still alive; and when he is quickened spiritually by Christ, he will impart the highest life to the dead world.[32]

Rabinowitz stubbornly fought for the idea that a Jew who comes to faith in Jesus as Messiah does not need to give up his Jewish identity. How this came about is a story in itself. But first some remarks must be made about the quantities of words that were spent upon Rabinowitz and his movement.

Great quantities of words

Much material about and by Rabinowitz was channelled through the then existing journals of the missions to Israel in the various countries. Some people held the view that too much was being written. Thus de le Roi wrote in his major work on evangelical Christendom and the Jews: "About Rabinowitz and his ministry really much has been written, indeed to the harm of the movement too much."[33] Lhotzky, Delitzsch's former private secretary who in 1885 was sent to Kishinev and later kept up some contact with Rabinowitz, viewed the same matter from a financial perspective. Writing in his memoirs of 1904 on the subject of what was being written and printed in the missionary magazines by those who visited Rabinowitz, Lhotzky sarcastically commented: "Thus they blighted all that might at least have grown well in silence. Oh, those wretched mission reports..." and further: "Mission needs reports and money. Anyone who does not write reports cannot gather in money; anyone who does not gather in money cannot carry on mission. One may work in mission without spirit, but not without money."[34]

Lhotzky's remarks on the relationship between mission reports and money are delightfully provocative and in themselves worth reflecting upon. All the same, in this context they are overstated and highly tendentious. For Lhotzky is trying to cast the missionary societies - particularly the British ones - as the villains. But Rabinowitz did not fight shy of these societies or of the public's approbation of his person and work. On the contrary, it may be said that he sought this to enable him to realize his vision. Whether his links with the foreign missionary societies and the financial support he received from them damaged his movement is another matter. It will be discussed later (see Chapter 13).

But it is a grave distortion for Lhotzky to insinuate that Rabinowitz thought that too much attention was paid to his work in foreign periodicals. Actually, Lhotzky had written reports himself.[35] In a letter of 1885 he promised to fight for the movement.[36] He regarded the stirring in Kishinev as a "sign of the time".[37]

Our information about the main thrust of Rabinowitz's conception of faith comes partly from the theological documents which rapidly appeared and were translated into European languages, and partly from sermons, tracts, and booklets, which were also translated into European languages, even though primarily intended for a Jewish readership. Little exists in the way of articles especially intended for Gentile Christian readers. In 1896 Rabinowitz promised the Mildmay Mission that he would "occasionally" send reports of the Lord's work in Russia to that organisation's magazine, but not much came of this.[38] Nor was it his habit, as was then quite common, to recount in detail the conversion stories of those who came to him for help. A few times, though, he did make exceptions from this rule.[39]

An important source is the material which was drawn up and published by those who, for various reasons, visited Rabinowitz in Kishinev. But he was known not least through his more or less private letters, in which he described his work. For to a great extent his letters were published in the missionary magazines. This correspondence forms important source material for posterity. Even though some facts were naturally reserved for the leaders of these organisations, one is surprised by the kind of personal matters and thoughts which were sometimes made available in this way to a wider circle of readers. Not all delicate and caustic comments were censored.

But without the contemporary missionary magazines containing Rabinowitz's letters it would not be possible for us to give such a detailed picture of him and his activity as we now can. We may feel frustrated that, for instance, the archives of the Institutum Judaicum in Leipzig were lost during the Second World War. To a large extent the original correspondence that was in the possession of the British missionary societies must probably be regarded as lost. Yet there is some material in the archives of the Church's Ministry among the Jews (earlier the London Society) in the Bodleian Library, Oxford. But I shall not rule out the possibility that somewhere a dusty pile of letters from Rabinowitz or something similar may be lurking. It has sometimes been a handicap that I have had to make do with secondary translations without being able to collate them with the Hebrew originals. Fortunately, the first documents from the movement, for instance, do exist in Hebrew. The same is the case with some sermons etc.

Despite persistent efforts, I have not succeeded in laying hands on some few sermons and booklets. In such cases, too, I have had to make do with translations or the mere awareness of the existence of certain works. I have seen the most important material in Hebrew in the Jewish press in Russia. But I gave up in advance the idea of reading Russian newspaper material in the original language. When such are quoted, this is done on the basis of contemporary translations and the selection that was made then. The great interest in Rabinowitz gives a reasonable guarantee that the most important newspaper material in Russian by and about Rabinowitz was translated. Yet there is undoubtedly in the Russian material some information that might shed further light upon not unimportant details. A forthcoming book by John D. Klier will deal with a number of articles from the Russian press (see the end of Chapter 8 below).

Nor have I succeeded in finding a complete set of the annual reports which from 1888 were issued about the work of the movement by the London Council for Rabinowitz. But excerpts from these were reproduced in various periodicals.[40]

Thus there is some quantity of material that has been lost, or which I have been unable to trace. But it is not lack of material that has prevented any major account of Rabinowitz's life and work from appearing hitherto. There is in fact a large amount of material, so that it has been necessary to be quite selective, which I had not envisaged when I began the work.

In our century Rabinowitz has been included in any book dealing with 'famous' Hebrew Christians of the 19th century. I. Fauerholdt is probably the most recent to have published a small booklet which deals solely with Rabinowitz. That was in 1914. The modern - brief - accounts are comparatively stereotyped and uncritical. Many are content to transcribe common sources without going to the primary sources. The highly uncritical use of sources in D.A. Rausch's book on Messianic Judaism of 1982 is remarkable, for it is a treatise in which a different approach might have been expected.[41] In general many people have been very sparing with the questions they have asked. In this account an attempt has been made to make up somewhat for this deficiency.

At the beginning of the twentieth century some attempts were indeed made to demolish certain over-simplifications: some people tried to put paid to the pious picture of Rabinowitz which had become more or less fixed at his death in 1899. But the use which, for instance, the German H. Lhotzky made of Rabinowitz in his memoirs in 1904 and which was repeated by the Danish missionary to the Jews S. Volf in 1906 must, viewed from a sober historical angle, be described as misuse of his name.[42] This, among other things, will be demonstrated in the following pages. But in any case these attempts have not affected the pious picture of Rabinowitz that has been portrayed in modern accounts of 'famous' Hebrew Christians. On the other side there are in these accounts some distortions due to abundant source material being left out of account.

Also the Jewish portrayals are relatively stereotyped and only to a slight degree are they based on Rabinowitz's own writings. This is the case with e.g. Sh.L. Tsitron (Yiddish and Hebrew 1923),[43] Zalman Rejzen (Yiddish 1929)[44] and Saul M. Ginsburg (Yiddish 1946).[45] As will be demonstrated below, the result is a very defective presentation when the description of Rabinowitz's faith is based solely on the so-called *Thirteen Theses*, which is what these three authors do. For they leave out - or do not know - the existence of the most important material about Rabinowitz's faith formulated by himself. In his work from 1987 Steven J. Zipperstein includes more sources than the writers mentioned above although sources important for the understanding of Rabinowitz's view of the faith have also escaped his notice. Zipperstein only uses an abridged version of Rabinowitz's Autobiography.[46] Some inaccuracies in his presentation of certain historical details could have been avoided if he had used the unabridged version. A critical examination of Zipperstein's use of the sources which have been at his disposal shows that some of the conclusions he arrives at concerning essential issues have no support in the source material. This is a shame since Zipperstein's contribution is one of the first - if not the first scholarly contribution - which, from a Jewish point of view, tries to see Rabinowitz in his historical context. In summary, Zipperstein writes about Rabinowitz:

> Rabinovich did not merely remain attached to things Jewish after his discovery of Jesus; paradoxically, he arrived at his own conclusions about the nature of Jewish salvation for peculiarly Jewish reasons and out of an overriding sense of commitment to his people and their destiny. Personal ambition, greed, and thwarted desires may very well have influenced him, but probably not much more than such factors influenced his more respectable contemporaries. To acknowledge that he occupies a place in Jewish cultural history, however minor, perhaps raises methodological questions as to the boundaries of Jewish historical research. To place Rabinovich outside these boundaries, however, is both unrealistic and unnecessarily vindictive.[47]

Whatever one may think of missionary reports, and sometimes they should be taken with a grain of salt, these reports are not "wretched" when a picture is to be drawn of Rabinowitz and the reactions of his contemporaries to his movement. On the contrary, through the mission magazines a rich source material has been preserved by and about Rabinowitz. Like everything else, they are not beyond all criticism or interpretation. Compared with the Hebrew originals, the translation of the correspondence is indeed only a second best. But when the best has been lost, we must rejoice that the second best has been preserved, and that in abundance.

Not only do there exist many words about and by Rabinowitz in the mission periodicals of the time. But information about him and the Messianic movement was also disseminated with enormous speed through these channels, among others.

Knowledge spread with great speed

Even though they may not always say so directly, some accounts give the impression that Rabinowitz publicly proclaimed his new faith in Jesus immediately after his return home from Palestine in 1882. This impression will be queried in the following chapters. He did not immediately speak out in public, but doubtless allowed something of his new conviction to filter out. As we shall see, it was not until the end of 1883 that he made contact with R. Faltin, the Lutheran clergyman in Kishinev. But then the debate was immediately triggered off in Jewish periodicals and Russian newspapers. In March 1884 a conference was held in Kishinev with the participation of Delitzsch's close collaborator W. Faber and representatives of the British Society. In the early summer of 1884 the first documents were published in German by Delitzsch; in the autumn of 1884 they began to appear in English. Particularly an article in The Times on 23 August 1884 contributed to Rabinowitz's name becoming known outside the circles of missions to Israel. The topic was dealt with in The Jewish Chronicle (e.g. 12 September, 28 November 1884 and 22 May 1885). At the beginning of 1885 Delitzsch published more documents about the movement. By that time Rabinowitz had conducted his first worship, and his name and activity were being made known, particularly in the periodicals of Israel missions. In English, James Adler published a book about Rabinowitz at the end of 1884 (The First-ripe Fig). It contained some of the material Delitzsch had published. In 1885 a new impression came out with a different title and accompanied by John Wilkinson's interview with Rabinowitz in Germany in 1885. In the same year G.A. Krüger issued a book in French with similar material that Delitzsch had published. In 1886 a book came out in Danish about Rabinowitz. Much else could be mentioned.

The rapidity with which the new reports were printed is shown by the following example: On 10 January 1885 R. Faltin, the Lutheran clergyman in Kishinev, wrote a letter to F. Delitzsch in Leipzig. Delitzsch at once forwarded it to the Norwegian Israel Mission among others. It was translated and printed in the Norwegian mission magazine - in the January issue![48] Much else might be cited, but there is no need to go into detail here. The material we shall be dealing with will make it plain that knowledge of the movement was disseminated extremely swiftly. But, be it noticed, not until after Rabinowitz had taken his public stand. In this connection it would be difficult to overestimate Delitzsch's involvement in the matter. Even though Rabinowitz was given the greatest financial support by English and Scottish mission supporters, he had Delitzsch to thank for the great attention which was given to him and his movement so quickly after its appearance. In his large biography of Delitzsch, S. Wagner treats the relationship between Delitzsch and Rabinowitz in an extremely brief and uncomprehending way.

Wagner underplays Delitzsch's enthusiasm for Rabinowitz by merely mentioning that Rabinowitz and his movement far from always met with Delitzsch's approval, whereas Faltin's work was constantly supported (see also the end of Chapter 10).[49]

In February 1885 The Jewish Herald could claim without exaggeration that the movement in Bessarabia "has been noticed by the Press throughout the world" and it was added that "before us [we have] English, German, French, Italian, American magazines, secular and religious, Jewish and Christian, for and against, but all more or less interested in it..."[50]

The story of Rabinowitz's conversion in the Holy Land was good copy and was retold again and again. It will be recounted here once more, but this time accompanied by some questions and observations which were previously skated over, either because they were felt to be uninteresting, or because no time was taken even to just leaf through the sources.

Chapter 2

THE JOURNEY TO THE HOLY LAND IN 1882

In the late 19th century conversion stories were popular reading-matter in the journals of the missions to Israel. They were not always marked by restraint. At a conference in 1895 Professor H.L. Strack felt it necessary to point out that conversion stories ought to keep to the absolute historical truth![1] The story of Rabinowitz's conversion was one of the more popular ones that were told and retold. It contained within it the ingredients for an edifying narrative. But it was vexing to discover that there were gaps in the story which Rabinowitz had intentionally left blank. For instance, there was some obscurity surrounding his thoughts about and attitude to Christianity before his conversion. Nor had it ever been made quite clear what happened to him on the Mount of Olives.

For lack of a better term, we here apply the word conversion to what happened to Rabinowitz on his journey to Palestine in 1882. This was the word used by his contemporaries. It is appropriate, in that his life was given a new turn. The content of his new faith in Jesus was not, however, settled once for all, as some later descriptions might mislead us into thinking. Firstly and supremely, his conversion did not mean that he ceased to regard himself as a Jew. Nor was his conversion of such a character that he took the very first conceivable opportunity to trumpet it abroad publicly; on the contrary, it would seem that he gave himself time for a closer study of the New Testament and for a period testified of his new faith only to a restricted group, before taking a public stand.

That aspect of the matter as well as other historical questions were of no particular interest to those who found the edifying story sufficient in itself. It is also difficult to avoid the conclusion that he did sometimes express himself in a way that suggested, or at least left the impression in people's minds, that he returned from Jerusalem to Kishinev with a clear idea of his new faith and his new task. In a letter of September 1884 he does, however, make it clear that he reached greater clarity after his journey.

> ... since my feet have trodden the holy city of Jerusalem, and I beheld the place where they pierced Him [Jesus], the Lord has opened my eyes to see in the Law, the Prophets, and the Psalms, concerning the salvation; and I have tasted a little of the secret ... which is still, to the great sorrow of my heart, hidden from the most of our Jewish brethren till now.[2]

But almost a decade later, in 1893, he wrote about the same journey:

> This journey became the means of my own salvation; there on the
> Mount of Olives I found him of whom Moses and the prophets wrote,
> Jesus the Messiah; I found true rest for my soul. On my return from
> Jerusalem to Russia I was a new man; instead of travelling as one sent
> by the Jews, I came as one sent back to them, sent by Jesus Messiah
> to witness to great and small about him, the crucified and risen one,
> our true Messiah.[3]

In 1896 he said in Scotland:

> ... and it was as I stood upon the Mount of Olives that the Prince of
> Life, the Lord Jesus Christ, revealed Himself to me as the Messiah of
> God, and when I descended the Mount I felt that my soul was restored
> to life, and I was brought to acknowledge that I had a living God, a
> living Book, and a living nation. Since then I have had the deep
> conviction that God is not the God of the dead, but of the living, "for
> all live unto Him" (Luke xx.38). I returned home to Russia a new
> creature. I began to testify of what I had found to my brethren and
> neighbours in the hope that they also might obtain the life that I had
> obtained. At that time I had no idea of what was going on in the
> Churches of Christ. I did not feel the need, therefore, of any
> instruction from them, for I had my instruction from the Chief
> Rabbi, Jesus Christ Himself. I looked however, upon the Churches
> with friendly respect, as a little child sometimes calls every acquaint-
> ance Uncle. But when I saw so many uncles, I felt that what I needed
> was brethren rather than uncles - for as I grew in knowledge of the
> Lord Jesus, I yearned not so much for the patronage of uncles as for
> the sympathy, and love of brethren especially as my own brethren,
> according to the flesh, had forsaken me and cast me out.[4]

It would be unfair to require Rabinowitz to include every detail when
describing his conversion. Nonetheless it may well be argued that, in the two
last quotations particularly, the course of events is compressed and simplified
considerably. The reality was more complicated than these quotations
would immediately suggest. Not necessarily in opposition to the edifying
picture which has been drawn earlier, we shall now put in a few lines and
touches to make the portrayal of Rabinowitz and his conversion slightly less
romantic. We must hope that it can be done without making the picture of
his conversion any less revolutionary. It is difficult to describe exactly what
happened on the Mount of Olives; this is bound up with the fact that it was
not a mathematical formula which dawned upon Rabinowitz. But that
something happened which, other things being equal, must be regarded as
the decisive turning-point for "the Herzl of Jewish Christianity" is beyond

dispute. But the pace of it all was not nearly so rapid as is usually suggested. A look at some details may shed fresh light on the matter.

When he left home

In more than one sense the atmosphere was tense for Russian Jews at the start of the 1880s. On 2 March 1881 the Czar Alexander II was murdered; under his successor, Alexander III, there was a tougher line towards the Jews.[5] From 15 April 1881 and, with brief respites, until the end of April 1882, a series of pogroms swept through south-west Russia. On 20 April 1881 Kishinev too was the scene of such a pogrom (the Russian word for persecution of Jews). From this pogrom in Kishinev there are no reports of anyone being murdered, as there were later, in 1903 (see Chapter 19).[6] The pogroms at the beginning of the 1880s did not have the same episodic character as, for instance, those the Jews had undergone in Odessa in 1825, 1841, and 1871. With the 'provisional regime' or 'May laws' of 3 May 1882 the government put a temporary end to these pogroms. But the 'protection' brought about by this regime had to be paid for by the Jews: further restrictions were imposed upon them, e.g. they might not settle outside towns and villages - except on agricultural colonies. The size of villages was not defined precisely. They were also forbidden to carry on trade on Sundays and Christian festivals etc.[7]

So it was not surprising that Zionist ideas were given fresh impetus, particularly among young Jews. Groups of Zion-lovers (*Chovevei Zion*) had started up with the purpose of supporting an emigration to Palestine.[8] 1882 was later designated the year of the first *Aliya*, the first immigration to Israel. The first Jewish colony Rishon Lezion was formed in that year. It was also the year in which Leon Pinsker published in German his book *Autoemanzipation*. In it this Jew from Odessa made himself the spokesman of those known as territorialists. These considered that it did not matter where a Jewish state was set up, the important thing was for one to be formed. Later Pinsker favoured the idea of colonizing Palestine.[9] Instead of going to Palestine, others were looking to another 'promised' land, i.e. America. From 1 July 1881 to 30 June 1882 over 17,000 Russian Jews emigrated there.[10] Rabinowitz was later to speak his mind about the Jews' situation in America (see Chapter 14). Even before he left for Palestine he was opposed to this solution. It would be like a horse with a sore on its back running to get rid of flies swarming around the sore. It would merely take its troublesome enemies with it, to use Rabinowitz's own imagery.[11]

But the Palestine idea did appeal to him. He set off to see for himself and get an impression of whether emigration to Palestine might be the solution to the Jewish problem. Just when he began his journey and how long it lasted are questions that remain unanswered in the articles which recount Rabinowitz's conversion to Christian readers. According to Strack, Rabinowitz's application for permission to set up a Jewish agricultural colony in Bessarabia (see Chapter 3) was turned down on 6 March 1882, so the journey to Palestine must have begun after that date, and perhaps it was commenced during the persecutions, as some later sources indicate.[12] If so, it must have been before the end of April 1882. This fits in with Tsitron's piece of information that Rabinowitz set off immediately after Passover.[13] In 1882 Passover fell before the middle of April. A couple of letters which were formerly overlooked by Christian readers of the periodical Hamelitz, doubtless because in them there is no hint that Rabinowitz had become a Christian, give a pointer to the answer to these questions. For on May 6/18 1882 he sent from Constantinople a letter to the editor of Hamelitz.[14] [See "Technical Details" at the back for an explanation of dates.] This shows, for instance, that he had visited Rumanian towns, and he apologizes for not writing before. In other words, he must have been on his way for at least a couple of weeks. In the same letter he reports that he expects to obtain permission from the Turkish authorities to travel to Jaffa the same day, i.e. 18 May. He came back to Kishinev on 24 June/5 July.[15] Depending upon whether he was given an entry permit and left Constantinople on 18 May, he can scarcely have stayed in Palestine more than a month. According to Sh.L. Tsitron Rabinowitz did not stay more than two weeks.[16] It would not be a wild guess to assume that Rabinowitz left Kishinev in the second half of April 1882; it is also certain that he had returned from his journey by 5 July.

Another question is how official Rabinowitz's journey was. His words in 1893, referred to above, indicate that he had been sent by the Jews. According to an account of a speech he made in Leipzig in 1887, he was chosen by a commission to go to Palestine to investigate conditions on the spot.[17] Tsitron relates that a group of about twenty persons requested Rabinowitz to go.[18] Rabinowitz's travel report to Hamelitz, sent from Constantinople on May 6/18, tends to suggest that he was not merely travelling as a private person but as the representative of a group. Hamelitz uses the very word "delegate" in its Hebrew text.[19] It is the more surprising then that in his (presumably) last contribution to Hamelitz, written in Kishinev on 27 June/8 July 1882, he is at pains to play down, indeed denies, that he was a delegate of Israel's congregation in Kishinev; he was travelling as a private person in accord with the wish of a few closely related brethren.[20] It might be appropriate to cite the article in its entirety:

KISHINEV. JUNE 27. To the editor of Hamelitz, Mr. A. Zederbaum. On Thursday, the 24th, on my return home from my journeys to Jaffa and Jerusalem, tired out from the rigours of the journey, despondent at the sight of the critical situation facing my people, I became even more distraught when I read Hamelitz no. 22 in which there appeared your article "Mah Achartanu" [What Disturbs Us!]. I was surprised at you Erez [Zederbaum's nickname - meaning "cedar tree"] who has known me for many years - as you yourself acknowledged in Hamelitz no. 21. How have you changed so quickly and falsely suspect me, unjustly taking away from me your friendship which you have always shown to me since the time we knew each other. Just now, I am not able to repond to your article. But, God willing, after a little time to regain my strength and my composure from the rigours of the journey, I will open the bundle of writings in my travel case and will produce all the written evidence which I have to expose the plans of those opponents who are trapped in folly and envy. Further, when I stood in the Valley of Jehoshaphat opposite the Temple Mount, I made an oath to wage war against those writers who profit from the situation of our people - for their own pleasure and gain - and I am confident that God will help me to redeem my vow. And now, Erez, you have always known, right from the first day of our acquaintance, that I have never profited from my Hebrew writing, nor have I ever taken anything, God forbid, from the communal funds, nor have I acted disloyally to my people or trespassed against anything holy to it. Even now, I did not travel as a representative. My journeys, there and back, were carried out on my own private initiative, with the agreement of a few of my friends who consented to contribute towards the considerable expenses involved, since the project was of importance also to them. Heaven can testify that I spent out of my own pocket more than 300 roubles in the interests of Jewish settlement in Eretz Israel. I therefore consider it just and obligatory upon me to tell the wider community everything that I saw and heard. This without any favouritism or attempt to hide anything of the truth, since in such a holy matter every liar and cheat is a serious sinner. But alas! to whom can I turn today? Where is there another journal among all the rest like Hamelitz which, from the first day of its publication, was the only one which did not look for scandal, and was never afraid of wicked libel mongerers who defaced the seal of the Holy One which is Truth? Is it then possible that "the cedar" which is so strong and unafraid, can turn in its old age into a reed upon which one cannot lean? Or has my unfortunate lot turned your back against me? To whom can I now send all the information and important news which I have gathered in with great difficulty during all my travels? To whom can I now produce clear evidence that, either through the stupidity or even through the deliberate planning of some writers, nihilists and missionaries met in Jerusalem, and that the lawless and the non-believers have made a covenant between them to injure the Lord of Hosts and to "cut down the plants"? And now Erez, I completely

forgive you for the insult and the shame which you dealt to me in
Hamelitz. I have only one request: Honour the truth, as was your
wont, and give me a chance to publish my writing. Do not add or take
away anything, since I bear the responsibility for what I write. Also
let me know if you wish to publish in Hamelitz an account of the
burden of my journeys. JOSEPH RABINOVITCH, KISHINEV.[21]

Rabinowitz might have written about his 'conversion' in Jerusalem, but
does not. But he does give an impression of disappointment that the contents
of his letter sent from Constantinople on 6/18 May had been strongly
criticized in some subsequent issues of Hamelitz.[22] With the pessimistic view
of a Jewish exodus to Palestine which his journey had given him, it is
understandable that immediately after his homecoming he played down the
idea that he had been an official emissary. Whether his experience on the
Mount of Olives also played a part in this context is a question we may ask.
Not until after he had become known to the public for his new faith does he
own to what he was when he left, but which he played down on his return
from Palestine: a Zion-lover who had been sent out by some like-minded
people to investigate conditions in Palestine. Steven J. Zipperstein finds a
contradiction between what Rabinowitz later says about his transformation
in Palestine and the negative words about missionaries in the article cited
above.[23] However, it is not obvious what Rabinowitz is alluding to, for
which reason it seems wise not to build too much on it.

Not just while he was in Palestine, but already on his way there
Rabinowitz had run into some problems.

On the way to Palestine

Equipped with letters of recommendation to influential groups in Palestine,
Rabinowitz set out on his journey. First he went north and west to Bukovina
and Galicia, where he consulted with the emigration committees which had
been set up there. He also visited the famous wonder rabbi in Sadogora who
was, however, unable to support the project.[24]

Then he went on to Constantinople. He met there a group of Jews
who were on their way to Palestine; they were stranded there because the
Turkish authorities would not, according to Rabinowitz, give them entry
permits to Palestine. He also had to make up his mind about Laurence
Oliphant. This Zionist-minded Englishman, who in 1867 had given up his
seat in Parliament in order to study occult and other topics, had in 1879 made
himself spokesman for a Jewish settlement in Gilead. His interest in Zionism
was partly stimulated by his religious mysticism, partly by his wish to
improve economic and cultural conditions in the Turkish possessions in the
Middle East so as to secure peace in Europe. He had contact with Russian and

Rumanian *Chovevei Zion* groups and tried to influence the Sultan in Constantinople.[25]

Rabinowitz rapidly took stock of Oliphant. In his letter of 6/18 May he assailed him strongly and made clear in no uncertain terms that Oliphant did not enjoy the influence with the Sultan and his ministers that people imagined. Also, he had no money to help, either. The English *Bar Kochba* was a *Bar Koziba*: the son of a star was a son of a lie, he said. The Turkish government had blocked Jewish immigration to Eretz Israel. Rabinowitz felt that his message should reach the ears of anyone thinking of emigrating: it was not sufficient to consider that the land was rich; it ought also to be borne in mind that the country was closed by the Turkish government, which "holds in its hand the keys to the empty portals of Palestine".

Rabinowitz's onslaught upon Oliphant evoked consternation in Russian emigration circles. In several items in Hamelitz, Rabinowitz was criticized in a heated debate which went on while he himself was in Palestine.[26] On his return he could not conceal his disappointment that the editors had taken sides against him in this matter, as has been touched upon above.

When Rabinowitz's feet touched the soil of the Holy Land, he knew nothing of the debate which his travel letter had sparked off. Probably one day in the last third of the month of May in 1882 he arrived in Jaffa.

Encounter with Palestine

Even Jaffa, the Mediterranean port where he arrived and whose name in Hebrew means the beautiful, was a disappointment to Rabinowitz. The town did not live up to its name. On the contrary, it seemed to him one of the most squalid towns he had ever seen. Not much better was his meeting with an emigration committee who had filled the Jewish magazines with their 'advertisements'. It turned out - as Rabinowitz is reported to have related to some students in Leipzig in 1887 - that the committee consisted of only two men. In their work to get as many Jews as possible to Palestine he saw but an attempt to further their personal financial interests. He felt it to be humbug, he said.[27]

These first experiences were already persuading him that the problems of the Russian Jews could not be solved by emigration to Palestine. Nevertheless he continued his journey towards Jerusalem in order "to fulfill his commission anyway"; here he was accompanied by a secretary of the well-known Sir Moses Montefiore. In Jerusalem his first impressions of the Jews' squalid conditions in Palestine were only reinforced.

The Muslims, he said in 1887, showed the deepest contempt toward the Jews and oppressed them in every way. On Friday evening, at the commencement of the Sabbath, he found himself at the Wailing Wall, where the Jews were gathered for prayer. He witnessed that the Jews could not even weep at the Wailing Wall without being exposed to the jibes and harassments of the Muslims. Under such conditions Rabinowitz found it hard to imagine that the Jews could settle in Palestine in peace.

However, Rabinowitz's pessimistic conclusions about the immigration of Russian Jews to Palestine did not prevent many from settling there. Even the group which he had met in Constantinople in May reached Palestine in the autumn of 1882. Other Jews shared Rabinowitz's negative view of the matter at that juncture, without for that reason considering themselves bad Jews. Naturally, it is pointless to ask what significance it would have had for Judaism if Rabinowitz had settled in Palestine and worked there for the formation of a Hebrew Christian congregation. It was actually some poor Russian Jews, who came to Jerusalem in May 1882, who set on foot the formation of a Christian colony in Artuf, 18 miles south-west of Jerusalem, in 1883.[28] And in the mid 1890s Rabinowitz himself had ideas of transferring his work to Palestine (see Chapter 17).

Whether Rabinowitz was particularly unfortunate in the exceptionally poor representatives of the Jewish settlement policy he came across, or whether on an objective view his account is biased, is of little importance in this connection. It certainly lacked any subtle shades. But the most important thing is that the disappointments, as Rabinowitz experienced them, led him on to his new discovery: Jesus is the King and Messiah of the Jews.

Rabinowitz on the Mount of Olives

"On the Mount of Olives I found Jesus," Rabinowitz told Venetianer in 1887.[29] But strangely enough he does not mention the Mount of Olives and what happened there at all in his *Autobiography*, which was printed in 1887. Delitzsch published it and wrote a foreword for it. In this Delitzsch could not conceal his vexation that towards the end the autobiography was so brief. Delitzsch had indeed tried to get Rabinowitz to give a fuller account of "the origins and emergence of his Christian conviction". But unsuccessfully. Rabinowitz gives no reasons for this, merely that it was done quite deliberately.[30]

It is scarcely odd that Delitzsch should have been vexed and surprised about this. When Rabinowitz went to Leipzig in 1887, he was not minded to expand the ending of his biography. But that did not stop him telling about it orally! At a meeting in London on 11 January 1887 he had told the story of his 'conversion'.[31] Against the background of his experiences at the Wailing Wall in Jerusalem, he came to think of 2 Chron. 36:14-16 with the words "till there was no remedy". In the Hebrew Bible these words are in the last chapter of the last book. Like a light from heaven he saw that the suffering of the Jews and the laying waste of Palestine were due to their persistent rejection of Christ. The remedy was to be found in Him. His description of this presupposes that he already had some knowledge of the New Testament and its teaching.[32]

The article relating this, which was presumably based on Rabinowitz's own account in London, does leave certain details unclarified. But we are not completely in the dark, certainly not if a report of the meeting in Leipzig on 13 February 1887 is reliable. It was made by a student called de Renesse who was studying at the Institutum Judaicum. On that occasion Rabinowitz did yield to the unanimous request of the gathering for him to tell about the events which led up to the emergence of the Messianic movement in southern Russia.[33]

After telling of his disappointments in Palestine, Rabinowitz related his experience on the Mount of Olives. One evening before sunset he had gone up there and seated himself on the slope by Gethsemane, filled with mournful thoughts about the hopeless state of his people. The report of his address continues:

> Suddenly a word from the New Testament, a word he had read 15 years before without heeding it, penetrated his heart like a flash of lightning: "If the Son therefore shall make you free, ye shall be free indeed" (John 8:36). From that moment the truth that Jesus is the King, the Messiah, who alone can save Israel, gained power over his soul. Deeply moved, he immediately returned to his lodging, seized the New Testament and, while reading John's Gospel, was struck by these words: "Without me ye can do nothing" (John 15:5). In that way, by the providence of Almighty God, it came about that he was enlightened by the light of the Gospel. "Yeshua Achinu" (Jesus our brother) was from then on his watchword, with which he returned to Russia.[34]

As we have said, these words are based on a report. They are probably the closest we can get to a description of Rabinowitz's 'conversion'. At all events this description came to fill the gap which many felt that his *Autobiography* had left. This account does not define the content of his new faith. We shall be returning to that theme.

The report suggests a sudden and unexpected conversion. At the same time, it may be observed that Rabinowitz had evidently had the New Testament with him in his luggage. Our spotlight will first be directed at this circumstance. The question is whether his bringing along a New Testament indicates that his 'conversion' did not come so unprepared as has usually been depicted. It is not easy to give a simple answer to this question.

The New Testament in his luggage

It must be regarded as certain that Rabinowitz had a Hebrew version of the New Testament with him on his journey. Perhaps it was the same copy he was given by a friend in the 1850s (see Chapter 3). Some sources tell us that he took his New Testament with him among other 'guidebooks' in order in that way to get information about the Christian holy places.[35] But, if so, we are not told who gave him this advice. In itself it causes no difficulty to envisage that an Enlightenment Jew like Rabinowitz might have followed the advice of other Enlightenment Jews on a point like this. His having a New Testament in his luggage does not necessarily mean that Christian thoughts were already burgeoning in his mind. It is hard to reach certainty on such a question.

Some obituaries and later descriptions are on the verge of depicting Rabinowitz as a seeking Jew visiting the holy places - the Christian ones! - with the New Testament as his guide. According to one of the British obituaries of 1899 Rabinowitz wandered around Jerusalem with his New Testament - unopened indeed - in his pocket, until he finally opened it on the Mount of Olives.[36] Or, as is said elsewhere: "He reached for the New Testament, and while he was reading it at the holy places where Jesus had walked, he felt convinced that the Truth was to be found here."[37] An account of 1984, after mentioning that Rabinowitz wanted to revisit the Mount of Olives once more before his departure, says, "He took out his NT and, amid profound ponderings, experienced a spiritual breakthrough."[38] But these and other similar descriptions are not based on independent examination of the sources.

A lithograph depicting Rabinowitz's conversion also suggests that he had his New Testament with him (see picture at the beginning of this book). The picture, which was made by a W. Webb, was reproduced in the February 1886 issue of The Jewish Herald.[39] It was later reproduced many times elsewhere.[40] The picture portrays Rabinowitz on the Mount of Olives, where he is standing looking out over the Kidron Valley towards Jerusalem. In his right hand he has a stick, in his left his hat; his overcoat is buttoned except for the top button; a book, no doubt the New Testament, is tucked into the unbuttoned coat. There is every evidence that Lhotzky is referring to this particular picture in his memoirs of 1904. He says there:

> With a New Testament in his hand and with lowered head turned towards Jerusalem, he is visibly converting. Such things Rabinowitz used to lay before me silently, but with an indescribable smiling of the eyes, shoulders, hands, indeed his whole body, as only a Jew can smile.

Lhotzky may be detected in other inaccuracies. When he alleges that the picture in question shows Rabinowitz with a New Testament in his hand this must be due to a lapse of memory.[41]

In a later chapter we shall discuss how Lhotzky used this example to show how foreign missionary magazines misused Rabinowitz - an allegation that must of course be offset by information from primary sources. But it is not unthinkable that Rabinowitz derived great amusement from seeing his own 'conversion' portrayed. Who would not?

The picture obviously wanted to link his conversion - and his Christian conviction - with the reading of the New Testament. And if it is not possible to draw a whole cartoon strip, and if everything has to be included therefore in one picture, then the New Testament must be put in somewhere. However, most indications are that Rabinowitz did not have his New Testament with him on every walk he made in Jerusalem.

It may seem rather finicky to wish to decide whether Rabinowitz had his New Testament with him or not that evening on the Mount of Olives. The important thing must be that he had a Hebrew New Testament in his luggage, and that he made use of it. Finicky or not: most evidence indicates that his New Testament remained in his lodgings on that particular evening. So we are justified in being critically wary of those accounts which turn Rabinowitz into a seeking pilgrim. They represent the pious embellishments of later times.

But this is not tantamount to asserting that the New Testament did not play any part in connection with his conversion. There are sources which allege that he had read it only sporadically before his journey, as well as those that say that he was familiar with it. We shall return to this in the next chapter. The question that arises here is whether he was more familiar with the New Testament before his journey than is openly acknowledged. In his addresses in London and Leipzig in 1887 he hinted that he had read it before he went to Palestine.

However, it is quite certain that after his journey to the Holy Land he did become very well acquainted with the New Testament indeed. At the same time he had an unshakable conviction that it could be efficacious to distribute it to Jews and others. As early as 1888 the spokesmen of the Israel Mission in Leipzig were giving him this good testimonial: "The dissemination of the New Testament in Hebrew has, through Rabinowitz, reached a completely new pace."[42] In one of his last letters to the Mildmay Mission he asks for 200 copies of the New Testament in Russian for distribution among Jewish soldiers.[43] He had previously done similarly.[44] The work of distributing the Bible could be taken as a hint that Rabinowitz was convinced that even a superficial reading of the New Testament might have great effects.

At any rate, as early as 1883 he gave his nephew Samuel Rabinowitz a New Testament in Hebrew with the following comment: "Read it, and do not be afraid of the name of Jesus." The nephew was baptized in December 1885.[45]

The Jewish Herald printed the following excerpts from his address at a meeting in London on 18 January 1887, which also reveal something of his view of the importance of the New Testament:

When a Jew asks me as to what he is to do, and what way he is to take,
then I tell him to read the New Testament. When he says, "I have done
that," then I say to him as a physician would to a patient under his care,
who is getting better by taking the medicine prescribed: "Take
another bottle, and another, and another." So I say to the sin-sick Jew,
"Read the New Testament again, and again, and it will in the end have
the desired effect.[46]

Back home with new expectations

Rabinowitz had set out on his journey with Zionist expectations. He had got
no further than Constantinople when these expectations were put to the test.
It dawned upon him there that it was the Turks who had the key to the empty
portals of Jerusalem. In the Holy Land his Zionist expectations were
crushed. But he still retained his hope of the national gathering of the Jews
in Palestine (see Chapter 9). When he returned to Kishinev, his expectations
had a strong social leaning. The Jewish question, he considered, could not be
solved without "our brother Jesus". Or to use an often quoted turn of phrase,
whose precise meaning few have taken the trouble to define: "The key to the
Holy Land lies in the hands of our brother Jesus" (see further Chapter 9).

We shall return to the way in which these expectations found
expression. But first we shall outline the course of Rabinowitz's life before
1882. A clear impression of his relationship to Christianity has not yet been
given, and perhaps we shall have to make do with less, with asking some
questions. In this context it is important to investigate whether before 1882
Rabinowitz was a man who was taken seriously in trend-setting Jewish
circles. To achieve a balanced view of his criticism of his fellow Jews after he
made a public stand as a Messianic believer, it may be appropriate to take
note of his criticism and vigorous comments upon his fellow Jews before
1882. Jewish self-criticism is not, of course, an expression of anti-Semitism.

Rabinowitz himself gave a fairly full account of the shape of his life
before 1882. The main points may be checked in Jewish sources. The sources
which, at the beginning of the 1880s, expressed their opinion on Rabinowitz
and his activity before the journey to Palestine, are particularly interesting
in this connection.

For if the information given by these sources is correct, then the
picture of Rabinowitz in some modern works of reference has to be
considerably revised.

Chapter 3

RABINOWITZ'S LIFE BEFORE 1882

Rabinowitz wrote his *Autobiography* at the suggestion of Delitzsch.[1] It appeared in German in 1887, translated by Delitzsch. In its entirety or in excerpts it was soon translated into other languages.[2] Originally it had been written in Hebrew and completed in November 1886. In an afterword Delitzsch had to admit that he had not always used the official designations when Russian state matters were referred to, and that Rabinowitz might perhaps "here and there" feel that certain expressions used about him in German were overdone compared with the Hebrew original.[3] This might suggest that Rabinowitz had seen the translation before it was printed, and had criticized some points.

Some of the statements Rabinowitz makes in his *Autobiography* may be checked in various ways. In particular, some articles by him which were published in reputable Jewish papers and periodicals are evidence that he enjoyed some degree of recognition. In a bibliographical lexicon of 1881 covering Jewish literature of the time, C.D. Lippe wrote about Rabinowitz that he was a "*Privatgelehrter*" (self-taught man) and adds the following in Hebrew: "Some valuable articles by the honoured scholar mentioned above have been printed, which all do honour to their author." There is then reference to an article in Haboker Or (see below).[4] In the first counterblast in Hamelitz to Rabinowitz's negative opinion of Oliphant, which he had expressed in his travel letter dated 6/18 May 1882, he is referred to as "the learned writer";[5] that was why there was so much consternation at his assessment of Oliphant.

To make the course of events as Rabinowitz himself presents it easier to follow, we shall first highlight some information which was published about him in Hamelitz. We shall later return to the polemical context in which these data are found (see Chapter 4). It was the editor, Alexander Zederbaum, who wrote this account of his former fellow-writer or correspondent for Hamelitz; it was written after it had become known that Rabinowitz was in touch with the Lutheran clergyman in Kishinev; a friend was writing about a friend he had long known. So this source is of immense importance for understanding Rabinowitz's position before 1882.

Profile of an esteemed Jew

The Rabinowitz case was dealt with in a front-page article in Hamelitz on 20 January/1 February 1884.[6] The editor reproaches Rabinowitz for not letting him know about his new faith, and challenges him to own up to it. For there is a rumour abroad that he has links with the Lutheran faith, that he has been led astray himself and is now leading others astray. Of course, says the editor, he does not believe that Jesus is the Son of God, but he does believe that he is the Messiah. The editor has more to say, and for the sake of clarity we shall pick out the relevant statements:

- it was difficult for us to believe these things about a man like him;

- he has been known by us for about 20 years, including while he was living in Orgeyev;

- we know him as a man versed in the Law;

- he writes and speaks both the Hebrew and the Russian languages;

- he loves his people and is zealous for their faith and enlightenment (Haskala);

- he is a scholarly and moral human being;

- he was highly esteemed in the Jewish congregation in Kishinev when he settled there;

- many listened to his proposals for setting up a society for promoting agriculture among the Jews of Bessarabia;

- when the Jewish persecutions broke out he expressed to his fellows his notion of settling in Eretz Israel;

- he travelled via Constantinople and Jaffa to Jerusalem;

- he was attacked in Hamelitz for his polemic against Oliphant, but his polemic was due to his zeal for his religion and his people.

Against this background it is not surprising that the editor asks: "How were we expected to believe those who said that a man like this had changed his convictions at his advanced age?" He then openly admits that at first he did believe it was a rumour put about by some of Rabinowitz's enemies.

The facts that emerge are quite clear. Among Enlightenment Jews Joseph Rabinowitz's name was a good one and he was well esteemed. So beneath the surprise there is also an undertone of pain and bitterness at his new conviction. At the same time, these statements do confirm the main points of Rabinowitz's life as he set them down in his own *Autobiography*.

From Rabinowitz's *Autobiography*

Joseph ben Rabinowitz was born on 11/23 September 1837 in the small town of Resina in Bessarabia. Both parents were of rabbinical families; hence of course the name: son of Rabbi - Rabinowitz. His mother died in his early childhood and the family moved from the town. But Joseph remained in Resina, where he was brought up by his maternal grandfather, who was a zealous adherent of Chassidism, in which Joseph was brought up. At the same time he learnt to love the Torah, the Talmud, and other good Jewish books. Three times a year his grandfather brings him along to Rabbi Salmina, the *zaddik* in Raschkov. When he was six he could recite the whole of the Canticles by heart, when seven the whole of the Mishna tractate *Sukkot*.

Owing to his grandfather's advanced years, from 1848 he was placed in the care of his paternal grandmother in Orgeyev. In his second decade he studied the Talmud under a handsomely paid rabbi and was still under the influence of Chassidism. He was captivated by it and had no taste for the amusements of those of his own age and kept well away from walks and games. When he was 15 the marriage-arrangers loomed, and in July 1853, a few months before attaining the age of 16, he was betrothed to his bride-to-be. In accordance with current custom, the wedding was to take place within three years. Before that happened - probably towards the end of 1855 - he became acquainted with western European ideas then reaching Bessarabia. These "waters began gradually to calm and quench the fire in my heart", the heart which had been fervent for Chassidism. Also, the Russian authorities began to require all Jewish children to learn to speak and write Russian. Acquaintance with the writings of Moses Mendelsohn and Reform Judaism also had an effect. Through Mendelsohn's writings he learnt the essence of logical thinking. He also got to know recent Jewish literature and interpretations and felt that through this he was awakening from the dreams which his Chassidic teachers had given him.

In other words: the 16-18 year-old teenager was on the move away from Chassidism. The cultural trends from Europe were having their effect upon him, as on so many other Russian Jews.

According to Delitzsch's translation of Rabinowitz's *Autobiography* Rabinowitz was married on "7 Tebeth in the year 5615 (1856)".[7] However, the Jewish year 5615 does not correspond to the year 1856.[8] Perhaps the figures have been confused so that it should have been 5616 (1855). If that is the case, Rabinowitz was married in mid-December 1855, about three months after he had completed his 18th year. After meeting Rabinowitz John Wilkinson writes, in the spring of 1885: "He was married about thirty years ago."[9]

However that may be, before the marriage Rabinowitz mentions his links with Yechiel Zvi Herschensohn. This man was a Talmudic expert who was then living in Kishinev, and was in touch with people who were understood to be 'enlightened'. He opened Rabinowitz's eyes to how the Jewish Kabbala had befogged the Jewish outlook. "My soul", wrote Rabinowitz, "became more and more knit to the soul of this my friend Herschensohn. Days and nights we sat in love by one another's side in order with deliberation to search out divine and human law and make clear to ourselves the true way to bliss."

One day Herschensohn brought a Hebrew New Testament to Rabinowitz in Orgeyev. He had been given it by the clergyman in Kishinev. Herschensohn had taken it in order to find out what Jesus of Nazareth had taught and what Gentile Christians profess to believe. He passed it on to Rabinowitz with the words: "Who knows? Perhaps it is really he whom the prophets have foretold." Rabinowitz adds that he still has this copy of the New Testament.

His study of older Jewish writings on religious philosophy, his zeal to learn Russian and German, and not least his friendship with Herschensohn, who was regarded by many within Chassidic circles as a free-thinker, provoked in Rabinowitz a breach with his teacher and with Chassidism. Against that background he felt obliged to leave Orgeyev. He moved home to his father in the village of Mashkovitz. He there studied recent scholarship and spoke his mind critically "to anyone and everyone" about Chassidism. His father placed no obstacles in his way but supported his son on his new path.

Rabinowitz's eyes were now opened to there being a world of nature created by God; he enjoyed seeing the peasants working on the soil, made contact with both Jewish and Gentile traders who came to the village to fetch wine and tobacco. "I broke out of the circle which had held me captive till then, and I saw that there are other callings in this world than studying and devoting oneself to barren speculations."

Then, probably in December 1855, Rabinowitz was married to the 17 year-old Golde, whom the match-makers had found for him some years previously; "Where was there a son in Israel who later troubled his head about what his father had already set in hand?" As was the custom, the newly weds spent the first year and a half in the home of the girl's parents. That was in Orgeyev, the place from which Rabinowitz had moved away not long before. Rabinowitz says of this period that he spent all his time meeting with his friend Herschensohn, who was also living with his wife in Orgeyev at this time, "otherwise I only attended Beit Hamidrash where I prayed morning and evening." (It must be commented here that this is the last time that Herschensohn's name appears in the autobiography, and that no mention is made of the fact that Rabinowitz's sister married none other than

Herschensohn. Nor is there a word to show that at the time Rabinowitz was writing his autobiography Herschensohn had long been a believer. We shall be making a few comments on these noteworthy omissions later).

Not quite a year after the marriage, the first son Vladimir was born; after living for a year and a half with his in-laws, Rabinowitz bought a little shop in Orgeyev into which they moved. But in 1859 the shop and the dwelling were reduced to ashes in a fire. "All my possessions, books, and furnishings fell prey to this great fire ..."

Amid bitter deprivation, and under pressure of these circumstances, he now tried to master the Russian language and study the laws of Bessarabia and Orgeyev in order if possible to function as a legal consultant or solicitor. By 1860 he was occupying a respected position and advising many, so the experi- ment was a success. He was now also sending written contributions to Jewish newspapers in Odessa. Altogether, he was regarded as a "friend of the Jewish people", for instance because he took the lead in the setting up of a Talmud-Torahh school to train Jewish boys both in Hebrew and Russian and in scriptural knowledge and knowledge of the Talmud "according to present-day scholarly requirements", it is added. He also took the lead in improving moral conditions among Jews and received appropriate recognition for this. "Authors asked me to recommend their books, writers of a liberal-minded persuasion asked for my collaboration in their undertakings. My impartial activity for the welfare and well-being of the people of Israel was recognized by all parties," he says.

In 1866 Rabinowitz became the proprietor of a large grocery shop; in 1869 he became the first Jew to be elected to the provincial diet of Orgeyev. He also became a member of a committee to select jurymen. His political work "crowned the third decade of my life". He says of the aim of his visions and his work: "It was the greatest wish of my heart to see my beloved nation happy in its Russian homeland."

The means to this end was "enlightenment". He had expectations that the spirit of the new age would set the Jews free and give them the same civic and social rights as other people. "But," he says, "my faith in Israel's salvation through enlightenment and the modern spirit was weakened." He cites some events which had shaken him. France under Napoleon III suffered defeat at the hands of Germany, even though the French "are the standard-bearers of enlightenment more than any other nation." He also mentions the persecutions of the Jews in Odessa in 1871; Christian fellow citizens were silent spectators as a fanatical mob went on the rampage. "It then became clear to me that it was far from true that enlightenment could save the Jews from the hand of their enemies." The Jews in Odessa, he says, were the first to give themselves over to enlightenment, but they were also the first to be threatened with annihilation. Finally, Rabinowitz mentions that through his political work he has become convinced that the inhabitants of the country have good relations with the Jews only when it is to their own advantage; otherwise they spurn them. "The future of Russia's Jews appeared to me like a sky covered with black clouds." He took the consequences of this new insight. He gave up his political posts in Orgeyev and, in November 1871, moved to Kishinev "as if to begin a new life".

In Kishinev he set up as a legal consultant or lawyer. In 1872 the youngest of his four daughters succumbed to cholera. The eldest child, his son Vladimir, was attending the grammar school in Kishinev when the family moved there. The law practice prospered. In 1873 he had the means to build a large house. Besides helping people with their legal and financial affairs, he spent his time at home reading the Holy Scriptures and giving tuition in Hebrew and Russian. Only on the Sabbath and the Jewish festivals did he participate in the rites of the Jewish congregation. Every Sabbath, cultured people from Kishinev gathered in his home to hear his opinion on religious and general scholarly questions. Or to hear general news about Judaism.

From this time - the beginning of the 1870s - he became a correspondent for a couple of Jewish periodicals which were published in St Petersburg. Among these was Hamelitz already mentioned. He submitted items about the spiritual and civic needs of the Bessarabian Jews. The war between Serbia and Bulgaria on one side and Turkey on the other also made an impact. After Serbia's and Bulgaria's independence in 1878 the hope was kindled in Rabinowitz that the nation of Israel might achieve the same form of independence.

In 1878 he wrote a long article which was published in the Hebrew periodical Haboker Or in 1879.[10] In this he asserted that the state of the rabbinate had to be improved. If this did not occur, then the spiritual state of the Jews in general would not be improved either. With others, he was also taken up with ways of getting the Jews to take an interest in agriculture. He gave lectures on farming and was the co-founder of a society which drew up a plan for a Jewish society which would support poor Jews who went in for horticulture. With a depth of feeling which seems amusing today but scarcely caused a smile on the lips of Jews at the time, he told of how he himself cultivated the garden by his house "in the view of people who bodily were stronger" in order to take the lead with a good example:

> For only by work in house and field which is done using all our strength can we save the honour of Israel and silence the hatred which is harboured against us. There is work of the mind which may rightly be called work, but only work which demands bodily effort and sets moving all man's strength makes a people skilled and protects it against one-sidedness.

So by the 1870s Rabinowitz had reached the conclusion that it was not sufficient to think and speak. Practical action was called for. He said about the Jews in general: "They are rich in words, but the poorer in action." In his battle against the "stultification" he sees among his fellow Jews who are victims of inactivity and ignorance, he published articles in Hamelitz so that Jews elsewhere in Russia might imitate his project by stimulating agriculture. He started participating in religious life again. He was involved in the setting-up of a handsome prayer-hall in Kishinev where skilled singers were used to make the services more solemn with choral singing, "and all that was tasteless and offensive was removed from the order of service". He was, he relates, assigned a leading position in this congregation.

In 1874 and 1876 their sons David and Nathan were born. The last comment he makes in his *Autobiography* about his views on the Jews intimates that they are not so good at matters of trade as they themselves think. He had discussed this in an article in Hamelitz in 1880.[11]

In conclusion, events are mentioned which are connected with the emergence of the south Russian Messianic movement. He "tortured" himself to find "the solution of the Jewish question" from three circumstances which are briefly mentioned: the death of "our righteous Czar Alexander II" (1881); the pogroms in various regions of Russia (1881-1882); and the persecuted Jews' flight and emigration to America and Palestine. Without explaining these circumstances, Rabinowitz continues:

> These occurrences helped me at length to recognise Him of Whom Moses and the Prophets did write, Jesus of Nazareth, Who said of Himself (John 18:37), "To this end was I born and came into the world, that I may bear witness unto the Truth. Everyone that is of the Truth heareth My voice," whom I now recognise as my Lord and my God.

With these words Rabinowitz laid aside his pen, lifting his eyes to him who sits at the majesty on high, asking him if he would for ever be angry with his people, asking to be granted to hear that God has promised his people and his saints peace, and ending with the conviction that the help of the Lord is nigh unto those who fear him.

Thus far Rabinowitz's *Autobiography*. It is not difficult to recognize the main lines which Rabinowitz himself traces, set alongside the facts which the editor of Hamelitz passed on to his readers at the beginning of 1884. The main lines of Rabinowitz's life are also confirmed by Jewish writers Sh.L. Tsitron,[12] Z. Rejzen,[13] and Saul M. Ginsburg.[14] All emphasize Rabinowitz's Chassidic upbringing, his subsequent rupture with the same, his life as an esteemed Haskala Jew with public tasks in the Jewish community, his journey to Palestine and his criticism of Oliphant.

An esteemed, zig-zagging, Enlightenment Jew

There can be no doubt that before his journey to Palestine Rabinowitz was
an esteemed Enlightenment Jew. Any Jewish circles who were opposed to
him were also opposed to other Enlightenment Jews who had wandered
away from their upbringing, whether this had been Chassidism or Orthodox
Judaism. In a postscript to one of Rabinowitz's articles in Hamelitz in 1880,
in which the editor expressed disagreement with Rabinowitz's views,
Rabinowitz is nevertheless described as "the beloved writer", a man of
understanding", "the enlightened author", and "this learned author".[15] He is
directly designated "rabbi" (Ha-Rav), although he was not an ordained
rabbi.[16]

In reporting Rabinowitz's death in 1899, The Jewish Chronicle avers
that his "entry into public life is associated with the never-to-be-forgotten
anti-Jewish excesses in Southern Russia in the years 1881 and 1882."[17] This
is to play down his previous activity. Whatever assessment one may wish to
make of his journalism, there is no getting round the fact that he had made
his entry into the public arena long before 1881-1882.[18] Referring to his
article in Haboker Or of 1879, The Jewish Encyclopaedia of the beginning
of this century asserts: "This was his only contribution as a Jew to Hebrew
literature".[19] If Rabinowitz had not become a Messianic believer, perhaps he
would have been given rather more credit as a writer. In passing it may be
mentioned that Rabinowitz's letter dated 6/18 May, Constantinople, and
printed in Hamelitz is included in a book published in Israel in 1982 as a
document on the history of the Love of Zion movement.[20] In this connection
Steven J. Zipperstein makes a very precise observation about Rabinowitz:
"Had he not undergone a radical religious transformation, he would probably
be remembered today as a Zionist who was the first outspoken critic of
Oliphant and whose commitment to the rebuilding of Palestine was based
on a peculiarly intense if idiosyncratic set of religious convictions."[21] We
shall, however, give examples below of how, soon after his conversion, he
was declared to be "uneducated". But that does not alter the fact that before
1882 he was an esteemed and respected Jew concerned with solving the
"Jewish question". Zipperstein rightly characterizes him as "a respected
Jewish communal figure before his turnabout in the early 1880s".[22]

Rabinowitz himself made it plain to Lhotzky that he had not passed
any examinations or attended any publicly recognized schools. Lhotzky says
that in Germany, where only people who have studied are recognized as
lawyers, Rabinowitz would be described as a "Winkelschreiber" (pettifogger).[23]
He stressed that Rabinowitz had a "great talent for languages", speaking and
writing classical Hebrew as well as Russian. Rabinowitz told his overseas
friends that he understood and read English, German, and French.[24] It
became customary for him to write his letters in Hebrew. When a letter
written in German in 1884 was published, Delitzsch made known that the

style had been corrected, as Rabinowitz did not write German as fluently as Russian, Hebrew, and Yiddish.[25] Later he sometimes corresponded in English, assisted by his daughter Rachel.[26] Even though his proficiency in speaking English was no doubt improved by his close relations with England and Scotland, his Scottish friends described it as a fiasco when he delivered an address in English in Edinburgh in 1896 (see Chapter 14). But the sources leave no doubt that Rabinowitz could take in information in English and French - and even better in German. Later he received periodicals in these languages from the leaders of the missions to Israel in these countries.[27] In 1889 he translated an English hymn by Horatius Bonar into Hebrew.[28]

In 1897 S. Wilkinson of the Mildmay Mission described Rabinowitz as an "omnivorous reader"[29]. This applied not only to Jewish literature and mission literature, but also to the reading of anything to do with the trends of the time. Rabinowitz's thirst for knowledge seems not to have been affected by his becoming a Messianic believer. He knew what Renan and Strauss stood for.[30] James Pirie in Prague speaks of him as "Dr.".[31]

It has already been mentioned that in Hamelitz of 1882 Rabinowitz was given the title of "Rabbi" by writers who criticized his article sent from Constantinople. But he hardly held an official position as rabbi either before or after 1882. Zipperstein holds that when Rabinowitz wrote his article *Masters and Rabbis*, published in Haboker Or 1879, "he still hoped to be elected to the position of crown rabbi of Kishinev," a position he never captured.[32] Probably on the basis of what Rabinowitz had himself told, an English source of 1887 mentions that his father-in-law wished him to be a rabbi.[33] But he does not seem to have become one, and so it is misleading when in 1896 Rabinowitz was described as "the Russian ex-rabbi" in the journal of the Scottish Free Church.[34] Some Christian sources occasionally call him a "Christian rabbi".[35] In 1885 the word "rabbi" is put on the Hebrew title-page of the first two sermons which were published by Jakob Wechsler (see Chapter 6). There can be no doubt that the Jews around him did not recognize him as a legitimate rabbi. But since the "prayer house" in which he later functioned as preacher was regarded by the Russian authorities as a synagogue and Rabinowitz presumably as a rabbi, it cannot be ruled out that Rabinowitz occasionally used this designation himself. But he does not seem to have flaunted it. In his sermon anthology of 1897 he wrote "preacher" on the title-page. "He is regarded as a Rabbi, but one who teaches what he likes", wrote the Scottish church leader A.N. Somerville in his "chronicle" of his visit to Kishinev in 1888.[36] In any case, neither before or after 1882 was he an ordained rabbi. Nor did he become an ordained clergyman.

Rabinowitz's withdrawal from Chassidism and embracement of enlightenment may be designated his first "conversion". After this he zigzagged between various models for the amelioration of Jewish conditions in Russia. When he writes of his hopes and disappointments, he seems honest, sometimes a bit naive, which perhaps says more about a later generation which views the matter from a historical distance. A characteristic trait of his personality - one that recurred in his life as a Messianic believer - was that he did not allow his activity to be paralyzed once he had realized that his expectations had not been fulfilled. He at once sought new paths. We shall give an example of this from the period just before his journey to Palestine.

In November 1881, with his brothers Yankel (Efraim Jakob) and Meir he sent an application to the governor of Bessarabia for permission to set up a Jewish agricultural colony.[37] First the adverse conditions of life of the Bessarabian Jews were depicted. It was mentioned that many of them, in their despair, were ready to discard the precious religion of their forefathers, reference being made to the Spiritual Biblical Brotherhood which was formed in Elisabetgrad (see below); others were ready to leave their beloved fatherland and go to America or Palestine. Against this background, application was made for 437 hectares of land for a Jewish agricultural colony.

The first paragraph of the draft articles of association for the agricultural colony says that the latest methods will be used. By cultivating and shaping the natural resources of their fatherland the Jews can make a living. Through their fellowship and religious life such Jews may be an example to other Jews to live modest, honest, and industrious lives.

On 22 February/6 March 1882 the authorities' rejection of the application came in, no grounds being given. And shortly afterwards Rabinowitz was on his way to Palestine to explore the possibilities for a Jewish settlement there! That some people regarded him as a "delegate" shows that he was not suspected of looking for the solution to the "Jewish question" in Jesus the Messiah.[38] But before any further comments are made about the difficult question of Rabinowitz's attitude to Christianity before 1882, we need to briefly mention his relations to a couple of other reform movements which arose in the early 1880s.

Rabinowitz and some Jewish reform movements

In 1880 Jacob Gordin had founded the Spiritual Biblical Brotherhood, which was a Jewish reform movement. This rejected post-Biblical Judaism; the Bible, interpreted rationalistically, was viewed as the source of an ethical way of living, and they disapproved of Jews engaging in trade. But they saw in farming a new possibility of improving the lot of the Jews. In an article in 1881 Gordin asserted that the Jews' love of money and their concern with trade were the causes of Russian anti-Semitism.[39]

It is not difficult to see that some points of Rabinowitz's criticism of Jewish mammon interests and of his suggestion for an agricultural colony, coincided with the views of Gordin. However, his words in the application of November 1881 (see above) tend to suggest that he regarded the movement as such as apostasy from the precious religion of the fathers.

Another movement, New Israel (*Novi Israel*), was founded by Jacob Priluker in Odessa late in 1881. He made himself the spokesman of a universal religion in which Jewish circumcision and the Sabbath were to be abolished. Nor was the Talmud to have any importance.[40] It cannot be completely ruled out that Rabinowitz may have sounded out Priluker before he left for Palestine. But all the same Priluker's movement, Novi Israel, and Rabinowitz's Messianic movement must be kept distinct.

It is amazing that The New Standard Jewish Encyclopedia (1975) not only asserts that Rabinowitz founded the Jewish-Christian sect Novi Israel in 1882 and wrote its book of statutes in which he explained his adoption of Christianity while retaining Sabbath observance and circumcision (!).[41] The same work also avers, under the entry *Novi Israel*, that Priluker wished to move the Sabbath to Sunday and abolish circumcision, after which it is alleged that the movement in 1884 "was renewed in Kishinev by Joseph Rabinovich, who also became a Christian in 1885, when the sect's activity ceased."[42] But the Encyclopedia Judaica (1972) gets it right when it asserts that Rabinowitz's movement must not be confused with Novi Israel, which was founded by Priluker.[43]

Rabinowitz gave his movement the name Israelites of the New Covenant (see Chapter 6). This name might be confused with New Israel. Even though the movements must be kept distinct, the name New Israel was actually applied to Rabinowitz's movement in his own time. For instance, according to the German rendering in *Saat auf Hoffnung*, it occurs in some Russian newspapers of 1885 and 1886.[44] Similarly, the minister of the Scottish Free Church, A. Moody, wrote from Budapest that Rabinowitz's movement "bears the designation 'New Israel' or 'Israel of the New Covenant'".[45] De le Roi, too, must be criticized for his choice of words in his large work on evangelical Christendom and the Jews. This asserts that a number of Jews followed Rabinowitz and joined together in a covenant, "for which they chose for themselves the name New Israel or Biblical Brotherhood."[46] The designation "New Israelites", which Zipperstein claims Rabinowitz called his followers, is not precise either.[47]

As far as can be judged from Rabinowitz's own works, he never used the designation New Israel himself about his movement. It is certain at any rate that this was never the official name of the movement. In a booklet written in Yiddish and published in 1894, Rabinowitz states his mind on this question.[48]

In the booklet "What is an Israelite of the New Covenant?" Rabinowitz has two rabbis discuss various questions in connection with the name of the Messianic movement. Rabbi Jakob is the outsider, Rabbi Israel is an adherent of Rabinowitz - though unbaptized. Thus, in the dialogue between the two rabbis, Rabbi Israel is the mouthpiece of Rabinowitz.

One of the questions Rabbi Jakob asks is: "Why do you call yourselves - I mean Rabinowitz and his movement - the New Israel?"

Rabbi Israel replies that Rabinowitz has never called his movement New Israel, but Israel of the New Covenant. That is the name to be seen, says Rabbi Israel, on all the documents published by Rabinowitz. And, he adds, in all his printed sermons in the sacred language - Hebrew - the expression Sons of Israel, sons of the new covenant, is found. Regarding the term New Israel, Rabbi Israel states that that is what some people in Odessa and Elisabetgrad have called themselves. But they are without faith in God and are inspired by some philosophical ideas from the nineteenth century. They are also without faith in God's Holy Scriptures, without faith in God's Son, Jesus the Messiah, and without faith that the Messiah Jesus shed his blood to make a new covenant with Judah and Israel. Rabbi Israel sets the work of Rabinowitz in contrast to this. It is based on the true faith. He argues that Rabinowitz teaches that the Jewish nation cannot be renewed unless it repents and believes that the God of Israel long ago made a new covenant with the Jewish people through the blood which Messiah Jesus shed on the cross in Jerusalem nearly 1900 years ago.

Rabbi Israel may answer for himself. For he is himself a *Ben Israel*, a true son of Israel. Through this dialogue Rabinowitz is putting a clear distance between his movement and Priluker's Novi Israel.

Attitude to Christianity before 1882

Delitzsch was disappointed that Rabinowitz did not give more details in his autobiography about "the origins and breakthrough of his Christian conviction".[49] This disappointment may be extended to cover the whole of Rabinowitz's attitude to or ideas about Christianity before 1882. Was there no more to relate than the mention in the autobiography that in his youth he had been given a New Testament by a friend? Or is this mention actually a hint that there were circumstances which had been consciously toned down or blacked out in the autobiography? The material which has been unearthed does not give an unambiguous answer to this. But the question must be kept in mind, even though A.S. Poulsen, in his book of 1886, says that it will remain unknown what earlier thoughts Rabinowitz had had about the relationship between "Israel's Holy Scriptures and the teaching of the New Testament."[50]

After his 'conversion' Rabinowitz tried vigorously to counter the view that his new faith might have been a product of a link with Christian missions. We shall return to this theme. But for that reason it cannot be ruled out in advance that any 'odd' contacts with Christian missionaries before

1882 may have been deliberately passed over in the autobiography. Rabinowitz might have had his reasons for playing down any contacts with Christians before 1882. Such contacts may also, of course, have been passed over because they were regarded by him as unimportant. On the other hand, Christian missionary societies might exploit any chance links with Rabinowitz to legitimate their missionary endeavours. And not only that. When some people 'took the credit' for his conversion, it was done in a power struggle with others, in which they were trying to substantiate that they had more right to him than others had. In the service of this cause, an exaggeration of certain circumstances might be involved.

It would hardly be a case of deliberate lying. But when the matter was presented, there were omissions, shifts of memory, subjective 'truths' and interpretations of the course of events. As we now shall see, on an objective view, everybody cannot be equally right in their interpretation of certain events and their significance for Rabinowitz's conversion.

Two contradictory views find expression in the material. The first stresses that Rabinowitz reached his new conviction without help from Christian missionaries to Israel. For instance, Delitzsch says this in Germany[51] and A. Saphir in England.[52] This was also stressed in the British Mildmay Mission.[53] In the periodical The Christian, this viewpoint was clearly expressed in 1887: "No society has the slightest ground for claiming him as their convert. His conversion was the work of the Holy Spirit alone."[54] This view is clearly aimed at the British Society, where a contrary view was maintained. It also gives a glimpse of the rivalry that existed among British societies over Rabinowitz (see Chapter 7).

This second view was already being put forward in March 1884 by J. Dunlop, the secretary of the British Society, who met Rabinowitz before any other representative of a British society. He summed up the "links in the chain" that led to Rabinowitz's conversion. Firstly, Rabinowitz's visit to Odessa is mentioned "where he met with our missionary and had presented to him a portrait of the Saviour as given in the Old and New Testaments." Secondly, "his residence in Kischinew, where he breathed a Christian atmosphere through the presence there of Pastor Faltin and his flock". "Had there been no British Society's missionary in Odessa and no London Society's agent [Faltin] in Kischinew, Joseph Rabinowitz might not have been converted." Thirdly, his trip to Palestine is mentioned, "which resulted in his spiritual birth and public confession of Christ."[55]

Unfortunately I have not succeeded in finding further details about the meeting between B. Ben Zion and Rabinowitz. Ben Zion was the British Society's missionary in Odessa. In some Jewish sources, his name is found connected with the mention of Priluker's reform movement Novi Israel (see below).[56] It is conceivable that Rabinowitz enquired into this movement in Odessa and in this way met Ben Zion a while before his journey to Palestine.

When representatives of the British Society arrived in Kishinev in March 1884, Ben Zion was among them. This might suggest that Ben Zion had at least kept informed about Rabinowitz and gave his society the first reports of his movement (see further Chapter 5).

But the London Society also has its version of its share in Rabinowitz's conversion. This is linked to O.J. Ellis's work in Warsaw, where he took over the leadership in 1877. The account of Rabinowitz says that he received the first impulse towards a favourable attitude to Christianity through reading the New Testament "a copy of which had been sent to him by Dr. Ellis, the Society's missionary."[57] After this the trip to Palestine is mentioned.

Faltin, the Lutheran clergyman in Kishinev, whose relations with Rabinowitz will be more fully described in the following chapters, also has his version. He mentions that "many years ago" he gave a Hebrew New Testament to a person in Kishinev. This person passed it on to Rabinowitz when he was living in Orgeyev.[58]

Faltin's version comes closest to the account in Rabinowitz's autobiography. It is certain that the unnamed person in Faltin's description is identical with Herschensohn. According to Rabinowitz himself, he had been given a Hebrew New Testament in Orgeyev by Herschensohn, who had received it from the clergyman in Kishinev, "the local pastor". But as Faltin did not go to Kishinev as a clergyman until 1859,[59] Rabinowitz cannot have received any New Testament by this route back in the mid 1850s, which is what his own words convey. This may be due to a slip of memory, for he spent several periods in Orgeyev. But at any rate Rabinowitz chooses his words in such a way that one does not immediately suspect the giver - Herschensohn - of being the henchman of Christian missions. Regardless of how many New Testaments Rabinowitz was given, he had a special relationship to the one he received through Herschensohn. When he wrote about it in 1886, he added that he still possessed it. As it had been printed in London, it was in all probability a new translation that was published in 1838. In 1877 Delitzsch's translation of the New Testament into Hebrew was published. Rabinowitz immersed himself in this after his return from Palestine, so it is necessary to modify G. Harder's assertion that Rabinowitz was "converted to Christianity" through Delitzsch's translation.[60]

In other words: if it is correct that Rabinowitz received his first New Testament in Hebrew from Herschensohn, who had been given it by the clergyman in Kishinev, he cannot have received it before 1859. At all events, Rabinowitz draws a veil over Herschensohn's attitude to Christian faith. When we set these omissions alongside information from other sources, fresh light is shed on Rabinowitz's relation to the Christian faith before 1882.

When we read in the autobiography about the close friendship between Rabinowitz and Herschensohn, it may surprise us that Rabinowitz does not drop one hint that his sister became Herschensohn's wife. She died shortly after the marriage, but all the same they had been brothers-in-law.[61] Zipperstein follows Sh.L. Tsitron uncritically when he maintains that Herschensohn did not marry Rabinowitz's sister until 1878.[62] Tsitron even goes so far as to say that Herschensohn left her in Russia and that sometime during the 1890s he gave her a certificate of divorce in London [sic], where she looked him up and presumably discovered that he had married another woman.[63] Whatever one may think about such stories, the late date is highly improbable. Herschensohn was in London in 1872.

It is even more remarkable that Rabinowitz, in his autobiography, totally passes over the fact that Herschensohn came to faith in Jesus as the Messiah during the very period in which Rabinowitz sets their close friendship and intense conversations. In his account, Rabinowitz does not give the impression that in the mid 1850s Herschensohn was baptized and - yes indeed! - tried to form a Hebrew Christian congregation. Nor does Rabinowitz divulge that in the same year in which his autobiography was written (1886) Herschensohn was appointed to the Institutum Judaicum, whose leader was Delitzsch, who translated the *Autobiography*.

At the beginning of the 1850s Herschensohn was confronted with the Christian faith. He gathered a group of friends around him to study the New Testament. In 1855 he baptized himself together with some friends in a river near Jassy. "At that time he gave the first New Testament to Rabinowitz", writes de le Roi.[64] He tried to form a Hebrew Christian congregation in Skolian, in the adjacent province of Moldavia. In October 1868 Herschensohn turned up in Leipzig and presented Delitzsch with a book in Hebrew which he had had printed with the name of the author given as J.Z. Lichtenstein. It had been written from a Hebrew Christian viewpoint and by Delitzsch it was regarded as an exceedingly significant book. Delitzsch states that the book was the fruit of 12 years of work.[65] If this is correct, it takes us back to 1856, a time just subsequent to the close relations between the two brothers-in-law in Orgeyev. After his meeting with Delitzsch, Herschensohn/Lichtenstein was appointed to a post in an English missionary society to Jews. In 1872 he was baptized again in London.[66] Zipperstein erroneously characterizes Herschensohn as "an unbaptized Christian since 1855". But the source which he mentions in support of this speaks about Isak Lichtenstein not Yechiel Zvi Herschensohn/Lichtenstein.[67] Before Herschensohn became permanently attached to the Institutum Judaicum in Leipzig in 1885, he had been a missionary in Poland, a teacher at a proselyte institution in Neuendettelsau, and attached to the Berlin Society 1874-1879, after which he returned to Russia.[68]

Against this background, it is an obvious assumption that in the mid 1850s Rabinowitz had discussed Christian topics with Herschensohn and had perhaps joined in the group around Herschensohn, in which they read the New Testament. It does not sound very likely that Herschensohn merely confined himself to an aside that Jesus might be the Messiah. In 1890 P. Gordon wrote that Rabinowitz learnt the truths of Christianity through his brother-in-law, and in an account of Lichtenstein's life of 1912 it is said that he "conveyed" his knowledge of Jesus as the Messiah to his brother-in-law Rabinowitz.[69]

Also, after his meeting with Rabinowitz in 1885, J. Wilkinson states that a brother of Rabinowitz was baptized by "Dr. Ewald nearly thirty years ago".[70] Once again, this takes us back to the mid 1850s. It is improbable that Rabinowitz did not form some kind of opinion about this.

Even though Delitzsch stated most definitely that missionaries had no influence upon Rabinowitz's conversion, already in 1884 he was open to the possibility that Rabinowitz's movement was a vibration stemming from the impulses which emanated from Herschensohn's attempt to form a Hebrew Christian congregation.[71] A closer study of the life of Herschensohn/ Lichtenstein would no doubt shed a clearer light upon his significance for Rabinowitz's position regarding the Christian faith.

But there is adequate reason to assume that in the mid 1850s, through his connection with Lichtenstein, Rabinowitz had concerned himself in an existential way with the Christian faith. And not only that: he may at that time have been involved in the discussions about a Hebrew Christian congregation. At any rate, in a letter written in Kishinev on 31 March 1884, W. Faber informed Delitzsch that if the Sabbath and circumcision could be retained as national distinctives, then 100 families in Kishinev would join. And he goes on: "Rabinowitz has been working on the idea for 25 years".[72] Such a remark is exactly the kind of thing that is said when the 'conversion' has taken place and the question has been 'pondered' before.

The data we have gathered here suggest that a time-honoured view of Rabinowitz's attitude to the Christian faith before his journey to Palestine in 1882 will have to be revised.

Not only as a Haskala or Enlightenment Jew did he acquire some knowledge of the Christian faith prior to 1882. But there seem to have been at least periods in his life when in an existential way he had to ponder the question. Herschensohn/Lichtenstein's new faith can hardly have left him unaffected. When he says that a word from the New Testament, which he had read 15 years before, flashed upon him on the Mount of Olives in 1882, this testifies to a certain familiarity with the New Testament.[73] Some sources do say that he had become familiar with it before 1882.[74] Other sources claim that he only made superficial use of it.[75] Compared with the thorough study of the New Testament which he undertook after his return from Palestine, his earlier reading of it was naturally superficial.

Because Rabinowitz would not link his movement to any existing church or any missionary society, he also played down in his autobiography the influence that emanated from his close friendship with Herschensohn/ Lichtenstein.

We must also stress in this connection that Rabinowitz did not follow Herschensohn in the 1850s. This may have strained the relationship between them. The Dane Axel Bülow, who studied at the Institutum Judaicum in Leipzig in the mid 1880s, confirms that the two were brothers-in-law. But Bülow adds: "The former friendship between the two brothers-in-law was transformed into a bitter hostility when Lichtenstein turned Christian. Rabinowitz persecuted and harmed him now in every way. A couple of years ago he himself did of course learn to bow the knee to the Lord Christ and, it is to be hoped, now regrets his former hardness."[76] Although Faber refers to Lichtenstein as "brother-in-law and friend of our Joseph Rabinowitz",[77] Bülow's word can be interpreted that the two brothers-in-law did not rush into one another's arms after Rabinowitz's breakthrough of faith. At any rate, Rabinowitz does not vouchsafe a word about Herschensohn/ Lichtenstein when he recounts his later visits to Leipzig, where Lichtenstein was teaching at the Institutum Judaicum. In the letters from Rabinowitz to Delitzsch that have been preserved Rabinowitz sends no greetings to his brother-in-law.

Although there were periods before 1882 when Rabinowitz was concerned with Christian questions, there is nothing to suggest that in the years just before 1882 he was seeking the solution to the 'Jewish question' in Jesus. In that sense he was not a 'seeker' and was not taken by others to be a 'seeker', nor did he travel to Palestine with the idea in mind of searching for Jesus. As such his 'conversion' came unexpectedly both to himself and those around him.

It is not easy to strike a balance in matters of conversion. It may well be that there were several links in the chain, to use J. Dunlop's expression. Herschensohn was an important link in this context. The close friendship with him shows that Rabinowitz's conversion did not come so unprepared as some have made out. But that his conversion was prepared for, is not tantamount to its being expected - in 1882. When it became known later, it did not only reverberate but had a shock effect upon Jewish friends in the Jewish cultural world of that time.

When Rabinowitz returned from Palestine in 1882, his eldest son had been baptized in St Petersburg, where he was a student.[78] History does not relate whether Rabinowitz had been expecting that.

Portraits of Rabinowitz

No portrait of Rabinowitz has been found dating from the period before 1882. But from 1884 onwards there are a number which it may be useful to note here. They are reproduced at the beginning of this book.

In November 1884 J. Wilkinson, the leader of the Mildmay Mission, sent his portrait to Rabinowitz, who immediately returned the compliment.[79] In June 1885 it was announced in the magazine of the Mildmay Mission that it may be purchased. The same issue mentions that Rabinowitz has sent Wilkinson a picture of his whole family.[80]

We shall not decide whether the photo mentioned is the same as that which Rabinowitz has autographed and which is found, e.g. in the December 1885 issue of the Swedish Israel Mission's magazine (fig.1)[81] or whether it is the picture printed in the Mildmay Mission magazine in 1899 along with the obituary.[82] The latter (fig.2) is described as poor in the next issue and a better one is printed (fig.4).[83]

During the visit to England in 1887 a new portrait photograph was taken by "Eason & Co. Photo" (fig.3).[84] During the last visit to England in 1896 a photo was taken by Elliott and Fry which was printed in the Mildmay Mission magazine after Rabinowitz's death in 1899 (fig.4). In its obituary the Swedish Israel Mission also printed a picture (fig.5).[85] There are probably other portraits.[86]

In connection with the inauguration of Somerville Memorial Hall in 1890 two pictures were sent abroad, one of the outside of the new prayer house, one of Rabinowitz on the pulpit (see the beginning of this book). Mention can also be made of the lithograph of Rabinowitz on the Mount of Olives, already discussed and also reproduced at the beginning of the book.

The sources reveal that Rabinowitz had grey or blue eyes and was of the blond type.[87] He had a black beard, wrote A.S. Poulsen in 1886, who is further of the opinion that Rabinowitz "more resembles an Englishman than a Jew". Poulsen adds that in those parts many other Jews have blue eyes.[88] In 1885 W. Faber wrote from his visit to Kishinev that there was a rumour abroad that Rabinowitz was not a Jew at all. But Faber added that it was not even believed by those who spread it. It was only an outworking of fanatical hatred, he added.[89] Also, Rabinowitz limped because of a foot deformity which he seems to have had from birth.[90]

But his limping gait did not prevent him from walking the road and taking the steps that were necessary for a Messianic movement to be formed. He took some first steps when he met R. Faltin.

Chapter 4

THE FIRST MEETING WITH FALTIN
AND THE THIRTEEN THESES OF 1883

Three days after his homecoming from Palestine at the beginning of July 1882, Rabinowitz, as the Kishinev correspondent, had sent in an item to Hamelitz. It might be taken as an expression of chagrin at being attacked for his criticism of Oliphant. The fact that he no longer wrote for Hamelitz could be taken as merely the result of personal disappointment or resentment. But less than 18 months after his return from Palestine any reader of Hamelitz knew what was the actual cause of the silence of its Kishinev correspondent: Rabinowitz had changed his faith.

The sources yield only scanty information about Rabinowitz in the period after his return from Palestine and before his first meeting with Christian missions and his subsequent public stand as a Messianic believer at the end of 1883. Some particulars from this period of almost 18 months have been preserved, however, thanks not least to the data which R. Faltin, the Lutheran clergyman in Kishinev, passed on. The meeting with Faltin and the drawing-up of the Thirteen Theses were two important events for Rabinowitz in 1883. But even before Rabinowitz's name was mentioned in West European missionary magazines, there was a debate going on in the Jewish press in Russia. A glimpse of this debate must be given first. When it is set alongside Faltin's and W. Faber's data, it is possible to trace the outlines of Rabinowitz's development in the year 1883.

An early Jewish reaction

By 20 January/1 February 1884 Rabinowitz was already under attack in the Jewish periodical Hamelitz.[1] The editor's words about his friend and correspondent Joseph Rabinowitz have been quoted (see Chapter 3). They were occasioned by a letter sent to the editor which was printed on the same occasion. In it Rabinowitz is attacked for being in contact with Lutheran missionaries. He is zealously proclaiming the foolish teaching that the only solution to the Jewish question is for the Jews to accept Lutheran doctrine. Together with his friends, the letter goes on, he is holding meetings with the Lutheran pastor, in which plans are being made to draw Jewish souls into Luther's net. It is asserted that the Jews in Kishinev have met Rabinowitz with silent contempt; unfortunately the same has not been the case in other towns of Bessarabia, where Rabinowitz's words have struck root and where he has helpers. The anonymous letter-writer maintains that Rabinowitz's change of faith is due to his strong sympathy for Kabbala and Zohar. In these Jewish writings he finds warrant for Christian doctrine. The editor should not believe that this is a slander against his "dear friend and correspondent". Rabinowitz's apostasy has been "known long enough". Besides, Rabinowitz would not himself deny what was earlier written about him in Woschod, a Russian-language Jewish periodical.[2] The writer of these lines even knew instances of Rabinowitz attempting to persuade the editor's staff to join his movement.

Some of the details in the letter are strongly slanted and tendentious. This particularly applies to the allegation that Rabinowitz's aim is now to get Jews to change to Lutheranism. As we shall see, right from the start, Rabinowitz did all he could to counter this misunderstanding, but in vain. The introductory words of the editor, A. Zederbaum, that Rabinowitz does not acknowledge Jesus as the Son of God, but only as the Messiah, also seem to be wide of the mark, even though the editor probably meant this comment kindly. None the less, this front-page article gives clear evidence that Rabinowitz's change of attitude had been known by some people from at least the turn of the year 1883-1884 and by the Jewish public from the beginning of 1884. The letter also gives evidence that Rabinowitz had not been keeping silent. For it says that Rabinowitz "from the time he came back from Palestine became converted in his views."

Some Christian sources of an early date give us an inkling of what Rabinowitz had been doing after his return from Palestine and in the year 1883.

Christians on Rabinowitz in 1883

W. Faber, Delitzsch's close collaborator, visited Kishinev at the end of March 1884. He states that Rabinowitz's legal practice had suffered a reverse, because it was mainly Jews who had previously employed him.[3] That means that Rabinowitz continued his work as a lawyer after his homecoming from Palestine. This is also confirmed by Faltin, the Lutheran pastor in Kishinev; he writes about this in his annual report for the period 31 October 1883 - 31 October 1884.

Without giving precise dates, Faltin writes that Rabinowitz openly and with much enthusiasm spoke about his new convictions to his fellow Jews. The Hebrew New Testament lay on his desk next to the Hebrew Old Testament.[4] Those who consulted him as a lawyer were told of his new conviction: that the Jewish question could only be solved by the Jews as a people accepting Jesus, their brother.

Before his public stand, Rabinowitz had studied the Scriptures thoroughly. He obtained a clear perception of what his conversion must lead to by combining Psalm 105 with Romans 11: God's wonderful way with Israel was that they were going to turn to him as a nation (J. Wilkinson claims that it was Faltin who had drawn his attention to Psalm 105, but this contradicts Faltin's own words).[5] In this connection the idea was also contemplated of forming a Hebrew Christian congregation. There were thoughts of this even before his first personal meeting with Faltin. It is not known definitely whether in this period he sought contact with his brother-in-law Herschensohn/Lichtenstein. But it is not inconceivable in view of our findings in the last chapter. The Jewish source mentioned above also bears witness that his ideas found a hearing in many people. In his annual report for 1883-1884 Faltin mentions that before he met Rabinowitz some people had been influenced by him in this matter. But no exact number is mentioned. It is certain that some members of Rabinowitz's own family sympathized with him early on. Thus his brother, Efraim Jakob Rabinowitz, a tobacconist, attended a conference about the Messianic movement on 26 March 1884. Later the same year he made his house available for his brother to hold public worship services.

The question of the number of Rabinowitz's followers rapidly became a topic of hot debate. It requires separate treatment (see Chapter 5).

The Thirteen Theses, which Rabinowitz published at the end of 1883, give an insight into some of the thoughts which preoccupied him in the period after his return from Palestine. But before we take a look at them, for the sake of lucidity it will be useful to give an account of his first personal meeting with the Lutheran pastor in Kishinev.

The meeting with Rudolf Faltin

On 17 February 1859 Rudolf Faltin had been installed as pastor of the small Lutheran congregation in Kishinev; part of his assignment was to be "divisional chaplain" for Lutheran soldiers in the Russian army, and pastor for the German settlers in the area. This job entailed considerable travelling. But it was not long before he actively entered into work among the Jews of Kishinev. He was highly esteemed for this work.[6] Particularly the story of the baptism of R.H. Gurland, the former rabbi, in 1864 had made Faltin well-known. That conversion also made a good story for the supporters of missions to Israel.

For Gurland had given Faltin lessons in Hebrew on the stipulation that the pastor was not to use the opportunity for proselytizing. Nevertheless it came about that, while reading Isaiah 53, Gurland began to ask questions and came to faith. After his baptism he took a theological training in Berlin and returned to Kishinev in 1867. He worked with Faltin there for some years, before being transferred in 1871 to Kitau in Kurland. He later went to Odessa, where he died in 1905.[7] The close relationship between Faltin and

Gurland was lifelong. That between Faltin and Rabinowitz was to turn out differently, although it began well enough.

Faltin was well-known for his work among the Jews of Kishinev. He was able to celebrate 25 years there in February 1884 just as the first information about Rabinowitz was coming in to Delitzsch in Leipzig. It was also Faltin who sent the Thirteen Theses to Delitzsch.[8] He was in close contact with the Norwegian Israel Mission after 1868, when this mission began to support his work financially; in 1869 half of the funds of the Norwegian Israel Mission went to the work in Kishinev.[9] In 1874-1890 the London Society supported him too;[10] from 1873 he received support from the Swedish Israel Mission, and others.[11] In his annual report for 1883-1884 he regretted "the circumstance rather embarrassing for us" that the usual sizable contribution from the Norwegians had not come in.[12] Shortly before Christmas 1884 a large sum was granted, and the accounts of the Norwegian Israel Mission itemize considerable sums for Faltin's work in these years.[13] Faltin's frequent dispatches were much used in the magazines of the various Israel missions. In Russia, for instance, his annual reports were published in German in the magazine St. Peterburgisches Evangelisches Sonntagsblatt.

Thus to meet Faltin and obtain his favour was to link up with the most esteemed Christian personality in Russia working for the cause of Israel. For Rabinowitz, however, the meeting with Faltin for which he took the initiative entailed some problems.

We are here concerned to chart the first personal meeting between these two. The question is of particular interest because, as shown above, the Jewish press connected Rabinowitz's new faith with the Lutheran church. Elsewhere too, Rabinowitz was accused of changing religion for the sake of the money he received from the mission (see Chapter 8).

In May 1884 Delitzsch briefly states that Faltin had first become acquainted with Rabinowitz personally "about six months ago".[14] In the same context it is stated that the "proselytes" who had been won over in Kishinev through Faltin's labours were almost without exception outside the new movement. Finally Delitzsch stresses that Rabinowitz had not been under missionary influence in connection with his 'conversion'.

According to these statements, Faltin and Rabinowitz must have met personally for the first time in November or December 1883, not quite 18 months after Rabinowitz's return from Palestine.

This seems to be confirmed by the annual report quoted above for 1883-1884. In this context it may also be commented that in a lecture Faltin gave in Berlin on 21 June 1883 there is not the slightest hint of the existence of the new movement.[15] As Faltin was dealing in depth with his work in Kishinev and Jewish missions in Russia in general, this must be evidence that Faltin did not at that time know anything about Rabinowitz. It may also be taken as an indication that Rabinowitz was working unobtrusively.

In Faltin's frequent bulletins reproduced in the magazine of the Norwegian Israel Mission the first news about the existence of the movement comes in the report for March 1884.[16] Whether he had written about it earlier to his Norwegian friends or not, the following paragraph is, as far as I can see, the first to be published, even though Rabinowitz's name is not mentioned directly. It runs:

> In connection with the Hebrew-Christian movement here, a conference was held at which an attempt was made, along with the most important of its leaders, to reach clarity about the aims of the movement. May God bless this significant movement among the Jews!

We shall return to this conference (see Chapter 5). In the annual report already cited for 1883-1884 Faltin goes into some details about what preceded it. He maintains - and with justification - that there can hardly be anyone who has such a good insight into the new movement as he has. Rabinowitz, he says, is in warmest fellowship with him, although he modestly adds that he does not wish to attribute any merit to himself in this matter.[17] Faltin does not give the exact date of the first meeting between him and Rabinowitz; it can only be deduced that it took place after 31 October 1883 when the report begins.

At the time the report was being written, his relations with Rabinowitz were the best possible. When the report was reproduced in Norwegian, the editor said in an introduction that it was interesting to see "how Rabinowitz's first impression of Christianity is linked to Faltin's work".[18] Although this seems to contradict Delitzsch's word, as cited above, this is not the case, for the editorial comment goes on: "especially the New Testament disseminated by him [Faltin], for the publication of which of course some of our country's mission contributions have been applied." It is plain what the editor is up to: to the mission supporters he is proving that the mission's money has been well spent, and he is giving Faltin all that is his due in connection with Rabinowitz's conversion; in justice to the editor, he does not make any statement about a personal connection between the two men.

In his report Faltin clearly reveals how Rabinowitz's "first impression of Christianity is linked to Faltin's work". In a wondrous way, he says, God has led them together. He mentions that "many years ago" he gave a Hebrew New Testament to a person who later underwent baptism. It is plain that Herschensohn/Lichtenstein is in mind here, though Faltin avoids mentioning the name. And this person passed it on to Rabinowitz when he was living in Orgeyev, says Faltin, "as I learned not long ago".

This evidence is close to Rabinowitz's account of the same matter in his autobiography, as was discussed in Chapter 3.

Faltin goes on to relate that for a long time Rabinowitz only used this New Testament "superficially". After briefly recounting Rabinowitz's journey to Palestine and his using his legal practice for telling about his new conviction, Faltin says: "At that time we were not known to each other personally, nor had we seen each other."

But they were to do so.

The first meeting on neutral ground

How the first meeting came about is itself a story worth the telling. Both parties knew how to act diplomatically, as the situation required. An intermediary got the meeting arranged on - as they say - "neutral ground".

An unnamed teacher and owner of a private school, who often visited Faltin and also attended his church services, told him about Rabinowitz. This teacher also had contacts with Rabinowitz and came to act as an intermediary between the parties. At any rate, Faltin relates that through this teacher Rabinowitz requested a meeting with him. But Rabinowitz stipulated that the meeting must not take place at the parsonage. It was to be on "neutral ground" so as not to arouse suspicion that he was seeking contact with the pastor for instruction and that he was thinking of being baptized.[19]

Faltin reveals that he gladly agreed to such a meeting, which must be dated in November or early December 1883. The neutral venue was found in the home of G. Ziegler, Faltin's brother-in-law. This and later meetings did not, however, prevent Rabinowitz from being accused of pleading the cause of Lutheranism, as we have already recounted. Besides the intermediary, only Faltin and Rabinowitz were present at the meeting. They prayed together and Rabinowitz narrated in some detail his life story and his conviction that the time had come for Israel to gather into a Christian congregation retaining national customs. "How this was to happen, we could not determine", comments Faltin. But through their conversation they arrived at a joint conviction that they were knit together in their faith. The meeting was closed with prayer in which the matter was committed to God.

Against this background it must be regarded as certain that Faltin and Rabinowitz did not meet before November or December 1883. Faltin's share in Rabinowitz's conversion was the indirect one of having given a New Testament to a person who had passed it on to Rabinowitz.

At the close of the first meeting Rabinowitz handed Faltin thirteen theses written in Hebrew. Faltin describes them as "a result of his researches and the conviction of those likeminded with him." Faltin sent these to Delitzsch, who translated them. Thus Faltin had a large share of the credit that Delitzsch early on was made aware of and got involved with the new movement. Without anticipating the course of events, we may mention here that some years later Faltin sharply criticized Rabinowitz, which resulted in a breach between the two (see Chapter 10).

The Thirteen Theses give some impression of the thoughts that had preoccupied Rabinowitz in 1883 - before his first meeting with Faltin.

The Thirteen Theses

Rabinowitz told Isidore Goldstern, who visited Kishinev at the end of April 1885, that it was about 19 months since he made a public stand, i.e. around October 1883.[20]

In the Thirteen Theses the date 5644 by Jewish reckoning appears, i.e. they were written after the Jewish New Year, which in 1883 fell on 2 October. They were written before the meeting with Faltin, which took place before Christmas 1883, as is revealed in a letter to be mentioned in the next section. The crucial question is whether the theses are an adequate expression of Rabinowitz's view of Christianity at the end of 1883, or whether they were formulated with a different purpose in view. This question will be discussed later. The theses were sent by Faltin to Delitzsch in Leipzig before Faber got back from his stay in Kishinev, which ended in mid April 1884. A German translation of them was published in the second issue of *Saat auf Hoffnung* 1884.[21] Already in the April issue of the Swedish Israel Mission's magazine the existence of the theses is mentioned; a few extracts are given in Swedish translation.[22] In May 1884 they were published in Hebrew and German in the first documents about the movement which Delitzsch issued.[23] Already on 29 February 1884 Delitzsch had mentioned the existence of the movement when commenting on Faltin's celebration of 25 years as pastor in Kishinev.[24] In 1884 the theses were translated into English, and in 1885 into French.[25]

The first theses describe the plight and need of the Jews and distance themselves from various proposals for solving the Jewish question, some of which Rabinowitz had himself advocated earlier. The content of the various theses may be summed up as follows:

§1 The present moral and material condition of the Jews in Russia is very bad.

§2 For us to sit idle and inactive at such a time is tantamount to consenting to the total ruin of our Jewish brethren in Russia.

§3 An improvement of the conditions cannot come about through the money of the rich, or the teaching of the rabbis, or the enlightenment of the learned. Such people do not think of the welfare of Israel, but only worsen the conditions.

§4 It is of no help to leave our native land of Russia and emigrate to Eretz Israel, and of just as little help to become assimilated with the Gentile population of Russia.

§5 Salvation and help can only be obtained here in Russia by our own efforts and with the aid of the Lord who is mighty to save.

§6 The material state of the Jews cannot be improved until they are healed of their moral and spiritual depravity.

§7 To put right the moral state there must be a deep spiritual renewal. Our idols, love of money, must be cast out, and instead our hearts must have love of truth and fear of evil.

§8 For this renewal a leader of firm character is needed.

Although there is no mistaking the criticism here, there is nothing in these first eight theses which necessarily place Rabinowitz outside the Jewish national community. The Russian Jews were familiar with self-criticism if anyone was. If these first eight theses are compared with Rabinowitz's articles before 1882 we discover that his wording about the material and spiritual situation of the Jews is the same. The criticism of the Jews' material and spiritual plight in these theses does not make Rabinowitz anti-Jewish or anti-Semitic, if it is possible to be the latter when one is a Jew. It is worth remembering these observations. Otherwise one may easily fall into misinterpreting Rabinowitz's later criticism of his fellow Jews as it was developed in his sermons.

We may imagine an unsuspecting Haskala or Enlightenment Jew nodding in approval at the description and criticism of the Jews' situation on reading through the first eight theses. Not until reading the ninth thesis would the unwary Jew begin to suspect something, and on coming to the tenth thesis he would probably fling them aside because the name of Jesus is mentioned. The name Jesus is rendered in its historically correct form of Yeshua; the name is also emphasized, being written with larger letters in theses 10-13 (see further Chapter 9).[26]

The leader whom thesis 8 adumbrates is described in more detail in the following theses, which we shall now summarize:

§9 This leader must be of Jacob's lineage, love Israel, and have given his life for God's holy name's sake and for the sake of the law and the prophets. He must be a man known by all the inhabitants of the earth. On the one hand he must have an understanding of his brethren who boast of the promises given to Abraham, Isaac, and Jacob, and who pride themselves on the knowledge they have received through the law of Sinai. On the other hand he must be acquainted with their tendency, in good times, to forsake their heavenly Father, the living God, and choose new gods for themselves: love of money and power over impoverished brethren through knowledge and mammon.

§10 After thorough searching in the historical books of our people, we have found the man who fulfills all this solely in the man Jesus of Nazareth, who was killed in Jerusalem before the destruction of the last temple.

§11 The wise men of Israel could not at that time understand the good counsel he gave to his brethren the Jews to keep the law in matters concerning the intellect and heart, and not to lay stress on outward acts which may alter according to the locality and the political situation of the Jews. We Jews who live in the year 5644 can positively see that Jesus is the man. Only he sought the true welfare of his brethren and spoke peace to their kindred.

§12 We feel bound by our great love for our brethren to keep holy and to honour the name of our brother Jesus and to study his holy words which have been recorded in the renowned writings, the Gospels. These should be inculcated into our children at school; wherever we are with people, we should speak about them, and the Gospel writings should be gathered as a treasure in our homes along with all the holy scriptures which have been handed down to us as a treasure by our wise men in all generations.

§13 We hope that the words of our brother Jesus, which were spoken in righteousness, love, and gentleness to our brethren, will take root in our hearts. The fruit of righteousness and salvation will be love of truth and goodness. Then the nations and the governments will change their attitude and permit us existence and establishment among the other living nations, overshadowed by the European laws which derive from this our brother's spirit, him who gave his life so that the world might thrive and to keep wickedness from the earth.

"Their acknowledgement of Jesus Christ is not yet central," wrote Delitzsch in connection with the publication of the Thirteen Theses in German. Nevertheless he rejoices at hearing Jesus named as "our brother" by Jewish lips. In the Thirteen Theses, "the small congregation" has formulated "its creed", he said.[27] But the question is whether Rabinowitz viewed his theses as a creed. In there being thirteen theses, some have seen confirmation of this, and pointed to Maimonides' 13 articles of faith, a comparison that proves nothing in itself.[28] Perhaps it is doing Rabinowitz an injustice to call these theses a creed instead of viewing them as a declaration in which he is primarily addressing his fellow Jews and clarifying his view as to how the Jewish question should be solved. Understood in this way, the theses do not necessarily say everything about Rabinowitz's conception of his faith in the autumn of 1883.

However, there is no mistaking the strong emphasis in this declaration on the positive social and political effects of a Jewish acceptance of Jesus. If this was indeed the main feature of Rabinowitz's conception of Christianity at the end of 1883, it was to alter amazingly rapidly. Zipperstein maintains that Rabinowitz "had lost faith in the prospect that changes in Jewish behavior would alter the attitude of gentiles... Rabinovich did not stress such social or political benefits of conversion, at least not in his earlier writings about Jesus. Rather, their acceptance of Jesus would win the favor of God, and He, and only He, would put an end to Jewish suffering."[29]

But here Zipperstein is turning things upside down. It is precisely in Rabinowitz's early writings from 1883 that the social and political benefits of the Jews' acceptance of Jesus are mentioned. In his writings from 1884 and onwards they are not mentioned. In this context, we must correct another misunderstanding for which Delitzsch is partly to blame. When he published the Theses along with other material in May 1884, he was in possession of information that Rabinowitz had at that time formulated his creed.[30] But other people could be misled into thinking that the Thirteen Theses and the other material published had in principle the same value. However this was not so. By the time the Theses were published in May 1884, and thus became known to Western Europe, Rabinowitz had reached quite a different kind of firm ground than can be read out of his Thirteen Theses.

A factor contributing to this may have been a letter he received shortly before Christmas 1883.

G. Friedmann's reaction to the Theses

Most Jews were bound to react unfavourably to Rabinowitz's Theses, because the solution to the Jewish problem was found in Jesus. Others might react on quite different grounds. Whether Faltin had a hand in it or not, he was in full accord with the ideas which G. Friedmann, a former catechist, expressed in a letter to Rabinowitz. Faltin sent this letter with the Theses to Delitzsch, who concurred with the criticism.[31] In his letter, written a few days before Christmas 1883, Friedmann, a Hebrew Christian, expresses a wish that Rabinowitz and those like-minded might realize that Jesus did not come to the world to give the Jews political equality with other nations, but to atone for sin. The letter, which was couched in a brotherly tone, refers to

Thesis 13, and Friedmann does not conceal that Rabinowitz's viewpoint is deficient. According to Friedmann it is not enough to acknowledge Jesus as the Son of David and the Messiah of Israel, he must be confessed as the Son of God and the Lamb of God who bears the sin of the world. Friedmann clearly expresses his joy at the pathway which Rabinowitz and those likeminded had trodden, but does not neglect to express the hope that they may enter upon the right road which leads to "the heavenly Jerusalem". "Beloved brethren," he writes, "you are not far from the truth and the way of peace, but you have not yet entered upon it. Moses' veil has been lifted from your hearts, but not yet completely removed."

Thus Friedmann puts his finger on an underplaying of the person and work of Jesus in the Theses, and a related overplaying of the political consequences which the Theses claim a Jewish acceptance of Jesus would have for Russian Jews. As mentioned, both Faltin and Delitzsch backed up this criticism, but like Friedmann they did not forget to express their joy at the good beginning that had been made.

Some 18 months after his return from Palestine, Rabinowitz's conception of his faith contained strong political overtones. There can be no doubt about that. The question must remain whether he had arrived at a greater knowledge of basic Christian truths than he displayed in the Theses. If the Thirteen Theses are an adequate expression of his basic stance at the end of 1883, we shall have to admit that he developed at amazing speed. In March 1884 he put forward in writing some material in which he reveals a basic attitude which, in quite a different way, accords with e.g. Delitzsch's understanding of the Christian faith. Either Friedmann's letter had the desired effect, or allowance must be made - as Friedmann did not - for the possibility that Rabinowitz's Thirteen Theses were not intended to give a full account of the content of his faith.

At any rate these observations show that at his homecoming from Palestine Rabinowitz did not have a ready-made view of his Christian faith. It developed. Zipperstein gives an incomplete picture of Rabinowitz's faith, however, when he maintains: "It is at some midway point between heresy and apostasy that Rabinovich must be placed, closer to the former and further (until 1885, at any rate) from the latter."[32] The borderline for Rabinowitz's alleged "apostasy" lies earlier that 1885, namely towards the end of 1883 or the beginning of 1884.

In March 1885, when he met John Wilkinson, the leader of the Mildmay Mission, he was asked the question when he first definitely trusted in the Lord Jesus Christ for salvation. According to Wilkinson, Rabinowitz said: "A year ago last Rosh Hashana". This was explained by Wilkinson as being about 18 months before, as the Jewish New Year fell in the autumn.[33] If this is the meaning, Rabinowitz's mind had been made up in the autumn of 1883, before the meeting with Faltin.

But most indications are that Rabinowitz made his final decision after the meeting with Faltin and after receiving Friedmann's reaction to the Thirteen Theses. He received that reaction about Christmas 1883, i.e. around New Year 1884 by our calendar. Would it be a facile explanation that when Rabinowitz answered Wilkinson's question using the Hebrew expression *Rosh Hashana*, he was referring to New Year 1883-1884 by the Christian calendar? However this may be, the underlying tone of the material Rabinowitz put out in March 1884 had changed. And most important: this new tone was to be his keynote for the rest of his life.

In 1885 Rabinowitz had this to say about his own development: "I first honoured Jesus as the great human being with the compassionate heart, later as the one who desired the welfare of my people, and finally as the one who bore my sins."[34]

Chapter 5

THE MOVEMENT TAKES SHAPE IN 1884

A few days before Christmas 1883 (i.e. 24 December 1883/5 January 1884) Rabinowitz had received Friedmann's letter. As we mentioned in the last chapter, it had been written in a brotherly spirit. All the same, there was no mistaking the criticism of Rabinowitz's conception of his faith. On Christmas Eve the following year (1884) Rabinowitz received a letter from the Russian authorities with permission for public gatherings of "Israelites of the New Covenant". Between these two "Christmas letters" significant events occurred around the Messianic movement.

The year 1884 was an eventful one. The main historical occurrences will be outlined here. At the same time the contours of Rabinowitz's faith will be plotted out with certain key words. There will be a fuller account in Chapter 8. In this context it is important to note that from March/April 1884 Rabinowitz had reached such clarity of mind about his faith and vision that the keynote had now been struck for his subsequent activity. This is particularly surprising when we think of the views he had put forward in the Thirteen Theses at the end of 1883. Friedmann's letter had taken effect. And shortly after that he was required to give answer to foreign representatives of some missions to Israel. This already occurred at a conference or meeting held in Kishinev on 14/26 March 1884.

The conference in Kishinev on 14/26 March 1884

After the first meeting between Rabinowitz and Faltin, the latter wrote to Delitzsch in Leipzig enclosing the Thirteen Theses and Friedmann's letter.[1] W. Faber, Delitzsch's confidential co-worker and the travelling missionary and PR-man of the German Central Agency arrived in Kishinev on 21 March 1884. A.S. Poulsen (and others) wrote that Faber was sent by Delitzsch "to Kishinev to obtain fuller information about the remarkable movement."[2] However, it would seem that, prior to Faber's departure, Delitzsch had only been presented with the plan for a journey to Breslau - to which he had given permission.[3] In an account of his life written by A. Wiegand in 1911, he says of Faber: "Faber's restless spirit electrified everyone."[4] From Kishinev it electrified Delitzsch too, as we now shall see.

The day after his arrival in Kishinev as well as 24 March, Faber had profound discussions with Rabinowitz. On 25 March he wrote a postcard to Delitzsch: "Today three representatives of the British Mission Society suddenly arrived from England to investigate the movement." On the same card he had written: "The matter is very important, but in quite a different way from what I had imagined. Rabinowitz is a very important person; Lichtenstein knows him." Faber regards it as "divine leading" that he is in town just then. "How strange that I here meet with the Englishmen who want to investigate the matter."[5]

Faltin presents the matter differently. In a wondrous manner, he says, the Lord had the Englishmen come to Kishinev, because "they wanted to get to know me personally."[6] Well, it may be that the Englishmen said that to Faltin, but that was not, in fact, the main purpose of their journey.

The Englishmen acted swiftly. On the very day of their arrival an appointment was made for a conference the following day. Later, representatives of the British Society seldom missed an opportunity to stress the significance of their presence. It was claimed that the formation of "the Hebrew branch of the Christian church" in Kishinev would not have occurred at that juncture if they had not been divinely led to visit the town. It is also emphasized that the meeting came about because of their visit.[7] This was undoubtedly correct. Faber's postcard supports this understanding. Delitzsch had no hand in this, apart from the not unimportant one that his right-hand man Faber happened to be on the spot anyway.

The conference as such was unprepared and was arranged from one day to the next. As Rabinowitz was able to present some written documents, this indicates that he had not been idle but was already busy mapping out the lines of the movement. The articles which were discussed were not "formulated" at the meeting, as Zipperstein says,[8] but were submitted by Rabinowitz. This is also confirmed by Faber on the postcard of 25 March. For on this he says that Rabinowitz has already almost drawn up "a Christian Siddur", i.e. prayer book, presumably with the order of service, and that he wishes to bring this, along with "much else", back to Delitzsch. Part of the material which was presented at the meeting on 26 March was some of the "much else" which Faber brought back to Germany.

From the minutes

The minutes that were taken give a good record of the course of the meeting.[9] G. Friedmann was assigned to write them. On 31 March he had still not finished writing them up, Faber relates.[10] The meeting which was held in the evening of 26 March was not held on "neutral ground". Evidently Rabinowitz realized that his connections with the Lutheran pastor could not be kept secret; almost two months previously Hamelitz had been trumpeting it abroad. Faltin was an obvious participant and chaired the meeting. The visitors from abroad were W. Faber and the three Englishmen from the British Society: the secretary J. Dunlop; the treasurer F.Y. Edwards; and the Society's missionary in Odessa B. Ben Zion. The seven other participants all came from Kishinev, although it was disingenuous of The Jewish Herald in its report of the meeting to describe them as representatives of "The Sons of the New Covenant".[11] The majority were office-holders in and were attached to the Lutheran church, as the following shows:

- G. Ziegler, member of the church council and Faltin's brother-in-law
- H. Rathminder, member of the church council and a grammar-school teacher
- A. Wachnitz, teacher at the Lutheran school in Kishinev
- R. Finkelstein, colporteur and a Hebrew Christian
- G. Friedmann, teacher and a Hebrew Christian

The last two participants were the grocer or tobacconist Efraim Jakob Rabinowitz and - of course - his brother, Joseph Rabinowitz, the main protagonist. These two had not yet been baptized. The copy of the minutes which are in the Bodleian Library, Oxford, bears the signatures of all those present, apart from G. Ziegler.[12]

After an opening hymn in German and a prayer by Faltin, he read from Acts 2:1-4. These words about the first Christian Pentecost in Jerusalem set the tone for the meeting. It was held with 'Pentecostal' expectations. After open prayer before the negotiations, they began by reading aloud "The Twelve Articles of Faith of the Israelites of the New Covenant."[13] These had been drawn up by Rabinowitz and had much more theological substance than the Thirteen Theses. In the Twelve Articles of Faith, the social and political consequences of the Jews' acceptance of Jesus had been deleted. We treat these more fully in Chapter 8.

The Twelve Articles of Faith were intended to be a draft of the articles of faith of the Messianic movement. At the conference they came to form the basis of discussion. The minutes give a good insight into the main topics of the subsequent discussion.

The debate at the meeting

Firstly, the question of the Trinity was discussed. The first Article of Faith said: "I believe, with a perfect faith, that the Creator, blessed be His name, is the living, true and eternal God, who hath made by His Word, and His Holy Spirit, heaven and earth, all things visible and invisible; that He is One, and all is from Him, through Him and to Him." The expression, "that He is One", gave rise to fuller discussion. The word for "One" in the Hebrew text was *Echad*, which was left unamended. But Rabinowitz consented to the sentence possibly being rendered into English "that He is a Unity". In German "*Einer*" was amended to "*Einiger*", making the same emphasis possible. However, the whole matter was reduced to nonsense in the magazine of the Norwegian Israel Mission, which stated that the expression "one" had been replaced with "some"![14]

During this discussion, Rabinowitz also stated that the doctrine of the Trinity was suggested at the end of the first Article by the words "all is from Him, through Him, and to Him". In an explanatory note which was laid before the conference in writing, Rabinowitz elaborated upon this question (see Chapter 8).

Rabinowitz was also called upon to give his views on the observing of Jewish customs. The cause of this was that at the meeting he had stressed that he and those like-minded with him desired liberty to observe Jewish customs handed down from their fathers in so far as these were not at variance with the spirit of Christianity. From a 'religious' point of view, he and his adherents believed that the law had been perfectly fulfilled by the Messiah. But from a 'patriotic' point of view, they felt obligated to keep the law as far as nationality and circumstances made it possible.

This gave rise to a debate on two main themes: the keeping of circumcision and the Sabbath. The Gentile Christian participants saw a danger that Hebrew Christians would nevertheless keep these commandments not merely from national but also religious motives. To reach clarity about Rabinowitz's attitude, the question was put whether a Christian Jew who did not circumcise his child would be committing a sin. Rabinowitz's reply was: "He does not commit a sin, but he thereby estranges himself from his people." He gave a similar reply to the question whether Christian Jews who do not keep the Sabbath were committing a sin.

Finally the meeting gave Rabinowitz an opportunity to explain what seemed so obvious to him: that the distinctive features of the various nationalities may be retained when the various nations receive Christ. Regarding the New Testament, he declared that it had the same canonical status as the Old Testament. On the other hand the Talmud and other rabbinical writings had no authority at all. He regarded these works as remnants of the time when Israel was walking in darkness and hardness of heart. He declared that his view of the sacraments was in accord with Lutheran doctrine.

The secretary of the British Society, J. Dunlop, mentioned an instance of an English Hebrew Christian who observed the 'Abrahamic covenant' in the case of his children by having them circumcised. The meeting closed with a prayer by Faltin and by everyone saying the Lord's Prayer together in Hebrew.

That is what the minutes have to tell us.

Faber remains in Kishinev

With this conference, the first international links of a personal kind had been forged. And in them lay the germ of rivalry over Rabinowitz among the various countries' missions to Israel. A. Wiegand commented in 1911 that if Faber had not been present, the dependence of the movement upon Britain and British money would probably have been greater.[15] But it is questionable whether Wiegand's view was sufficiently balanced. Financial support from Germany remained comparatively low (see Chapter 13). It was not until later in 1884 that correspondence was started with John Wilkinson, the leader of the English Mildmay Mission. This contact was to have considerable significance. It was not with unalloyed enthusiasm that the British Society had to acknowledge that the upstart among English missions to Israel had made this contact - and made a scoop (see Chapter 7).

The three Englishmen left soon after the conference. But Faber remained in Kishinev for some weeks. Besides speaking in the Lutheran Church, he studied the Messianic movement closely. He wrote to Delitzsch on the day after the conference that the journey he was making, and which had led him to Kishinev, had given him material for 50-100 talks![16]

On this postcard, and in a letter of 31 March, he tells of his other travel plans. Now that he has become acquainted with the movement in Kishinev, he feels it important to continue the journey to Palestine to get to know the Hebrew Christian colony of Artuf.[17] But Delitzsch now vetoed this; he replied swiftly making his colleague see reason; Kishinev must be the end of the line, says Delitzsch, all the rest is superfluous: "Come back as quickly as possible, the journey was improvised hastily."[18] Faber did so. The two quickly got over the disagreement caused. After the autumn of 1884 the previous formal "*Sie*" (for "you") is replaced by the informal "*Du*" when they correspond.[19]

Before returning to Leipzig in April 1884, Faber was able to keep the Jewish Passover, Pesach, which he celebrated with the Messianic Jews using a communion liturgy which Rabinowitz had drawn up (see further Chapter 8). This experience made a favourable impression upon Faber. But so had Faltin's daughter Luitgard or Luita. He was betrothed to her on his departure.[20] All the same, later in the year Delitzsch had to put pressure upon Faber to get him to return to Kishinev. They were not married until 1886. This link is not without interest in this context. As we have already intimated, Faltin later broke with Rabinowitz. His son-in-law - Faber - had to make up his mind about this. And as we shall see, the decision went in favour of Rabinowitz.

But the British visitors also went home from Kishinev encouraged. J. Dunlop recounted a story which Rabinowitz had told at the close of the conference. Dunlop described it as the "crown of the conference".

A story from the conference

J. Dunlop gives Rabinowitz's story the heading "The parable of the Wheel":[21]

A few foolish people driving in a four-wheeler happened to lose a wheel. Finding that the car moved along heavily, they looked about and found that a wheel was missing. One of the foolish men jumped down and ran forward in search of the missing wheel. To everyone he met he said, "We have lost a wheel. Have you seen a wheel? Have you found a wheel?" One wise man at last said, "You are looking in the wrong direction. Instead of looking in front for your wheel, you ought to look behind." That is exactly the great mistake the Jews have been making for centuries. They have forgotten that in order to look forward aright, they must first look behind aright. The four wheels of Hebrew History may be said to be Abraham, Moses, David, and Jesus. The Jews by looking in front, instead of behind, have failed to find their fourth wheel. Thank God, that "the Sons of the New Covenant" have found the Supreme Wheel - Jesus. Abraham, Moses and David are but beautiful types and symbols of Jesus. They were, and still are, the repositories of His energy; they were, and are still, moved and managed by Him, as truly as are the Cherubim and Seraphim. Thank God, we have found Yeshua Achinu, our Brother Jesus, our All, "who of God has been made unto us, wisdom, righteousness, sanctification, and redemption;" from whom alone we have found divine light, life, liberty, and love, for the great Here and the greater Hereafter. And now with bright eye and jubilant heart, we are looking forward to the pulsing splendours of His appearing.

The public debate in 1884

In May 1884, less than two months after the conference, Delitzsch was able to publish the first documents about the Messianic movement. Before this, some scattered notices about the movement had already reached the west European press. Thus in April the magazine of the London Society could quote what the correspondent of the Daily News in Odessa had written in the paper on 3 March and which The Christian repeated on 6 March:

> Considerable excitement has been aroused in the Jewish communities of South Russia by the appearance at Kischineff of an energetic Reformer named Joseph Rabinovitch. He declares Christ to have been the real Messiah, supporting his theories by numerous citations from the Bible and the Prophets. Rabinovitch is an enthusiastic and eloquent preacher, and is winning numerous proselytes. He is anathematized generally by the Jewish Press.[22]

The British Society, which had taken part in the conference in Kishinev in March, did not print the same information until May;[23] in June more information was given in the Society's magazine about what it calls "one of the most remarkable conferences we have ever attended".[24] Nevertheless J. Dunlop later feels able to claim that "the first account of this movement was given in England by us", pointing out that this was done at the Society's 41st annual meeting on 13 May 1884.[25] Onward from October, translations of documents and other material are printed. The London Society began a month earlier, in September (see Chapter 1).

But it was a fairly brief article in The Times which really set the debate going and also influenced the debate in Russia, both in the Christian and the Jewish press, which particularly drew a caustic riposte from Delitzsch. Viewed from a distance, the debate sparked off by the article in The Times is a textbook example of how easily parties to a dispute can talk at cross purposes. Not all those who expressed opinions about the article in the months following its appearance had in fact seen it. Delitzsch seems only to have known the contents from the reports of others. Rabinowitz was sent it by J. Wilkinson.[26]

The article, which occupies no more than about half a column, appeared in The Times on 23 August 1884. It was written by J.H. Titcomb on 20 August in Hamburg. Titcomb was Bishop Coadjutor for the English Church in Northern and Central Europe. He based his article on Delitzsch's information as it appeared in the first documents about the movement from May 1884, and said that his attention had been drawn to it by a clergyman named Hefter in Frankfurt.[27] In his article Titcomb does not provide any information that is particularly new, compared with Delitzsch's. But Titcomb does write concerning the attraction of the movement that the words "our brother Jesus" have proved to possess such attractive power that "they have not only awakened the hearts of all in Kischinew - his [Rabinowitz's] own place of residence - but many also in other parts of Bessarabia". And Titcomb continues with some words which were later warmly discussed: "More than 200 families have now joined in one communion under the title of "The National Jewish New Testament Congregation".

In Britain this article was commented upon in The Jewish Chronicle on 12 September in a letter sent in under the pseudonym "One who knows" and written on 8 September. While acknowledging the scholarship of Delitzsch, his missionary activity is regarded as narrow-minded. The writer of this letter is more concerned with the channel through which the information about the new movement was presented than with the movement itself, as he himself admits. Concerning the reliability of Titcomb's information he has to admit that "it is impossible out of Russia to arrive at a trustworthy conclusion".

The item in The Times found its way into Russian newspapers, apparently being copied in at least three papers in September.[28] In Hamelitz no. 71 for autumn 1884 the matter is discussed on this basis. Rabinowitz is there characterized as "an old man who has forgotten what he learnt". This old man, "who has lost his wits" has however succeeded in dazzling the eyes of "such a learned man as Professor Delitzsch", who is known to be a reader of Hamelitz. According to The Times, 250 families have joined the movement, but Hamelitz can state that there is not one single family who has adhered to the new prophet in Kishinev. It maintains that Rabinowitz is a fool who has read some books which have made his brain sick; he is a phantasist without any general religious education. The writer of the article has a sure premonition that the information appearing in The Times had Rabinowitz as its source. And the claim about the 250 families who were supposed to have joined him, is regarded as an expression of Rabinowitz's own dreams and fancies.[29]

Also in an article in Jüdische Presse, later reproduced in English in The Jewish Chronicle on 28 November 1884, Delitzsch is declared to have been made the victim of "a base lie" if he believes that Rabinowitz has succeeded in founding a movement that is daily spreading and already numbers 200 families. This article concludes: "After having strictly investigated the matter, I am enabled to affirm that such a society exists only in the imagination of Mr. J. Rabinowitz, and that in reality he has not succeeded in winning over one Jewish soul to his ideas beyond the family of his own brother."[30]

At about the same time Delitzsch published a sharp protest against the way Hamelitz had dealt with the matter in issue no. 71 of 1884. We shall summarize the contents of this.

A sharp reaction from Delitzsch

In a tone that for Delitzsch was unusually caustic, he made his reply in "Continued Documents", which appeared in 1885, the preface being dated November 1884.[31] The tone of his reply is undoubtedly an expression of his anger at reading that Rabinowitz had dazzled the eyes of such "a well-intentioned and learned" man as Professor Delitzsch. In four paragraphs introduced with the words "It does not surprise us", Delitzsch goes on the counter-offensive.

It does not surprise us, writes Delitzsch, that the same Rabinowitz who had been formerly described in the same periodical as a learned Jew and friend of his nation should now - after believing in Jesus the Messiah - be declared a doting fool and seducer of his people. Anyone who confesses the Crucified One must also take his cross upon him, and reference is made to Hebrews 13:13. Even before the time of Jesus, the synagogue cast out those who followed the true prophets. But such outcasts are comforted by the prophets, and he quotes from Isaiah 66:5.

It does not surprise us, continues Delitzsch, that Rabinowitz, who was formerly regarded as a man of good sense, should now be declared overwrought and distracted when he professes faith in the Crucified One, reference being made to 1 Cor. 1:23. The synagogue's centuries-long hatred of Jesus is mentioned, reference being made to some passages in the Talmud and the Gospel travesty Toldot Yeshu, which for instance makes Jesus out to be the illegitimate son of a soldier. Among educated Jews this attitude has changed into some esteem for Jesus, says Delitzsch. But proud monotheism cannot ignore Jesus's blasphemous self-deification and considers him a seducer who leads people to apostasy from the one God. Referring to John 8:59, which tells how people took up stones to stone Jesus, Delitzsch asserts that these stones are still to be found in the hands of his people. And anyone who lets the stones fall from his hands - as Rabinowitz has done - counts as a fool who has fallen away from Judaism and gone over to the religion of the false Messiah, which is semi-paganism.

It does not surprise us, writes Delitzsch thirdly, that such is the state of the matter, though it would be more prudent for present-day Judaism to adopt a different attitude to Christianity from that of the Middle Ages. It would be more prudent, because the Jews are among people who have Christianity as their religion, and because they have obtained varying degrees of civic rights. Then they would not be adding fuel to anti-Semitic agitation. But the least one may ask of the Jews is not to refer so woundingly to that which is sacred to Christians, says Delitzsch. And he continues in the same vein, asserting that the Jews ought to make the concession to Christianity that it possesses sufficient persuasiveness that a Jew can become a Christian without at the same time becoming a fool, and unclean, and a criminal.

But the article did not surprise us, concludes Delitzsch, also because we know the deadly hatred which the Jews of eastern Europe have against Hebrew Christians who are regarded as an outlaw band. What surprises us is that a periodical like Hamelitz tries to deny the movement's existence and restrict it to embracing only one man: Rabinowitz, who has so disgracefully succeeded in duping Delitzsch concerning the extent of the movement.

Viewed from a distance, Delitzsch's arguments are not all equally endearing; his irritation at being personally attacked led him away from a reply which might have been more judicious. Particularly he is - without wanting to admit it - in retreat on the fourth point: the size of the movement.

Discussion about the size of the movement in 1884

With hindsight, Delitzsch ought to have done at least two things when he made reply in Hamelitz. He ought to have admitted that it did the cause no service that he had used the expression "joined" when he mentioned the number of Rabinowitz's adherents. Secondly, he ought to have got hold of a copy of The Times for 23 August 1884.

He did neither. As regards the notorious number 250 which was bandied about in the debate, Delitzsch was able without a qualm to declare that this information from The Times was not derived from "our 'Documents'".[32] He thus put the blame on Titcomb's article in The Times. But Delitzsch was allowing himself to be tricked on this point. For the irony is that the number 250 does not appear at all in the article in The Times. Concerning numbers, Titcomb writes exactly what Delitzsch had done in

May 1884, i.e. 200. It was not until the translation process into Russian, or from Russian to Hebrew, that the 200 adherent families became 250. That with this number of 250 the movement was being "in no small degree looked at under a magnifying glass" was being admitted by A.S. Poulsen in his book as early as 1886.[33] But characteristically, Delitzsch's reputation did not suffer at all. It is Titcomb who has to take the brickbats. However, a sober appraisal suggests that in the situation at the time it makes little difference whether the number was given as 200 or 250.

In his preface to the first documents of the movement, Delitzsch had in May 1884 written that Rabinowitz's words had an attractive power not only in Kishinev but in the small Bessarabian towns. "There are now said to be more than 200 families who have joined the new Hebrew Christianity..."[34] In his reply he claimed that he had expressed himself more indefinitely than the article in The Times, i.e. he was talking about the adherents of the movement both in Kishinev and in other Bessarabian towns.[35] Not until an article in 1885 did he produce a clear admission: the circle around Rabinowitz was both narrower and wider than he had first stated. He continues to rebut the idea that the movement does not exist at all, but goes on: "But it is true that the firm nucleus of the congregation consists of the families of the Rabinowitz brothers, altogether 15 persons."[36] It was W. Faber who had brought this information back to Delitzsch from his stay in Kishinev at the beginning of 1885. Earlier, in a letter dated 31 March 1884, Faber had written that 100 families would go over to the movement if circumcision and the Sabbath could be kept as national signs. With this number he was referring to Jews in Kishinev.[37]

In his reply Delitzsch says that it is insulting to insinuate that Rabinowitz was the origin of the information about the numbers in The Times, and that it is a hateful lie to say that Rabinowitz stands alone. Delitzsch remarks that he does not need to ask Rabinowitz but refers to Faber's observations when he was in Kishinev - in March 1884. There he had not only met Rabinowitz and like-minded brethren and others who headed the movement, but Faber had also seen with his own eyes the stir that the movement was causing and that Jews even came from remote parts to find out about the movement.[38] In the article of 1885 Delitzsch also states that the movement is not restricted to Kishinev but has reached out further and mentions the towns of Batum, Elisabetgrad, Jekaterinsoslav, Berditschev, Schitomir, St Petersburg, which is partly confirmed in an article in the Jewish magazine Hamagid in autumn 1885 in which a warning is given against a person in Kiev who is under the influence of Rabinowitz's writings.[39]

Because Delitzsch had started out by talking of "adherents", he was vulnerable to Jewish criticism. This sidetracked the debate right from the start. Public meetings had not yet been held and the criteria for "adherence to the movement" had not yet emerged. So the Jews might with some justice maintain that in 1884 nobody had adhered to Rabinowitz's movement. But when these facts were brought up in the heat of debate, no indication was given that Rabinowitz had at least aroused some sympathy in Jewish circles. In Hamelitz of 20 January/1 February 1884 it had been admitted that the movement, at least outside Kishinev, had gripped so many Jews that there were grounds for warning against it. The subsequent months also showed that Jews took quite a serious view of the Rabinowitz affair, more serious than if he had been a lone figure, "the new calf of Kishinev", as he was called in Hamelitz no. 71 of 1884.

In a lengthy letter to Faber, on 16/28 October 1884, Rabinowitz gave an account of the debate. Concerning the number 200, Faber had himself seen that 200 fellow Jews had approached the Christian faith. But on the other hand Rabinowitz was unwilling to enter into mathematical calculations. He says that he does not regard himself as a general who has to gain a military unit of at least 200 families. Nor is he the promoter of a company who has to get 100 or 200 shareholders. Nor has it been his intention to offer to the Lord a new meal offering of exactly 200 men, so that if one was lacking the Jewish newspapers might hold him up as a liar. He claims that thousands of his brethren in various places are deeply interested in his cause. Likewise he claims that among the Russian Jews there are many Nicodemus Christians who love Christ in secrecy.[40]

Rabinowitz's literary productivity and other labours aimed at realizing his visions are evidence that he did not spend all his time counting adherents. We shall return to this. But first we must sketch the events which resulted in Rabinowitz being able to hold public gatherings. The public debate had meant that the Russin authorities could not ignore the movement.

Rabinowitz and the imperial authorities

In May 1884 Delitzsch had published the first documents in Hebrew and German. Already on 13 June 1884 Rabinowitz was able in a letter to thank Faber for the reception of the first five copies, which had passed the Russian censors. He owns to these writings, calls them "his", and gives thanks that there is someone who will pay for them.[41] On 4/16 September he thanks Delitzsch for some books and tells him that the rest of the consignment are with the censors in Moscow.[42]

In a letter of 24 October/5 November 1884, Faltin writes to Delitzsch that one of the results of the agitation against the movement has been that attention has been paid to it on the highest level: the documents have been translated into Russian and have been submitted to the ministry and the ecclesiastical authorities in Kiev. Faltin adds that "yesterday", i.e. 4 November, Rabinowitz received a letter from the censorship committee. On the minister's behalf it gave permission for Rabinowitz to disseminate these writings in Russia and even others which he had written in Hebrew. This permission was given, writes Faltin, "without any action being taken from here."[43]

But action was taken now. The day after receiving this permission, Rabinowitz visited Faltin to show him an application addressed to the governor which he had drawn up. It is a "document", writes Faltin, which is quite well composed. Faltin expresses his assurance that the petition will be granted. Against this background it may be doubted whether, already in the spring of 1884 Rabinowitz had submitted a petition for permission to form a Hebrew Christian congregation - as some people suggest.[44] However this may be, according to Faltin in November 1884 Rabinowitz applied for permission to gather in their own premises as a "branch" of the Jewish population under the name "Israelites of the New Covenant" in order, without interference from other Jews, to be able to be edified in God's Word of both the Old and the New Testaments and in this wise to devote themselves in love to Jesus of Nazareth, whom they regarded as their and the world's Saviour.

Application was also made for a section of the Jewish cemetery to be allotted to them so that they might bury their dead there. Faltin does not say how many joint signatories of the petition there were, only that there were some. It must be observed that Rabinowitz was applying to the authorities for permission for the right of assembly as a Jew.[45]

In his letter Faltin also says that the meeting-hall has already been decided upon. It is to be on the top floor of the house in which Rabinowitz's younger brother - Efraim Jakob - lives as a tenant and which is not far from the Lutheran church.

Faltin proved right in his supposition that the petition would be granted. It even seems that the permission to hold public gatherings came in more quickly than expected. In a letter of November 1884 to J. Wilkinson, Rabinowitz writes that he does not expect to get the permission until about Easter 1885, so that he will be able to go to London after the New Year (see Chapter 7). He expresses his gratitude to the Russian authorities. According to the laws it is forbidden to preach publicly and hold meetings without the sanction of the Government "and these laws stand till now in my way, preventing me from doing my work to any large extent," he writes. He also says that he has sent his tract *Kol Kore* to the censors in Odessa applying for permission to publish it.[46]

It was not until 12/24 July 1886 that the special burial ground for Israelites of the New Covenant could be opened.[47] Permission to hold meetings came more rapidly. Rabinowitz's application to the government on 3 November 1884 was accompanied by a supporting letter from the governor of Bessarabia, which resulted in Rabinowitz's movement being recognized as a distinct Jewish sect.[48] Similarly, in February 1885 the Spritual

Biblical Brotherhood got permission to open its own synagogue and to elect its own rabbi, but after Jacob Gordin's emigration in 1891 to America the authorities did not comply with the sect's application for permission to elect a new rabbi.[49] So the permissions granted to Gordin as well as to Rabinowitz were given to them personnaly and were not automatically transferrable to others. When people abroad wrote about the permission Rabinowitz had obtained, it was not always made clear that this did not entail that Rabinowitz might work as a clergyman. No permission had been given for the formation of a congregation proper. According to Faltin, Rabinowitz also applied for that in autumn 1884.[50] Rabinowitz does not mention this himself in his letter to Wilkinson.

Before the arrival of official permission to gather in a special place, there may have been unofficial intimations that this permission was on its way.[51] At least, the first legal and public gathering could be held on the evening of the very day on which the written permission arrived. This was on Christmas Eve. But preparations for this first meeting had already been made.

Christmas Eve 1884

On 24 December 1884 by the Russian calendar (= 5 January 1885) permission from the Interior Ministry arrived for Rabinowitz to hold public gatherings. The first one was held that same evening. Two sources which mutually confirm and supplement each other, give a good account of the course of the evening. Faltin, who according to his own testimony usually put letter-writing aside on Christmas Day felt compelled to take up his pen on 25 December (r) to tell Delitzsch about this red-letter day.[52] The Russian newspaper Odesski Listok on 30 December/11 January carried a report written in Kishinev on 28 December/ 9 January.[53]

Both sources relate that the Christmas gathering was held in the house of Joseph Rabinowitz's brother at 9pm and had attracted a large crowd. Faltin says that there were a couple of hundred in the packed room, which he reached after finishing his Christmas duties. The visitors were both Jews and Christians. Faltin also relates that some persons from the authorities were there and that policemen were standing at the door to limit the numbers attending.

Faltin does not omit to mention that the programme for the Christmas celebration had been made by Rabinowitz "together with me". Further proof of the good relations between these two was that Faltin had allowed the Lutheran church's harmonium to be loaned for the occasion. It was installed in the side room. It was not particularly "Jewish" to use an organ for a service. In his worship premises later Rabinowitz did not use an organ. But it was on a list of requests he sent to J. Wilkinson in January 1885.[54]

Assisting at the Christmas Eve gathering were the "proselytes" of the Lutheran church and some children in the singing.

Concerning the programme for the evening we discover that first a Christmas carol was sung. Then Rabinowitz, according to Faltin, read various Messianic prophecies from the Old Testament about the coming of the Messiah. This was done - naturally - in Hebrew. Then the Christmas gospel was read out in Hebrew. Rabinowitz then gave an address - according to the Russian newspaper in Yiddish lasting about an hour and a half - in which he applied the readings to his Jewish audience. He called upon them to receive Jesus, the one who had come from them and whom neither the Pharisees nor the Sadducees had received, although the shepherds in the field had. According to the Russian newspaper, he also touched upon "a happy co-incidence", that he had that very day received permission from the Interior Ministry to open a congregation for Israelites of the New Covenant.

After this address, another hymn was sung, and Rabinowitz read out a poem he had written. In conclusion Faltin took over, expressing among other things his great joy that, on that 25th Christmas Eve (or was it the 26th?) which he could celebrate in Kishinev, he was a witness of this which he regards as a fulfilment of his prayers. To Delitzsch he also relates that at the conclusion he had opportunity to hand out some literature.

Rabinowitz's Christmas sermon was published in Yiddish in 1886, and so was a Hebrew translation. Unfortunately it has not proved possible to trace a copy. From the information which Delitzsch gives in 1887, in his Christmas sermon Rabinowitz dwelt upon the question which is otherwise used in the Passover Haggada in the Jewish tradition.[55] The question: How is Passover night different from other nights? had, in this Christmas sermon, become: How is Christmas night different from other nights?

From about Christmas 1884 there is a poem, dated 21 December (r) 1884. The original text in Yiddish was published in German in connection with the obituary for Rabinowitz in 1899.[56] Here is also the information that the song exists as an appendix to a draft for an order of morning services for weekdays and Sabbaths. "The song of the birth of Yeshua Mashiah" was reproduced in, at least, Norwegian and Danish and can be found in the magazines of the those Israel Missions, in 1900 and 1906 respectively.[57]

It may be mentioned already now that Rabinowitz's prayer-hall after its restoration and inauguration in May 1885 was given the name "Bethlehem". That was also the name of the church in which Rabinowitz was baptized - in March 1885 - which, for reasons we shall return to, he could not possibly have foreseen.

Chapter 6

THE MESSIANIC MOVEMENT IN KISHINEV
AT THE START OF 1885

From 1871 Rabinowitz and his family had been living in Kishinev. Before this "lawyer apostle" (as the French periodical Chrétien évangélique[1] called him in May 1885) took a public stand as a Christian, overseas supporters of missions to Israel knew of the town's existence, not least because of the work of the Lutheran pastor R. Faltin. With the emergence of the Messianic movement the town was mentioned even more. Not until 1903 and 1905 did the town become known to all who kept abreast of the history of the Jews and anti-Semitism, when the Jews of the town were victims of two horrible pogroms (see further Chapter 19).

Before we glance at the names of the movement and its first worship services in Kishinev in 1885, it may be appropriate here to say a few words about Rabinowitz's town.

The town of Kishinev

In 1818 Kishinev had become the capital of the government of Bessarabia. The town grew rapidly and, being the centre of trade and industry that it was, it attracted many Jews. Throughout the 18th century there was a Jewish burial ground near the town and in 1774 a Jewish congregation was formed numbering 144 members. In 1847 there were over 10,000 Jews (about 12% of the total population), in 1867 there were over 18,000 Jews (around 22%). In 1897 the Jewish population had grown to over 50,000 (about 46% of the inhabitants).[2] In the period of Rabinowitz's activity as a preacher the Jewish population had thus grown from around 30,000 to 50,000 Jews.

At the end of the 19th century most Jews in Kishinev were engaged in trade, craft, and industry. The area was well known for its tobacco, fruit, and wine, and a fair number of Jews were employed in processing these products. Of the total of 38 different factories, 28 were in Jewish hands in 1898. Many Jewish workers were also employed in some large commercial firms and printing-works owned by Jews. At the same time Kishinev had a large number of poor Jews who were supported by various Jewish philanthropic institutions.

In 1816 the foundation stone was laid for the large Jewish synagogue in the town. In 1838 the first secular Jewish school was opened. As already suggested through Rabinowitz's autobiography, there were some

'Enlightenment Jews' in Kishinev, although what is known as the Haskala movement had not gained much of a foothold in Kishinev.

According to W. Kahle, in 1889 there were one synagogue and 29 prayer houses in Kishinev. There were 18 Orthodox churches, two 'Old Believers', one Armenian, one Roman Catholic, and finally a Lutheran church.[3] From 1859 R. Faltin had been the incumbent, but the town had obtained its Lutheran pastorate back in 1837. Besides ministering to incoming Lutherans, the pastor was a 'divisional chaplain' to the Lutheran soldiers in the Russian army.

In 1903 49 Jews lost their lives and over 500 were wounded and many more lost their homes in the first serious pogrom in Kishinev. In 1905 a fresh pogrom broke out in which 19 were killed and 56 were wounded. In memory of the victims in 1903, E.M. Lilien made a picture in which he depicted a Jewish martyr dying on a 'cross': the martyr is bound to a stake with his *Tallit* (prayer shawl) and an angel is shaping his wings into the crossbar.[4] On these occasions Christians who had been involved with Rabinowitz's work also acknowledged how hard it was to proclaim the gospel of the cross of Jesus against the background of the Christians' 'crucifixion' of the Jews in these pogroms (see Chapter 19).

Under the Peace of Versailles after the First World War, Kishinev passed into Rumanian hands in 1918. In June 1940 Russia annexed the town. In mid-July 1941 Kishinev was occupied by German and Rumanian forces. Many Jews were deported or killed. It is estimated that of the approximately 65,000 Jews living in the town in 1941, 53,000 were killed.

We shall not elaborate on this tragic tale here. Even though there were tumults and riots in connection with Rabinowitz's first emergence, these were of quite a different nature from the 'Christian' slaughter of Jews. But all did not pass off quite calmly in Kishinev in 1885 when the Messianic movement began its public activity. Although what are called the 'May laws' continued to apply to followers of Rabinowitz, the Israelites of the New Covenant were regarded by their fellow Jews as traitors (about the May laws, see Chapter 2).

Versions of the movement's name

The city of Kishinev had acquired a new movement with the official name of "Israelites of the New Covenant". This is a fairly adequate rendering of the movement's Hebrew name. It was already being used in autumn 1884 in connection with Rabinowitz's petition to the Russian authorities for permission to hold public meetings.[5] The name reveals a good deal about the movement's self-image. But there were of course other more unofficial names going about, which we must first comment upon. We have mentioned above that Rabinowitz was careful to distance himself from the designation "New Israel", for instance (Chapter 3).

In the western European world F. Delitzsch also came to set his mark on the name of the new movement. The first documents were published as: "Documents from the national-Jewish Jesus-believing movement in South Russia".[6] (He often calls it "The South Russian Christianity movement").[7] When Gentile Christian readers are in mind, the former appellation is fairly descriptive of the matter. It conveys that this is a movement of Jews who wish to keep some national distinctives while confessing faith in Christ. So Delitzsch is also able to use such an expression as "the new Jewish Christianity".[8] In a number of contexts, however, he omits to point out that "they themselves" call themselves "Israelites of the New Covenant".[9]

At the beginning Faltin often used this designation.[10] He also used more unofficial versions, e.g. "the local new Israelite congregation", "the Christian movement among the Israelites/Jews" etc.[11]

Often a geographical epithet is used to characterize the movement, as Delitzsch does, e.g. "the South Russian Christianity movement", "the South Russian Bessarabian movement" and the like.[12] The name of Kishinev often gets included in such designations: "The so-called Kishinev Christianity movement",[13] or simply "the Kishinev Christianity movement";[14] or as Delitzsch writes in one place: "The Christ-believers of Israel in Kishinev".[15]

Of course his own name was often included in the descriptions of the movement. Already in January 1885 B. Ben Zion, a missionary in Odessa for the British Society, used the term "the Rabinowitz movement".[16] On the formation of "the London Council for Rabinowitz" in 1887, the name of Rabinowitz was stressed more than the programme which was contained in the movement's Hebrew name. A natural consequence was that "the Rabinowitz movement" became increasingly common;[17] and when Faltin mentions Rabinowitz's death in 1899 and calls the movement "the so-called Rabinowitz movement",[18] the expression has negative undertones.

The fact that the movement gradually came to be identified with its founder, which affected more or less unofficial names, is something which has occurred in many other movements with a prominent leader, regardless of how much or how little the leader has approved of this development.

Some people have incorrectly asserted that the movement in Kishinev called itself the national-Jewish movement.[19] However legitimate this description, it is and remains a re-phrasing that arose in western European circles. Rabinowitz did not use it himself, and it was not the official name.

The official name: Israelites of the New Covenant

In Hebrew the official name of the movement was rendered as *Bnei Israel, Bnei Brit Chadasha*. Directly translated: Sons/Children of Israel, Sons/Children of the New Covenant. A more idiomatic, and quite adequate, rendering is Israelites of the New Covenant. *Brit Chadasha* may mean both "new covenant" and "new testament". In Hebrew the book of The New

Testament is called *Brit ha-Chadasha*. And of course that is what Rabinowitz calls the book. In West European languages some preferred to render the name of the movement as "Israelites of the New Testament" or similar.[20]

The name Israelites of the New Covenant indicates the belief that the God of Israel has through Jesus the Messiah established a new covenant with Israel. It also underlines that a Jesus-believing Jew remains a *Ben Israel*, a son of Israel. The Russian laws applicable to Jews continued to apply to Rabinowitz and his adherents from a legal point of view.[21] His worship services were 'Jewish', his meeting house was regarded as a Jewish house of prayer, and right until his death his passport described him as a 'Jew'.[22] Rabinowitz himself held on to his Jewish identity, although the Jews around him contradicted him. Until his death he thought of himself as a son of Israel. On the title-page of a Hebrew anthology of sermons of 1897 stand the words: "By J. Rabinowitz, preacher to the congregation of Israel (*Edat Israel*), the Sons of the New Covenant (*Bnei Brit Chadasha*)". Compare this with the Hebrew subtitle on the first documents which were published by Delitzsch in 1884: "The congregation of the Sons of Israel (*Edat Bnei Israel*), those who believe in Jesus the Messiah in South Russia". On his tomb, by his own wish, was to be inscribed: "An Israelite who believed in Jehovah and his Anointed, Jesus of Nazareth, the King of the Jews. Joseph, son of David, Rabinowitz".[23]

While on the subject of names, a couple of comments should be made on Rabinowitz's Hebrew use of words for Christ and Christian. This may shed light on why, instead of using the term 'Christianity movement' we prefer to speak of 'the Messianic movement'.

When Rabinowitz is speaking of Christ, he naturally uses the Hebrew *Mashiach*, cf. our Messiah. When translating this into European languages, we can give it a Jewish flavour by rendering it Messiah instead of the Greek-derived Christ; Delitzsch's translations do not always bring out this flavour.

The commonest word for Christian in Hebrew is *Notzri* (plural *Notzrim*). Derived from this is *Natzrut* for Christianity. In 1884 the periodical Hamelitz writes of the sect "*Yehudim Mitnatzrim*",[24] i.e. "Jews who have (or have been) converted to Christianity". The expression's negative ring in Jewish ears is not fully expressed by Delitzsch's translation "*christgläubige Juden*"[25] (Christ-believing Jews). In passing we may note that Christian Jews using *Ivrit* (modern Hebrew), nowadays customarily use the term *Yehudim Meshichiyim*, i.e. Messianic Jews, to describe themselves.[26]

Based on an analysis of Hebrew texts by Rabinowitz, the following summing-up can be made: Rabinowitz uses the word *Notzri/Notzrim* both of the first Gentile Christians and about contemporary evangelical churches and their faith.[27] For instance, the expression "*Notzrim* of the uncircumcised".[28] The word *Meshichi/Meshichiyim* is also used of the early Gentile Christians as well as churches of Gentile origin.[29] Thus it may be noted that the expressions "the first *Notzrim*" and "the first *Meshichiyim*" are both applied to Gentile Christians. The Twenty-four Articles of Faith say (e.g. in Article 6, see Chapter 8), that the Israelites of the New Covenant celebrate Passover and Pentecost at the same time as the *Meshichiyim* do, i.e. they follow the (Gentile) Christian calendar of festivals.

The word *Meshichi/Meshichiyim* was thus not restricted to Christian Jews. On the other hand, the word *Notzri/Notzrim* is not found used as a description of Rabinowitz's followers. In Jewish ears, this term was too reminiscent of Gentile Christianity and was too tainted. Instead of a fixed designation for Christian, Rabinowitz employs a number of circumlocutions, in which the word "believer" generally occurs. Although *Meshichi/Meshichiyim* is used about both "Gentile Christians" and "Hebrew Christians", there are grounds for calling the movement "the Messianic movement". This stresses its Jewish flavour. In 1885 Jakob Wechsler translated a couple of sermons into Hebrew which Rabinowitz had preached in Yiddish. In his preface Wechsler uses the expression "*ha-Tnua ha-Meshichit*",[30] "the Messianic movement". Delitzsch translates: "Christianity movement".[31] Wechsler looks forward to "a large Messianic congregation in Israel". Delitzsch renders this: "a large Christ-believing congregation in Israel".

To elucidate the term *Meshichi*, we may finally quote a poem of 1885 by the same Wechsler entitled *Ha-Meshichi weha-Yehudi*.[32] Delitzsch translates this as "The Christ-believer and the Jew".[33] Objectively, this is a correct rendering, although the terminology does not have a particularly Jewish aroma. A better rendering is: "The Messiah-believer and the Jew". The expression *Yehudi Meshichi*, which is nowadays used as a self-description by most *Ivrit*-speaking Christian Jews in Israel, has not been found. This is one of the particular points which make it regrettable that so many of his letters in Hebrew have been destroyed. But the title of Wechsler's poem is the closest we can get to it. I have not, in the material I have analyzed, found any support for Gabe's claim that Rabinowitz in Hebrew called his congregation *Yehudim Meshichiyim Bnei Brit ha-Chadasha*.[34]

However, the official name was "Israelites of the New Covenant". An adherent was a son of Israel and a son of the New Covenant which the God of Israel had established through Jesus. Through faith in him a Jew did not, according to Rabinowitz, lose his Jewish identity. He remained a *Ben Israel* or rather: he now became a true son of Israel.

"The Israelites of the New Covenant" had held their first gathering on Christmas Eve 1884, i.e. 5 January 1885 by our dating. A few days later they were able to hold their first legal observance of the Sabbath - in Jesus' name.

The first worship services and riots in Kishinev in 1885

On 10 January 1885 the group around Rabinowitz was able for the first time to observe the Sabbath "in a Christian sense", as Faltin expresses it.[35] He remarks that Rabinowitz does not take any steps without first consulting him. Thus, the previous day Rabinowitz had laid before him the "formulary for the Sabbath service". It had been tried out, and Faltin says that the premises may be used as a place where people can search the Holy Scriptures "and edifying entertainment and lectures can be held". In a PS to the letter about this, he mentions that he has just come back from the Sabbath service at 12 o'clock. "The room was packed. The Lord gave rich blessing." He goes on to say that the Lutheran Church's harmonium had been lent and a small company of singers from the Lutheran Church had assisted at the service.

Faltin makes no mention of disturbances in this connection. But Faber does write (though at second-hand, as he did not get to Kishinev until mid January 1885) that at the first two services "thousands of Jews had turned up, who thronged around the completely filled house".[36] A rather distorted picture of the state of affairs in Kishinev emerges in a report of an address Faber gave in Uppsala on 26 September 1885. "At the first sermon which the respected Joseph Rabinowitz delivered in Kishinev, around 4000 people were gathered, although the premises could not hold more than 600-700".[37] The reader might get the impression from this that 4000 Jews were positively interested - a huge exaggeration, whether due to Faber or the reporter.

There is however no reason to query that there were crowds of people in and outside the room at the second Sabbath service on 17 January. One source mentions that not only was the hall thronged, but that people were also in the adjoining rooms and on the stairs.[38] Outside the hall, a large crowd had gathered. Faltin signalled to Rabinowitz to curtail his address. With the help of the local police, order was maintained. But as Rabinowitz left, the police had to come to his aid when he was attacked. The next day a crowd assembled outside his house. Finally they got him to come out. He called on them to believe in Jesus as the Messiah and gradually the crowd dispersed.

On 5 February when Rabinowitz drove out in a carriage with his daughter, a street demonstration broke out against him. Accounts of these things may differ: Faber, who at this time was in Kishinev, mentions that there were "about 2000 Jews against him".[39] A Russian newspaper sets the number - no doubt more realistically - at 200-300.[40] Snow was thrown at him and other "less cleanly ammunition", as Poulsen puts it.[41] Rabinowitz got out of the carriage and told the crowd that even if he were to cease speaking, others would preach the same things. He did not suffer any violence on this occasion either, which Faber seems to have seen through a magnifying-glass.

With a fairly tranquil mind he was able to read about his own murder. This rumour was spread by, for example, the Jewish Chronicle, which on 30 January 1885, stated that reports of Rabinowitz's murder were coming from Odessa - citing as its source the Vienna correspondent of The Daily Telegraph.[42] This rumour was vigorously denied in the magazines of the European Missions to Israel.[43] Professor Strack could not determine whether this rumour was due to fear, wishful thinking, or journalistic imagination.[44]

Faber writes that while he was in Kishinev the excitement had waned, apart from that street demonstration.[45] In a letter of 15 February (r) Rabinowitz relates that the premises are much too small to accommodate all those who wish to listen to the Gospel. He reveals that the police were having to stand at the door to prevent disorder and disturbances at the services.[46]

Through press reports (whether favourable or unfavourable) the news about the "Israelites of the New Covenant" in Kishinev spread. Faber writes that many "hidden groups of Christians" in Russia "have ventured to lift their heads and emerge into the light of day" because of Rabinowitz's activities. He goes on: "During my stay in Kishinev letters were coming in to Rabinowitz almost daily from such circles."[47] In his correspondence with J. Wilkinson in England, Rabinowitz mentions in January 1885 that he is daily receiving letters from Jews all over Russia.[48] Faltin confirms that shoals of letters were coming in both to himself and to Rabinowitz.[49]

As Rabinowitz was unable to reply in detail to the many letters, he requested the editor of the newspaper Odesski Listok to print a reader's letter, which did in fact appear on 1 February 1885.[50] In this he replied to three matters. Firstly, many people had asked about the "rites" of the Israelites of the New Covenant. In reply he refers to the documents which Delitzsch had published. Secondly, it had been asked how the Russian laws would apply to the Israelites of the New Covenant and whether they would be at an advantage compared to other Jews. In his reply he is content to refer to John 8:31,32,36, e.g., with the words: "If the Son therefore shall make you free, ye shall be free indeed." Thirdly, people had asked whether members of the Israelites of the New Covenant might count on financial support. The categorical reply is that "the capital of our congregation does not consist in corruptible gold or silver" (see further Chapter 13).

In April 1885 Rabinowitz returned to Kishinev from his journey to Germany as a newly baptized believer (see next chapter). At the end of May they were able to hold the first services in the freshly restored premises (see Chapter 11). But we must first mention a favourable reaction to Rabinowitz's preaching. It is supplied by Jakob Wechsler and gives an picture of how some Jews who had first met Rabinowitz with hostility, changed their minds.

Who would have believed it before?

In 1885 the Jew Ben Jakob Haisraeli, alias Jakob Wechsler, translated two sermons into Hebrew. Rabinowitz had preached them in Yiddish on 8 and 29 June (r) 1885. Wechsler wrote an accompanying preface which included a description of his reaction to Rabinowitz's public stand.[51] First he mentions how we can be gripped with wonder at the miracle of creation when we look at a drop of water or the wing of a butterfly under a microscope. The invisible becomes visible. Similarly, the divine word can aid our shortsightedness. That which previously appeared to be something unimportant we now see to be something great, so that we are compelled to exclaim in holy wonder: "How great indeed are Thy works, Lord!" and Wechsler continues:

A few months ago who would have believed that the Messianic movement which is emerging among us would have assumed larger and larger dimensions from day to day? As an honest man [Nathanael] asked the honest question over 1800 years ago: "Can any good thing come out of Nazareth?", so many asked: "Can light come forth from Kishinev and the Word of the Lord from Bessarabia?" Others said: "This movement has no viability, it will soon be blown out and extinguished". But the words of the Lord the Messiah still apply: "If these should hold their peace, the stones will cry out", in this case the stones of the prayer house, Bethlehem, which Mr Rabinowitz has erected - these shout and proclaim for time and eternity. They give our hearts hope of soon seeing a large Messianic congregation in Israel. Who would have believed before that around 100 Israelite men would each Sabbath assemble in a house built in honour of Jesus the Messiah? Who would have believed before that a Jew would hear from the mouth of his Jewish brother the name of Jesus the Messiah being lauded on his lips without pursing his lips and stopping his ears...?

Wechsler goes on to tell of his earlier opposition to Rabinowitz, but also of how he came to change his mind. He was one of the first in Kishinev to polemicize against Rabinowitz. He sometimes went to services to gather more material so as to be better able to oppose the cause. But the convicting words of Rabinowitz cut him to the heart. He admits that he had disparaged Rabinowitz without really having known him. Although from childhood he had known the Holy Scriptures, it was not until he heard Rabinowitz's preaching that it dawned upon him that the key to a right understanding of the Scriptures is to be found in the word: "The Messiah is the end of the Law" (Rom. 10:4). In an adroit way this is precisely what Rabinowitz is stressing.

Wechsler concludes by relating that after this he went to the services every Sabbath, eagerly soaking in the sermons, indeed making notes so that he could show them to other Jews who were ashamed to attend the services themselves. He expresses the hope that such might find faith through them.

It is an interesting detail that Wechsler sees Paul's words, "The Messiah is the end of the law", as the key to understanding the Holy Scriptures and asserts that Rabinowitz stresses this. Along the way the new movement was attacked for wanting to hold on to Jewish customs. In another context we shall return to this key word (see Chapter 8). Since the Messiah is the end of the law, Rabinowitz concluded that he was free to remain a Jew.

When this was written Rabinowitz had been baptized. But he did not consider that this meant that his Jewish identity had been drowned. We shall now describe the circumstances around his baptism.

Chapter 7

TRAVEL PLANS AND THE BAPTISMAL JOURNEY TO GERMANY IN 1885

On 14 March 1885 Rabinowitz was baptized under extraordinary circumstances in Berlin. Although everyone interested in Rabinowitz agreed that he had to be baptized at some time, it nevertheless came as a surprise that it should occur on this particular journey. Whether he had already planned it before his departure from Kishinev is a question that may justly be asked.

Prior to this journey to Germany in spring 1885 various travel plans had been laid. Far from all of them proved feasible. But by viewing matters on the basis of these travel plans, a picture may be formed of Rabinowitz's interest in making personal contact with key persons in the existing missionary societies - and vice versa. Particularly this gives us an impression of the missionary societies' anxiety among themselves not to be shunted into a siding in this matter. Although all the parties involved desired what was best for Rabinowitz, we may discern some rivalry between the societies and individuals. It was of course possible to make different assessments, and this was not necessarily due to petty sectional interests.

Fulfilled and non-fulfilled plans for travel

Even before the conference in Kishinev, Rabinowitz had plans to travel to Germany. The previous day - 25 March 1884 - Faber was writing to Delitzsch that Rabinowitz would visit Leipzig for a while "this summer".[1] Some days later, 31 March, Faber writes: "He will come, I hope, to Leipzig in the late summer."[2] On 13 June of the same year Rabinowitz wrote to Faber that it was necessary for him to leave Kishinev for a brief period and go away to stir up interest in the movement. "Perhaps it will be possible for me", he wrote.[3] If this was meant as a hint to send him money for the journey from Leipzig, he was disappointed. He did not go on any travels that summer. Nevertheless, on 3 October 1884 Delitzsch was able to write that "it is absolutely necessary for us to get acquainted personally".[4] Referring to Faber's having plans for this, he says that they will wait for God's pointer to the right moment.

At this juncture the British Mildmay Mission had also entered the scene. The link with this rapidly growing society, which had been founded in 1876 after John Wilkinson had left the British Society, his former employer, and set up a new one, was to shape developments in this context.[5] At the very time of Rabinowitz's ministry, the Mildmay Mission was expanding strongly and threatening the position of others. In autumn 1885, on a journey in Sweden, Faber could write to Delitzsch that the most important result of his trip was that from now on the Swedes would no longer send their missionaries to Wilkinson but to Leipzig to be trained for missionary service.[6] Delitzsch was realist enough to assess that he could not carry on the work in Leipzig without the good will of the Mildmay Mission This is revealed in a letter to Faber in June 1888, when the latter was just about to set off for England. He is told to convey greetings to the Mildmay Mission "from old Delitzsch" and he enjoins Faber: "Stir up interest in Britain for this international and interdenominational institute!" And concerning the continued existence of this institute, i.e. the Institutum Judaicum, he says in the letter: "Without British support it cannot continue to exist. Britain is the land of the Bible and mission."[7] According to Delitzsch both the Institutum Judaicum and the cause of Rabinowitz needed British financial support.

There was no getting around the Mildmay Mission, whatever one might feel about this upstart among the established societies. Whatever one's opinion of faith missions might be, it was effective.

At the beginning of September 1884 John Wilkinson, the founder and head of the Mildmay Mission, wrote to Rabinowitz. It is interesting to notice that the date of the first acquaintance with the movement is carefully recorded. Two or three months before the article in The Times Wilkinson's attention had been drawn to the movement's existence. In mid July he had referred to it in a lecture.[8] In his first letter Wilkinson asks among other things for a complete account of the origin and development of the movement.[9] Rabinowitz sent him a letter and the first documents in German/Hebrew.[10] The material was translated and printed. In the second letter which Wilkinson sent to Rabinowitz he apparently wished for further information. At any rate, Rabinowitz wrote in his letter of 8 October 1884 that for the time being he cannot manage to write statistics about the number of adherents or describe in detail the services and their liturgy.[11] But in his letter Wilkinson had also raised the question whether Rabinowitz was willing to make a trip to London for one or two months with board and lodging paid and with arrangements already made for an interpreter and places to preach. Wilkinson says that he is also ready to go to Bessarabia with the missionary James Adler and then bring Rabinowitz back to London.[12]

Rabinowitz immediately falls in with the idea. Wilkinson only has to send him £100 to cover travel expenses and the family's keep for three months.[13] In a letter from the first half of November Rabinowitz still stands by the offer to come to London.[14] He can come in the period after Christmas until shortly before Easter. He does not omit to point out that he must have the matter settled a month before he is to leave Kishinev - a clear signal to Wilkinson to make up his mind!

And Wilkinson did. As Rabinowitz had not yet been granted permission by the authorities to erect a special hall for services, Wilkinson found it inexpedient for him to pay a visit now. It would have to wait until the work in Kishinev had been consolidated. Winter weather and other circumstances also meant that the suggestion of him and Adler visiting Russia had to be deferred - until the spring of 1885.[15]

The initiative taken by Wilkinson fluttered the dovecotes of the more established societies. So on 28 November 1884 three persons from the London Society negotiated with Wilkinson about this matter. They expressed apprehension that a visit to London might damage Rabinowitz's work. On the other hand they had no objections to Wilkinson and Adler going to Kishinev. But Wilkinson would make no promises as to how he would act. He maintained that a personal visit to Rabinowitz would be an encouragement to him and yield information for the Mildmay Mission as to how he could be helped. And a visit by Rabinowitz to London would give him Christian friends who would assist him, and interest in the salvation of Israel would be increased. The interest of British Jews in the Christian faith would also be augmented by such a visit, Wilkinson claimed.[16]

In Britain it was not only the London Society which reacted unfavourably to Wilkinson's plans for bringing Rabinowitz to London. There were also protests from the British Society. F.Y. Edwards, who had attended the conference in Kishinev earlier in the year, set the ball rolling in the December issue of The Jewish Herald by arguing that Wilkinson's plans for a trip to Russia would not bring in more information about the movement than was already available to British Christians. On the contrary such a journey would "neutralize that element of secrecy" that was necessary for the advance of the movement in Russia.[17]

In the same issue of the society's magazine a similar view was expressed by E.O.C. Roeder, who had translated the documents of the movement into English. He claimed that a visit to Kishinev at present "even by the most eminent Christian men of this country" would hinder more than help Rabinowitz in his relations with the Russian authorities. According to Roeder it was fully adequate for Rabinowitz to communicate with Delitzsch and consult him about "all matters connected with the movement".[18] It is clear enough that Roeder is making a point against Wilkinson when he states that at the start of the movement J. Dunlop, F.Y. Edwards, and Faltin were present in Kishinev. The implication was that Wilkinson had not been there. And in the January 1885 issue the well-known Hebrew Christian theologian Alfred Edersheim supported the views for which Edwards and Roeder had made themselves spokesmen. He viewed with disfavour both the plan to bring Rabinowitz to London and Wilkinson's plan to go to Kishinev.

The work which God had begun should not be imperilled by publicity or by introducing alien elements into the matter, said Edersheim.[19] In March 1885 J.E. Neuman wrote in the magazine that anyone who wanted to help the movement ought first to consult the secretary and the treasurer of the British Society. "Again, the Secretary should not communicate with Mr. Rabinowitz directly, but through the good Pastor Faltin of Kischinew."[20]

Without depreciating the motives behind these warnings to Wilkinson, the items quoted arouse the suspicion that they were compositions produced more or less at the behest of the editors. For the irony is that in the same issues of the magazine there are not only translations of the movement's documents but the latest information about the movement is printed. Nor does the society express any disapproval when it is learned that Delitzsch has sent Faber to Kishinev.

Wilkinson was in a strong position when, already in December 1884, he commented upon the fear expressed by others that it would damage and compromise Rabinowitz if he went to Russia. He has no difficulty in dismissing this fear, which "sincere friends" have expressed. For Rabinowitz had already compromised himself in Russia by publicly confessing his faith in Jesus. Nor will Wilkinson agree with those who think that by bringing Rabinowitz to England they will "puff him up" into believing he is something special. That depends on the kind of Christians with whom Rabinowitz links up, says Wilkinson. All the same, on the basis of this debate he has again sent a letter to Rabinowitz asking him for his opinion whether an exchange of visits would help or hinder his work. At the end of 1884 Rabinowitz's reply was being awaited.[21]

It will not have been solely because preparations for the first Christmas Eve service laid so much claim upon Rabinowitz's time that Wilkinson did not get a prompt reply. Concurrently with the public discussion in Britain - and perhaps stimulated by it - Delitzsch was revealing his plans in Germany. We have already mentioned that he wrote to Rabinowitz in October and pointed out the importance of a meeting between them. While Delitzsch was waiting for God's pointer about this, he was also putting enormous pressure on Faber to get him to go to Kishinev again. This is shown by preserved correspondence between the two of them, correspondence which was not published at that time. Compared with the situation that spring, the roles have been reversed by December 1884. Delitzsch wants Faber to operate in Kishinev for about six months beginning at New Year 1885. In that way Faltin's request for help in his work could be met. At the same time Faber could give Delitzsch first-hand briefing about the Messianic movement.[22]

But Faber was not minded to set out on a journey, not even though his fiancée lived in Kishinev, a factor which entered into the discussions with Delitzsch. Of course Delitzsch succeeded in getting his will in the end, although Faber's visit to Kishinev was of shorter duration than Delitzsch had first requested. For four weeks from mid January 1885 Faber was again in Kishinev, about 9 months after he had last left the town. This visit meant that other people's travel plans were shelved.

In a letter dated 10 January 1885 Faltin wrote about Rabinowitz that he was ready to travel and was leaving for Leipzig on 15 January.[23] Faber's arrival in Kishinev thwarted this plan. Shortly afterwards Delitzsch was writing that Rabinowitz had followed his advice about not going to England. They are on close terms with each other, but not so close that Rabinowitz does not take some steps without Delitzsch's consent, writes the latter.[24] In his letter Faltin does not conceal his motives for wanting Rabinowitz to make a journey. He could not indeed envisage how he would be able to cope with the burden of work in Kishinev without Rabinowitz's help. Nevertheless it is necessary for Rabinowitz to spend a couple of weeks in Leipzig to be together with "faithful, pious Christian people", writes Faltin. He gives expression to its being necessary for Rabinowitz to be instructed in many dogmatic questions. Faltin has of course given him books, but there has not been any regular teaching, although the two of them have had many conversations. According to Faltin, Rabinowitz wishes to consult Delitzsch about the future ecclesiastic shape of the movement.

In his letter Faltin makes known that he expects some of the new congregation to be ripe for baptism a couple of months after Rabinowitz - along with Faber, it is expected - returns from his journey. Then the permission of the authorities will be sought for this. Other sources intimate that Faltin had expected that he would be the one to baptize Rabinowitz (see further below). At about the same point of time, the beginning of 1885, Wilkinson was negotiating with a representative of the London Society and A. Saphir, a well-known Hebrew Christian, who later through "The London Council for Rabinowitz" became a warm advocate of the Messianic movement. In these negotiations the question of baptism was discussed. It was decided that Rabinowitz should not be pressured into an early baptism, but that the matter should be left to his own judgement and conscience. All agreed that he should be baptized, but he had to take responsibility for the timing himself.[25]

Interestingly, there were efforts in the London Society to have Rabinowitz attached to the society as an "agent". In a letter of 12 December 1884 Faltin had recommended the employment of Rabinowitz "as a missionary of the Society". The committee rejected the proposal on the grounds that Rabinowitz had not been baptized: "... it is contrary to the Rules of the Society to employ an unbaptized agent - but ... the Committee desire to stand on the most friendly and brotherly relationship with Mr. Rabinowitz - assuring him of their earnest prayers and sympathy, and of their deep interest in the movement he represents."[26] The magazine Word and Work, which reports this on 9 April, mentions that this obstacle will probably not apply much longer. (By the time of publication Rabinowitz had in fact been baptized). But the magazine adds this parting comment on the proposal: "Nevertheless we trust the attempt to put the Jewish reformer in harness will not be repeated." Rabinowitz can be helped in a thousand other ways, without being tied, it says.[27]

But it was not only other people who had baptismal plans for Rabinowitz. At that time he too was preoccupied with the matter. During Faber's visit to Kishinev at the beginning of 1885 the question of baptism was discussed. Faber mentions that Rabinowitz has laid before him the plan to be baptized in Leipzig, which however Faber had rejected at once. Another plan was that Rabinowitz should be baptized in the hall of the Messianic movement by Faltin using a Hebrew baptismal formulary, an idea which Faber was able to support. According to Faber the question of baptism was a main issue for the future of the movement: he points out that among Jews and Christians Rabinowitz's baptism was regarded as a touchstone for the viability of the movement.[28]

A month after Faber wrote this, Rabinowitz was baptized. Not in Kishinev or Leipzig, but in Berlin. This journey was planned and financed by Wilkinson.

On 10 February 1885 Wilkinson sent a letter to Rabinowitz, which the latter acknowledged in a letter of 15 February - immediately after Faber had left Kishinev.[29] Rabinowitz stresses - in the words of Paul - that Christ has not sent him to baptize but to preach the gospel. A few days after receiving this letter, on 24 February, Wilkinson sent a cheque to Rabinowitz along with the time and place of the planned meeting in Germany.[30] For the enlightenment of readers of the Mildmay Mission magazine, the March issue reveals that Wilkinson has suggested to Rabinowitz to meet in Leipzig or Berlin around 12 March.[31] A few days before, on 7 March, Wilkinson received a reply from Rabinowitz. He had received the cheque, is preparing for the journey and looking forward to the meeting, planning to leave Kishinev for Germany on 10 March "to the Hotel which you have appointed". Further, Rabinowitz mentions that when the negotiations in Berlin have been completed, they must go to Leipzig together to visit Delitzsch, whom he will personally inform about the journey by writing directly to him.[32]

This planned journey was made. It was financed by the Mildmay Mission (see further Chapter 13). Neither Rabinowitz nor Wilkinson indicate that the purpose of the journey was to be Rabinowitz's baptism. It is no easy task to untangle all the threads in this affair.

Negotiations in Berlin and Leipzig in March 1885

On Friday 13 March John Wilkinson, Dr Dixon, and James Adler arrived in Leipzig - roughly half way between Kishinev and London. Rabinowitz had booked in at the hotel before them. The same evening they conversed with and about Rabinowitz, his family, and his work, after praying and reading the Scriptures together. They met again on Saturday 14 March, reading the Scriptures, praying, and talking together. Wilkinson's diary entries give quite a good picture of his impressions of the meeting. We shall here confine ourselves to the negotiations, as other relevant impressions will be included elsewhere.[33]

On Saturday evening F. Hausig, the secretary of the Berlin Society, attended, having been at the hotel before the Britons' arrival with a letter asking for a meeting. After a brief conversation with Wilkinson, Hausig negotiated with Rabinowitz, "for I saw that he wished chiefly to see Mr. Rabinowitz," comments Wilkinson very realistically. On Sunday and Monday 15 and 16 March there were discussions with, among others, Strack, "a most intelligent Christian gentleman, and warmly interested in Israel." On the Monday he negotiated with Wilkinson for 1½ hours and - again quite significant - for 3 hours with Rabinowitz. Strack complained to Wilkinson about British missionary societies sending missionaries to the Jews in Germany. Wilkinson agreed that the work ought to be done by German Christians, so that there would be no room for missionaries from other lands. But - and this is also very expressive of Wilkinson: "In the meantime somebody must preach Christ to the Jews."

In the nature of the matter Wilkinson could not reveal anything about the negotiations between Rabinowitz and Strack. Thus there are no certain data as to whether the question of Rabinowitz's baptism was discussed in Berlin. But we are better informed about the talks in Leipzig, where the baptism issue was thoroughly discussed.

On 17 March the three Britons and Rabinowitz arrived in Leipzig. That evening Delitzsch came with his two young assistants W. Faber and H. Lhotzky. The talks continued on 18 March with Strack joining in. At the first meeting Delitzsch put forward "some eight or nine Theses" concerning Rabinowitz and his work. In the course of the discussion they became ten theses.[34] Early the next morning Dixon and Adler translated them into English, while Wilkinson sought God's guidance in prayer. He writes in his diary that they could not sign some of the theses, and that the way they were formulated had apparently upset Rabinowitz. This disagreement mainly concerned the question whether money from abroad for Rabinowitz's work should be sent to Faltin, who would then give an account of the monies received. The thesis implied that unity and concord on this point was "absolutely necessary". Even if the formulation at Wilkinson's request was changed to "very desirable", he himself did not want to accept even this![35] He wanted rather to send the money directly to Rabinowitz, which incidentally is what Rabinowitz, in a letter of 6 April 1885, requested him to do.[36]

However, the talks did lead to their agreeing on a number of points at the meeting on 18 March 1885. Wilkinson sums up these principles.

Firstly, Rabinowitz is to have complete freedom to lead the movement. Neither in questions of doctrine or practice must there be any interference from outside. Secondly, Rabinowitz's continued observance of Passover, circumcision, and the Sabbath should not be a cause of his being refused sympathy and help, in so far as he does not put his trust in these things but solely in Christ for salvation. Thirdly, Rabinowitz can be baptized into the evangelical church and in the manner he wishes. If so, he is to be regarded as a member of the church of Christ and not as a member of the denomination to which his baptizer might belong. Fourthly, they agreed that they cannot recognize the existence of a Hebrew Christian church in Kishinev until Rabinowitz, his brother, and their respective families receive holy baptism and thus become members of the church of Christ.

At the meeting on 18 March it was proposed that Wilkinson should baptize Rabinowitz, but he refused. He feared that many Christians would lose their interest in Rabinowitz if the person who baptized him and the way it came about did not match to their views. Another reason for his refusal was that he thought that the time was premature for baptism just then. This last item is rather obscure, particularly in the light of the fourth point that had been agreed that day. As regards the fourth point, it may be remarked that it had more the character of a declaration and a stressing of the importance of baptism than actually foreshadowing the future situation. On the one hand they 'recognized' Rabinowitz's work even before his whole family had been baptized; on the other hand this fourth resolution never achieved full outworking for the simple reason that at a later point of time the Russian authorities made it clear that they would not recognize Rabinowitz's congregation as a separate church with the right to baptize.

On the same day, 18 March, the three Britons left Leipzig. Rabinowitz bade them farewell at the station. "One of his last words to us was," writes Wilkinson in his diary: "I have learnt one thing since we came together - I have learnt to pray." Not until the Britons had left was the final decision made about Rabinowitz's baptism. That happened the next day.

According to Strack, Rabinowitz had declared on the morning of 19 March that it was his wish to be baptized as quickly as possible and before he left for Russia again.[37] In the afternoon Delitzsch designated Berlin as the most suitable place for the baptism.

The minutes show that Faber and Lhotzky also attended the meeting where this decision was made, as well as Delitzsch and Strack.[38] Rabinowitz must have been outside the door of this internal meeting. The minute begins by saying that the Kishinev Christianity movement has full liberty to develop on its own without any of the existing "particular" churches seeking to absorb it. It is also argued that Rabinowitz himself has expressed a wish to be baptized before his journey home. Against that background, it was found most fitting that he should be baptized somewhere where the baptism would appear as his own decision without influence and responsibility from the friends of Israel at that particular place. In accord with his internal and external relations with the evangelical Christians in the churches of Germany and England it is to be done by an English-speaking clergyman. Strack had declared his willingness to arrange the necessary matters for the baptism to take place in Berlin. It is added finally that in this way the act of baptism may take place quietly and without attracting attention.

As mentioned, Rabinowitz was not at this meeting. But when the resolution was presented to him, he showed - says Strack - what he had written in his notebook while he was waiting: "I have determined to do what my King, the Messiah, determines for me." Rabinowitz took the result reached at the meeting as an expression of this.

A few minutes later Rabinowitz and Strack were sitting in the train on the way to Berlin.

Rabinowitz's baptism in Berlin

On 24 March 1885 Rabinowitz was baptized in Berlin. The following details show that they had done everything to prevent anyone from getting the idea that he had been baptized into any particular denomination: Rabinowitz was baptized in the Bohemian-Lutheran Church 'Bethlehem' in Berlin by the Congregational (Methodist) clergyman and Professor C.M. Mead from Andover in Massachusetts, USA, and in the presence of the church's incumbent P.J. Knack and a few invited guests (not "many" as a German magazine claims), among them Hausig, Strack, and Lhotzky, who was attending on Delitzsch's behalf.[39] David A. Rausch follows Louis Meyer uncritically and repeats the latter's erroneous statement that Rabinowitz was baptized "in the presence of Franz Delitzsch, John Wilkinson, Adolph Saphir ...".[40] But together with his travel companions Wilkinson had returned to England before the baptism, and Adolph Saphir had not even been present at the preceding negotiations.

On 22 March Lhotzky wrote enthusiastically to Wilkinson about the imminent baptism.[41] For that reason it is hard to fathom that in 1904 he could write the following about the same matter: "As a Lutheran theologian Delitzsch could not be present at this interdenominational baptism, but as he wanted to be there anyway, he sent me."[42] Lhotzky thus gives the impression that Delitzsch only half-heartedly approved the outward framework of the baptism. But the minutes of the meeting on 19 March and Strack's accompanying comments show with all clarity that Delitzsch did not merely agree to it reluctantly, but that he shared responsibility for it, if indeed he was not the prime mover. In 1888 Delitzsch made no apology for his close friend Professor Mead baptizing Rabinowitz.[43] To put it another way: Delitzsch recognized Rabinowitz's desire to become a member of the church of Christ without becoming a member of a particular denomination, so that he might continue to be a Jew.

It may also be remarked that after declaring himself to be in full agreement with the Apostles' Creed, Rabinowitz was nevertheless baptized upon a creed which he had drawn up in Hebrew for the use of the Israelites of the New Covenant (see Chapter 8).[44]

From Berlin Rabinowitz informed the Russian authorities in Kishinev of his baptism. He returned to Kishinev on 1 April 1885. On 2 April he told a Bessarabian newspaper of his baptism. But the rumour had gone ahead of him and had reached Faltin and the Hebrew Christians of the town before Rabinowitz returned home.[45]

But before he went back to Kishinev, Rabinowitz paid another visit to Leipzig, staying there from 26 to 29 March. With Delitzsch he discussed such questions as the setting-up of a congregational school. The question of the Sabbath was discussed once more, probably raised by Delitzsch. Other sources make it clear that even though Delitzsch did not wish to make this into a test question, he found it difficult to accede to it. Strack - who presumably was not present himself - reveals about these talks that the Sabbath was to be observed as a memorial to the deliverance from Egypt, with reference to Deuteronomy 5:15. Sunday was to be kept as the Lord's Day, i.e. a day of remembrance of his resurrection and was to be hallowed by worship. Circumcision and the Sabbath were to be national distinctives, which however must not obscure that Christ is the end of the law and that justification is solely through faith in him.[46]

There is no doubt at all that Rabinowitz was able fully to accede to this theological interpretation. Even at that time the words of Paul that Christ is the end of the law had become one of his key words. Neither this discussion nor his references to this word of Paul in other contexts prevented him, however, from later being taken to task on this point.

It does not emerge clearly from Strack's account whether Rabinowitz gave a promise to hold services on both the Sabbath and Sunday. The usual thing was - and remained - to hold services on the Sabbath. In a letter of 27 March/8 April 1885 Rabinowitz told Strack that at the first Sabbath service after his journey to Germany the prayer-hall was filled with people listening reverently. Yet many Jews were also in the prayer-hall on the following day, Sunday. But the most straightforward explanation is that that particular Sunday was Easter Day. For the first time, writes Rabinowitz, in a Jewish house of prayer the mighty words: "Christ is risen" were heard.[47] Other sources show that he later also held services at the great Christian festivals, e.g. Good Friday, Easter Sunday, and Easter Day. Sometimes he held his Sabbath services not only on Saturday morning but also Saturday evening.

But it would probably be a bit too facile to assert that in this way he was able to hold services on Sunday according to Jewish reckoning, by which the new day of course begins after sunset. The Sabbath remained the primary day for services for Rabinowitz - even after the conversation with Delitzsch in Leipzig in 1885. Everyone who kept up with events knew this, doubtless including Swedish supporters of missions to Israel, although it will have confused them that a few times the editor of their magazine translated "Sabbath" by "*söndag*" (Sunday) and "*altsabbathlich*" by "*söndagligen*" (on Sundays)![48] When Louis Meyer says about Rabinowitz that it was only "for a time he clung to circumcision and the observance of the Jewish Sabbath," he gives a wrong impression.[49]

The act of baptism itself passed off with little fuss in Berlin. But when it became known that Rabinowitz had been baptized, it caused a stir. The reactions to it require a section to themselves.

Some reactions to Rabinowitz's baptism in Berlin

Rabinowitz was in quite a strong position on his return from Germany. Faber - Faltin's future son-in-law - who a few months previously had most definitely rejected the idea of Rabinowitz being baptized in Leipzig, had been involved in the decision to baptize him in Berlin. Lhotzky had done the same; he arrived in Kishinev on 3 April, sent by Delitzsch as a helper for Faltin. These two young men will hardly have contributed greatly to the negotiations, but all the same they had been there. But particularly because Delitzsch had actively helped to make his baptism in Germany possible, on his return to Kishinev Rabinowitz was in a strong position against the critics of this decision. Both Lhotzky and Faltin participated in the first Sabbath service Rabinowitz held after his return from Germany.[50]

Faltin's report of April 1885 and Lhotzky's account of the situation - written down in Kishinev in Whit week of the same year in Kishinev - give a picture of the confusion which prevailed among many people because of the new situation.

In his report Faltin attempts to give an objective account and refrains from presenting his own opinions. But we know these from his letter to Delitzsch written on 10 January 1885. In this it is quite apparent that Faltin had assumed that he was going to baptize the Israelites of the New Covenant. This view had the support of Faber while he was in Kishinev. In his report of April 1885 Faltin relates that Rabinowitz has been baptized and that he brought back, in addition to his baptismal certificate, a strange letter from Professor Strack. According to Faltin, Strack wrote that now that Rabinowitz had been baptized himself, he also had the right to baptize others. In support of this opinion, Strack invoked the right of any Christian in an emergency to function as a priest for others. He compared the group around Rabinowitz with people banished to a desert island without a clergyman in their midst.[51]

Faltin also gives the interesting information that Strack's letter and Rabinowitz's baptismal certificate had been sent to the authorities with an application for permission for Rabinowitz to discharge the office of a Christian clergyman. In his report for the month of May Faltin intimates that the possibility is to be reckoned with that this permission will be given - without divulging his own opinion.[52]

Concerning other reactions to Rabinowitz's baptism, Faltin relates in his April report that it has made a confusing impression upon "the Israelites", i.e. those around Rabinowitz, and on many Christians. He points out that some of the "Israelites" had expected to be baptized with Rabinowitz in the Lutheran church "as the idea had been at first". These did indeed desire a national church, says Faltin, but with a decidedly evangelical-Lutheran creed; yet they were willing to allow their "weak brethren after the flesh" the right to retain peculiarities like circumcision and the Sabbath, as these matters have no significance after baptism. "In brief, they wish to be national Christians with a Lutheran creed," says Faltin.

We shall return to the open conflict which later broke out between Faltin and Rabinowitz (see Chapter 10). So it is the more important to note Faltin's public utterances just after Rabinowitz's baptism. Though he is disappointed at developments, his fair words about Rabinowitz are not necessarily dissembled. At any rate he ends his report for April 1885 by communicating that after his return Rabinowitz continued to hold services in his brother's house, "and they are always well attended". Of Rabinowitz he says: "He preaches Christ, the crucified and risen one, Saviour and Lord of sinners... The faithful Lord will in grace add his blessing to the word." In his May report which mentions that Rabinowitz has held his first service on 18/30 May 1885 in the remodelled premises, Faltin writes: "May the house become a place of blessing in which many hearts in Israel turn to their Lord and Messiah. We commend this congregation as also our work to the prayers of our friends."

These and other comments by Faltin indicate that, although he did not approve of the circumstances around Rabinowitz's baptism in Berlin, he did not directly use this as an occasion for open conflict. On the contrary, he had not abandoned hope that it might be possible to find a solution. In his May 1885 report he writes: "We continue to have friendly relations with Mr Rabinowitz, as before."[53]

Lhotzky's account agrees in all essentials with Faltin's. Lhotzky, who on his arrival in Kishinev on 3 April 1885 had dropped into the middle of this unfolding affair, said that Rabinowitz's baptism had created a "distressing impression" upon both Christians and Jews. It had been expected, he writes, that Rabinowitz along with his family and followers would have had themselves baptized by Faltin. "But now things have turned out otherwise, and some confusion prevails." He avers that many Jews, i.e. people who were otherwise supporters of Rabinowitz, now see Rabinowitz's Christianity as a mixed religion, and prefer to become Christians in the normal manner. And many Christians, by which is probably meant Faltin and the Lutheran congregation with its proselytes, have become downhearted. But this downheartedness is on the wane, partly because of his own efforts in the matter, writes Lhotzky at Pentecost 1885.[54]

Delitzsch in Leipzig was following the course of events as well as he could, and was oscillating between forebodings and hopes for the situation in Kishinev.[55] In his address at the annual meeting on 2 June 1885 he nevertheless spoke in enthusiastic terms of the new movement in Russia. He stressed that the congregation around Rabinowitz was not a Lutheran congregation. He touched briefly on Rabinowitz's baptism: Rabinowitz did not think he should be baptized by Faltin "which would have been closest at hand", but was baptized in Berlin not as a member of a particular denomination, but into the church of Christ. After these brief comments upon this inflammable topic, Delitzsch hurried on to ask the question: "Where will he take the sacrament of communion for the first time?"[56]

If Rabinowitz had obtained the authorities' permission to function as a clergyman, this question would not have been any problem. But he was never given this permission. Before the rejection was received, he continued his preaching activity. On 18/30 May 1885 it was possible to hold the first worship service in the restored premises. He still had enthusiastic adherents. Along the way he was going to have to make up his mind about baptism, communion, and church membership. An actual formation of a church or congregation never came about. The Russian authorities refused this. Some temporary expedients to solve the baptism problem for Rabinowitz's adherents, which might have been tolerable, encountered obstacles that others placed in the way. In this matter Faltin was neither neutral nor on Rabinowitz's side.

Some corrections and a question

The way Lhotzky deals with the circumstances around Rabinowitz's baptism in his 1904 account is good evidence that some data given in his memoirs must be taken with a grain of salt. A. Wiegand's words about Lhotzky's article are indeed true: "We discover there much that is not in any mission report."[57] Wiegand means this favourably, for he characterizes the article as "exceedingly worth reading." But if we go to the primary sources, they contradict Lhotzky on some important points, although he had been personally at the centre of events. A couple of examples:

Lhotzky asserts that Wilkinson requested "a secret conversation" with Rabinowitz somewhere on the continent.[58] But it can be ascertained that Wilkinson mentioned it in his magazine before the meeting was held.[59]

Besides alleging that Wilkinson encircled and watched over Rabinowitz when they met, Lhotzky maintains that Wilkinson "had a need" to get Rabinowitz baptized in order to have some good mission reports.[60] But this is contradicted by Wilkinson's attitude, for he did not find the time to be ripe for baptism just then, and he refused to carry out the baptism.[61] Lhotzky also avers that it was the Englishmen who stipulated that an Englishman should baptize Rabinowitz and that it must not be done in Leipzig.[62] The sources referred to above show that it was Delitzsch with three other Germans (including Lhotzky) who appointed the venue and were those responsible for this. Wilkinson had left Leipzig early in the morning of 19 March 1885 with the impression that Rabinowitz would return to Kishinev unbaptized. When he was informed that Rabinowitz had been baptized, he feared that "undue pressure had been exercised from some quarters".[63] In a letter of 2 April Strack, however, writes the following to Wilkinson:

> When you left Leipsig, we were agreed as to the necessity for Rabinowitch to take time to consider respecting baptism. The next morning (19/3) he declared that he was resolved to be baptised before returning to Russia. Therefore, in the afternoon, Prof. Delitsch thought it better to have him baptised in Berlin and not in Leipsig; not by a Lutheran clergyman, but by a clergyman of Great Britain or America. Without the least pressure Rabinowitch was willing to return with me to Berlin. A friend recommended Prof. Mead, formerly Pastor of the Congregational Church, Andover Theological Seminary, Mass. U.S.A., as an earnest Christian. After due information Prof. Mead consented to baptise Rabinowitch, and the latter consented to be baptised by him...[64]

In the same letter Strack draws attention to Delitzsch's attitude to the relationship between Rabinowitz and Faltin. Strack writes:

> I am convinced that I may assure you, that Prof. Delitsch is not willing to give over Rabinowitch and his movement into the hands of any Society. Prof. Delitsch wishes Rabinowitch should be absolutely independent of Pastor Faltin and of the various Societies... Now I agree with you, that the unknown - at least to us (in Leipsig) - position of Pastor Faltin creates a great difficulty. How can Pastor Faltin be an impartial medium between the different Societies and Rabinowitch, if he is an agent of the London Society?[65]

It is hard to give an unambiguous answer to the crucial question whether Rabinowitz went to Germany with the clear purpose of being baptized. In 1904 Lhotzky argues that his link-up with the mission meant that Rabinowitz for his own part found the question of baptism brought home to him and that Rabinowitz "had perhaps never before thought of baptism".[66] To do Lhotzky justice, it must be mentioned that he is not here speaking directly of the journey to Germany. It is certain that Rabinowitz discussed this question with Faber in January-February 1885. The connection with Faltin makes it natural to assume that the baptism issue had obtruded earlier. But if so then the blame cannot to be laid upon the British societies.

But did Rabinowitz go to Germany with baptism in mind? In 1904 Lhotzky cites that during the talk with Rabinowitz in Leipzig there was one person who did not wish him well who asked the question whether he intended to get baptized.[67] But it is hard to find one of those present who did not wish Rabinowitz well.

However this may be, the primary sources make it clear that Rabinowitz desired baptism once he was in Germany. At some time during the negotiations, Rabinowitz had, according to Wilkinson, expressed his wish to accompany Wilkinson to England and be baptized in London, something Wilkinson could not consent to.[68] When Strack describes the intention behind Rabinowitz's journey, he mentions three matters: he came partly to get baptized, partly to get personally acquainted with Wilkinson, and partly to visit Delitzsch in Leipzig.[69] Well, all three things happened. Nevertheless it is impossible to rule out completely that Strack's words may have been influenced by the actual course of events, rather than expressing Rabinowitz's intention and plan when he agreed to meet Wilkinson in Germany. Later mentions of it aver that Rabinowitz journeyed to Berlin in order to be baptized, which is to rationalize after the event.[70] The claim that Rabinowitz was baptized in Kishinev by Faltin betrays historical ignorance, although it is made by a Hebrew Christian from Kishinev.[71] The assertion that Rabinowitz in Leipzig went over to Protestantism, as the Jüdisches Lexikon (1930) maintains, is an interpretation which goes against Rabinowitz's intention.[72] This understanding is common in Jewish presentations.[73] And that Rabinowitz on his baptism day ate roast pork to prove his evangelical liberty? Well, it may be, but I have found no evidence for this in primary sources.[74]

It is certain that Rabinowitz's baptism took Faltin by surprise. And it is hard to imagine that Faber received the suggestion with enthusiasm (even though he did not oppose it when it came up at the meeting), when it is recalled that shortly before he had rejected the possibility of Rabinowitz being baptized in Leipzig. No definite evidence has been observed in the sources that Rabinowitz before his departure from Kishinev informed Delitzsch or Wilkinson that such was his intention.

But all the same it may have been in the back of his mind, particularly because we know that a little earlier he had been mulling over plans to be baptized in Leipzig. So the possibility must be kept open that, before he went to Germany, in his secret soul Rabinowitz saw the journey as an opportunity to get baptized. What is important in this connection is that prior to his journey he was convinced that baptism was both right and necessary, which has been substantiated above. Baptism was not "a sudden and surprising decision", as Zipperstein argues when he claims that Rabinowitz was probably influenced by promises of financial aid for his movement and by the excitement of being courted by Delitzsch and by other Christian dignitaries.[75] It is also to keep in mind that Rabinowitz did not feel pressed to be baptized. In a letter to John Wilkinson of 6 April 1885 Rabinowitz writes:

> Now I am going to reply to your letter. As regards the holy baptism, I can only say a few words; it is done, and everything is done by the guidance of the Holy Spirit. And I say it distinctly, that I did not receive baptism because I was in any way, or by anybody, pressed to do it; but, as I told you long ago, because it was absolutely necessary for me to take that step. I now had a good opportunity of being baptized in Berlin by Professor Mead, who is an American, and made up my mind to be baptized there. The Government does not like to see thousands of its Jewish subjects join the German-Lutheran Church, and I again assure you, that the goodwill of the Government is of greater value to me than that of ten Lutheran Professors.[76]

At all events, Rabinowitz had succeeded in getting his way and being baptized in Germany. He had obtained a baptismal certificate without being baptized into a particular denomination and without giving up his status and identity as a Jew. Nor was it unimportant that Delitzsch bore the main responsibility for Rabinowitz's desire to be baptized in Germany being achieved.

Chapter 8

MAIN THEOLOGICAL VIEWS 1884-85

Before we continue to trace the historical events, it may be appropriate to give a resumé of Rabinowitz's main theological views as he presented them in written form in 1884-1885. At the conference in Kishinev in March 1884 he had been called to account for them, and the outlines of the topics discussed then have already been given (see Chapter 5). He made several attempts at formulating a Creed or Symbol for the Israelites of the New Covenant and did write twenty-four articles of faith. In these and in the Creed we find lasting expressions of the faith he held. It should be noted that some sources mention twenty-five articles.[1] The twenty-fifth article, which is about the Oath, is rendered in an English translation from 1885.[2] A French translation also from 1885 has only twenty-four articles,[3] and the same is the case with the *Tefila* which Rabinowitz had reprinted in Kishinev in 1892. As this is the situation in 1892, we shall refer to this document as the *Twenty-Four Articles*, although it may at some time have contained twenty-five.

The *Twenty-Four Articles of Faith* were not, however, given the same publicity as previous drafts. They were written in Hebrew and seem not to have been known by all those who at that time expressed their opinions about Rabinowitz. We may add that some critics were not always capable of differentiating between the value of the *Thirteen Theses* and later expressions of Rabinowitz's basic stance, but - erroneously - regarded the *Thirteen Theses* as in principle on a par with the later material. Descriptions of Rabinowitz's faith by Jewish writers, e.g. Sh.L. Tsitron,[4] Z. Rejzen[5] and Saul M. Ginsburg,[6] only mention the *Thirteen Theses*, which means that they are precluded from a deeper understanding of Rabinowitz's faith. That they were not even anywhere close to the *Thirteen Theses* is revealed by the fact that they claim that Rabinowitz in these articles advocates the retention of circumcision and Sabbath. These are not even mentioned in the *Thirteen Theses*. As we have already shown (see Chapter 4) Rabinowitz found a firm basis for his faith in 1884 and amplified this in credal statements up to his baptism in March 1885.

Enough material is available for us to make up our minds about the theology of Rabinowitz. But we shall definitely be led astray if we assign the same importance to the *Thirteen Theses* as we do to statements drawn up later.

Rabinowitz's articles of faith

Rabinowitz formulated some articles of faith on four occasions. The first two came about in spring 1884, the last two doubtless in spring 1885.

A draft of articles of faith was presented at the conference in Kishinev on 26 March 1884. They are called the *Twelve Articles of Faith*. These were accompanied by *An Exposition*. Shortly before the conference, Rabinowitz composed a document in 10 points, which we shall here call the *Ten Articles of Faith*. It was these which Delitzsch published in May 1884, accompanied by *An Exposition*, the same one which originally accompanied the *Twelve Articles of Faith*. According to Delitzsch, the *Exposition* had been written in great haste in one afternoon.[7]

After Rabinowitz's promising negotiations with the authorities in St Petersburg in December 1885,[8] Delitzsch wrote to him: "So now it is a matter of drawing up liturgies for baptism, marriage, and burial."[9] As permission to perform them was not officially granted, these liturgies were never written.

Before his baptism in Berlin in March 1885, Rabinowitz formulated a Creed or Symbol, which can also be called the *Seven Articles of Faith*. At about the same time, he had also drawn up the *Twenty-Four Articles of Faith* which he conveyed to, among others, John Wilkinson when they met in Leipzig in March 1885.[10] These, with the *Creed*, are found printed in the *Prayer Book* which was re-issued in 1892. This indicates that it was these two which expressed Rabinowitz's lasting basis of faith. But the first two statements are not unimportant in giving an overall impression of his faith and how this developed. It is particularly significant to trace the models he followed. Earlier accounts have not shown much interest in this question.

In style the *Twelve Articles of Faith* are very close to Maimonides' thirteen articles of faith which were formulated in the 12th century.[11] These are often read by Jews after the morning prayer proper. Like Maimonides, Rabinowitz introduces each of the twelve articles with the words: "I believe firmly and assuredly" - or, as it is rendered in the English translation in The Jewish Herald: "I believe, with a perfect faith." Then, by Jewish custom, there follows a word of praise in §§1-9: "Blessed be His name!" Also in content there are clear points of contact with Maimonides. Thus Rabinowitz's §2 - that God is not corporeal - is identical to §3 of Maimonides. The belief that God rewards and punishes (§8) and that there will be a resurrection from the dead (§12) is also to be found in Maimonides (§11 & §13). Rabinowitz also adopts the words of conclusion:

For Thy salvation have I waited, O Lord! I have waited, O Lord for
Thy salvation. O Lord! for Thy salvation have I have waited.

In both, the belief in God's unity is set out in §1. But Rabinowitz goes further and stresses that God has created everything "by His Word and His Holy Spirit." This entered into Rabinowitz's considerations about the concept of the Trinity (see below).

Belief in the truth of the prophets' words is also set out in both (§6). In Maimonides, the stress is placed on Moses being the greatest of the prophets (§7), on the given Torah coming from Moses (§8), on the Law being immutable, and on their never being given any other Torah (§9). Rabinowitz follows a different path. He first mentions Abraham. It is Abraham to whom God gave the promise of the land of Canaan as an eternal possession and also the sign of the covenant, circumcision (§3). This is an eternal sign. Not until after this is it said that the Sabbath and Passover are an eternal law given through Moses. The Ten Commandments are mentioned in §5 in Rabinowitz.

Not surprisingly, the greatest difference between Maimonides and Rabinowitz is to be found in the articles about the Messiah. Maimonides writes in §12: "I believe firmly and assuredly in the coming of the Messiah, and should he tarry I shall nevertheless hope every day for his coming." In Rabinowitz, the Messiah is the fulfilment of God's promise to David (§7), and Jesus is mentioned by name (§§9-12). In this context, we may note the 'Jewish' and Old Testament phraseology: Messiah is the horn of salvation (cf. 1 Sam. 2:10; Luke 1:69), the righteous Zemak (*Zemak* = shoot: Jer. 23:5 and Messianic name: Zech.3:8; 6:12), he is the saviour, whose kingdom shall have no end (§9). In §10 the passion, death, and resurrection of Jesus are mentioned, but it may be noted that the virgin birth is not mentioned. In §11 the hardening of Israel's heart is mentioned. In §12 the belief in the resurrection of the dead is linked to the resurrection of Jesus from the dead.

So there cannot be any doubt at all that Rabinowitz formulated the *Twelve Articles of Faith* with a sideways glance at Maimonides' work.

We shall now render the *Twelve Articles of Faith* in E.O.C. Roeder's translation from 1884.[12] There is also a Norwegian translation.[13] The Bodleian Library, Oxford, has a hand-written copy of the *Twelve Articles of Faith*.[14]

The Twelve Articles of Faith: a draft

§1 I believe, with a perfect* faith, that the Creator, blessed be His name, is the living, true and eternal God, who hath made by His Word, and His Holy Spirit, heaven and earth, all things visible and invisible; that He is One, and all is from Him, through Him and to Him.

§2 I believe, with a perfect faith, that the Creator, blessed be His name, is not corporeal, that we cannot apprehend Him by the corporeal senses, and that there is no likeness to Him.

§3 I believe, with a perfect faith, that the Creator, blessed be His name, has made a covenant with our father Abraham, to be his and his children's God, and to give him and his descendants the land of Canaan for an eternal inheritance, and that the sign of this covenant is circumcision in the flesh, a sign of an eternal covenant.

---

*The word "perfect" carries unintended overtones in English; as stated earlier, this could have been translated, "I believe firmly and with assurance".

§4 I believe, with a perfect faith, that the Creator, blessed be His name, has, according to His promise, brought out the children of Israel from Egypt with a strong hand through Moses, His chosen one, and commanded them [us] to keep holy the Sabbath and the Passover, as a law forever.

§5 I believe, with a perfect faith, that the Creator, blessed be His name, gave us on Mount Horeb the Ten Commandments written with His own finger on two tables of stone, and enjoined us to keep these laws and ordinances in the land which He has given us as our inheritance.

§6 I believe, with a perfect faith, that the Creator, blessed be His name, raised up prophets in our midst from among our brethren, and that all their words are true, and not one of them shall remain unfulfilled.

§7 I believe, with a perfect faith, that the Creator, blessed be His name, promised to David, the son of Jesse, of Bethlehem, that He would make his name great, and that his throne and kingdom should endure for ever and ever.

§8 I believe, with a perfect faith, that the Creator, blessed be His name, rewards those who observe His commandments and punishes those who transgress them.

§9 I believe, with a perfect faith, that the Creator, blessed be His name, in His infinite mercy, has raised up in the house of his servant David, a Horn of salvation, the Righteous Zemah, the Saviour, the Lord Jesus Christ of Bethlehem, and that He reigns over the house of Jacob forever, and of his kingdom there shall be no end.

§10 I believe, with a perfect faith, that according to the will of the Creator, our Messiah, Jesus, was persecuted and crucified; that He poured out His soul unto death for our salvation; that He rose from the dead, and now sits at the right hand of God the Father.

§11 I believe, with a perfect faith, that in accordance with the counsel of the Creator, our forefathers hardened their hearts and rejected their Messiah, Jesus, and that this was permitted in order to provoke other nations to jealousy, to bring salvation to the whole world; that the Gentiles also might believe on our Jesus through the preaching of His messengers of peace, whom we rejected and drove from our midst, so that the whole world might be filled with the glory of the Lord, and that He might be the King of the whole earth.

§12 I believe, with a perfect faith, that when it shall please our heavenly Father, there will be a resurrection from the dead, even as our Lord Jesus rose from the dead and became thereby the first-fruits of the resurrection.

For Thy salvation have I waited, O Lord! I have waited, O Lord for Thy salvation. O Lord! for Thy salvation have I have waited.

We shall later summarize the views with which Rabinowitz accompanied these articles in *An Exposition*. But first a word about the *Ten Articles of Faith*.

The Ten Articles of Faith: a tract on salvation history

Krüger maintains that Faber did not bring the *Twelve Articles* with him when he returned from his visit to Kishinev.[15] But he did bring other articles of faith or basic articles of the Israelites of the New Covenant. The *Ten Articles of Faith* were published by Delitzsch.[16]

Compared with the *Twelve Articles*, the style of the *Ten Articles* lacks the same solemn and credal character. Delitzsch named them "articles of faith", so we retain the term here. They are more like a ten-point tract on salvation history. In content, it is easy to find similarities with the *Twelve*.

§1 The unity of God, and his not having a body are stressed here (cf. §§1-2 of the *Twelve*). He creates everything by his Word and his Holy Spirit.

§2 God's eternal covenant with Abraham contains the promise that God will be the God of Abraham's offspring and will give him Canaan as an eternal possession. The covenant sign is circumcision.

§3 In Egypt Jacob and his sons multiplied. The Lord sent Moses and delivered the people. In that connection he gave them the everlasting commandment to keep the Sabbath and the Passover.

§4 On Mount Horeb the Lord gave the tables of the Law to Moses, later the laws and ordinances as they are written in the Pentateuch. The Lord also promised his people that a prophet would be raised up out of their midst, to whom they should hearken (Deut. 18:15-19).

§5 God kept his promise and led Israel into the promised land where he raised up seers and prophets whose words are written in the books of the prophets. Their words shall not return void (Is. 55:11).

§6 After the first king of Israel rejected the Lord, the Lord also rejected Saul. The kingdom passed to David, the son of Jesse, of Bethlehem. Through the prophet Nathan God gave David the promise that he would establish his house and kingdom and throne for ever (cf. 2 Sam. 7).

§7 Because of their sin, Israel was sent into exile. Judah too was sent into exile in Babylon, because they did not keep the commandments of God.

§8 Both while Judah was in captivity and after their return, all the true prophets concurred in promising that:
1) the covenant with David shall never be broken, but the son of David shall be a light to the Gentiles, who shall flow to Zion,
2) the son of David shall bring about everlasting righteousness,
3) those who receive him shall be called a holy nation and from them the message will be preached unto the Gentiles,
4) those who do not receive their preaching shall be confounded,
5) the Messiah, the son of David, shall suffer and yield himself unto death and bear the sin of many.

§9 The word of the Lord to Abraham our father, to Moses our prophet, to David our king, and to His servants the true prophets, was fulfilled around 70 years before the destruction of the second temple. (After this the ministry of Jesus is described in accordance with §§9-10 of the *Twelve Articles*).

§10 Israel's hardening of heart is an expression of God's mysterious wisdom (cf. §11 of the *Twelve Articles*). But now the times of the Gentiles have been fulfilled (Luke 21:24), so that we descendants of Abraham may all come and be blessed through faith in the Lord Jesus the Messiah. The God of Abraham, Isaac, and Jacob has again looked in mercy so that the branches broken off have again been grafted onto the holy stem, in Jesus. Thus the whole of Israel shares in the eternal salvation, and Jerusalem, our holy city, and the throne of David will be raised up once more and endure for ever (cf. Rom. 11).

As may be judged from this brief summary, the content of these articles of faith is an elaboration of the ideas expressed in the *Twelve Articles of Faith*, merely being more systematically and less solemnly formulated than those. They are also significant as expressing Rabinowitz's view of his faith in 1884. But neither of these two statements of faith were included as such in the *Prayer Book* of the Israelites of the New Covenant. But the next two were, and we shall now take a look at them.

The Seven Articles of Faith: a short Creed

In connection with his baptism in March 1885, Rabinowitz drew up a *Creed*, or *Symbol* in Hebrew. Compared with the two groups of articles we have just discussed, this *Creed* is more 'Christian', i.e. there are no references to the specific distinctives of his congregation: the keeping of the Sabbath, Passover, circumcision etc. Also, belief in the virgin birth of Jesus and the Christian church and baptism is expressly stated. It was undoubtedly Rabinowitz's intention that this *Creed* should replace the Apostles' Creed.

The *Creed*, in James Adler's translation,[17] is as follows:

§1 I believe, with a perfect faith, that our heavenly Father is the living, and true, and eternal God, who created heaven and earth and everything visible and invisible through His Word and His Holy Spirit. All things are from Him, all things in Him, and all things to Him [cf. §1 of the *Twelve Articles*].

§2 I believe, with a perfect faith, that our heavenly Father has, according to His promise made to our forefathers, to our prophets, and to our king David, the son of Jesse, raised unto Israel a Redeemer, Jesus, who was born of the virgin Mary, in Bethlehem the city of David, who suffered, was crucified, dead, and buried for our salvation, rose again from the dead, and liveth, and sitteth at the right hand of our heavenly Father, from thence He shall come to judge the world, the living and the dead. He is the appointed King over the house of Jacob for ever, and of His dominion there shall be no end.

§3 I believe, with a perfect faith, that by the counsel of God and His foreknowledge, our fathers have been smitten with hardness of heart for sin and for rebellion against our Messiah, the Lord Jesus, in order to provoke the other nations of the earth unto jealousy, and to reconcile all through faith in Christ, by the word of His Evangelists, in order that knowledge of Jehovah should cover the earth, and Jehovah be King over the whole world.

§4 I believe, with a perfect faith, that through faith in Jesus, the Messiah alone, without the works of the law, a man may be justified; that there is but one God, who justifies the circumcised Jews by faith, and the uncircumcised through faith; and that there is no difference between Jew and Greek, between bond and free, between male and female. They are all one in Christ.

§5 I believe, with a perfect faith, in a Holy Catholic and Apostolic church.

§6 I confess one baptism for the remission of sins.

§7 I wait for the resurrection and renewed life of the dead, and for the life of the world to come. Amen.

> For Thy salvation, I wait, O Lord; I wait, O Lord, for Thy salvation,
> O Lord, for Thy salvation I wait.

This *Creed* was included at the close of the worship liturgy and came after the sermon and before the close with the Aaronic blessing (see Chapter 11). It was printed in the *Prayer Book* of 1885, reprinted in 1892. The *Twenty-Four Articles of Faith*, with which we shall now deal, were also printed there. This shows that they were intended to function in the life of the congregation.

The Twenty-Four Articles of Faith: Excerpts from the Thirty-Nine Articles of the Anglican Church

In 1885 Delitzsch translated into German the *Symbol* (i.e. the *Creed* just discussed) of the congregation. In a note he reveals that he also knows of the *Twenty-Four Articles of Faith*.[18] Elsewhere he says of these that Rabinowitz took as his pattern the *Thirty-Nine Articles of the Church of England* more than the *Augsburg Confession*.[19] Krüger translated them into French in 1885, mentioning that §1, which corresponds to §1 and §2 in the *Twelve Articles*, is a word-for-word rendering of the first part of §8 - he means §1 - of the Anglican Church's confession.[20] In his discussion of these Articles of Faith A.S. Poulsen says that Rabinowitz "seems to have had the Thirty-Nine Articles of the Anglican Church in view."[21] He did indeed, quite literally, rather more than Poulsen seems to have sensed.

In fact Rabinowitz must have had the *Thirty-Nine Articles* from the *Book of Common Prayer* - in Hebrew - actually in his hand. This book had been translated into Hebrew in its entirety in 1837, followed by a fully vocalized edition in 1841. Rabinowitz must have possessed this edition, having obtained it through Faltin probably, who had good relations with the

London Society, the publishers.[22] An analysis of the language shows that Rabinowitz adopts a number of expressions from the Hebrew translation of the *Thirty-Nine Articles*. And more than that, he takes over parts of the *Thirty-Nine Articles* word-for-word. Apart from the saving in time involved, as he did not have to formulate them for himself, he had also placed himself in an almost unassailable position. For if the Anglican Church was able to use the Hebrew version in its activity in, e.g. Jerusalem, Rabinowitz could hardly be attacked for using similar articles of faith - in Kishinev.

Once it can be established that Rabinowitz used the *Book of Common Prayer* in Hebrew (BCP), this gives us a unique chance of plotting his basic theological stance by examining the omissions and additions he made in the *Twenty-Four Articles of Faith*, reproduced here as R.

It may be confirmed that the first four articles of the *Twenty-Four Articles of Faith* are identical (except for a few mostly slight changes of language) with the first four articles of the *Seven Articles of Faith/Creed*. But the solemn "I believe, with a perfect faith," has been left out. The position and content of these first four articles indicate Rabinowitz's programme, amplified in the following articles. The following observations may be made about the most important omissions and additions compared with BCP:

R§1 The first part is almost word-for-word from BCP§1, *Of the unity of God*. But Rabinowitz omits mentioning that there are three persons of one substance in the godhead. Yet he affirms that God creates and upholds everything by his Word and his Holy Spirit.

R§2 *Of Jesus, the Redeemer of Israel*. The material has been taken from BCP§2, *Of the Word or Son of God*, which was made very Man, and BCP§4, *Of the resurrection of Christ*. BCP§3, *Of the going down of Christ into Hell*, is omitted by Rabinowitz. He introduces §2 by stressing that God has raised up the Redeemer of Israel according to the promises to the fathers. BCP§1 speaks of the Word of the Father, begotten of Him from everlasting. However, it is important that Rabinowitz says in §9 that the Messiah is "the Word of our heavenly Father, who was begotten by the Father in eternity". When Rabinowitz further describes Jesus in §2 (see §2 of the Creed above) he does not use the ecclesiastical and 'Greek' terms like 'substance', 'nature' and so on. The most important elements of the second article of the Apostles' Creed are included. In Rabinowitz's version there is not only a 'Jewish flavour' about the introduction but also about the conclusion, with its stress that the risen Jesus is king over the house of Jacob for ever. The same may be said of the emphasis that Jesus was born in the town of Bethlehem in Judah.

R§3 The article *Of Israel's sin and rebellion against the Messiah* has no counterpart in BCP, but the prominent place of this article is due to these being articles of faith for the Israelites of the New Covenant. Jesus is called the Lord; it is clearly signalled that his work avails for all peoples of the earth.

R§4 The article *Of justification* is given a prominent place by Rabinowitz compared with BCP§11. It is clearly stated that it is by faith alone and without the works of the law that a man is justified. Quoting Gal.3:28 shows clearly that there is no difference on this point between Jews and Gentiles, they are all one in Jesus the Messiah. As against §4 of the Creed, the following is added in conclusion: "In our faith in the Messiah we keep the Law (the Torah) and that is a great assuagement of the soul and full of comfort". This last Rabinowitz has taken from BCP§11, but there it is applied to the doctrine of justification by faith.

Rabinowitz omits BCP§5 *Of the Holy Spirit*, doubtless because it speaks in 'Greek' terms of the Holy Spirit proceeding from, and being of the same substance as, the Father and the Son.

R§5 *Of the sufficiency of the holy Scriptures for salvation.* Rabinowitz takes this article from BCP§6. The Holy Scriptures contain all that is necessary for salvation, and whatever is not read in them or can be proved from the Scriptures, is not to be required of anyone to be believed as an article of faith. Rabinowitz even adopts the BCP's term for the Old Testament (*Brit ha-Yeshana*), and also uses it in §6, whereas in §16 he uses the normal Jewish term *Tanakh* (*Torah* = the Pentateuch, *Nevi'im* = the Prophets, *Ketuvim* = the Writings). He does not, as BCP does, enumerate the canonical books of the Old Testament and does not express an opinion about the OT apocryphal writings. To Rabinowitz, the OT and the NT are the canonical books, and "they have been written by the Holy Spirit."

R§6 Parts of BCP§7, *Of the Old Testament*, have been adopted, but with important changes. Whereas BCP says that the OT is not contrary to the NT, Rabinowitz reverses this: the NT is not contrary to the OT, an understandable application, for that is the question that is a problem for Jews. Both stress that eternal life is given through Christ, who is the only mediator between God and man. Rabinowitz here follows BCP without however identifying Christ as "God and man". Both say that the law was given by God through Moses. BCP then speaks of Christians not being bound to keep the ceremonial law and the civil law, but being obligated to keep the moral law. Rabinowitz takes a different path. First he cites that the law - the Torah - has become "a schoolmaster to bring us to the Messiah, so that we shall alone be justified by faith in him" (cf. Gal. 3:24). Then the obligation is mentioned to keep circumcision, "because we are Abraham's offspring" and because God has enjoined this upon him. The keeping of the Sabbath is set in relation to the exodus from Egypt. Also the keeping of the Feast of Unleavened Bread (Passover) and the Feast of Weeks (Pentecost) is mentioned, which is to be done at the same time as the Christians celebrate these festivals. Christians celebrate these festivals solely in memory of the resurrection of the Messiah and the coming of the Holy Spirit, but they are also to be celebrated in memory of the exodus from Egypt.

Rabinowitz omits BCP§8, *Of the three Creeds*, i.e. the three Symbols of the Early Church (the Nicene, Athanasian, and Apostles' Creeds) are not binding upon the Israelites of the New Covenant as expressions of the faith.

R§7 *Of the Mishna, Talmud, and Shulchan Aruk*. This article - naturally - has no counterpart in BCP. No doctrine may be based upon the Mishna and Talmud, which are only a perpetual reminder of the greatness of that spirit of sleep which God made fall upon "us". The *Shulchan Aruk* is regarded as a hindrance and a snare which has prevented "our eyes" from seeing the ways of the living and true faith.

R§8 *Of original sin* is a shortened version of BCP§9. Original sin is defined as a corruption of the nature of every man, that is engendered by the nature of Adam. The flesh is inclined to evil and is contrary to the Spirit. It is therefore difficult to assume the yoke of God's law. BCP's rejection of Pelagius is omitted, but nothing can be deduced from this, as Rabinowitz consistently omits BCP's references to church fathers and heretics.

R§9 *Of free will* corresponds in content to BCP§10. Man cannot by his own strength and good works make his way straight and believe and call upon the name of the Lord. Only by God's grace in the Messiah, him who is the Word "begotten of the Father in eternity", is the good will granted.

Rabinowitz leaves out BCP§11 *Of the justification of man*, as he has included this article in §4.

R§10 *Of good works* has been adopted from BCP§12 with slight alterations. Living and true faith is known by good works, as the tree is known by its fruit. In the Messiah good works are well-pleasing to God, but they cannot put away sins or justify us or prevent God's judgement.

R§11 In this article Rabinowitz combines BCP§13, *Of works before justification*, with BCP§14, *Of works of supererogation*. Good works done before justification are not well-pleasing to God, they have the nature of sin. The whole idea of the possibility of works of supererogation is denied.

R§12 *Of the Messiah who alone was without sin*. This article corresponds to BCP§15. Only the Messiah was without sin in his flesh and his spirit. "Although baptized and born again in the Messiah, yet we still offend in many things."

R§13 *Of sin after baptism* corresponds to BCP§16, Rabinowitz first declaring that all sin that is committed may be forgiven by a full repentance of heart. But there is a sin against the Holy Ghost, which is unpardonable. What this is is not defined either in BCP or by Rabinowitz.

R§14 *Of predestination and election*. Here Rabinowitz follows BCP§17 in a lengthy disquisition on these questions. God's mysterious predestination in the Messiah is maintained. The predestined are those who are called, obey the call, and are justified freely and made the children of God.

Rabinowitz omits BCP§18 *Of obtaining eternal salvation only by the name of Christ*. This omission is probably not for theological reasons but because the matter has already been presented.

R§15 *Of the church*. In accord with BCP§19 the church of the Messiah (*Kehilat ha-Mashiach*) is defined as the congregation of believers, in which the Word of God is preached in purity and the sacraments administered according to the ordinance of the Messiah and the holy apostles. BCP's additional comment that the churches of Jerusalem, Alexandria, Antioch, and Rome have erred, both in their view of ceremonies and in matters of faith is omitted by Rabinowitz.

R§16 *Of the authority of the church* corresponds to BCP§20. The church has authority to decree rites and ceremonies, but in matters of faith nothing must be ordained that is contrary to God's Word in the Holy Scriptures (see also R§5 above).

R§17 Whereas BCP§21 says *Of the authority of general councils* that they may not be gathered together without the commandment and will of princes and must be governed with the Spirit and the Word of God and that they have erred even in matters of faith, Rabinowitz begins with the same words but uses the article to say that no general and special gatherings may take place except at the government's command and according to the will of the authorities. The powers that be do not bear the sword in vain (cf. Rom. 13).

Rabinowitz omits BCP§22 *Of purgatory, pardons etc.*

R§18 *Of ministering in the congregation* is a shortened version of BCP§23. It says bluntly that anyone is forbidden to minister the sacraments unless he is lawfully called and in accord with the laws of the government. It may be remarked that Rabinowitz does not say, as BCP begins by saying, that public preaching is forbidden unless one has been called and sent.

R§19 *Of speaking in the congregation in such a tongue as the people understand*. This article applies the intention of BCP§24 to the conditions of Russian Jews. Most of the children of Israel in Russia understand Hebrew, "the sacred tongue", and Yiddish. So services should be conducted in these languages.

R§20 *Of the sacraments*. BCP§25 says first that the sacraments are not only tokens of profession but also even more certain witnesses and effectual signs of grace. Rabinowitz turns this about. The sacraments which were ordained by the Messiah "are sure witnesses of God's grace and his will towards us. Through them he works in our midst in a hidden and wondrous way to awaken and confirm our faith in him, and they are also tokens of profession." He affirms that there are two sacraments: baptism and the Lord's supper. The sacraments are effective only as they are received worthily. Rabinowitz does not mention the five other matters which the Roman Catholic church regards as sacraments and which BCP rejects as such.

R§21 *Of the unworthiness of the ministers which does not hinder the effect of the sacraments.* Like BCP§26 Rabinowitz points out that the minister does not administer the sacraments in his own name, but in that of the Messiah, so that the effectiveness of the sacraments does not depend on the worthiness of the minister. The church is bound to investigate whether a minister is living worthily; if he is not, the congregation must depose him, after a just verdict has been reached.

R§22 *Of baptism* corresponds in content to BCP§27. Baptism is the sign of regeneration. By the water of baptism a person is grafted and immersed into the congregation of the Messiah. Baptism is the washing and purging away of all evil. Those who receive baptism are professing openly to all that they are assured of the forgiveness of their sins and that they are children of God. Finally the rightness of baptizing children is affirmed.

R§23 *Of the Lord's supper* takes its material from BCP§28. "The supper of the Lord is a sign whereby we remember the death of our Lord the Messiah until he comes the second time in his glory." Rabinowitz calls the bread "heavenly bread". By eating the bread and drinking the wine one partakes of the body and blood of the Messiah. Rabinowitz omits BCP's refutation of transubstantiation and other remnants of Roman Catholic theology, doubtless because these were not current problems for his congregation. In conclusion he states that the wicked do not partake of the Messiah when they receive the sacraments. The content is taken from BCP§29 *Of the wicked which eat not the body of Christ in the use of the Lord's supper.*

The next four articles from BCP are omitted by Rabinowitz, i.e. BCP§30 *Of both kinds* [both the bread and the wine are to be given to the people], BCP§31 *Of the one oblation of Christ finished upon the cross,* in which the Roman Catholic idea of a sacrifice of the mass is rejected, and BCP§32 *Of the marriage of priests,* with a rejection of celibacy for the ministers of the church, and BCP§33 *Of excommunicate persons,* how they are to be avoided.

R§24 *Of the traditions of the church* takes its material from BCP§34. Whoever breaks those practices of the church that are not repugnant to the Word of God shall be rebuked, as he is disobedient to the authority of the Magistrate. In conclusion it is asserted that every congregation has the right to ordain and change customs which are due to the taste of the congregation. But everything shall be done to obtain a greater knowledge of the Messiah.

The five remaining articles in BCP are omitted by Rabinowitz, except that BCP§39 *Of a Christian man's oath* appears as R§25 in the versions where this document has 25 articles (cf. the beginning of this chapter).

To sum up we may say that with the *Twenty-Four Articles of Faith* Rabinowitz has given a clear answer to traditional doctrinal questions, that in much - both in language and content - he follows the Christian tradition when this speaks biblically, but he seeks to avoid formulations taken from the Greek world of thought. The distinctive views of the Israelites of the New Covenant are expressed, but in the *Twenty-Four Articles* there is no detailed argument for the justification for a Hebrew Christian congregation. But such a congregation is assumed. It may also be remarked that he uses the word 'church', not 'synagogue' or similar, about his congregation.

The importance of these articles of faith for an appraisal of Rabinowitz's basic theology can hardly be exaggerated. He adhered to them for the rest of his life. Therefore it seems appropriate to render the entire twenty-five articles from James Adler's translation of 1885.[23]

Articles of faith of the new people of Israel - sons of the new covenant

§1 There is but one true and living God, not corporeal, without divisions, cannot be apprehended by the bodily senses, of great goodness, power and wisdom beyond comprehension, who creates, forms, makes and upholds everything by His Word and by His Holy Sprit. All things are from Him, all things in Him, and all things to Him.

§2 The true God has, according to His promise to our forefathers, to our prophets, and to our king David, the son of Jesse, raised unto Israel a Redeemer, Jesus, who was born from the virgin Mary, in Bethlehem the City of David, who suffered, was crucified, dead, and buried for our salvation, rose again from the dead, and liveth, and sitteth on the right hand of our heavenly Father; from thence He shall come to judge the world, the living and the dead. He shall be King over the house of Jacob for ever, and of His dominion there shall be no end.

§3 According to the counsel and foreknowledge of God, our ancestors have been smitten with hardness of heart to sin and rebel against the Messiah, the Lord Jesus, in order to provoke to jealousy the other nations of the earth, and to reconcile all the children of men, through their faith in Christ, by the ministry of His Holy Evangelists and Apostles, in order that the knowledge of God should cover the earth; and the Lord be King over the whole world.

§4 Through faith alone in Jesus the Messiah all men may be justified without the works of the law. There is but one God, who shall justify the circumcised Jews by faith, and the uncircumcised Gentiles through faith; and there is no difference between Jew and Greek, between bond and free, between male and female; for they are all one in Christ Jesus. By faith in Christ we fulfil the law, and that faith is a wonderful balm to our soul, and full of comfort.

§5 The Holy Scriptures contain everything necessary for our salvation. No one is bound to accept anything not found in them, nor made binding by them, as articles of faith, or as things necessary to salvation. By "Holy Scriptures" we mean the books of revelation Old and New Testament which have always been accepted by the Church as inspired by the Holy Spirit.

§6 The Scriptures of the New Testament do not contradict those of the Old Testament, for in both life everlasting is offered unto mankind through the Messiah, who alone is the Mediator between God and man. The law which was given by God through Moses was to lead us to Christ, that we might be justified through faith in Him. But we are the seed of Abraham according to the flesh, who was the father of all those who were circumcised and believed, we are bound to circumcise every male-child on the eighth day, as God commanded him. And as we are the descendants of those whom the Lord brought out of the land of Egypt with a stretched out arm, we are bound to keep the Sabbath, the feast of unleavened bread, and the feast of weeks, according as it is written in the law of Moses, whilst the (Gentile) Christians celebrate them only in commemoration of the resurrection of the Messiah from the dead, and the outpouring of the Holy Spirit from heaven.

§7 The Mishna and Talmud are not to be used for establishing any doctrines, but regarded only as an everlasting memento of the spirit of deep slumber which God has permitted to fall upon us; so that the "Schulchan Aruch" (*Megeeneh Erets, Joreh Deha, Choshen Mishpat* and *Eben Ezer*) became a net, a snare, and a stumbling-block to us, and have darkened our eyes so that we failed to see the ways of the true and life-giving Faith.

§8 Original sin is the cause of the corruption of every natural man born of blood and the will of the flesh, which always inclines towards evil. The lusts of the flesh war against the spirit, rendering it hard to accept the law of God.

§9 Man in his natural condition is unable to do good works, to walk uprightly, or to call upon God, unless there first be given to him the grace of God, which is treasured up in Christ, who is the Word of our Heavenly Father, and begotten of the Father from eternity.

§10 The good works of the sons of men are the signs of a true and living faith in the heart; as the tree is known by its fruit; and they are acceptable before God in Christ; but nevertheless they are unavailing to blot out transgressions, or to avert the severity of God's judgment.

§11 The works done prior to the bestowment of the grace of Christ and the reception of the Holy Spirit, are insufficient to secure, as a reward for merit, grace and righteousness for those who practice them; for undoubtedly they are defiled by the nature of sin, and there is no merit in deeds which originated with men, and who think they are doing more than is required of them. The foolishness and pride of men lead them to think that they not only do their duty towards God, but more even than that; though Christ says distinctly: "When you have done all those things which are commanded you, say, we are unprofitable servants."

§12 Christ alone was sinless in body as well as in spirit; but we, although baptized and born anew in Christ, still fail in many things; and if we say, we have no sin, the truth is not in us.

§13 Every sin, whether committed intentionally or unintentionally, is forgiven when the sinner repents with his heart and soul; and even after we have fallen into sin, we may by the grace of God rise and amend our ways. But a sin against the Holy Ghost is one which remains unforgiven.

§14 It was the secret counsel of God, and His will before the foundation of the world was laid, to save those from the curse and from judgment whom He chose in Christ, and to bring them through Christ unto everlasting salvation. Those upon whom this great goodness of God has been bestowed, are those who are called by His Spirit in due time; they also listen to the invitation by that grace; they are justified freely; they are accepted and made the children of God; they are fashioned to the likeness of His Only Begotten Son Jesus Christ. It is they who walk in fear, and do good works, and at last obtain by the grace of God the everlasting riches. Their meditation and study respecting their election in Christ is a source of great comfort to those who fear God, and who realize in themselves the power of the Holy Spirit, who subdues the works of the flesh and the natural evil inclinations, and who lifts up their hearts to things above, to things in the heavens. Such meditation greatly strengthens and establishes their faith in the everlasting salvation which they enjoy in Christ, and which kindles in them the flame of the love of God. It is the contrary with the proud who follow their own lusts; in them there is not the Spirit of Christ, and they do not lay to heart the judgment of God that by an eternal decree they are taken and made into children of Satan, who drags them down into the pit of despair, or into the practice of all uncleanness which is as bad as despair.

§15 The visible Church of Christ is the congregation of believers among whom the Word of God is preached in purity, and the holy ordinances observed in every detail according to the charge of Christ by the holy Evangelists.

§16 The Church is at lberty to introduce rules and observances. She is, however, not at liberty to introduce anything contrary to the Word of God, or to interpret one verse of Holy Scripture in such a manner as to contradict another. Neither is she at liberty to impose any doctrine outside the Old and New Testament Scriptures, as necessary to salvation.

§17 Without the permission of the Authorities neither a general nor special assembly is to take place; for the Government is ordained by God, as we are told in the Holy Scriptures, and in her hands God has placed all the concerns of the country, temporal as well as spiritual, to hold in check by the power of the sword of the State those who are bent on doing evil.

§18 It is forbidden for any one to officiate as minister unless he is authorised by the congregation and by the laws of the Country.

§19 The liturgy as well as the whole of the service must be conducted in a language understood by the people; and as the most of the sons of Israel in

Russia understand Hebrew, "the holy tongue", and the German jargon, therefore, it is decided that the service be conducted in these languages.

§20 The sacraments instituted by Christ serve us as faithful witnesses of the grace of God, and His goodwill toward us; and it is through them that He is working in us in a mysterious and wonderful way, to keep alive and to establish our faith in Him, and they are likewise chosen proofs that Christ is the desire of our souls and the glory of our heads. The Sacraments are two: Baptism and the Lord's Supper; the observance of them is only of real use when the communicant receives them in a right state of mind.

§21 As the minister is not ministering in his own name but in the name of Christ and on the strength of being sent by Him, it is our duty to listen to his proclamation of the word of God, and to receive at his hands the sacraments, although he is a sinful man himself. His sinfulness does not destroy the grace of the gift of God to those who receive; nevertheless, the congregation is bound to investigate carefully into the life and habits of their ministers, and if after an impartial inquiry it has been found that the minister is a bad man, it is the duty of the congregation to deprive him of his office.

§22 Baptism is a sign of the new birth. By means of water baptism, the baptized one is placed and planted in the Chuch, the Church of Christ. By means of water baptism there is the washing and cleansing from all evil, the baptized ones testify before all that they know their sins are forgiven and that they are the children of God. It is therefore quite right that little ones should be led into the Church by baptism.

§23 The Lord's Supper is a sign that we remember the death of our Lord the Messiah, till He come, and by partaking of that heavenly bread and wine we unite all our physical and spiritual powers with the body and blood of Christ which have been offered in this world for our salvation. Such are bound up in the bundle of life to shine eternally at the right hand of our heavenly Father. By faith the bread of which we partake becomes a part of the body of Christ, and the blessed cup a part of the blood of Christ. The ungodly, who have no living faith, eat it only with their mouths, but receive no part of Christ, and their sin is unforgiven.

§24 He who breaks intentionally any of the rules of the Church, although it is not against the word of God, is to be reprimanded as one who acted against the order of the Church; and against the permission of the Government. It is within the power of the general, as well as in that of a special assembly, to revise and to alter any Church rules which have only been framed by the wisdom of man. But any change must be for the edification of all.

§25 We acknowledge that false and thoughtless swearing is, according to our Lord Jesus Christ, and His apostle James, forbidden; but still we are of opinion, that according to the religion of Christ it is not forbidden, but allowed to take an oath in matters touching the Government, if one does it truthfully and in harmony with the law of God.

Before we describe how influential theologians reacted to Rabinowitz's basic stance, we shall give an outline of how he presented his views when he was not using a 'confessional' language.

An Exposition

As we have already recounted in Chapter 5, at the conference in Kishinev in March 1884 Rabinowitz's views were requested on the observance of circumcision and the Sabbath. In *An Exposition* he writes that circumcision is a sacred sign showing that a person is a descendant of Abraham. It offends nobody, as it is not performed publicly and some doctors consider that it may even be physically beneficial. Then, circumcision is not enjoined upon European nations. He believes that circumcision must be observed by Jews in order to retain their nationality or national affiliation. Both the Torah and the New Testament "make it incumbent" upon them to keep circumcision for this purpose. Circumcision "links us to our Jewish brethren, [but] it cannot justify us before God", after which he quotes Rom. 4:2: "For if Abraham were justified by works, he hath whereof to glory; but not before God." When Paul says to the Galatians: "If ye be circumcised, Christ shall profit you nothing" (Gal. 5:2), he is addressing only Gentiles who mistakenly believed that they could be justified by works of the law and Christ's grace. But according to Rabinowitz, the yoke of the law was never given to them.

Regarding the Sabbath, he refers to Ex. 20:8: "Remember the sabbath day to keep it holy." While it is incumbent upon the Israelites of the New Covenant to keep this commandment, they are at liberty regarding the laws that were conditioned by the possession of the land of Israel, by the temple worship, by the rulers holding office, by the hot climate, and by the need to keep down idolatry which has long since been rejected.

Regarding ceremonies of the new covenant, Rabinowitz stresses that only baptism and the Lord's supper are incumbent, but these are to be understood in accord with the pure Jewish spirit which finds expression in the Old Testament scriptures and according to the pattern found in the evangelical confessions in England and Germany.

He also makes statements about the Trinity. Again he contrasts the different backgrounds of Jews and Gentiles. The Gentiles, who were accustomed to polytheism, needed to have it stressed to them that the three persons in the Holy Scriptures are one. But the Jews find it exceedingly difficult to use the number three, although they well know from Scripture that the One God is three persons or personalities (*Partsufim*: faces, strictly speaking). And he continues: "The believing Gentiles call the three persons in the Godhead: 'Father, Son, and Holy Ghost'; we name them: 'One God, and His Word and His Holy Spirit', which is the same. Why should the

Christian Church burden Israel with doctrines, which were taught them by their fathers to keep them from false conceptions of the Godhead?" He emphasizes that the Jewish apostles did not lay this burden upon the Jews. "And we do not find anywhere in Holy Scripture, that the belief in 'Three persons' is to form a necessary part of our confession."

In conclusion he asserts that it is difficult to explain the virgin birth to Jews without anthropomorphizing the Holy Spirit. Rabinowitz considers that it is more honouring to God not to go into details, but only to keep to the formulation: conceived of the Holy Spirit (cf. Matt. 1:20).

This outline should have established that Rabinowitz learnt from the Christian tradition. But he did not follow the ecclesiastical forms of dogma when these spoke in a more Greek than biblical manner. This is the light in which Rabinowitz's attitude to the Christian doctrine on the Trinity must be seen. He recognized the divinity of Jesus. He was convinced that as to the subject-matter he managed to express in his Jewish terminology the essentials of the Christian doctrine on the Trinity. At any rate, Rabinowitz's thoughts about these matters are more complex than Zipperstein implies when he claims that "Rabinovich's most important departure, from the vantage point of his new Christian supporters, was his stress in his early (pre-1885) christological writings on the Oneness of God and his rejection of the Trinity".[24] As to the question of baptism, Faber had already mentioned, on a postcard to Delitzsch on 25 March 1884, that Rabinowitz's opposition to infant baptism had now changed as a result of the long debates they have been having about it.[25] He regarded baptism not only as an act of profession, but as a "sign of regeneration". To John Wilkinson, one of his most loyal supporters, Rabinowitz's view of the sacraments was even a mark of "sacramentarianism", which not only says something about Rabinowitz but also about Wilkinson. After the meeting with Rabinowitz in Germany in 1885, writes Wilkinson: "He seems to have much faith in sacraments, and thinks that souls may get life while partaking of the Lord's Supper in faith."[26] And when Wilkinson discusses the question whether Rabinowitz's doctrine is sound, he says: "Some parts of his 'Articles of Faith' have a strong flavour of Sacramentarianism and Sacerdotalism which may be accounted for by his surroundings, and which Evangelical Christians may reasonably hope he will in time outgrow. In the meantime he must not be lectured out of error, but loved into truth."[27] Later Rabinowitz was to castigate a Jew like Isak Lichtenstein, who professed faith in Jesus as the Messiah, but did not get baptized - at least not as an official act (see Chapter 14). From the beginning of his public preaching, the words of Paul in Romans 10:4 became one of his key words: "The Messiah is the end of the law." Wechsler, for instance, testifies to this (see Chapter 6). His sermons testify to it.[28] And not least: these words were written on the Torah scroll which lay in the prayer-hall (see Chapter 11). Finally, mention must be made of Rabinowitz's sharp criticism of the Talmud. He regards it as the true cause of the Jewish people's misfortune, for Rabinowitz emphasizes the contrast between the divine revelation and the rabbinical interpretation of it. Interestingly, Delitzsch criticizes Rabinowitz for this, considering that in the Talmud and other Jewish traditional literature there are ideas which are akin to the Christian faith. Delitzsch would wish that on this point Rabinowitz expressed himself with greater balance![29]

In this context it is relevant to draw attention to the fact that Rabinowitz had questioned the significance of Talmudic study and the binding character of the Talmud, already before he came to faith in Jesus. In an article in Haboker Or in 1879 he gives expression to this critical attitude to Talmud. Other Haskala Jews had done the same. That Rabinowitz "deemphasized the Talmud", as Zipperstein puts it,[30] is not a new stance conditioned by his new faith: it is an old concept which he holds on to. But it may be noticed that Rabinowitz does make use of Jewish tradition if it may serve the point he is wishing to make in his sermons. Sometimes he presents matters that are inspired by the Jewish Kabbala. When he met John Wilkinson in Germany in March 1885, he had given some examples of how it was possible, by following Kabbalistic principles, to interpret some Hebrew words christologically about Jesus. This did not meet with Wilkinson's approval. On the contrary, he showed Rabinowitz that it "was a rather dangerous principle, for the same letters might be taken to represent other words directly contradicting the point supposed to have been proved."[31] Kabbalistically inspired interpretations are not very prominent in Rabinowitz's writings after March 1884, although he still plays with such ideas orally, also in 1893 during his journey in America (see Chapter 14). In An Exposition from March 1884 he had expressed the view that allusions to the origin, birth, sufferings, death and resurrection of the Messiah were not merely to be found in the prophets and the Psalms but also "in the Talmud, Midrash, Sohar and Kabbala".[32]

The Passover Haggada: a communion liturgy

Before Faber returned to Germany in the spring of 1884, he had time to keep the Passover in Kishinev according to the Passover Haggada which Rabinowitz had just completed (see Chapter 5). It was intended to be a communion liturgy that the Israelites of the New Covenant were to use on Passover Eve.

The form is Jewish, the liturgy being shaped around the four cups which are part of the Jewish Passover meal; the content is 'Christian'. The pastor and the congregation take turns to read selected scripture portions. It may be noted that there is a pastor (or "shepherd") to conduct the proceedings. After the Lord's Prayer has been said, a dish containing three unleavened loaves, a flagon of wine, and cups for the communicants are placed on the table. The pastor fills the first cup with wine. (P = pastor; C = congregation).

First cup: The cup of Abraham, the chief ("head") of the patriarchs.

P: This night is to be kept by all the children of Israel, generation after generation. P: Ex. 12:42. C: Ex. 13:3. P: Is. 63:9. C: Is. 63:16. P: Matt. 26:17-19. C: Luke 22:15-18.

- Each takes his cup and says a prayer of thanksgiving for Abraham and the covenant given to him. The cup is drunk.

Second cup: The cup of Moses, the chief of the prophets.

P: Ex. 3:13-16. C: Ex. 14:30-31. P: Is. 63:11-12. C: John 5:45-47.

- Each takes his cup and says a prayer of thanksgiving for Moses, through whom God instructed Israel to love him. The cup is drunk.

Third cup: The cup of David, the chief of the kings.

P: Deut. 17:15,18b,20. C: 2 Sam. 7:18-24. P: Is. 55:3-5. C: Luke 1:30-33.

- Each takes his cup and says a prayer of thanksgiving for David the son of Jesse, to whom God revealed the things to come and gave promise that of his kingdom there should be no end. The cup is drunk.

Fourth cup: The cup of salvation of Jesus Christ.

P: Num. 9:9-11 and 7:2. Matt. 27:34. C: Deut. 8:3. P: Is. 33:13-14. C: Is. 33:15. P: Is. 33:16-17. C: Is. 53:5-6.

- The pastor puts the bread in order, each takes his cup and says a prayer of thanksgiving for Jesus, the saviour of the world, God's anointed, who shed his blood to bear the sin of many and grant an eternal righteousness. The pastor takes the dish with the bread and says the words of institution. Then the bread is distributed and the pastor says: "The body of our Lord Jesus the Messiah, which was given for thee ..." The wine is given with the words: "The blood of our Lord Jesus the Messiah, which was shed for thee ..." In conclusion he prays the Lord's Prayer.

This communion liturgy was tried out privately in 1884.[33] It does not seem that it was later used at the public services. The simple explanation for this is that Rabinowitz was not granted permission by the authorities to administer the sacraments.

"Sinai and Horeb"

Another literary work of the same year, 1884, should also be mentioned, although it was never printed and it is difficult to decide whether Rabinowitz later held the ideas which are expressed in it. This composition, *Sinai and Horeb, or Priest and King*, is mentioned by him in his letter to Delitzsch of 4/16 September 1884.[34] The work, which runs to around 12 sheets, deals with the problem that Deuteronomy, the prophets, and the Psalms all say that Israel was given the divine revelation on Mount Horeb, whereas it says at the end of Exodus and in Leviticus and Numbers that this happened on Mount Sinai. After Ezra's return from Babylon the name Sinai is used, cf. Neh. 9:13.

And Jewish tradition says: "Moses received the Torah from Sinai." Rabinowitz writes to Delitzsch that he has found the solution, but he does not say what it is. But it will shed light on biblical passages that are difficult to understand, e.g. Deut. 18:15-16; Mal. 4:4; Acts 3:22; Gal. 4:25 as well as on the three Jewish parties, the Pharisees, Sadducees, and the Essenes at the time of the second temple. But Rabinowitz has decided not to publish it without consulting Delitzsch. Perhaps the time has not come for that.

In his letter of 3 October 1884 Delitzsch comments upon the matter, although he has not seen the work, but he asks Rabinowitz to bring it when he comes to Leipzig. But Delitzsch wishes to say in advance once and for all that in the scholarly forum only the grammatical-historical method is valid. The Reformation broke with allegorizing and any haggadic interpretations. He informs Rabinowitz that recent Pentateuch research has shown that the "Yahwistic Deuteronomic view is the prophetic one, the Elohistic is the priestly one."[35]

According to Lhotzky, Rabinowitz took his treatise with him to Delitzsch on his "baptismal journey" in March 1885. Lhotzky avers that Rabinowitz had no knowledge of scientific source criticism. But in Scripture Rabinowitz finds a peculiar opposition between a priestly and a prophetic conception. Jesus is placed in the Horeb line, the Sadducees and the Pharisees in the Sinai line.[36] Delitzsch mentions the book in 1887. To Rabinowitz Horeb is the expression of the original law-giving, Sinai expresses the priestly, unprophetical "and as it were Pharisaical expanded law-giving". Hostility to Jesus proceeded from this priestly line. So it is quite consistent of Rabinowitz to regard the Talmud as the true source of the Jewish people's misfortune, adds Delitzsch (see above).[37]

According to Lhotzky, the battle against biblical criticism raged hotly when Rabinowitz brought his work to Delitzsch. "You outdo all of them! You go much farther than Wellhausen!" Delitzsch is supposed to have told him. (Wellhausen was the leading advocate of the documentary hypothesis of Pentateuchal origins.) And Lhotzky continues: "Rabinowitz later kept the actual treatise to himself."[38]

With the strong confidence in biblical inspiration which he later expressed (see e.g. Chapter 14), it would seem that he was willing to learn and at least kept his explanation of this problem to himself. These ideas were never referred to in the debate around Rabinowitz. But there were enough other points for Gentile Christian theologians to fall foul of.

In a letter to C.A. Schönberger of 25 July/6 August 1888 Rabinowitz gave answers to some questions which G.A. Dalman had asked, particularly on other people's behalf.[39]

Firstly, Dalman wanted to clarify whether Rabinowitz had understood Paul on the subject of circumcision and the Sabbath. Rabinowitz referred to Gal. 6:15 and did not consider that he gloried in being circumcised. But

Dalman should not forget that, as one uncircumcised, he had no advantage either. Rabinowitz did not wish to write about the Sabbath, as Paul did not speak of it. In a note Dalman refers to Col. 2:16; Rom. 14:5; and Gal. 4:10, but points out that Rabinowitz has said often enough that Sabbath observance is not regarded as a work of the law.

Secondly Dalman asks whether Rabinowitz thinks that Christ is first and foremost the Messiah of Israel or the saviour of the world. Rabinowitz quotes John 3:14-16. God has loved the whole world, and there is only one mediator between God and man, the man Jesus Christ, quoting 1 Tim. 2:5.

Finally Dalman asks whether Rabinowitz regards the history of the Christian church as precious and valuable. Dalman rejoices that the Gentiles have come near to God by virtue of Christ's blood, but he has himself some pain that Israel has not achieved what it was seeking (Rom. 11:7). His eye and heart are directed at the history of the Christian church, and that has taught him that through the crucified Christ "in one Spirit, we both have access to the Father" (Eph. 2:18), but in the new Jerusalem there will also be a "Jewish street", and he cites Num. 23:9 supplemented with Rev. 21:27.

In his reply Rabinowitz can scarcely conceal his surprise, bordering on irritation, that he is being asked questions and tested out on points on which he has already given replies in other contexts.

It may be appropriate here to give a brief outline of the debate about Rabinowitz's basic tenets. Some examples will be given from the early phase, supplemented with some tenets from the 1890s. In this last period the arguments against Rabinowitz were mainly taken from the first documents without paying much attention to e.g. the *Twenty-Four Articles*.

Some glimpses of the theological debate around Rabinowitz

Franz Delitzsch was not merely sympathetically disposed to Rabinowitz and the Messianic movement, he rejoiced over it, indeed was actually "electrified" by the good news from Kishinev and defended Rabinowitz when he was attacked.[40]

Delitzsch welcomed Rabinowitz's effort to build an independent Hebrew Christian congregation in which the believers might mould their profession and link their worship to that of the synagogue.[41] He did not regard Rabinowitz's keeping of circumcision and the Sabbath as being at variance with Paul, although in his opinion these matters "are difficult to reconcile with Christianity's character as a world religion."[42] He does not cover up this disagreement, but is the first to stress that these things are going to be kept as national distinctives, and that Rabinowitz stresses justification by faith.

In general Rabinowitz has to an extreme degree the same view of the ceremonial laws as Paul and Luther, the German Paul.[43] Rabinowitz recognizes Sunday as the holy day for mankind. But he wishes to keep the Sabbath as a day of remembrance of the exodus from Egypt, so that the creation of the Israelite nation may be a day of worship for the Jewish congregation. He repudiates the Pharisaical way of keeping the Sabbath according to the ceremonial laws. Correspondingly, circumcision is retained by Rabinowitz as a national sign. Delitzsch expresses the hope that Rabinowitz, with his Pauline attitude, will finally draw the Pauline conclusion and abandon this view. "Israel's national distinctiveness must be maintained and will be maintained without circumcision and with Sunday instead of the Sabbath," says Delitzsch.[44] On 30 December 1885 he writes to Rabinowitz that it is understandable that, with regard to the synagogue, they wish to retain the Sabbath, circumcision, and the Hebrew language. He expresses mixed feelings about this motive, "but we hope that within these forms there will grow up a congregation of a Christian essence."[45]

These critical tones did not, however, prevent Delitzsch from regarding Rabinowitz as "a phenomenon of church history".[46] He is convinced that Israel will be saved as a people. If only 10 persons of this nations join together and form a national Christian congregation, Delitzsch must welcome this as a prelude to the salvation of all Israel. And he will rejoice at it and not allow "petty criticism" to mar this joy. In the introduction to the first documents, Delitzsch concludes by calling upon the church and the synagogue to live up to the prophetic word: "Destroy it not; for a blessing is in it" (Is. 65:8).[47]

Concerning Rabinowitz's *Creed*, Delitzsch was already saying in 1885 that it was much closer to the catholic (i.e. universal Christian) Creed than the Ebionite creed (of the past) or the modern Unitarian one. Rabinowitz attempts to formulate it differently, but Delitzsch affirms that Rabinowitz does profess the triune God, the "man of God" and "the lamb of God" who bears the sin of the world.[48] In the conflict between Faltin and Rabinowitz, Delitzsch made his voice heard, and it was unambiguously in favour of Rabinowitz (see Chapter 10).

Among other influential German theologians, H.L. Strack also supported the formation of independent Hebrew Christian congregations.[49] G.H. Dalman also took Rabinowitz's part when he was attacked by Faltin (see Chapter 10). But there were also critical voices to be heard.

P. Greve was one of the first to react critically to Rabinowitz in 1884.[50] On the one hand, he says, he can rejoice at the emergence of the movement, but on the other he is alarmed that in Rabinowitz's statements he sees an expression of Jewish pride of race. In a superficial way he regards Rabinowitz as departing from the church's Gentile Christian development: Rabinowitz twists Romans 10:6 (presumably 10:4 is meant) and regards the doctrine of the Trinity as not a necessary element in the confession of faith. When Rabinowitz, instead of speaking of Father, Son, and Holy Spirit, speaks about the one God, his Word, and his Holy Spirit, he is overlooking that the expressions Father, Son, and Holy Spirit derive from the Hebrew Christian apostles, not from Gentile Christians as he alleges. Nor does Greve find the communion liturgy satisfactory. He expresses the hope that Rabinowitz's friends will be able to convince him that a man must be humble to be able to enter the Kingdom of God. In Christ Jesus there is neither Jew nor Greek. For that reason there is no room for "carnal pride".

De le Roi too, the author of the great work on evangelical Christendom and the Jews, became one of Rabinowitz's critics. In this work the criticism is still slight, and Rabinowitz is praised for having taken Jesus from the periphery into the centre of Jewish life.[51] But in 1896 he spoke out critically of Rabinowitz's view of the law,[52] reacting against the sentiments put forward by A. Wiegand at a mission conference in 1895.[53] Wiegand backed Rabinowitz. In his address he had stated that according to the New Testament there was full liberty for Hebrew Christians both to keep and not to keep the Jewish law. A voluntary keeping of the Jewish law was, Wiegand thought, to be recommended. Space does not permit us to delve further into this interesting debate.[54] In 1897 de le Roi clearly expresses his disapproval of Rabinowitz's enterprise. He is being threatened by corruption "through the leaven of a false nationalism", writes de le Roi, and he is astray in asserting that Jews who enter the Christian church are not given the required nurture there.[55]

In his book on Lutheran missions (1895), O. Hardeland attempts to be fair.[56] He maintains that it is a fact that a mighty Hebrew Christian movement has gone out from southern Russia. Nevertheless there is no mistaking his criticism of Rabinowitz. The main question must be: what does Rabinowitz say of Christ? Hardeland refers to the *Ten Articles of Faith* and *An Exposition* of 1884. He finds that there is no room for the idea of the Trinity in Rabinowitz's general view.

He cannot, he says, sufficiently deplore the split in the church which an observance of the Sabbath and circumcision will cause. And Hardeland also considers that developments in church history and the history of dogmatics have something to teach Rabinowitz, and cannot be said to apply to Gentiles alone. The importance of the movement does not depend on a Christian congregation with a Jewish character being set up. Hardeland finds that the greatest significance of the movement is that it has brought out that Christ and Christianity are not alien to the Jews and their nation.

In an article in 1896 A. Wiegand strongly repudiates Hardeland's portrayal as well as an article written by a clergyman in Mecklenburg in 1895, which was based on Hardeland.[57] According to Wiegand, the Hebrew Christian movement is a danger neither to the church nor to Hebrew Christians. It is true that Christianity is international, but he argues that it is not anti-national. Rabinowitz does not use formularies taken from Gentile Christian dogmatics, such as 'person', 'divine nature'. But nor did Paul or John. But the matter itself, that the one God is three persons, has been clearly affirmed by Rabinowitz. Wiegand considers that missions to Jews ought to learn from Rabinowitz and tell the Jews: "Keep circumcision, the Sabbath, and the food rules if you like! That is not what Christianity is about, it is solely about Christ, and the soul's salvation, and a new heart."

These examples have shown the main points in the criticism of Rabinowitz. It may be noted that even those who took a critical view of his theology and the formation of independent Hebrew Christian congregations recognize his efforts as a preacher - and commend him for it. This was true of F. Heman in Basel, for instance.[58] His criticism was rebutted by G.A. Krüger in France, who in his book of 1885 had already argued the case for such congregations.[59] Even R. Faltin recognized the significance of Rabinowitz's sermons, even when he was inveighing against his life and teaching (see Chapter 10). The importance of Delitzsch's assessment of Rabinowitz's orthodoxy can hardly be exaggerated. His assessment was conveyed to Denmark through A.S. Poulsen among others, who was chairman of the Danish Israel Mission from 1890. P. Wolff, a Hebrew Christian and a missionary of the Swedish Israel Mission, translated Poulsen's work into Swedish in 1891. At the request of the same mission, another Hebrew Christian, P. Gordon, published a booklet about Rabinowitz in 1896. In the magazines of the Swedish and Norwegian Israel Missions there are frequent reports about the movement. When J.G. Blom, the editor of the Norwegian magazine, visited Kishinev in 1892, he got a favourable impression of Rabinowitz (see Chapter 11). In the English-speaking world Rabinowitz was backed up by the Mildmay Mission. The British Society also viewed him favourably. With the setting-up of the London Council for Rabinowitz (see Chapter 13) Rabinowitz obtained lasting moral and economic support, without this council interfering in his theological views. The Hebrew Christian Testimony to Israel, a movement founded by D. Baron and C.A. Schönberger in 1893, had the support of Rabinowitz - and Isak Lichtenstein -[60] as one of its main objects. The London Society showed an interest at the start, but later dissociated itself from Rabinowitz's distinctive views, as their obituary of him in 1899 makes clear (see Chapter 18).

At the end of the 1880s the London Society still tries to balance between Rabinowitz and Faltin. In a letter from the autumn of 1888 the Committee advises Faltin "in a Christian and brotherly spirit to abstain from interference with Mr. Rabinowitz".[61] In a later letter, of February 1889, the Committee assures Faltin "that there was not the least intention of reflecting upon himself personally, when the Committee offered their advice respecting Mr. Rabinowitz".[62] At no time was the London Society Rabinowitz's "major financial backer", as asserted by Zipperstein[63] (see further Chapter 13). In Scotland Rabinowitz found support in circles attached to the Free Church of Scotland. But the Church of Scotland also showed an interest and invited him to speak at their General Assembly in 1896 (see Chapter 14). In America he was given support by A.C. Gaebelein among others.

As in the Western world, opinions were divided also in Russia. The Russian press branded Rabinowitz as a Christian missionary "in order to discredit him before traditionalists and maskilim alike", as Klier puts it.[64] Among the number of newspaper articles which Klier has collected with reactions to Rabinowitz's movement from Christian quarters[65] there are examples of sympathy for Rabinowitz because of the movement's rejection of the Talmud.[66] The Orthodox philosopher Vladimir Soloviev expressed as his view that just as it took decades to develop the doctrines of early Christianity, the Church now ought to show toleration so that the new movement might find its own way along the path to truth.[67] But there are also examples of a vehement opposition to Rabinowitz's movement from spokesmen of the Orthodox Church. For one thing they could not accept a movement whose leader was closer to Protestantism than to the Orthodox Church,[68] and besides they could not recognize a movement which could not embrace the basic dogmas of the Orthodox Church.[69] After his baptism in 1885 it appears that Rabinowitz tried to obtain the government's permission to have foreigners of the Anglican faith to minister to the movement, a requst which was turned down. The head of the Holy synod maintained in his statement to the government that if Rabinowitz's propaganda could be restricted to the Jewish population alone, one might wish it as broad a spread as possible. But as it could be feared that the movement might be captured by less desirable elements, such as the Baptists, who would then operate under its banner, Rabinowitz's application could not be supported.[70]

After this outline of Rabinowitz's tenets - and reactions to them - a few comments must be made about Rabinowitz's use of the term "brother" for Jesus. It will be shown that this did not stand in isolation, as some accounts suggest. This will shed further light on Rabinowitz's understanding of the person Jesus.

Chapter 9

'OUR BROTHER JESUS' AND THE KEY TO
THE HOLY LAND

After outlining in the previous chapter the main points of Rabinowitz's basic theological views, this is an appropriate point to consider Rabinowitz's use of the designation "brother" about Jesus, a designation which caught the attention of western observers right from the start (see Chapter 1).

In May 1884 Delitzsch wrote in his preface to the first documents about Rabinowitz: "He returned from Palestine with the watchword: `The key to the Holy Land lies in the hands of our brother Jesus'". And Delitzsch goes on to assert that in "the two words *Yeshua Achinu*" (Yeshua/Jesus our brother) lies the centre of gravity in Rabinowitz's creed and "doubtless also" the attractive power of the movement.[1]

For reasons which will become apparent, it will be convenient to deal first with the brother appellation without paying attention to the whole "key" sentence.

Our brother Yeshua/Jesus

Rabinowitz always uses the Hebrew name *Yeshua* for Jesus when writing Hebrew, and never Yeshu, which in large parts of the Jewish tradition is taken as a pejorative name which is only used of Jesus of Nazareth. Also, many Jews found a curse in the Yeshu form: "May his name and memory be blotted out".[2] The form *Yeshua*, which must indeed be regarded as the historically correct name of Jesus,[3] was stressed in various ways by Rabinowitz, both in the first documents and in some sermons. Sometimes the name is emphasized by being written in larger letters, sometimes by the letters being spaced out. On the 'altarpiece' in his prayer house (see Chapter 11 and photo at the beginning of the book) the name *Yeshua* is picked out in capitals. In his sermons he sometimes makes a play on words between the name *Yeshua* and the word for saviour (Moshia) or other nouns and verbs of the same root. He was no doubt inspired by Matt. 1:21 with its underlying wordplay on *Yeshua Yoshia*, i.e. Jesus shall save. In his "Kishinev song" in Yiddish he sets it out plainly in one line of verse: "Jesus is the same as *Yeshua*".[4]

By using the name *Yeshua*, Rabinowitz was not only signalling that for his own part he had acquired a new relationship to him whom the Christians call "Jesus" and Jews normally call "Yeshu", but also that this *Yeshua* is a Jew who will save his people. For above all *Yeshua* is the brother of Israel and the Jews.

There is no shadow of doubt that Rabinowitz launched the phrase "our brother Jesus". It resounded afar, often being quoted in the western world. But the question must be asked whether this gives an adequate picture of Rabinowitz's lasting view of the person of Jesus. He did indeed, as we shall see, defend the usage in June 1885. Nevertheless it would be wrong to consider the term "brother" in isolation without allowing for other terms he used to describe Jesus. If it was used as a motto at the beginning, then its life was very brief. If this is correct, it creates a quite different picture from that found in earlier accounts.

The phrase is mainly found to occur in earlier material from Rabinowitz's hand, including the *Thirteen Theses* (§12 & 13) of 1883, in a Hebrew poem (stanza 17) of 1884,[5] in the appeal *Kol Kore* of autumn 1884,[6] and in *Joseph's Misfortune* (see Chapter 21) of 1884-1885, reproduced by K.J. Gottlieb. Here Rabinowitz says that he returned from the Holy Land with the glad message: "Jesus is our brother". The phrase is only occasionally found in correspondence material, e.g. in a letter to Faber of 16/28 October 1885.[7] The report of the account he gave of his conversion (Leipzig 1887) runs: "Yeshua Achinu (Jesus our brother) was from now on his watchword, with which he returned to Russia" (see Chapter 2). The phrase also occurs in some of the first sermons to be published (cf. below).

It may also be remarked that the phrase is not found in the various articles of faith which Rabinowitz drew up in 1884-1885. But it is used in *An Exposition to The Ten Articles of Faith* (1884). In sermons and writings produced after 1886 it occurs exceedingly rarely, if at all. It is true that it is found in the anthology of sermons of 1897, but only in the earliest sermons reprinted there in more or less revised form. It must also be mentioned that Rabinowitz's last written work was translated into English in 1898 with the title "Jesus of Nazareth, the King of the Jews", not the brother of the Jews. The appellation brother is not applied to Jesus anywhere in the work. In Rabinowitz's correspondence the term is used exceedingly seldom. This is not to say that it cannot possibly have occurred on Rabinowitz's lips. The memory of the term was vivid in the 1890s. In a report from his visit to America in 1893, it is said: "... many have been led to see in Jesus their Brother and King".[8] That he himself should have used an expression like this cannot, of course, be rejected.

All this evidence nevertheless leads to the conclusion that the term brother applied to Jesus is not well attested, at least in Rabinowitz's later writings. In these the Jews are sometimes termed "the brothers of Jesus" or "the brothers of Jesus according to the flesh".[9] Thus the primary sources contradict the impression created by practically all later accounts that the term brother applied to Jesus was a motto which Rabinowitz kept throughout his active life. This is not the case. But it is true that it was an important concept at first, although it does require defining.

Delitzsch rejoiced at the expression and regarded "Jesus our brother" as words which the Lord had given to Rabinowitz.[10] N.I. Mossa, after reading the first documents, responded with a poem to "the brethren in Bessarabia" entitled *Yeshua Achinu* - but otherwise in German.[11] Others had misgivings, including P. Greve, who sent a report to *Saat auf Hoffnung* from the annual meeting of the German Central Agency on 3 June 1884: In a note he puts forward the view that the expression has "a tang about it which the Blessed one will hardly acknowledge".[12]

An American "kinsman and fellow-believer" also criticized Rabinowitz for this expression. In a letter to this unnamed person of June 1885 Rabinowitz explained and defended his use of the designation brother about Jesus.[13] This shows that he had been accused of demeaning the greatness of the Lord by calling Jesus "our brother" and the expression was said to run counter to Paul's words in 2 Cor. 5:16. "Though we have known Christ after the flesh, yet now we know him so no more."

Firstly, Rabinowitz points out that, owing to the distance between Russian and America, this person has not a full insight into Rabinowitz's conception of the being of the Messiah and the purpose of his coming. Nor has he understood Paul's words in 2 Cor. 5:16. Furthermore, he has not sufficient insight into the time, the place, and the people among whom the Messianic movement is taking place. Then Rabinowitz refers to Delitzsch, who has stated that the expression is the driving force of the movement. But besides he can assure his correspondent that he can say yea and amen to the Lord's testimony concerning himself: "I and the Father are one" (John 10:30), and: "For as the Father hath life in himself, even so gave he to the Son also to have life in himself" (John 5:26).

Rabinowitz goes on to say: "The Messiah is he who was and is and in eternity will everlastingly remain the same in his humiliation and in his greatness, in his flesh and in his spirit". He and his Father are constantly at work in our midst, partly in the Son of Man's guise as the one who has been given over for our transgressions, partly in the Son of God's guise as the one who has risen for our justification. Referring to Hebrews - Rabinowitz considered it was written by "the holy Paul" - he finds support for using the term brother (Heb. 2:11-12,17). It is emphasized at the same time that Jesus was without sin (Heb. 4:15), and Rom. 8:16-17 is quoted.

As regards the interpretation of 2 Cor. 5:16, Rabinowitz disagrees with the critic in question. He maintains that if we cannot call Jesus our "brother and Son of Man", then we cannot call a believing Christian a "man" either, for the verse begins of course: "Wherefore we henceforth know no man after the flesh". And then he makes short shrift of the matter: Paul really only means that everything has become new and that God has raised up among us the word of reconciliation.

And he goes on: "Do you not know, my dear brother, that your brethren after the flesh, the blind Talmud Jews, continue to besmirch the person of the Lord ...?" So that they shall not continue, like their fathers, to gnash their teeth and stop up their ears so as not to hear the name of Jesus (Acts 4:18; 7:57), it is necessary to use the same method as the early believers, i.e. to remind them of some "home" truths. This is exactly what Peter and Stephen did (Acts 3:22-23; 7:37) by quoting Deut. 18:15 with the phrase "one of your brethren".

It is thus for the Jews' "salvation's sake" that a "homely" word like brother can be used of Jesus. But the designation brother also has a point which may be turned against anti-Semitism, which tries to wipe out all that is reminiscent of Israel, considering that it is permissible to shed the blood of Shem. Rabinowitz writes about these anti-Semites at the conclusion of his letter:

> They have completely forgotten that their divine Saviour after the flesh was Israel's brother and that the ransom for their souls consisted in the blood which ran in Shem's veins. And this blood cries from the cross, praying down the forgiveness of sins for us Jews. It is therefore necessary in these dark times to remind them that this Jesus is our brother according to the flesh. They shall see the blood and pass over the houses of the children of Israel, the Semites, and not enter into them to destroy Israel's inheritance.

After this defence of the use of the phrase "our brother Jesus" one might expect Rabinowitz to continue to use it. But, as we have already intimated, this only happened to a small extent. The matter as such finds expression, and he goes on calling his listeners "brethren", but the phrase "our brother Jesus" was on its way out of Rabinowitz's language at the moment that it was really entering foreign accounts of him. Although he defended it theologically in 1885, it belongs mainly to the very early period.

On his return from Palestine, Rabinowitz used the brother-designation for Jesus and thus signalled that Jesus belonged to the history of Israel and was the answer to "the Jewish question". While the *Thirteen Theses* and their message were rapidly replaced by various articles of faith, the brother designation was supplemented by other terms for Jesus. As we have already shown, the *Thirteen Theses* cannot be taken as an adequate expression of Rabinowitz's view of his faith when he made his public stand as a preacher to the Israelites of the New Covenant (see Chapter 4). Correspondingly, no adequate expression of Rabinowitz's view of Jesus is given if we solely concentrate upon the appellation "our brother Jesus". It was a slogan, which he launched, became well known for, and also defended when he was attacked. But that does not alter the fact that even in his first sermons he used it relatively rarely and supplemented it with other descriptions of Jesus. The publicity given to this phrase abroad was quite out of proportion to its actual use in Rabinowitz's sermons!

A check on the matter in the four first sermons which were published in Hebrew in 1885 (in *Ha-Davar*, see Survey III.2) shows that the designation "brother" was only applied to Jesus four times. And in none of these cases does it stand alone, but is set alongside other descriptions:

- "...the Lord, our brother Jesus the Messiah's name..." 8 June (r)
- "...the name of our brother, the Lord Jesus the Messiah..." 29 June (r)
- "...the lamb of God, Jesus the Messiah, our brother according to the flesh..." 5 Oct. (r)
- "...your brother according to the flesh, Jesus the Messiah..." 5 Oct. (r)

Without going into details here, it may be mentioned that in these sermons there are, for instance, expressions like "Messiah", "Jesus, son of Joseph, from Nazareth", "the Messiah, the Son of God", "the Son of God, Jesus of Nazareth", "Our Lord Jesus the Messiah", "Prophet", "Son of David", "Son of Jesse", "King", "the Lord", "Our Lord Jesus the Messiah, the blessed one", "Saviour", "our Messiah Jesus of Nazareth, mighty God and Prince of Peace", "The man, God's Son, Jesus the Messiah", "the Teacher", "the true Messiah, Son of Man and Son of God", "Jesus the Nazarene who was crucified for our sins; for this Jesus is not a God who cannot save, for he is mighty to save", etc.

A rapid perusal of Rabinowitz's written production seems to show that there is no New Testament description of Jesus which he could not use. In a sermon about the good shepherd (5 July (r) 1886) he says: "Yes, Christ is everything. He is Israel, Israel's first - and only-begotten! He is the Tora! He is God!"[14] With this in mind, it must be described as unjust of his critics to launch an attack on a term like "our brother Jesus", not weighing it against other important names for Jesus, the more so as Rabinowitz had played down the use of the brother designation when his faith was more firmly based compared to the period just after his return from Palestine. The above-mentioned designations used by Rabinowitz about Jesus are also evidence that Steven J. Zipperstein simplifies the matter considerably when he argues that "... it was Jesus that Rabinovich embraced in 1883 and not specifically Christianity in any of its forms".[15] Zipperstein contends that, for example, the London Society minimized Rabinowitz's heterodoxy, but the quotations from Rabinowitz's own writings unanimously indicate that he was orthodox in his Christology.

Neither in the *Creed* (the *Seven Articles of Faith*) nor in the *Twenty-Four Articles of Faith* does the expression "our brother Jesus" occur. It is first and foremost these articles who show Rabinowitz's lasting basis of faith and enduring view of Jesus, not the phrase "our brother Jesus". This had its day and function as a slogan, and although throughout his activity Rabinowitz stressed the substance to which the phrase pointed, the actual use of it shows that he realized that a congregation could not be built up solely on such a phrase. He told Venetianer in 1887: "... and on the Mount of Olives I found Jesus, our Adon ha-Gadol (our great Lord)."[16]

So we have not only given a quite different picture of the facts of this matter compared with earlier accounts, but we have also prepared the ground for looking at the whole "key" sentence with fresh eyes.

The key to the Holy Land

Rabinowitz did not make extravagant use of the phrase "our brother Jesus", and even less so of the "key" sentence: "The key to the Holy Land lies in the hands of our brother Jesus". There is some lack of clarity in the centenary publication of the Norwegian Israel Mission when it says that Rabinowitz came back to Russia "where from Kishinev he raised up a singular Hebrew Christian movement under the motto: 'The key to the Holy Land lies in the hand of our brother, Jesus of Nazareth!'"[17]

When Delitzsch published this dictum in 1884, he did not reveal when and in what context Rabinowitz had promulgated it.[18] That is vexing! It is also vexing that we have not seen the precise wording in Hebrew. Consequently, the sentence is rendered slightly differently in contemporary translations. Some have the key *to*, others the key *of* the Holy Land; some have *is*, others *lies*; some have *hand*, others *hands*. These small differences have not been levelled: they will appear in the quotations below. In another context Delitzsch says that Rabinowitz "has said" these words.[19] Although the sentence is quoted in practically any contribution about Rabinowitz, very few people have taken the trouble to explicate it. The dictum as such seems to have had an exceedingly short life on the lips of Rabinowitz. But abroad people never tired of quoting it.

The "key" sentence must be regarded as authentic words first used by Rabinowitz in connection with his return from Palestine. In Constantinople, in the letter of 6/18 May 1882 which was later published in Hamelitz, he had written about the Turkish government that it "holds in its hand the keys to the empty portals of Palestine" (see Chapter 2). Although Rabinowitz's Zionistic expectations were disappointed, and in the *Thirteen Theses* he cannot recommend an emigration to Palestine, it does look as if he had not abandoned the idea of a re-establishment of a Jewish nation in the Holy Land. The land which the Turkish government now had the key to opening, will one day be opened by Jesus in connection with the Jewish nation's reception of Jesus as the Messiah.

This understanding of the "key" sentence finds clear expression in a notice in the magazine of the Mildmay Mission in 1903. This says: "The key to Palestine lies in the hands of Jesus Christ. So said the late Joseph

Rabinowitz, and we know that restoration to the land, and all the blessings therewith associated are bound up with the return of our Blessed Lord".[20] In an address on 5 November 1884 Delitzsch seems to have confirmed this interpretation. He says: "'The key to the Holy Land' Rabinowitz has said, 'lies in the hand of our brother Jesus'. With the same right we say that the key to the Jewish question lies in his hand."[21] Here, a literal understanding of the Holy Land is attributed to Rabinowitz, whereas Delitzsch turns it into a more general question, namely the Jewish question. It can hardly be completely ruled out that the latter may sometimes have been included in Rabinowitz's thinking.

In only one place have I found the sentence on Rabinowitz's lips, and that is in an interview which Lerner had with him in 1893. In this Rabinowitz is quoted as saying: "I return to Russia with the following word: The key to the Holy Land lies in the hand of our Lord Jesus Christ."[22] In passing it may be noted that "brother" has been replaced by a more churchy-sounding, but New Testament expression "Our Lord Jesus Christ". This may have been Lerner's re-write, but in view of the comments made above on the use of the designation "brother" about Jesus, it is very probable that in 1893 Rabinowitz expressed himself in exactly the way he is quoted. In the interview Rabinowitz maintains that the "key" sentence was a "word of awakening" he used, "portraying a general Jewish conversion to Christ as the only means by which the Jewish question could be solved." He goes on to admit that only gradually did he begin to realize that "the Jews' conversion requires a preparation step by step and that the Jewish question will not be solved unless the Jews are born again and in their very inner being become familiar with the true content of Christian doctrine." If they merely changed their names outwardly and obtained rights which they had not had before, that would be of no benefit, on the contrary it would "lead to greater hostility and animosity in the future."

Here Rabinowitz is standing by his development from the first awareness that found an outlet in the *Thirteen Theses* up to a later conviction. But this interview is not particularly illuminating for the understanding of the "key" sentence, as he speaks generally about the solution of the Jewish question and not about a return of the Jews to the Holy Land. But there is clear evidence that he had given this matter thought. It may be useful here to outline what he says about it in 1896.

In 1896 - on the return journey from his last trip to England and Scotland (see Chapter 14) - he visited the Berlin exhibition. In his letter about this to S. Wilkinson he says that he "could not help" visiting the Palestine stand, being on his way through anyway, "because I longed to see in reality the products of the land so dear to me, the land which the eyes of Jehovah are always upon." While mentioning his belief that Israel will be saved as a nation, he allows his thoughts to return to his first visit to England (1886-

1887), when "I saw a cold and indifferent expression on some faces when I said that I firmly believe and wait for the coming of our Lord in glory, in which is included the restoration of a national Israel in the holy land Palestine." After this he speaks of "lovers of Zion" and their activity - without criticism, for he rejoices at the greater understanding for this cause which he has now found during his visit.[23]

Rabinowitz says that from his first visit to England he has believed that a return of the Jews to Israel's land will occur in connection with the coming of Jesus. He may well have had this belief just after his return from the trip to Palestine - perhaps adjusted along the way. It can be confirmed that the belief in the restoration of Israel was already expressed in the *Ten Articles of Faith*, which were published in May 1884 (see Chapter 8). In these the hope is expressed that Israel as a nation, the branch broken off, will again be grafted into the stem, into Jesus, so that the whole of Israel will participate in eternal salvation, and Jerusalem "our holy city" will be built up again and the throne of David will be set up again for ever.

In conclusion we may say that the "key" sentence as a sentence was on its way out of Rabinowitz's usage before the Messianic movement as such made its debut. But throughout his life he adhered to the content of it, adjusted to the deeper knowledge which he had already attained in spring 1884. Perhaps P. Gordon expresses it most aptly when, in his devout style he plays upon the "key" sentence and says that Rabinowitz "in the crucified and transfigured king of the Jews" found peace "and the key to the heavenly Jerusalem, to the Holy of Holies, and the throne of grace." But, continues Gordon, the city of David belongs to the Son of David, Jesus Christ, and he who has him as saviour and king possesses citizenship there with him. With Jesus the people of Israel will be mighty. Once they receive Jesus Immanuel, they will again occupy Immanuel's land.[24]

As an adjunct to this it is natural to summarize the content of an article on anti-Semitism and Zionism. It was published in English in February 1899, shortly before Rabinowitz's death.

An article on anti-Semitism and Zionism

In a lecture in Stockholm, T. Lindhagen maintained that the Zionist movement had Rabinowitz as one of its forerunners.[25] But this assertion is only valid in the period prior to Rabinowitz's journey to Palestine in 1882. On the contrary, it must be asserted that after his journey to Palestine Rabinowitz - like so many others of the time - adopted a critical stance to Zionism and longed for Zion. In 1898 de le Roi cites him as saying of the Zionists that they do not return to the land as prodigal sons. They are fleeing from a bear and coming upon a serpent. Instead of fleeing to Jehovah, they are turning to the Sultan.[26] Similar ideas are expressed in a letter to W.E. Blackstone in 1887. Here Theodor Herzl and Max Nordau are criticized for

having forgotten God "during all the three days of their Congress in Basel".
The letter continues:

> The majority of the Russian Jews confess with assurance that they
> have a Father who is mighty to save His people yet "beloved for the
> fathers' sakes" and bring them back with joy to the Holy Land in due
> time. These orthodox Jews know assuredly that the help of Israel
> cannot and will not come from the hills of Switzerland at Basle, but
> from Jehovah, creator of heaven and earth.[27]

It certainly startles us to find, in an article of 1899, that Rabinowitz starts by
setting up anti-Semitism and Zionism as two comparable entities, indeed he
says that they are "plagues" as written about in Deut. 28:61. "Anti-Semitism
is an external pain which is destroying the body, and Zionism is an internal
malady crushing down the spiritual health."[28] This is not the place to
demonstrate that other Jews were of the same opinion at that time. But
Rabinowitz goes on to claim that both things may be factors in keeping some
Jews from receiving the word of God.

In this article, after mentioning anti-Semitism, and particularly the
Dreyfus affair, Rabinowitz takes a closer look at Zionism. There is, he says,
an internal debate within Zionism, adding that Zionism "is only whirling the
Jewish brains, making them stupid". Those who know of Zionism only from
the newspapers, rejoice about it; but those who really know the Jews must
regard Zionism differently. "Zionism is a combination of modern Jewish
ungodly literature with old Talmudical hypotheses, mingled with some
portions of mammon interest." The orthodox Jews, writes Rabinowitz, are
against Herzl's plans. The movement is carried on up by the young people
who do not care for all that "is holy and dear to the heart of their nation".
The writers in the newspapers who tell of the immense growth of Zionism
do not care about the truth. Just now, Rabinowitz goes on, one may sense
a mood of disappointment, partly because the Sultan will not permit Jews
to enter Palestine, partly because of the journey of the German Kaiser
Wilhelm II to Palestine (1898). Both these are "ignoring the thoughts of
Jehovah about Jerusalem, expressed by His true prophets," says Rabinowitz.

While representatives of Zionism sit in Basel discussing how the
Jewish nation can settle and find peace in Jerusalem, Rabinowitz feels it his
duty to unfurl the banner of Jesus Christ and invite any Jew to "rest under
the shadow of their true Messiah, the crucified and risen One". He sends this
invitation out to all those who feel offended by anti-Semitism and Zionism.
He does not think that his voice will be in vain, as there are still Jewish hearts
who receive "the love of the Father in the beloved Son Jesus Christ".

And then Rabinowitz continues by affirming that these "few precious
souls of Israel are witnesses that Jehovah is never forsaking His ancient
people, and indicate that, although this nation [Israel as such] is now
withered like grass, yet He will arise and have mercy upon Zion, for the set

time to come. All these events of this wonderful time encourage me much more to preach Christ Jesus the Messiah, and wait watchfully for the moment when all the nations, including the Jewish, shall fear the name of Jehovah, and all kings of the earth of the earth will glorify His Anointed One upon the Holy Hill Zion."

With this in mind, it may seem surprising that in the mid 1890s Rabinowitz was toying with the idea of transferring his activity to - Jerusalem! (see Chapter 17)

Now that we have traced some of the main points in Rabinowitz's faith, we shall return to the historical course of events.

Chapter 10

THE CONFLICT BETWEEN FALTIN AND RABINOWITZ

In March 1885 Rabinowitz had been baptized in Berlin. This took Faltin by surprise. He had expected to baptize Rabinowitz himself. Faltin openly admitted that tension had arisen. Nevertheless, in May 1885, he wrote that he was continuing to have friendly relations with Rabinowitz (see Chapter 7). So it did not lead to an immediate breach. That came some years later. It became public knowledge in the spring of 1888, after Faltin had publicly attacked Rabinowitz. The conflict broke out after A. Venetianer, a Reformed clergyman, had baptized some of Rabinowitz's followers. Through this conflict the foreign missions were compelled to make up their minds about Faltin's attacks. In general it may be said that Rabinowitz lost no sympathy abroad. Faltin's attacks were too poorly based for that. And Faltin's attacks did not, on the whole, bring any unfavourable repercussions upon himself. Abroad, Rabinowitz emerged as the "winner" in principle. But all the same he may be described as the "loser" in the conflict. For this conflict had an important harmful effect on the continued development of the Messianic movement. After the conflict it was quite clear that Rabinowitz would not be granted permission to administer baptism.

Faltin's comments on Rabinowitz 1885-1886

If Faltin is to be taken at his word in his public comments on Rabinowitz after his baptism, some disappointment may be detected, but there is no fundamental criticism of Rabinowitz's religious views.

In his annual report for 1 November 1884 - 1 November 1885 Faltin does not conceal that Rabinowitz's baptism in Berlin has cut across his plans.[1] He considers that the formation of an independent Hebrew Christian congregation has been rendered impossible for the time being by this special baptism. But he describes it as an error to think that it was in a spirit of opposition to Rabinowitz that he had taken some people who had previously attended Rabinowitz's services for instruction and had baptized them. He also maintains that for decades it has been his heartfelt desire to see the formation of a Hebrew Christian congregation on an apostolic-evangelical basis. Nor does Faltin in this annual report conceal his recognition of Rabinowitz's efforts. But he does not accept Professor Strack's interpretation of the baptism (see Chapter 7).

In the next annual report (1 Nov. 1885 - 1 Nov. 1886) Faltin mentions that the Christian movement among the Jews is proceeding quietly.[2] Referring to the "differences" mentioned in the 1884-1885 report, he writes that unfortunately no actual congregation has been formed. But it is noteworthy that - with thanks to God - he mentions results of this movement: the Israelite prayer-house in which Rabinowitz holds services, and the agricultural colony in Oneshti.

The colony had been set up in 1886. Its first leader was H. Lhotzky. Here both baptized Jews and Jews desiring baptism worked. But the Russian authorities soon put a stop to unbaptized Jews living there. Oneshti was close to the frontier and was therefore a prohibited area for Jews. In his annual report for 1886-1887 Faltin tells about it.[3] On reflection he has to admit that he is glad that now only baptized Jews are working there, pointing out that there had been problems with baptized and non-baptized working so closely together.

The agricultural colony was closed down in 1889 and Lhotzky left Kishinev. When Lhotzky arrived in Kishinev, he had advocated the setting-up of such a colony for Jews.[4] Before his 'conversion' Rabinowitz had toyed with similar ideas. The need for something like this increased along with the turmoil caused by the movement around Rabinowitz. In March 1885 he told John Wilkinson that he considered the setting-up of an agricultural colony which, at approx. 4000 roubles a year, would be able to support about one hundred families.[5] Faltin's words seem to be evidence that Rabinowitz actively participated in the setting-up of the colony. But there is nothing to indicate that Rabinowitz was otherwise involved in its work. The responsibility lay with Faltin and Lhotzky.

In his 1885-1886 annual report Faltin also mentions - in an appreciative way - Rabinowitz's rousing addresses and his considerable gifts as a speaker, as these are manifested in "the only prayer-house in the whole of Russia in which Christ, as the Son of God, the Saviour of sinners, is proclaimed each Saturday in a language intelligible to the Jews."[6] At the same time some matters come in for criticism: hitherto Rabinowitz has not proved to be a personality around whom a stable and definite group gathers, which according to Faltin is necessary for the formation of a permanent congregation. He also mentions that Rabinowitz's emphasis on some "Judaistic elements" (i.e. the keeping of the Sabbath and circumcision) which he intends to retain in his coming congregation, has not made the impression upon his people which he had hoped for. Finally Faltin mentions that the Russian authorities have not yet acceded to Rabinowitz's request for permission to form an actual congregation.

Faltin adds a comment about this lack of permission: More important than this permission, he feels, is the establishment of similar prayer-houses in other places than Kishinev, in which Hebrew Christians "under the supervision of a Christian clergyman might in Christian liberty proclaim God's word to their countrymen".

In one of his regular reports in 1886, Faltin claims that Rabinowitz has been negotiating with the authorities in Moscow and St Petersburg.[7] The outlook seems favourable to Rabinowitz, says Faltin. He expects Rabinowitz to be granted permission to proclaim the Word in various places, to found congregations, and to function as a clergyman.

Thus in 1886 Faltin's critical assaults upon Rabinowitz were still relatively mild. Earlier Delitzsch had warned against the danger of "Judaistic elements". Perhaps the criticism directed against Rabinowitz's person is more revealing of Faltin than of Rabinowitz. At the same time it may be mentioned that in 1866 Faltin mentions the Harmony of the Gospels which Rabinowitz had compiled and which was then printing.[8] Faltin expresses the hope that it may be widely used among the Jews and in this connection asks his readers to convey a "love gift" to Rabinowitz.

None the less these public professions by Faltin have to be balanced against other information which suggests that in other contexts he expressed himself more critically of Rabinowitz.

Firstly, there are some interesting data in a letter from Faber to Delitzsch, dated September 1886 but not published until 1911.[9] Faber was in Kishinev. The main purpose of his trip was his marriage to Faltin's daughter, which took place on 6 October 1886. All the same, this is not what makes his heart exult, if his own words are to be believed! At any rate, he writes in his letter:

> Now for the most important matter, which has made my heart exult and rejoice. You know that, as regards Rabinowitz, I came here with a troubled heart, fearing that things were bad with him. But how surprised I have been! Early on Saturday evening I went to his prayer-house. There were nearly 100 listeners - by their appearance some of them richer Jews - who listened with tense attention to his truly hearty sermon. The prayer-house is fitted out in the loveliest manner. I shall certainly describe it all to you by word of mouth. Rabinowitz gave me a hearty welcome. I spend with him every moment of leisure I can obtain. The movement has made undreamt-of and immense progress...

Faltin's reports confirm that his future son-in-law visited Rabinowitz.[10] But we are left to guess why Faber went to Rabinowitz with a troubled heart. Perhaps we shall not be wide of the mark if we guess that he was affected by information he had been given by his future father-in-law, Faltin.

So even though Faltin had not openly criticized Rabinowitz in 1886, there was something smouldering under the surface, which later came out. In this connection we may also refer to a letter from Delitzsch to the Norwegian Israel Mission, dated 19 January 1887. This shows that Delitzsch possessed information that relations between Faltin and Rabinowitz were strained. In the letter Delitzsch makes the following comments upon the authorities' refusal of Rabinowitz's application to work as a clergyman:

> His application to the government for permission to baptize and marry has been rejected; I do not regret this, as the movement's organic link with Pastor Faltin may be re-established in this way, and Rabinowitz, who each Sabbath gathers a large audience around him, may now say with Paul in 1 Cor. 1:17: "Christ sent me not to baptize, but to preach the gospel".[11]

Rabinowitz was never granted the desired permission and had to be content to preach. But Delitzsch's hope that the rejection would bring Rabinowitz and Faltin back together was not fulfilled. On the contrary, in 1887 some events occurred which were to cause all that had been brewing up within Faltin to erupt openly.

Schönberger and Venetianer visit Kishinev in 1887

After the emergence of the Messianic movement, Kishinev began to attract visitors who were involved in mission to Israel elsewhere. Such visits had of course taken place before on account of Faltin's work, which was highly esteemed and fairly well covered in the magazines of the various missions to Israel. But although many visitors were now primarily interested in learning about the work of Rabinowitz, visits were also paid to Faltin. Initially after the appearance of the movement, it was quite natural for the two protagonists to be in close contact. Although Faltin seems to have been well in control of the visits, he can hardly have helped reflecting about who it was the guests had primarily come to see.

Nor does Faltin in his reports neglect to point out if, in his opinion, the visitors have not been given sufficiently clear insight into the situation. For instance, he says of C.A. Schönberger, a missionary in Vienna for the British Society, that his stay at the end of 1885 was much too brief, so that he "received only an inadequate and therefore scarcely correct insight into things". But he consoles himself that it may be deduced from such visits that "the dear Christian friends" have a warm interest in the work being done among Israel.[12]

Already in late summer 1885 Schönberger was reporting from Vienna that the Jews living there were deeply affected by the revival in south Russia.[13] In 1887 Schönberger was once again in Kishinev. On this trip he brought with him A. Venetianer, the Hungarian Hebrew Christian, who was at that time a Reformed pastor in Rohrbach near Odessa.[14] The aftermath of this visit was that Faltin made a public attack on Rabinowitz. Even during the visit Faltin had given the guests some impression that his relations with Rabinowitz were strained.

The evidence about this visit comes mainly from a booklet which Venetianer issued in 1887 and which in 1888 was augmented with a second part, in which he took stock of Faltin's attacks.[15]

In the 1887 booklet impressions are given of the meeting with Rabinowitz, both in the prayer-hall and at home. Venetianer was thrilled by the vitality of the activity there. On their visit in 1887 Schönberger and Venetianer also called upon Faltin. He is described as the "father of the mission among Israel in the Russian Empire". They wished to be briefed by this "experienced" man who was "knowledgeable about Jews and proselytes".[16]

What had been planned as a fifteen-minute chat turned into a two-hour discussion with Faltin. In the talk, he asserted that it was necessary to say openly of Rabinowitz that, "although we are brethren", he is making great mistakes, and he must become small and humble. There is no reason for Rabinowitz to be haughty, as everyone gives him the testimony that he is truthful, says Faltin. Schönberger offsets this by saying that when something does not fit our ideas we may call it pride. "Haughty [*hochmüthig*]! Did not Paul too - the second apostle - pass for being that? When we get to know it more, we may find quite a different term than haughtiness [*Hochmuth*] - perhaps it is a high spirit [*hoher Muth*] to which we will gladly bow," says Schönberger, with a play on words.[17]

A couple of months after this visit, Faltin had to write his annual report for 31 October 1886 - 31 October 1887. It was published in the St. Peterburgisches Evangelisches Sonntagsblatt in February 1888. All that had been brewing up beneath the surface for quite a while now appeared in print. What set it off was some baptisms which Venetianer performed before the annual report was written.

So what was agreed between Venetianer and Rabinowitz during the 1887 visit, and what occurred in the matter of baptism immediately after Schönberger and Venetianer's visit?

The baptism agreement between Rabinowitz and Venetianer   The discussion between Schönberger and Venetianer on the one side and Rabinowitz on the other in summer 1887 particularly concerned the question of baptism. Rabinowitz's application to the authorities for permission to baptize had been turned down. According to Venetianer's account, Rabinowitz unburdened himself to them: "Brethren, I thank God you have come just now in my great distress - it is certain that God has sent you. Give me advice now: what am I to do? Hundreds believe in our Mashiach and are linked with me and pray with me that the Lord our God will look upon us and help us so that they may be baptized."[18]

At the same time Rabinowitz makes it clear where his dilemma about baptism really lies: If the group around him get baptized by Faltin, then in the eyes of the government they count as Lutherans. "And is that the solution to the Jewish question, that the Jews should become Lutherans? If the Orthodox clergy baptize us, then we also cease to be Jews. My brethren, I tell no one where he should be baptized - I preach and let everyone go whither he will."[19] In the same connection, Rabinowitz mentions that there are already many to whom he has spoken who have been baptized by Faltin or other clergymen.

According to Rabinowitz, anyone from the group around him may be baptized where he wishes, "... he may become Lutheran - Russian or Roman - but my people, my congregation, which the government has permitted me to found, cannot and must not become German, Russian, or Roman! They have no reason to become something first; they are Jewish, my people is Israel. Who is to baptize us?"[20]

The discussion was not fruitless. Venetianer, who was pastor of the government-recognized Reformed congregation in Rohrbach near Odessa, made himself available to baptize Rabinowitz's adherents.[21] "The good news" immediately reached Delitzsch through Faber, who was in Kishinev in August 1887. Delitzsch also received letters from Rabinowitz about it. With approval Delitzsch recounts the new situation of the movement, "which God has in his hand".[22]

Shortly after the visit and this being written, the first people were baptized. It did not pass off quietly. Nor was it the start of a lasting solution of the dilemma facing Rabinowitz. The opposition was too strong for that. But as a consequence of these events, Faltin came out in a public polemic against Rabinowitz.

The first people are baptized by Venetianer in Rohrbach

In the summer of 1887, soon after Schönberger and Venetianer's visit to Kishinev, the first six people from the group around Rabinowitz set off for Rohrbach to receive baptismal instruction from Venetianer. Among them were Rabinowitz's three daughters, Sara, Rebecca, and Rachel, and Sara's husband, Joseph Axelrud.[23] Of the other men, one of them - a "Mr R" - was fetched back to Kishinev by his wife! The other, Abraham G, fell ill and was taken to hospital in Odessa.[24] But he did get baptized on 20 September/2 October 1887.[25] Venetianer had to admit that, because of the special circumstances, he was baptized before the expected permission had come in from the ministry.[26] Axelrud did not wish to be baptized together with his wife and two sisters-in-law.[27] The three daughters of Rabinowitz were baptized on 4/16 October.[28]

Prior to these baptisms, Rabinowitz expressed his great hopes in a letter to Schönberger. When the expected permission from St Petersburg came and the people concerned had been baptized, "great crowds will travel to Rohrbach with the same purpose." That would mean that a true Hebrew Christian congregation had been formed, wrote Rabinowitz.[29]

Venetianer relates that Abraham G. was given the baptismal name of Peter. Rabinowitz's three daughters also wanted new names: Fidelia, Spermanza, and Amantia, but on Venetianer's advice abandoned the idea. He states that the daughters were well versed in God's Word. Sara made a particular impression when they were going to sign the ministerial application for baptism. Something which he regarded as a formality, she turned into a solemn matter: she took the pen, laid it down again, rose and prayed a brief prayer that the baptism might be done to God's glory and "Baschem Adonênu Yeshua Hameschiach" (in the name of our Lord Jesus the Messiah).[30]

Venetianer also says that, while it was common knowledge that the three men and Rabinowitz's three daughters had gone to Rohrbach to receive baptismal instruction, something occurred that was not so well known in Kishinev: the wives of the men in question were visited daily by Faltin's henchmen who sowed dissension in their hearts by saying, "Rabinowitz is getting several thousand roubles from London for everyone he gets baptized, but you get none of it."[31]

Venetianer also reveals that at the baptism on 20 September/2 October 1887 one of Faltin's proselytes was present in Rohrbach. The following day he returned to Kishinev. A couple of days later the "anti-Jewish" newspaper in Odessa, the Novorossiiskii Telegraf, was able to discuss and criticize the matter in an article datelined "Rohrbach 20 September"(r), the very day on which the first baptism had taken place.

A newspaper item

This article, datelined 20 September (r) 1887, contains a sharp attack, partly directed against the act of baptism itself and thus against Venetianer, partly against Rabinowitz and his movement.[32] These matters are viewed in the light of Faltin's rights and baptismal practice.

It correctly asserts that Faltin is the only one of all the clergy in south Russia to have the Interior Ministry's permission to baptize Jews according to the rites of the Lutheran Church. It says of his baptismal practice that only 11 of roughly 200 Jews who desired baptism in the year 1886-1887 were baptized by him. Faltin's motive for refusing the many requests for baptism is given. If the Jews in question were unable to show how they would subsist, and if he judged that they desired baptism, not from genuine conviction but only on material grounds, they were rejected.

Then the article deals with the case of the baptisms in Rohrbach. It says of Rabinowitz that he was baptized abroad "in a quite unknown church" and that the government has refused permission to this "obtuse and completely uneducated Jew to found a new sect" in which they will retain both circumcision and the Sabbath. It is also claimed that Rabinowitz does not acknowledge the resurrection of Christ. He has now agreed with Venetianer to send five persons to Rohrbach for baptism, where this Reformed clergyman, who is also of Jewish descent, recently arrived. A Jew of Rumanian descent was also sent to Rohrbach by Rabinowitz (this was Abraham G. mentioned in the last section). But, continues the newspaper article, Venetianer evidently reckons that Rohrbach is so far from the government that as a clergyman and Russian subject he is not obliged to keep Russian laws. The baptism took place before the eyes of several thousand on 20 September (r) 1887, and the article asserts that many were discontented about this, "as they did not wish to have in their midst some people who mock Christianity". Against this background, it refers to the Act of 3 May 1882 (see Chapter 2) and the wish is expressed that the authorities may succeed in having "this vagabondizing Jew" removed, as Venetianer is called. In conclusion, the hope is expressed that this Russian article may be published in a German newspaper, so that the German-speaking colony may be notified that no such sect as the New Israelites exists (on this latter term see Chapter 3).

There is no mistaking the tone of all this. If the writer of the article had the slightest acquaintance with Rabinowitz, it is a gross insinuation to maintain that he does not recognize the resurrection of Christ. But Venetianer was in a weak position, for he had indeed baptized Abraham G. before the authorities' permission for this had been received. In 1888 Venetianer said of the anonymous writer of the article that Faltin had admitted to him that the chairman of the Lutheran Church Council in Kishinev, Mr Allendorf, might be the 'possible' author. "Enough about that", concludes Venetianer. "It is certain that it was written in Kishinev."[33] Later Faltin asserted elsewhere that he did not say that Allendorf wrote the article, while at the same time continuing to maintain that Rabinowitz's creed was heterodox.[34] (At all events, Allendorf does express criticism of Rabinowitz in an article in a German magazine in 1888).[35]

Regardless of whether Faltin approved of the letter being written, shortly after these baptisms in Rohrbach he burst out into a public attack on Rabinowitz. This was in his annual report for 31 October 1886 - 31 October 1887. Although there had been preliminary moves before, this was the first time Faltin had publicly made such a strong attack on Rabinowitz. The events in Rohrbach were undoubtedly the deciding factor.

Faltin's attack on Rabinowitz

In his lengthy account of the matter, Faltin makes it clear from the start that "the so-called Rabinowitz movement" is now completely separate from his own work.[36] The former close connection has been severed. He avers that this is due to the exclusive position and the altogether unclear and wrong direction which its founder has taken in "doctrine and life". Christians and Jews regard Rabinowitz as a Reformer, as he does himself. But the Jews do not need a Reformer or a Reformation, but Christ and new life in God, says

Faltin. He criticizes the accounts in foreign periodicals for not being discriminating enough. As he himself and others have been in error in this whole matter, he feels obliged now to clarify the affair around Rabinowitz.

To start with, he mentions three views which many people share but which are described as mistaken by Faltin.

First, it is wrong to think that Rabinowitz has gathered a large group of adherents holding to his religious opinions and agreeing with him in everything. There are no such people.

Second, it is wrong to think that the documents published in Saat auf Hoffnung (he means: Schriften des Institutum Judaicum) are the expression of the faith of an Israelite-Christian congregation under the guidance of Rabinowitz. No congregation exists, and he is solely responsible for the documents.

Third, it is wrong to think that an Israelite-Christian congregation exists with the name "Israelites of the New Covenant". Together with nine other men he has founded a Jewish community with its own burial ground. Under the law, other Israelites consisting of 10 men may do the same.

Faltin goes on to describe his first hopes about the movement, but also his own development. He had himself looked forward to a national-Israelite Christian congregation within the evangelical church in Russia. Such could be compared with the congregations in Russia that were formed of people of various nationalities. Each congregation was different as regards nationality, but they had a common basis of faith, professing one Lord, one faith, and one baptism. But Faltin was obliged to take exception to the retention of the Sabbath and circumcision, and the formation of a Hebrew Christian congregation outside the universal church, as Rabinowitz wanted. His experience in the last years had taught him that Jews do not wish such a "halfway house" as Rabinowitz was offering. They need not expunge their nationality. They can cultivate the Hebrew language and other customs, which are now viewed in the light of the gospel. Faltin concedes that he used to think that Jews who came to faith in Jesus Christ could retain the Sabbath and circumcision on the principle of nationality.[37] But sooner or later they would cease to hold such things. But, claims Faltin, such Hebrew Christians do not exist! It is therefore quite "artificial" for Rabinowitz to wish to build up such a congregation. In his views on Christianity he is theoretical and speculative. Nor has he the necessary theological training to hold a clerical post. He lacks a grasp of the laws which apply to a congregation, and he also lacks the object of his activity, namely the congregation!

Despite all this, Faltin asserts that Rabinowitz has permission to function as an evangelist. Through his preaching-activity he can be of much blessing to many, says Faltin.

In his comments on the baptism of Rabinowitz's three daughters and "a certain G", Faltin expresses his joy that they have been received into the

community of the triune God. As an excuse for Venetianer's action, Faltin
mentions that he wanted to assist in gathering a congregation. But, avers
Faltin, Venetianer has now reached a clearer insight and declares himself at
one with him in the view that above all there must be "lively, stable, believing
Israelite Christians" before there can be any question of forming a
congregation. Venetianer has also realized that there are not two persons
around who agree completely with Rabinowitz, avers Faltin.

All the same, the course of events in subsequent months was to show
that Venetianer had not changed sides. He was still willing to baptize
Rabinowitz's adherents.

Faltin's report meant that the breach with Rabinowitz had become
public knowledge. For his part Faltin had reached clarity and had no need
to hold out a hand to Rabinowitz. The gauntlet had been thrown down, and
Rabinowitz and others joined in the fray. If Faltin had restricted himself to
describing his own development and way of dealing with the problems, he
would have been in a stronger position. But he attacked Rabinowitz for
being on a slippery slope in his faith and life/conduct. But he had given no
instances of this. Therefore it seemed very wounding and unfair, like a blow
below the belt.

Nor did Rabinowitz rest content with merely quoting Hebrews
12:11: "All chastening seemeth for the present to be not joyous, but grievous:
yet afterward it yieldeth peaceable fruit unto them that have been exercised
thereby, even the fruit of righteousness." He did that in a letter to G. Dalman
on 4/16 March 1888.[38] But he also gave vent to other feelings.

Rabinowitz's reaction to the attack

In a letter to Schönberger on 2 April (r?) 1888, Rabinowitz not only expresses
his disappointment, but gives a sharp riposte. For us to understand this
counter-attack, it is necessary to deal with a couple of events which occurred
after the two baptisms in Rohrbach in October 1887.

In December Venetianer visited Kishinev. On 10 December (r) he
preached in Rabinowitz's prayer-hall. "I administered the Lord's Supper to
Rabinowitz and those of his people whom I had recently baptized. It was a
very solemn service," he wrote.[39] Many Jews were present and, what is most
remarkable, on the Sunday he was preaching in Faltin's church![40] Whether
this is to be taken as a final attempt by Faltin to avoid a conflict and a public
attack, or whether it is rather an expression of a peculiar double game, must
remain uncertain. At any rate, Venetianer expresses the expectation that
after this visit some people from the group around Rabinowitz's will come
to baptismal instruction in Rohrbach.

Ten days after Venetianer's departure from Kishinev, four men from
Rabinowitz's 'congregation' went to Rohrbach to be baptized.[41] Nothing
came of this, however. According to Rabinowitz, Venetianer was told by the

authorities in St Petersburg that he was not allowed to baptize them, "because his church is in a village, and in Russia Jews may be baptized only in the churches of the larger towns."[42]

In itself, the reasons given were not surprising. But if in fact in August/ September 1887 Rabinowitz had been given a hint from the authorities that the imminent baptisms would be regarded as baptisms into his congregation, his reaction is understandable.[43] If so, they had been close to reaching a solution, but the public polemics had spoilt the chances.

To Schönberger Rabinowitz writes first that he has received a letter from Delitzsch "filled with consoling words in which at the same time he assures me of his purpose to battle for me and my cause against these unholy insinuations from F[altin]." Rabinowitz goes on to refer to the strong words from Is. 7:4: "Take heed and be quiet; fear not, neither let thine heart be faint, because of these two tails of smoking firebrands, for the fierce anger of Rezin and Syria, and of the son of Remaliah."[44]

After this Scripture, which is strong in itself, he continues his letter to Schönberger with sharp attacks upon Faltin. His words in the report are like the chirpings and mutterings of familiar spirits and wizards who can do neither good nor evil. Faltin's love of Israel is purely theological, not springing from the depth of a man's heart, writes Rabinowitz.

Although it was a private letter, it was none the less published in the July issue of The Jewish Herald, the organ of the British Society, for which Schönberger was a missionary in Vienna. The same issue included a letter from Venetianer to Schönberger, dated 10 May 1888. Venetianer writes that it will be Schönberger's 'business' to acquaint Rabinowitz's English friends of Faltin's 'aspersions' and goes on to assure them of the importance of Rabinowitz's work.[45]

That Rabinowitz had not been knocked out, is shown by another letter to Schönberger, dated 14 May (r?) 1888, which was also printed in the same issue of The Jewish Herald. In this he writes that it is high time to get on with the building of a new prayer-house on the plot of ground that has long been ready.[46] But it was to be nearly two years before this work could be commenced (see Chapter 11).

In a letter of 8/12 August 1888 to Delitzsch, Rabinowitz also touched upon the same matter.[47] He regarded the calumnies which Allendorf had put forward, not as an attack upon himself but on God, who never abandons his people. He does not see himself as a teacher or reformer, but as a brother to his brethren in south Russia.

The conflict between Rabinowitz and Faltin also forced the leadership of the German Central Agency to make up their minds. The matter was not made any easier because for a number of years they had also supported Faltin's work in Kishinev. Nevertheless the upshot was in Rabinowitz's favour, as we shall shortly show.

Faber's and Delitzsch's appraisal of the conflict

Clear evidence has been preserved to show that Delitzsch did more than merely send a private consolatory letter to Rabinowitz, but also entered publicly into the fray along with Faber. In the Passover issue of Friede über Israel (newsletter from the Institutum Judaicum in Leipzig) of 1888, Faber comments upon the affair.[48] The first part of Faltin's annual report is transcribed, but not the part in which Rabinowitz is attacked. Referring to this, Faber asserts that Faltin has no direct connection with the national-Jewish Christianity movement started by Rabinowitz. Faber tells those who have themselves read Faltin's report, that "what is said there about Rabinowitz is expressed in a misunderstandable way." What "my father-in-law" has expressed is of course correct, that in Kishinev no actual large congregation has been organized around Rabinowitz. But the blame for this must not be put upon Rabinowitz, but on the circumstance that the Russian authorities have not given him permission to baptize. Faber summarizes his opinion of Rabinowitz "which, I scarcely need to remark, is in full accord with that of Professor Delitzsch" in four points:

1. The gospel is preached every Sabbath to a numerous audience, which is perhaps an event unheard-of since the days of the apostles. Rabinowitz's printed sermons have in Jewish circles disseminated a knowledge of the gospel in a shorter time than have the efforts of many years of many missionary societies. In remote regions of the Carpathians Faber has heard of a profound influence from Rabinowitz's writings.

2. The idea that by embracing Christianity Israel does not need to give up its nationality has through Rabinowitz found a response among the Jewish people. It is an experience which Faber has seen borne out on his journeys in Galicia. Though owing to circumstances in Russia Rabinowitz has been unable to establish a large congregation, the foundation has been laid in the community led by him. This consists of 10 men who have been permitted by the government to form a society with its own burial ground. Rabinowitz has shown that it is based on a Christian foundation.

3. Through Rabinowitz the dissemination of the Hebrew New Testament has greatly accelerated. From the farthest areas of eastern Europe Faber has received urgent requests to send New Testaments. Quite clearly, this knowledge of the New Testament has come through Rabinowitz.

4. As a consequence of this it may be indisputably claimed that the movement brought into being through Rabinowitz is of importance for church history. In a mighty way it will hasten the time when all Israel is ready to receive its Messiah.

Besides this vote of confidence, Delitzsch also expressed his opinion in the same periodical in which Faltin had had his annual report printed.[49] Delitzsch writes that it is a long time since he has had such a "painful surprise". In the prefaces to the documents he has had published, he has "as a Lutheran theologian" substantiated that the setting-up of independent Jewish-Christian congregations is a prelude to the fulfilment of Rom. 11:25-26. In reply to Faltin's assertion that a national Christian church must be built within "the evangelical church in Russia", Delitzsch asks: "The Lutheran or the Reformed?" And he continues with an argumentation which shows that he takes Rabinowitz and those like-minded seriously: "As they wish to retain the Sabbath and circumcision, how could a Lutheran or Reformed church government officially legalize this retention!" Faltin is also in error in asserting that Rabinowitz wishes to place himself outside the church, nor is it true that no Hebrew Christians exist who wish to retain the Sabbath and circumcision, as Faltin claims. Faltin's opposition is because Rabinowitz was baptized in Berlin by Professor Mead, whom Delitzsch regards as a dear friend. So Delitzsch cannot see that Faltin is being consistent when he now expresses his joy that Rabinowitz's daughters have been baptized by Venetianer. For both baptisms were done with the intention of helping to found and gather a congregation for the Israelites of the New Covenant. Delitzsch concludes with a reference to the four documents by Rabinowitz which he has had published. "Any unprejudiced reader of those writings must gain the impression that here we have a Jewish profession and effort that has not had its like since the time of the apostles."[50]

In German missionary magazines too it seems that Delitzsch made his voice heard in favour of Rabinowitz. In this way he kept the promises which he had made in his private letter to Rabinowitz (see above). But the matter was also touched upon by G. Dalman, who was now the editor-in-chief of Saat auf Hoffnung, the organ of the German Central Agency.

Dalman's treatment of the conflict

Without wishing to go into detail, Dalman does give ample coverage and assessment of the conflict in the first issue of Saat auf Hoffnung for 1889.[51] In this context we may pass over the observations on principles (see Chapter 13). Though Dalman does not refrain from criticizing Rabinowitz for receiving money from his British friends and also mentions Delitzsch's misgivings about Rabinowitz's retention of circumcision and the Sabbath, his sympathies are plainly on Rabinowitz's side. It is not Rabinowitz, but in fact Faltin, who has changed his stance, the same Faltin who welcomed the documents on and by Rabinowitz which Delitzsch had published. Rabinowitz is only doing what Paul did, who did not require of his fellow Jews that they should stop observing the Sabbath and circumcision. So Dalman will not reproach Rabinowitz and his believing brethren for continuing to be Jews as much as possible in their faith in Jesus. Also, Dalman catches Faltin out in the inconsistency of saying on the one hand that in word and conduct Rabinowitz is on a slippery slope, and on the other admitting that as an evangelist Rabinowitz can bring great blessing to his people.

Dalman winds up his contribution with a call to prayer for Rabinowitz and by stressing that earthly mistakes and human imperfection are to be found in any instrument God makes use of.

So Dalman too declared Rabinowitz to be the "winner".

Aftermath of the conflict

Though Rabinowitz might see himself declared the winner abroad, he became the loser in Russia. The polemics after the first baptisms in Rohrbach in autumn 1887 had their effect. When fresh baptisms were attempted at the beginning of 1888, they were banned. It is unclear whether Faltin made his influence felt in the corridors of power. At any rate, the chance of Rabinowitz's group being given special treatment in the matter of baptism was frustrated. It would be unjust to deny that there were theological issues at stake for Faltin too. But at the same time it is hard to avoid the conclusion that considerations of church politics were being 'theologized' by him in this case. In March 1888 Somerville could note in his diary that Faltin had said that Rabinowitz's hope to organize a church with the right to baptize, marry, and bury, was unfounded and the government would never grant him these rights.[52]

In British and German circles that had supported Rabinowitz before the conflict, Faltin's attacks had no appreciable negative impact. And, for instance, the Norwegian and Swedish Missions to Israel, which had formerly mainly supported Faltin and only given modest financial support to Rabinowitz, continued to support Faltin financially. From these quarters no more money flowed in to Rabinowitz, but this had no real effect, as the amounts previously sent were of modest proportions. Nevertheless, the magazines of these societies continued to give favourable information about the work of Faltin and Rabinowitz. A.S. Poulsen, later president of the Danish Israel Mission, aligned himself completely with Rabinowitz and in 1888 found that the wrong had essentially been on the side of Faltin and his party.

It may seem the more remarkable that the conflict did not harm Faltin much either, considering that people dissociated themselves from his attacks. In this context, the words of G.A. Krüger in the French-language Le Réveil d'Israël are very significant. Even though Krüger more than anyone aligned himself with Rabinowitz, he nevertheless says *a propos* of Faltin: "Alte Liebe rostet nicht" (old love does not rust).[53] Although people failed to understand Faltin's criticism, they did not blacklist him. For some this was bound up with their supporting on the one hand Rabinowitz's efforts, but on the other hand wishing to support Jews who voluntarily desired to renounce their Jewish identity after coming to faith in Jesus Christ. Such Jews might find succour and understanding with Faltin.

The authorities' ban at the beginning of 1888 on Venetianer baptizing Rabinowitz's adherents was a signal that Rabinowitz should not count on a special solution to the baptism dilemma for his particular group. The refusal of that which could have meant the formation of an actual Hebrew Christian congregation remained in force. And at the beginning of 1889 Venetianer left Rohrbach. After this time Rabinowitz did get his two youngest sons baptized by Pastor Kornman in Odessa in October 1888[54] - the same Reformed clergyman who buried Rabinowitz in 1899. In 1891 Rabinowitz's wife was baptized in Budapest (see Chapter 14). That Rabinowitz should have instructed his followers "to go to clergymen in Austria or Germany, most often it seems to Leipzig", as Zipperstein maintains, is without support in the source material.[55]

But the pain which Rabinowitz felt and the anger to which he gave vent after being attacked by Faltin did not render him passive. He continued his activity in Kishinev and kept up his international contacts, not least the English and Scottish ones, in an attempt to gather funds for building new and larger premises for the congregation (see below Chapter 14).

Before we expand on this, we shall briefly examine how relations between Faltin and Rabinowitz developed later.

Rabinowitz and Faltin after the conflict

There was never a reconciliation between Rabinowitz and Faltin. In 1889, for instance, Dr F.W. Bädeker, while on a visit to Kishinev, tried to arrange a meeting between them, but in vain.[56] Later they were both sent an invitation to attend as speakers a major conference in Germany in 1895. But they did not meet there either. Rabinowitz declined the invitation - on the grounds of illness (see Chapter 14).

After the outbreak of the conflict, Faltin rarely mentions Rabinowitz in his annual reports. In the report for 1887-1888 Faltin comments upon the many untruths going around about his attitude to Rabinowitz.[57] He declares that he has done no injustice to Rabinowitz either personally or by misrepresenting him. It seems to him that Rabinowitz's task is to prepare the ground as a missionary preacher and evangelist. He promises that in the future he is prepared to give him assistance for the furtherance of God's kingdom. In the 1892-1893 report, Faltin describes his attitude to Rabinowitz and Isak Lichtenstein and their work.[58] The reason that a radical conversion and the gathering of an Israelite Christian congregation have never come about is that the burning question is not: "What must I do to be saved?" That is not in the centre. But peripheral questions are. Anyone who loves his nationality, the traditions of his fathers, and their customs more than Jesus Christ is unworthy of him, says Faltin, adapting a well-known saying of Jesus. "In some manner these movements linked to the persons of Rabinowitz and [Isak] Lichtenstein are reminiscent of what happened in Galatia and Colossæ..." According to Faltin the words of Jesus: "Repent and believe the gospel!" are not in the centre with these men and their congregations.

In the 1898-1899 report, Faltin mentions Rabinowitz's death.[59] "How differently things have turned out from what we then hoped" - he says after referring to their mutual good relations at the start. And he goes on:

> Rabinowitz did not join the church; in Ebionite manner he wanted to set up a separate Jewish Christianity in which one should indeed believe in Jesus Christ, but not on the condition which Jesus lays down, i.e. "Repent and believe the gospel". What has the result been now? No Jewish Christian congregation has come out of it; he himself has become isolated in his peculiar view; abroad he is regarded as an evangelical Christian, at home as a Jew; until the last listed as a Jew of "the Mosaic religion" in his passport...

After this Faltin regrets that he was on a visitation when Rabinowitz was to be buried in Kishinev. He finds it sad that the "so-called Rabinowitz movement, which initially gave so many hopes, has apparently run into the sand." The worship hall is now unused, says Faltin, and exclaims: "God knows what it will later be used for" (see Chapter 19).

In conclusion, he praises Rabinowitz for speaking many fresh and powerful words to bring Jews out of their confusion. He is also praised for having distributed many New Testaments and Christian literature in general. Finally Faltin wishes that God in his mercy may protect him in eternity and add his blessing to the seed which he has scattered.

With the years Faltin's view of Rabinowitz became more and more negative. But his criticism of Rabinowitz does not seem to do Rabinowitz justice. Nor is he very consistent when he criticizes Rabinowitz for Ebionitism and at the same time praises him for his preaching. A suspicion is aroused that if Rabinowitz had kept to his preaching and had led his adherents into the Lutheran church under Faltin, no major objections would have been voiced by Faltin.

Shortly after his baptism in 1885, Rabinowitz wrote to Delitzsch that he honoured Faltin as an angel of God and that he was hoping for a peaceable collaboration despite their differing viewpoints.[60] Faltin's public attacks entailed that Rabinowitz could no longer regard him as "an angel of God", as is shown by his strong words about Faltin.

Chapter 11

THE MEETING-HALLS AND THE LITURGY

Rabinowitz conducted worship in two places in Kishinev, although we have to differentiate between three periods of services. The first worship services were held under makeshift conditions on the first floor of the house which Efraim Jakob Rabinowitz rented, but with the right to alter it. Already in the spring of 1885 it was remodelled. On 18/30 May 1885 the first service was held in the newly restored hall. Until the end of 1890 Rabinowitz's services were held there. The plan for further alterations to make room for a congregational school was never realized. On 15/27 December 1890 the Somerville Memorial Hall was brought into use. It had been built mainly with Scottish funds and was adjacent to Rabinowitz's new house.

The names of the premises

At the time, the foreign missionary magazines applied varying designations to these premises: meeting-room, assembly hall, worship room, church, temple, prayer-hall, synagogue etc. The terms applied to Rabinowitz's gatherings vary similarly: meetings and services etc. The usage was far from fixed and the very same organisation might use different terms. When some refer to Rabinowitz's sermons as "addresses", this rather plays down the fact that they were delivered in a liturgical context. But in this connection the most important factor is that Rabinowitz was never given permission to function as a clergyman. His premises were a preaching-point where baptism could not be administered. Only occasionally was communion held (see below).

The authorities regarded the premises as a synagogue. The laws applicable to Jewish synagogues also applied to Rabinowitz's prayer-hall. Although on this point too Lhotzky exaggerates in saying that there were about 100 synagogues in Kishinev which functioned with or without the authorities' permission, he does have a point when he continues: "nobody worried about this."[1] But people were concerned about Rabinowitz's synagogue. Other sources reveal that in 1889 Kishinev had one synagogue and 29 "prayer-houses".[2]

This particular term "prayer-house" or "prayer-hall" corresponds to the Hebrew *Beit Tefila*, which is also applied to premises where the Jews gather for prayer. The title page of the first two sermons which were translated into Hebrew by Jakob Wechsler, mentions that they were preached in the "prayer-house" (*Beit Tefila*) Bethlehem.

To make it easier to differentiate between the two preaching-places, the term prayer-hall is used of the restored premises in Rabinowitz's brother's house, and Somerville Hall of the building which was erected in 1890. Rabinowitz regarded this building too as a "synagogue".[3] Sometimes Rabinowitz himself used the name Somerville Hall,[4] as did his daughter Rachel in her letters to English and Scottish friends.[5] Krüger in France disapproved of this name.[6] It was hardly Rabinowitz's idea, but he accepted that the groups in Scotland who had financed the building had in this way obtained a memorial to the Scottish church leader A.N. Somerville, who had visited Kishinev shortly before his death in 1888.[7] In 1896 Rabinowitz mentioned the "Scotch atmosphere" of the building when he spoke to the General Assembly of the Free Church of Scotland. He said that £200 had been given for the walls by Campbell White (Lord Overtoun), someone else had given the candlestick, the Free Church in Edinburgh had given a small printing-press.[8]

It is only to be expected that the name Somerville Memorial Hall is most often found in English and Scottish sources. The name Bethlehem also seems to have been used in Kishinev after 1890.[9] In the Christmas poem of 21 December 1884 the Bethlehem motif is already clearly apparent (see Chapter 5). That in 1885 Rabinowitz was to be baptized in a church also called Bethlehem, was something he could not then know. But in all circumstances there were, for Hebrew-speaking Jews, the makings of some very obvious associations: Rabinowitz's *Beit Tefila* was *Beit Lechem*, house of prayer and house of bread. The brother and Messiah of the Jews had been born in Bethlehem. He it was who was preached in the hall called "Bethlehem".

Somerville Memorial Hall

In letters to friends abroad Rabinowitz more than hints at his wish to obtain new and larger premises than the prayer-hall. In May 1888 he was writing, for example, to Schönberger that it was high time to get a house built on the site that had been acquired long since and was ready for this purpose.[10] From his second journey to England and Scotland in autumn 1889 he brought back a promise from his Scottish friends that they would finance the new building (see Chapter 14).

In May 1890 Rabinowitz laid the foundation stone of the building, which "is consecrated in the name of the Lord Jesus the Messiah, who ever rules over the house of Jacob", as the foundation-stone document says.[11] This also quotes Heb. 3:4; Ps. 118:3; and Zech. 4:6, and mentions that the building has been financed by "the Lord's friends in London, Edinburgh, and Glasgow." On 31 October the same year The Christian announced that the building had been completed.[12] But not until 23 December did official permission arrive for it to be used. This happened after "a long and painful suspense".[13] The same day a New Year card was drawn up with the motto for 1891 (Ps. 80:4 and 34:4a). This card announced that the new building would be inaugurated on 27 December, as indeed it was.[14]

Interestingly, the building was designed by an architect in Odessa who was Faltin's brother-in-law.[15] It looks as if Rabinowitz took the drawings with him on his journey to England and Scotland in the autumn of 1889 (see Chapter 13). The oblong service hall was about 13 metres long, 6½ metres wide and practically 5 metres high.[16] The building also had two projections, the right-hand one - as seen from the street - served as a vestibule, the left-hand one as a vestry and bookstore. On the site was also the home of the Rabinowitz family, and two other buildings "belonging in whole or part to him and his work", says S. Wilkinson in 1897.[17] It is difficult to say definitely how the ownership was defined (but see Chapter 19).

The site was enclosed by railings. According to Dalman, Somerville Hall did not resemble a church building.[18] But in the photo that has been preserved we can see that the large windows were mullioned to suggest a cross. Along the side of the large hall, facing the street, were written some words from Acts 2:36 in gilt Hebrew and Russian letters: "Therefore let all the house of Israel know assuredly, that God hath made that same Jesus, whom ye have crucified, both Lord and Christ."

In a letter to Dalman, Rabinowitz rebuts the idea that these words would intensify the hatred of surrounding Christians for the Jews. The honoured name "Israel" is indeed reserved in the New Testament for the Jews and is not there used of other nations - an interpretation which Dalman disagrees with, by the way. According to Rabinowitz, the inscription is an invitation to the Jews to acknowledge their sin and believe in the Messiah. But it is not an expression of flattery towards Gentile Christians. The other nations, "Europeans, highly educated and distinguished people," who fancy that it is they who have made Jesus Lord, will be reminded through this that it is God who has done this. These peoples, who had no citizenship in Israel, have by the blood of Jesus come nigh unto God, Rabinowitz emphasizes.[19]

For over eight years Somerville Memorial Hall was the setting for Rabinowitz's worship services. We shall later take a look at the uses to which it was put after his death in 1899 (see Chapter 19). Shortly after its inauguration, two photographs of the exterior and interior of the new building were sent abroad.[20] These, together with more or less detailed descriptions of both the prayer-hall and Somerville Hall, enable us to describe the arrangement of the rooms.

How the prayer-hall and Somerville Hall were arranged

Already in a letter of 5 November 1884 Faltin wrote to Delitzsch about Rabinowitz's plans for fitting out the room in his brother's house.[21] It was to be furnished as a Lutheran church, says Faltin. On the back wall there was to be a plaque with gilt letters with some scriptures which Faltin encloses on a slip of paper, asking for Delitzsch's opinion about them. It must remain uncertain whether this was actually done in the hastily fitted-out temporary premises. Organ music accompanied the singing at the first services. This was not particularly Jewish, and we do not hear of the use of organ music subsequently. The Jewish Chronicle writes of the first Christmas Eve service: "The altar was decorated according to Lutheran custom and on it was placed a Lutheran Bible."[22] The surprising expression "a Lutheran Bible" must refer to a Hebrew New Testament.

We are comparatively well informed about the lay-out and furnishings of the prayer-hall and Somerville Hall. In September 1886 Faber wrote to Delitzsch from Kishinev: "The prayer-hall is fitted out in the loveliest way. I shall certainly describe it all to you exactly by word of mouth."[23] The same year A.S. Poulsen described the lay-out of the hall in considerable detail.[24] He had not indeed seen it himself, but when we put his description alongside those of e.g. Venetianer (1887)[25] and Somerville (1888),[26] we get the impression that he has more or less hit the mark. To avoid too many repetitions the lay-out of the prayer-hall and of Somerville Hall will be described together. As regards the latter we have fairly ample descriptions by visitors, e.g. J.G. Blom (1892),[27] the journalist Lerner (1893),[28] and S. Wilkinson (1897).[29] Then Rabinowitz himself and his co-worker R.F. Feinsilber also wrote about the lay-out of the new building.[30]

The hall will have had about 150 seats. Sometimes there were more listeners than seats. Somerville Hall had about 200 seats, and most often that was ample (see further Chapter 12). In the prayer-hall "a kind of altar" had been erected, says A.S. Poulsen. Towards the left - seen from the congregation - on this table there lay a written Torah scroll. On it there stood in Hebrew letters: "The Messiah is the end of the law" (cf. Rom.10:4). From his visit in 1887 Venetianer narrates that there was a reading from this scroll.[31] Such a Torah scroll is not mentioned for Somerville Hall (see below). Towards the right on the altar in the prayer-hall there was a "Gospel Book", presumably a New Testament. According to the plans which Faltin mentions to Delitzsch there were to be, besides a written Torah scroll, an Old Testament and a New Testament bound in one volume. Lerner mentions that in Somerville Hall a Bible lay in a beautiful casket. S. Wilkinson says that on the table there is "simply a Bible, bound in red plush, raised so that one can read the gold letters upon it: Kitvei Kodesh" [should be *Kitvei ha-Kodesh*: the Holy Scriptures]. This actual Bible was still in use in Kishinev as late as 1936! (see Chapter 20).

At the top of the back wall of the prayer-hall were two plaques or tablets with the Ten Commandments. Under the Ten Commandments there was, according to Poulsen, a violet wall-hanging "which also carries inscriptions". Feinsilber, Rabinowitz's helper at the time, also writes of a hanging in Somerville Hall on which the Ten Commandments were embroidered with golden lettering.[32] This is probably an error which has crept into the translation from French and which Dalman also repeats.[33] The photograph of the interior of Somerville Hall shows that the Ten commandments were written on two plaques. The descriptions by Blom and Wilkinson suggest the same. In the prayer-hall the second article of faith from the Creed for the Israelites of the New Covenant was written above the Torah scroll.[34] The article of faith deals with statements about Jesus. In the photograph of Somerville Hall it is legible. It may be remarked that the name of Jesus (*Yeshua*) is written in larger Hebrew letters than the rest of the text. Above the "Gospel Book" there was in the prayer-hall the Lord's Prayer in Hebrew, says Poulsen. This is also mentioned for Somerville Hall and it has to be assumed that it was written on the extreme right of the plaque. Lerner also mentions these two things, although it must be regarded as a slip when he says that the whole creed was written there.

Between these two plaques above the Torah scroll and the Gospel Book respectively there were in the prayer-hall a number of verses from the Old Testament. It must be presumed that they were written on a plaque too. Feinsilber's words - however imprecisely they have been translated - suggest that the whole "altar section" - "the synagogue section" - already embellished the old worship room, i.e. the prayer-hall. According to Poulsen the following lines were on the board above the centre of the table:

- O Lord, my rock and my redeemer (Ps. 19:14)

- Hear, O Israel, the Lord our God, the Lord is one (Deut. 6:4)

- Thou shalt love thy neighbour as thyself (Lev. 19:18)

- The Lord thy God will raise up unto thee a prophet from the midst of thee, of thy brethren, like unto me; unto him ye shall hearken (Deut. 18:15)

- Remember ye the law of Moses my servant, which I commanded unto him in Horeb for all Israel, even statutes and judgements (Mal. 4:4)

- He bare the sin of many and made intercession for the transgressors (Is. 53:12).

On the altar in the prayer-hall were the words from Jeremiah 31:31: "Behold, the days come, saith the Lord, that I will make a new covenant with the house of Israel, and with the house of Judah."

No evidence has been found that the altar in Somerville Hall had this inscription. This may be pure chance. The preserved photograph perhaps rather suggests that this inscription was not on the altar in Somerville Hall. Nor does it seem that anything was written on the pulpit in the new building. But there was in the prayer-hall, where there were lecterns to both right and left of the altar. Poulsen says that prayers and the liturgy were read out from the right-hand lectern. This bore the inscription: "Faith, hope, and charity" (1 Cor. 13:13). The preaching was done from the left-hand lectern. On this were the words: "I am the way, and the truth, and the life" (John 14:6). Writing about the prayer-hall's decor, Faltin says that the altar and pulpit were adorned with scriptures from the Old and New Testaments, thus confirming Poulsen's testimony. Venetianer says that after the Scripture reading and the prayer for the Czar and the powers that be, Rabinowitz stepped up to the lectern on the right side (right must be viewed from the altar, not from the congregation). Poulsen also states that when preaching was going on, a hanging piece of cloth was fixed to the pulpit with the Hebrew words: "Search the Scriptures". Poulsen asserts that this piece of cloth in some way took the place of the priest's vestments, adding that Rabinowitz spoke in his usual black attire. In the photograph of Somerville Hall these words can be read on the piece of cloth. They are also mentioned by S. Wilkinson. On the other hand, no scripture words are discernible on the pulpit.

Thus some few alterations can be traced in the way Somerville Hall was arranged compared to the prayer-hall. These alterations were slight, however, against the fact that the central "altar section" - or perhaps better the *Aron Kodesh*, The Holy Ark with the curtain with tassels, the *Parochet*, to use the synagogue terminology - seems to have been moved over from the prayer-hall into Somerville Hall. Krüger regrets that there was no chalice on the altar table, the explanation being that the authorities had not given permission for the sacraments to be administered. He presumes that the empty space to the right of the altar table was reserved for a font.[35] This sounds very likely, and is a sign that Rabinowitz had not completely given up hope of getting government permission to administer baptism.

In 1895 Rabinowitz writes the following about his synagogue:

At our synagogue the Jews are called upon by me to yield to Jesus Christ solely by the power of the pure Word of God. Here I do not possess any attractive means used in ordinary missions. I have no medical help, no dispensary for the poor sick Jew, no school for the poor Jewish children, nor any store of old clothes to clothe the poor naked and starved Jew. In the interior of the Hall the Jew does not find any attractions to gratify his curiosity, as there are no organ and choir. He only sees before him pews and tables, upon them the Holy Scriptures; Old and New Testament; hears the preacher praying, clearly reading the psalms, and expounding the Scriptures, proving at the same time its everlasting power and significance, how it will bring us Jews and all the nations to the knowledge of that truth which was embodied in Jesus of Nazareth, who gives life eternal to all true believers in Him.[36]

Before we give a sketch of the order of service or liturgy, it may be apppropriate to give a couple of examples of how visitors described their experience of Rabinowitz's services.

Visitors' experience of Rabinowitz's services

By 1884 Rabinowitz had drawn up a *Siddur*, an order of service.[37] Faber tells from his visit in 1885 that the service proceeded in a dignified way, but there was no participation by the congregation in the liturgy, Rabinowitz reciting it all on his own.[38] In his book of 1886, Poulsen asserts that the congregation did not join in very much in the liturgy, as they were still not well-versed in its form.[39]

A favourable account is given by Venetianer from his visit in 1887, which also contained some elements of surprise.[40] He was surprised that Rabinowitz - on a Sabbath - drove to the prayer-hall. He had no objection to this himself, but he knew of many who used this as a weapon against Rabinowitz. After the service, when he noticed that the samovar was lighted in Rabinowitz's home, he was about to say: "Excuse me, but isn't it the Sabbath?" The words were not spoken, because he observed Rabinowitz lighting up a cigarette! (Making fire on a Sabbath is of course forbidden by Jewish tradition.)

Venetianer writes that the hall was full for the service; some stood up, others sat, a few were old, most middle-aged, but there were also many young boys and several uniformed soldiers. Somebody from the congregation handed round Hebrew New Testaments. People sat or stood bare-headed when the Torah scroll was unrolled and there was a reading from it in the sacred language, Hebrew. Venetianer describes Rabinowitz as a "liturgist".

First the Torah text for that particular Sabbath was read in Hebrew, afterwards in Russian. Then James chapter 1 was read, first in Hebrew in Delitzsch's translation, then in Russian. Then followed a prayer in Russian for the Czar and the government. Before the sermon Rabinowitz prayed from the other lectern an extempore prayer in Yiddish. "This form of jargon has always seemed atrocious to me - but I had to join in praying," says Venetianer. And he continues: "Now began the sermon. So doubtless must the apostles have proclaimed the Word. From each sentence the message rang out: `God hath made this man both Lord and Christ!'" Rabinowitz had chosen as the basis of his sermon Ps. 119:120-136.

During the service there was a constant coming and going of listeners. The sermon is described as long. At one point a group of young people had to be asked to keep quiet during the sermon. A little later a group - consisting mostly of boys - left the hall "with cheeky expressions and heavy steps which resounded through the hall." Venetianer suspects that they had been ordered into the hall with this demonstration in view. "The service lasted a solid two hours," he says. Rabinowitz gives the same period for the whole service in 1890.[41] In 1885 Faber felt that it spoilt the overall impression that Rabinowitz spoke "unusually quickly" and claims that the sermon usually lasted two hours - was Faber exaggerating, or did Rabinowitz become briefer later?[42]

The Scottish church leader Somerville also comments from his visit in 1888 that Rabinowitz spoke quickly in the Yiddish sermon, which lasted "an hour all but four minutes"(!)[43] He also mentions that Rabinowitz used a liturgy but also had "a long extempore prayer". There was neither hymn-singing nor any other form of music. Somerville felt that there was some form of sadness to be discerned on the faces of those present. This is explained by the restrictions which the authorities had imposed on the work.[44] In his diary notes Somerville mentions that there was a candlestick on the table/altar, that Rabinowitz kissed the "Law", i.e. the Torah scroll, and that he bowed before "the tablets on the wall" when he read the name Jehovah.[45]

From his visit in 1889 Schönberger says that Rabinowitz's "Bethlehem is still the only synagogue in Russia where on every single Jewish Sabbath Jewish services are held in Jesus' name and where the gospel is proclaimed to Jews in the Jewish language."[46]

J.G. Blom and Gustav Jensen got a good impression of Rabinowitz's "whole personality" on their visit to Kishinev in 1892.[47] Blom describes the hall as "beautiful" and recounts that at first he misunderstood the paper lying by each seat, because it said 9 May. A little later it dawned upon him that, by the Russian calendar, it was that very day, 21 May. On the sheet were printed in Hebrew the sections of the Bible "with which the day's address was going to deal". They were Lev. 25:47-55; Josh. 24:14-28, and Luke 16:13-17. They were unable to follow the sermon, as it was in Yiddish. The sermon ended with a common prayer and the Aaronic blessing. "It was stirring to hear this in the old Hebrew tongue," writes Blom. In the conversation with Rabinowitz afterwards, the Norwegians spoke to him about Jewish missions and Judaism and Christianity. "Here, he emphasized repeatedly, 'no compromise' applies. He asked us finally to greet the mission supporters in Norway: 'Tell them that God has a great ministry with Israel, but it is going slowly, slowly!'" The next day they attended a service with Faltin. His son-in-law Faber, who was travelling through, had had a children's service arranged beforehand. The musical Gustav Jensen had the chance to show his skill at the organ. There had been no opportunity for that with Rabinowitz.

The journalist Lerner from Odessa gives a detailed description of the service led by Rabinowitz on 27 February/11 March 1893.[48] He had become acquainted with the movement earlier, although it was now ten years since he had last been in Kishinev. He says that the service did not last long, but does not define his terms. The service included some short prayers in Hebrew, which were enunciated in a clear voice without any of the intoning that is usual in Jewish synagogues. Lerner also makes clear how Rabinowitz responded to the tetragram, i.e. the four-letter name of the Lord, YHWH. He did not pronounce it "Adonai", as is usual, but said "Jehovah". According to Lerner, he showed by this pronunciation that the Messiah had already come to Israel. For the orthodox Jews think that the name YHWH cannot be uttered until after the Messiah has come and after the restoration of the temple worship in the Holy Land, explains Lerner. He believes that Rabinowitz's manner of saying the name may awaken the Jews to consider the matter (Rabinowitz's use of "Jehovah" is confirmed in his sermon *Rede* of 1890 published in German.).

Lerner also reveals that Rabinowitz read three Psalms in Russian, one of them Ps. 92, the psalm for the day, he says (but see next section). After praying for the Czar Rabinowitz began to preach. Lerner thought it was interesting. But he does not omit to point out that for him there was no accord between the passage of the Bible taken from the synagogue calendar and the theme which Rabinowitz took up. But Lerner apparently regarded the lesson from Ex. 39 as an introduction, for he could see from the programme handed out that there were other matters to be dealt with. Also on the programme were, e.g. Is. 60 and Eph. 4.

About the style of preaching Lerner tells that Rabinowitz preached in a simple Jewish jargon, i.e. Yiddish. Bombastic turns of phrase were avoided, and he wished to make his sermons easy to understand for the ordinary listener. Despite the "unpolished Jewish jargon" it was a well-formulated sermon. And, adds Lerner, his humour came out even amid the seriousness, and as a whole his sermons made a strong impression.

Lerner also reports that the Bible (OT and NT) in Hebrew, Russian, and German, as well as a German programme, were available for the visitors. Everyone sat bare-headed.

And finally a couple of glimpses which S. Wilkinson gives of his visit in 1897.[49] He openly admits that the service contained "somewhat more of ritual" than he had expected. The first part of the service, which was conducted from the "platform surrounded by a railing, on which is a table which conveys instinctively to one's mind the idea of an altar", lasted about half an hour. It was in Hebrew and Russian and consisted of prayer and readings from the Psalms. Sometimes Rabinowitz kissed the Bible which lay on the table; once he held it up in front of the congregation while saying in Hebrew: "Thy word is a lamp unto my feet and a light unto my path" (Ps. 119:105). The text for the day was taken from the synagogue lectionary and was read in both Hebrew and Russian, the congregation standing. "The service includes, of course, no singing." People came and went as is "common also in our mission meetings in London." He reports that the Hebrew Bibles which are available to visitors are bound up with Delitzsch's translation of the New Testament into Hebrew. Also available are programmes and other literature printed in Rabinowitz's own printing-press, which is in a building behind the hall.

These excerpts give a basis for maintaining that Rabinowitz's services had a liturgical character and are to be accounted more than mere "lecture meetings". Throughout his ministry he drew upon the Old Testament passage which was being used in Jewish synagogues on that particular day. In conclusion we shall now give a brief outline of the order of service which Rabinowitz was already working on in 1884.

Rabinowitz's order of service

Even as early as the conference in March 1884, Faber was able to reveal that Rabinowitz had drawn up "a Christian Siddur",[50] i.e. order of service. In 1885 Delitzsch revealed that the liturgy for the morning service on the Sabbath and weekdays had already been brought into use, and it was probably printed in 1885.[51] At any rate, Krüger was able to give a French translation of it in his book of 1885.[52] The liturgy was re-issued in Hebrew in 1892. Unfortunately we have had no opportunity to see the Hebrew text of 1884-1885. First we shall reproduce the service translated from the French rendering. Then we shall add some comments about the variations which the 1892 editions seems to evidence. This will clarify some of the obscure points left by our survey of visitors' descriptions.

According to Krüger the order of service in 1885 looked like this:

The Cantor says in a loud voice:
Repent, for the Kingdom of Heaven is at hand (Matt. 3:2)

The congregation's confession of sin:
Come, and let us return unto the Lord... (Hos. 6:1-3 followed by a set confession of sin).

The Lord's Prayer

The Cantor:
Bless the Lord, the only (God)!

Congregation:
Blessed be the Lord, the blessed one!

Recitation of Psalm 33:
Rejoice in the Lord, O ye righteous...

Then (expanded) Shema Israel:

Hear, O Israel: The Lord our God is one Lord. And thou shalt love the Lord thy God with all thine heart, and with all thy soul, and with all thy might. And thou shalt love thy neighbour as thyself (Deut. 6:4-5; Lev. 19:18).

On weekdays Psalm 103 is recited:
Bless the Lord, O my soul...

On Sabbath days Psalm 92 is recited:
It is a good thing to give thanks unto the Lord...

The Cantor is handed the New Testament and says:
Out of Zion shall go forth the law (Torah), and the word of the Lord from Jerusalem (Is. 2:3c).

The Cantor is handed the Torah scroll and says:
This is the law which Moses set before the children of Israel (Deut. 4:44).

The Cantor reads from the law of Moses and the New Testament. The Torah scroll and the New Testament are returned to their places. He says:
And when it (the ark of the covenant) rested, he said: "Return, O Lord, unto the many thousands of Israel" (Num. 10:36).

Common Prayer for the Czar.

Sermon upon God's Holy Word

Afterwards, Psalm 40:4-6 is recited:
Blessed is that man that maketh the Lord his trust...

The Sabbath hymn Lekah Dodi[53]

The Aaronic Blessing

Between Krüger's rendering of 1885 and the Tefila which was published in Kishinev in 1892 it seems possible to trace a few differences, although the main elements are the same. A.S. Poulsen (1886) also asserts that the service was introduced with the usual prayers prayed in every synagogue, quoting Num. 24:5; Ps. 5:7; and 69:13.[54]

The following comments may be made, based on the 1892 version: It is not indicated that the congregation recites the introductory confession of sin. The *Shema Israel* is also here expanded compared with the Jewish tradition, cf. Jesus's summary of the law in Matt. 22:37-39. No handing-over of the Torah scroll takes place, but of the Holy Scriptures, i.e. a Bible containing both OT and NT. This suggests that the Torah scroll was not moved to Somerville Hall. On handing over the Bible, the Cantor quotes Is. 2:3c and Deut. 4:44 - as before. After the Sabbath hymn and before the Aaronic blessing come the *Seven Articles of Faith* (see Chapter 8). These are ended with the words: "For Thy salvation I wait, O Lord; I wait, O Lord, for Thy salvation. O Lord, for Thy salvation I wait." (cf. Ps. 130:5).

It is not hard to discern the Jewish strain in Rabinowitz's services. At the same time the confession of sin clearly expresses that it is for the sake of Jesus the Messiah, our Lord, that the God of Israel may be called a merciful father. We may also remark that it is not a "priest" but according to Jewish custom a "cantor" or precentor who leads the service. James Adler renders it "minister" in his English translation,[55] Krüger has "L'officiant" in his French translation.[56] In the Christianized Passover Haggada, on the other hand, it is a "shepherd", i.e. pastor, who faces the congregation.[57] Formally Rabinowitz never became a clergyman. Correspondingly it can be difficult to define the status of his adherents. In the eyes of the authorities they were still Jews. As they could not be baptized by Rabinowitz, there are difficulties about precise estimates of the number of Jews who joined his movement. But it is possible to say something about the numbers attending the services in Kishinev. We shall now take a look at this question.

Chapter 12

RABINOWITZ'S HEARERS AND ADHERENTS

There was considerable curiosity about the first services that were held at the beginning of 1885 (see Chapter 4). At the three services which Faber attended at the beginning of 1885 the numbers present fluctuated between 80 and 200.[1] But after the first curiosity had faded, the attendance at the services stabilized. But it was not easy for everyone to keep a level head when addressing the question of attendance levels: some exaggerated, some understated, and Steven J. Zipperstein mixes up information about the size of Rabinowitz's group as it was in the end with information about the beginning to such a degree that the result is a misrepresentation of both the 1880s and the 1890s.[2] It may therefore be useful in this context to divide the period into two. During the first part, from 18/30 May 1885, services were held in the restored premises accommodating about 150. During the second part, the services were held in the hall known as Somerville Hall, which was inaugurated on 15/27 December 1890; in this about 200 could be seated.[3]

Hearer and/or adherent

The number of hearers at Rabinowitz's services was not necessarily the same as the number of adherents. Particularly in the first period there were among his audience a number of people who turned up out of pure curiosity. Others came to pick up arguments against Rabinowitz. Of these some became adherents. Thus it is easier to give a fairly definite figure for the number of hearers than for the number of adherents. It is more plausible to identify the number of hearers with the number of adherents for the latter part of Rabinowitz's ministry, as compared with the former. But there is evidence that even as late as 1893 there were still people attending his services out of simple curiosity.

Rabinowitz's failure to obtain permission to form an actual congregation also makes it more difficult to describe the ratio between hearers and adherents in detail. In the foreign missionary magazines no clear distinction between the two groups was always drawn. So the numerical strength of the movement might easily be assumed to be greater than it was. In this context too the enthusiastic language (as we may call it) of mission was adopted. So it was possible to speak of full houses, so that readers of foreign missionary magazines could hardly fail to think that the accommodation was nearly always strained to the limit.

Nevertheless, from the whole period there is so much scattered evidence coming from different eye-witnesses and from other sources that a fairly realistic picture may be drawn of the number of hearers. So how many people did come along to Rabinowitz's services after the first curiosity had abated? Did no more than 10 'meshummadim' (apostates) attend Rabinowitz's services at first - a number which was further reduced until at last there were only Rabinowitz himself and his brother Efraim Jakob, as Tsitron claims?[4]

The number of hearers

If we piece together the scattered references found in the material investigated, it would seem that on average there were more people at services in the prayer-hall Bethlehem in 1885-1890 than at Somerville Hall in 1891-1899. There are sufficient testimonies for us to assume that, during the first period, it was not unusual for there to be between 100 and 150 hearers. Doubtless this is the kind of number intended when it is stated in general terms that Jews "were flocking" to Bethlehem, that the room was "full", and that the premises could not "hold" all the hearers.[5] There is no reason to doubt that more people than this might attend some services - thus Venetianer mentions 200 on his visit in 1887. He gives a lively description of how people were both sitting and standing up.[6] But it is a wise precaution to assume that a number like that does not err on the low side. There was also opportunity for various estimates, not because people could not count, but because some of the listeners came and went - as was customary in many synagogues.

On his visit in 1887, the clergyman E.H. Leitner counted 150 at the service.[7] The same year Rabinowitz wrote a letter of thanks to the Swedish Israel Mission and said that there was need of a larger room for services, not only for 150 but for 500.[8] But Somerville Hall did not give him this. And the approximately 200 seats that were there did prove sufficient. In 1888 Faber mentions the number 60-80, in 1889 70-80, and another eyewitness 30-40, asserts F. Heman.[9]

In 1891 Strack mentions that on average 50 people come to Rabinowitz's Sabbath services.[10] This declining number is perhaps very realistic, though it may be too low. There were more at least on special occasions like the Christian festivals. In connection with the inauguration of Somerville Hall, the following Sabbath service, and the services on Christmas Eve and New Year in 1890-1891, it is related by Rabinowitz's helper at the time that there were 546 people present in all.[11] It must be assumed that this is an overall total. Saphir reports from about the same time that at eight services there were a total of about 900 people present.[12] In 1892 the Norwegians J.G. Blom and Gustav Jensen visited Kishinev and reported 100 attenders.[13] In 1893 Lerner in a conversation with Rabinowitz referred to the suggestions in the

Russian press that the Israelites of the New Covenant had faded out. This was strongly denied by Rabinowitz, who pointed to what Lerner himself had seen at that day's service. "You saw today that I did not preach to empty pews."[14] But the exact number of attenders is not given in that context. But Lerner does mention that among those attending are some who come out of curiosity. The inauguration of Somerville Hall also drew in a number of hearers who had not previously heard Rabinowitz preach.[15] J.R. Axelrud, Rabinowitz's son-in-law, mentions in his book that from the inauguration of Somerville Hall on into the spring of 1893 - he dates the preface June 1893 - more than 6000 Jews attended the services.[16] That makes an average of about 50. For the year 1894 the London Council for Rabinowitz relates that 68 services were held with a total attendance of about 2700, giving an average of around 40.[17]

It is instructive - and amusing - to trace the effect of this information about the average of 40 attenders in 1894. In Le Réveil d'Israël, February 1885, the number stated is 90.[18] This is noticed by A. Lempert, who on behalf of some "proselytes" in Kishinev protests against this in a letter to the Russian press and also informs the London Society about it.[19] In the letter Rabinowitz is asked: "Where are the ninety persons who attend your chapel every Sabbath?... we know that twenty persons attend your house of worship..." Lempert argues: "The readers of the above referred article [in Le Réveil d'Israël] must gain the impression that his followers amount to hundreds of thousands" - a bold assertion when the point of departure is 90! And he goes on: "But alas the real facts do not come up at all to the overdrawn picture and in fact the real truth is in entire disagreement with his statement." Zipperstein uses Lemper's statement as support for his claim that "several Christians" found it improbable that Rabinowitz should have 200 Jews within the orbit of his group. But this statement by Rabinowitz dates back to 1884 (see Chapter 5) and does not allow for a decrease in the attendance. The letter from Lempert (whom Zipperstein calls Lampert) is from February 1895 and cannot be said to be a response "to a similar report" in Le Réveil d'Israël, as Zipperstein does. There is a difference between 200 and 90. That the article in Le Réveil d'Israël is not from "February 1889", as Zipperstein writes, but from February 1895 contributes to blur the picture that Zipperstein draws.[20] The irony of the whole matter, which also has influenced Zipperstein's presentation, is that the information in Le Réveil d'Israël in February 1895 is due to a misprint! In April 1895 this error is corrected. Instead of 90 it should have been 40.[21]

In 1895 Faber is quoted as saying that hundreds of Jews are flocking to Somerville Hall.[22] That is of course true, if they are added together! When he is speaking more precisely, the number of those attending is given as between 40 and 80.[23] In 1895 Rachel Rabinowitz writes that Somerville Hall is filled every Sabbath.[24] But she herself reveals that there was still room for more, for she expresses the hope that even more will attend at the forthcoming Jewish festivals, i.e. the Jewish autumn festivals. In 1896 the same Rachel in another letter writes that on the previous Sabbath her father preached to a large company of people.[25] The Swedish missionary Paulus Wolff relates from his visit to Kishinev in the spring of 1896 that each Sabbath Rabinowitz preached to many of "our brethren". He expresses his joy that "a large company" of the children of Israel were able to hear a powerful sermon by Rabinowitz on Good Friday 1896. On 4 April he himself brought along 34 Jewish soldiers to the service in Somerville Hall, which he calls Bethlehem. Indeed, he could even write: "For the whole Passover, both theirs [the Jews'] and ours, 'Bethlehem' was so overfull of Jewish hearers that they could scarcely find room in the prayer-house."[26] The same year the Mildmay Mission news reports that 150 were coming to the services.[27] Although such a statement must be taken with reservations - the same issue of the magazine reports that funds for the work in Kishinev have dropped off - it is natural to allow for some fluctuations, which may be due to circumstances now difficult to trace. From his visit to Kishinev in 1897, Samuel Wilkinson relates that the audience consisted of "50 or more Jews, probably more", noting that the Jews had not abandoned their custom of coming and going as they did in their synagogues and which actually they also did during the mission's meetings in London.[28]

In 1896 Rabinowitz writes himself - in the form of enthusiastic language: "Somerville Hall is filled every Saturday by Jews, young and old, eagerly listening to my sermons."[29] In 1898 the London Council for Rabinowitz recounts that 59 services have been held with a total attendance of about 3000.[30] That makes an average of about 50. Unfortunately it has not proved possible to trace similar exact information from Rabinowitz himself for all the years.

Although examples have been found of Rabinowitz himself using the language of enthusiasm when speaking of the number attending, the last figure quoted indicates that he was honest in his statements. Although in Kishinev too there were "great" days of services throughout his ministry, the number of listeners did drop in the latter years. A balanced estimate of the numbers attending Rabinowitz's services has to assume that at the prayer-hall Bethlehem attendances of 100-150 were not unusual, with more on special occasions. At Somerville Hall there were sometimes similar numbers, but in general appreciably fewer. For the period 1885-1890 the number 100 may be taken as a starting-point, with the trend pointing clearly upwards for the first years, but downwards towards the close of the 1880s. For the period 1891-1899 the average would have been around 50. This last number is virtually unassailable. Axelrud testifies to it for the first period of Somerville Hall's history and the London Council testifies to it for 1898. The credibility of this number is strengthened, because it might well sound rather low to those who supported Rabinowitz's work.

Even in January 1885, at the start of the services, A. Saphir (not Rabinowitz, as Zipperstein erroneously maintains)[31] was saying that the importance of the Messianic movement should not be estimated by its numerical strength, but by its intrinsic character.[32] It is certain that it set off chain-reactions which cannot be evaluated on the basis of attendances at Kishinev.

Many reasons may be adduced in an attempt to explain why Rabinowitz's movement did not continue to expand. One doubtless important reason was that the Russian authorities did not give him permission to form a proper congregation. Some of those who initially sympathized with Rabinowitz, were baptized by Faltin, and probably did not continue to come to Rabinowitz's services.[33] For instance, in his annual report for 1891-1892, Faltin mentions that he had baptized one person who used to go to Rabinowitz's prayerhouse.[34] Priluker, the founder of the New Israel movement (see Chapter 3) writes that a certain Abraham Wechsler had for a time been linked with Rabinowitz's work in Kishinev, "but he left it in 1889 and joined the New Israel company in Odessa".[35] It may be envisaged that along the way there were others who left him, e.g. poor Jews who were disappointed if they expected material benefits (see Chapter 13). Faber relates of his visit in 1885 that most of those attending services belonged to "the poorer classes of people".[36] In 1886 he saw among the 100 attenders also some richer Jews, to judge by their appearance.[37]

In 1899, reporting on Rabinowitz's death, The Jewish Chronicle says: "The sect never numbered more than between 30 and 40 members; in recent years it fell into decay, and nobody now knows whether it still exists."[38] In 1912 a Jewish-edited newspaper in Kishinev wrote that the adherents Rabinowitz had "consisted of only [as we well remember] about eight or ten people, all of whom were in some way dependent upon him".[39]

Just as Delitzsch in 1884 may be criticized for not having, in his enthusiasm, defined what was meant by a "following" (see Chapter 5), so may the above quotation be criticized for obscuring the fact that right up to his death Rabinowitz did have people attending his services. However, the London Council for Rabinowitz does not conceal that the attendances were dropping off in the final years. But that is not the same as saying that "the sect's activity ceased" when Rabinowitz "became a Christian" in 1885, if we are to quote The New Standard Jewish Encyclopedia of 1975.[40] Such a verdict is only possible if people wish to deny the facts or have not examined the source material on the subject they are pontificating about.

Chapter 13

THE FINANCIAL ASPECT

Just before his journey to Palestine in 1882, Rabinowitz had been earning a living as a legal consultant or lawyer. In March 1884 he was still maintaining himself in this way. But his practice had suffered a setback because of his public profession of faith in Jesus. From the beginning of 1884, when his new faith became known, he was accused of being paid by Christian missions.[1] But there is nothing to suggest that Rabinowitz changed his views out of financial considerations. His social standing in the years prior to 1882 was far better than the average for Jews in Russia. It is true that he lost his house and his household goods in a fire in Orgeyev in 1859 and for a time lived in poverty. But in 1866 he was the owner of a big grocery in Orgeyev, and in 1873 he had a house built with six spacious, comfortable rooms, which implied a certain social status.[2] Steven J. Zipperstein attaches so great importance to the fire in 1859 (of which he mistakenly makes Rabinowitz's father's wealth the victim)[3] that he thinks Rabinowitz in the late 1870s "probably would have commanded a more important position in Jewish communal life had his family's wealth not been lost".[4] This is misleading about Rabinowitz's social status and financial circumstances at that time. At any rate, it is hardly reasonable to use an event which occurred twenty years earlier as an argument for Rabinowitz's financial situation in the late 1870s. Also in the history of the Messianic movement the issue of money quickly became a problem. Tsitron even claims, in 1923, that Rabinowitz received money from the Russian government, which is not very likely.[5] And Zipperstein intimates that promises of financial aid was one of the factors which influenced Rabinowitz in his 'conversion', i.e. his baptism in 1885.[6]

It may be asserted with assurance that Rabinowitz was not bribed into 'changing' his faith. But later he was given money from abroad for his work of leading other Jews to faith in Jesus. In this lay the seeds of renewed charges of a personal nature against Rabinowitz. As early as 28 October 1884 he wrote in a letter that it was repugnant to him to receive people who merely wanted to profiteer from the religion of Christ; he also reproached Jewish editors who pretended to believe that he was receiving a certain sum of money from missionaries, depending upon "the number of heads [*Gulgolot*] which I win for the law of Mount Golgatha" - with a play upon words. "But they know very well it is untrue," he wrote to Faber.[7]

Among Christians abroad opinions were also divided about making the Messianic movement dependent upon foreign money. But it cannot be completely ignored that a factor in some people's view of this question was their particular organisation's financial resources - or lack of them.

"The Jewish nature's love of money"

In 1906, Stefan Volf, a Danish missionary to Jews, wrote that Rabinowitz fell for the temptation to accept the large sums of money which English missionary societies were able to make available to him. And he continued with an unpleasant generalization: "The Jewish nature's love of money here seduced him into a step which he later regretted."[8] Lhotzky had drawn a similar picture in 1904, to which Volf also refers. Lhotzky made Rabinowitz out to be a Jew who, with a "cunning smile", pocketed all the money which he could so easily obtain from the societies. Above all else he desired freedom, and the freedom came with the gold from these societies, said Lhotzky. In return he gave, among other things, "his honourable Jewish name Joseph Rabinowitz as a display sign." Lhotzky too employed a distasteful generalization: "Gold is freedom, and a Jewish heart is very susceptible to incense. Rabinowitz needed freedom."[9]

First off, we are not concerned to weigh up whether Volf and Lhotzky were right in thinking that financial dependence upon foreign funds harmed the movement. This question must be kept separate from another: whether Rabinowitz felt constricted by help from abroad, or whether he sought it himself. The following shows that, right from 1884 until his death, Rabinowitz continued to request financial help for his work. So the assertion of Volf, for instance, that Rabinowitz later regretted his financial arrangements and withdrew from his connection with the missionary societies, is refuted by clear statements in sources that cannot be impugned.

It is certain that the money he received did enable him to devote himself entirely to his work for Jesus and Israel. There was a difference of opinion about the way he administered the money. All the same, it is a regrettable insinuation to assert that the financial support he received from abroad was an outworking of "the Jewish nature's love of money". Jews have no monopoly of that "nature".

The first money

The fitting-out of the temporary prayer-hall in Rabinowitz's brother's house can hardly have cost more than a modest sum; perhaps the group around Rabinowitz largely defrayed the cost themselves. But the remodelling required more money before the restored premises could be brought into use on 18/30 May 1885. Money came from abroad for this.

As early as November 1884 Delitzsch wrote that the Bessarabian brethren were turning to Christians in all places asking for help to erect a prayer-hall. He expressed the hope that this appeal might be heard, and declared himself willing personally to accept - and forward - gifts for this purpose; he was "electrified", as he wrote to Saphir, at the good mission news.[10] Similar appeals found a place in the following months in magazines of other countries' Jewish missions.[11]

In a letter of 12 December 1884, J. Wilkinson enquired how the Mildmay Mission could provide aid. To this Rabinowitz responded with the following reply with a detailed budget:

1. Support for the place of worship, about 1500 roubles.
2. Establishing a school for boys and girls, about 1500 roubles.
3. Setting up a fund to help poor brethren, about 1000 roubles.
4. Supporting the Rabinowitz family.
5. Bibles, both Old and New Testaments.
6. Organ for the place of worship.

"We would need this help," writes Rabinowitz, "for about two or three years, till our community becomes established, and able to meet all its needs without asking help from other quarters."[12]

However, money was not sent by the Mildmay Mission straight away. But it was from there that the first cheque was sent to Rabinowitz. This was done in a letter of 24 February 1885, the money being advanced for Rabinowitz's forth-coming journey to Germany.[13] It seems that Wilkinson brought a considerable sum for Rabinowitz when they met in Berlin. His aim was to take £500.[14] It is true that at the subsequent meeting in Leipzig all the parties involved agreed to encourage the new movement to be financially self-sufficient, although they would help for the time being.[15] This "for the time being" became something permanent, however.

In his account of the movement as he knew it at the beginning of 1885, Faber wrote: "But in general the Jews believe that Rabinowitz is paid by the mission, whereas hitherto he has received only comparatively small support."[16] If it is correct that Rabinowitz had in fact received some small support, then the words that he wrote to J. Wilkinson in a letter sent on 20 March/1 April 1885 - the very same day he returned from Germany - may be puzzling. For Rabinowitz wrote: "Beside your kind contributions, I have not received from anyone a single farthing, and our needs are great, as I told you in Berlin."[17] There is doubtless a sensible explanation of these divergent statements, even if we are not going to be able to discern it.

However that may be: immediately prior to his trip to Germany in 1885 J. Wilkinson was able to inform the readers of his magazine that the expenses of this journey had been met from a special fund, and that not a penny had been taken from the missionary budget or from the gifts that had been designated for Rabinowitz's work.[18] In the May issue of the same magazine, Wilkinson wrote that sufficient money had been sent in for present needs, and that it was wished to see how the work developed.[19] In other words: Wilkinson did not accede immediately to Rabinowitz's - indirect - request for more money, indicated in the letter just quoted. But later that year, in December 1885, Wilkinson did say that £300 had been sent off, half for personal use and half for the school.[20] But the latter project remained on the drawing-board.

Although the first money came from England, from the Mildmay Mission, it must also be assumed that Delitzsch's appeal produced results. The Jewish missions of other countries also became involved. It may be questioned whether money from the Norwegian Israel Mission was sent direct to Rabinowitz for the renovation of the prayer-hall, although this has been asserted;[21] large sums from Norway went to Faltin's work. On the other hand, there is clear evidence that the Swedish Israel Mission passed on money gifts in 1885-1888, for which Rabinowitz personally sent thanks.[22] In March 1886, for instance, he received £30 from a clergyman, which was conveyed through the London Society - and sent to Faltin.[23] On his first visit to Scotland in 1887 an envelope was pressed into his hand containing £100.[24] It may be concluded from these examples that money came in to him from various countries and individuals, and certainly from more than it is now possible to trace.

On the formation of the London Council for Rabinowitz in 1887 most of the money was channelled through this.

The London Council for Rabinowitz

The London Council for Rabinowitz was set up on 15 March 1887 (see Chapter 14), shortly after Rabinowitz's first visit to England. In this way the financial support for his work was put into a firmer framework. At about the same time, committees were set up elsewhere. Particularly those in Edinburgh and Glasgow were to play an important part in collecting funds for the work in Kishinev. These Scottish committees worked in close collaboration with the London Council for Rabinowitz.[25]

The London Council claimed that, as well as assisting Rabinowitz with advice, they would supply him "with the necessary material means to carry on his labours."[26] The sources leave no doubt that Rabinowitz himself urged them to do this.[27] But precisely because Lhotzky and others attempted to make the British the scapegoats in the financial game, it may be appropriate to point to Delitzsch's opinion about this. Publicly and in print the promoters of the London Council for Rabinowitz made known that Delitzsch had given his backing to the setting-up of the council and the financial support. At any rate, in 1888 A. Saphir wrote on behalf of the Council: "This step was taken some time ago, partly at the earnest request of Professor Delitzsch, who is in thorough sympathy with the movement, and who is convinced that only in England the requisite spiritual, moral, and financial support could be secured."[28]

In 1887 the Mildmay Mission estimated that he had an annual need of £500 to cover both family expenses and expenses in connection with the printing and distribution of Rabinowitz's sermons and booklets.[29] This budget does not appear to have changed much in subsequent years. At least, in 1891, A. Saphir could state that the budget was still £500. This sum also included a salary to a co-worker Rabinowitz had at that time. He also reported that more than 27,000 copies of Rabinowitz's tracts in Hebrew and Yiddish had been printed, and that the stockroom was almost empty.[30] In 1896 the London Council attempted to raise £400 for Rabinowitz's work, which included his allowance of £300.[31]

Besides funds for Rabinowitz's private consumption and running expenses, collections were made for special projects. In these the Mildmay Mission, for instance, also participated by setting up special funds while at the same time fully backing the London Council for Rabinowitz. A later chapter will describe an interesting project for railway evangelization (see Chapter 17). The money for the building of Somerville Hall, which was brought into use at the end of 1890, also mostly came from English and Scottish supporters and was channelled through the London Council for Rabinowitz (see Chapter 11).

In autumn 1889 it was suggested that £500 should be collected to erect a new prayer-house[32] (in 1887 the Mildmay Mission had estimated that £1500 would be needed for this plus a school).[33] The later history of Somerville Hall leaves it unclear whether Rabinowitz had both rights of use and of ownership in the building. In the spring of 1888 A.N. Somerville had visited Kishinev and had then brought a sum of money from Scottish mission-supporters.[34]

Although it is unlikely that Rabinowitz took the lead in naming the new building, he did so in drawing up the plans. It would seem that he brought the plans with him on his trip to England and Scotland in autumn 1889 (see Chapter 11). He had been campaigning for a new building for a long time. This can be proved by a couple of examples.

While visiting London in January 1887 he said that he wanted his own place to hold services in. "As I do not know how soon the Lord may call me away, I should like to look upon a house free from debt, where the glorious work would go on after my departure. I want, therefore, the Christians of England to help me by their prayers and gifts."[35]

In a letter of 26 April (r?) 1887 Rabinowitz thanks the Swedish Israel Mission for the 170 kronor sent. He does not omit to point out that the present prayer-hall is much too little, accommodating only 150 people. But as large numbers of Jews come to join in the services, he needs room for at least 500, he writes.[36] In May of the same year he informed A. Saphir that the prayer-hall was much too small for the large number who wanted to listen to the gospel, so a new house had to be built as quickly as possible.[37] In the same month he wrote to Saphir's son-in-law, C.A. Schönberger, in Vienna that it was high time to have a prayer-house built on the plot of land that had already been bought for the purpose.[38] It was at this point that the conflict between Rabinowitz and Faltin became public knowledge. But that did not hamper his plans for building. In his letter to Schönberger he went on: "How often will my Christian brethren and friends change their minds towards me, trying and testing me continually, though they know my work in the name of the Lord?"

The fact that the London Council for Rabinowitz channelled money to his work did not of course prevent others from sending money direct to Kishinev. For instance we have already mentioned a letter of thanks to the Swedes, which was sent after the formation of the London Council. At the beginning of the new year of 1888 he gives thanks for another sum.[39] G.A. Krüger, the editor of the French-language periodical Le Réveil d'Israël, an enthusiastic supporter of Rabinowitz's work, was able to report for 1887 that 350 francs had been sent to Rabinowitz and similar ministries.[40] For comparison, it may be mentioned that the annual budget of the French organisation was 1500 francs - and that Faltin was given 15 francs that year, which had been earmarked by the donor. Later it would seem that money collected through this French organisation was also channelled through the London Council for Rabinowitz. This is said expressly, for instance, about 125, 105, and 100 francs which were given to Rabinowitz in 1890, 1891, and 1894.[41]

There are also instances of his receiving money in connection with journeys abroad. In the summer of 1896, the last time he was in Scotland, where for instance he addressed the General Assembly of the Free Church of Scotland, £50 was subsequently voted to him "towards the promotion of the important work which he is carrying on at Kischineff."[42]

To confine ourselves to the main outline, we may assert that, after the formation of the London Council for Rabinowitz in 1887, most of the money was channelled through this, given by English and Scottish supporters. The size of the gifts which arrived by other routes is difficult to determine accurately. The conflict between Faltin and Rabinowitz may have also influenced the missions to Israel and individuals of other countries. At any rate it is a fact that the last letter of thanks printed in the magazine of the Swedish Israel Mission is dated the beginning of 1888. This could be an indication that they had taken sides in making their financial allocations. But it did not mean that they stopped printing information about Rabinowitz's work.

It is conceivable that the situation was similar elsewhere too. In this connection it is worth mentioning the London Society's attitude to Rabinowitz, the Society which Zipperstein describes as Rabinowitz's "major financial backer". He writes: "From the mid-1890s, even the London Society lost faith in Rabinovich and was hesitant to continue sending his movement an annual donation of £400. It is not clear whether or not it stopped payments but there was considerable support within the group to do so."[43]

Zipperstein has, however, not examined the source material carefully enough, which is the reason why he draws some wrong conclusions. The London Society had never before sent an annual donation of £400 to Rabinowitz. In 1896 J.E. Mathieson asks the Society, on behalf of the London Council for Rabinowitz, to consider giving to Rabinowitz's work. The annual expenditure for Rabinowitz is estimated at £400, but Mathieson assumes that also others will contribute, e.g. the Scottish churches.[44] On 25 September 1896 the London Society resolved "that whilst the Committee greatly sympathize with Mr Rabinowitz they are unable to make a grant".[45]

An examination of the repeated discussions held by the London Society's Committee of a grant to Rabinowitz's work reveals the weak foundation of Zipperstein's claim that the London Society was Rabinowitz's "financial backer". This claim is part of Zipperstein's argumentation when he concludes that Rabinowitz at his death in 1899 was "a largely forgotten and isolated figure" and "that Rabinovich died a failure with few Jewish souls to his credit having all but lost the goodwill of his Christian backers abroad".[46] The truth is that Rabinowitz never received his main income from the London Society but from the London Council for Rabinowitz, strongly supported by e.g. the Mildmay Mission, and these whole-heartedly backed up Rabinowitz until his death, both the cause itself and financially. Nor can the fact that the London Council for Rabinowitz had difficulties collecting the £400 in 1896 be taken as an argument that Rabinowitz should have "lost the goodwill of his Christian backers abroad". On 13 February 1885 the London Society had decided to grant £100 to their missionary, Pastor Faltin of Kischineff, for the promotion of Christianity in connection with Mr. Rabinowitz's work."[47] Not only must the money be forwarded through Faltin, but it can only be disbursed after Faltin has submitted his views as to the manner in which the sum may be appropriated. Having been on the agenda at several Committee meetings[48] the matter is recorded in the minutes on 14 December 1886: "Resolved that under the circumstances represented by Mr. Faltin, the Committee do not feel justified, as the matters now stand, in authorizing payment for the grant".[49] In a letter Faltin had accounted for his position and dissociation from Rabinowitz's baptism.[50] As late as in 1889 the question of the £100 is on the Committee's agenda. On 29 November 1889 they decide to invite Rabinowitz to an interview with the Committee.[51] Nothing became of the meeting, however, as Rabinowitz had already left London.[52] And the £100 that the London Society had granted in 1885 was never paid. The payment of the amount was bound to Faltin's assessment of Rabinowitz. On 18 January 1889 he writes to the London Society: "I solemnly declare, that this very moment no Jewish-Christian community with positive confession can be found in Kischinew."[53]

On Rabinowitz's death in 1899 the London Council published a booklet containing, among other things, the accounts of the fund. In a summary of this booklet, it expressed the hope that the work in Kishinev would continue. Nevertheless the Council was wound up, and it was proposed that the remaining funds should be used for Rabinowitz's bereaved family.[54]

The same proposal was made about another fund which the Mildmay Mission ran.[55] The railway evangelization project will be described later (see Chapter 17). Rabinowitz's death put a stop to the carrying out of these plans. But there is an abundance of documentation to show that Rabinowitz had plans for the money that was collected abroad.

How Rabinowitz spent the money collected

Even before Rabinowitz had received "a farthing" - or at least only modest sums - from abroad, he had to make up his mind whether the Messianic movement was going to set up a social and economic safety-net for Jews who came in contact with him. He sums up in the following way one of the questions most often asked in the many letters he received when the movement had first become known: Can future members count on getting material support from the new Hebrew Christian congregation?" He replied to this in a newspaper article on 20 January/1 February 1885: "...I say categorically that the capital of our congregation does not consist of 'corruptible gold or silver', but of 'the precious blood of Christ, of a lamb without blemish and spot', employing the words of 1 Pet. 1:18,19. He also saw it as his duty to declare publicly "that we do not have available to us the kind of funds that the envoys of the various foreign missions can spend" (see Chapter 6).[56]

At roughly the same time as these words were being written, there was however a collection going on abroad. The appeals for this collection mention not only money for the place of worship and the school, but also money to support impoverished Jews who came to faith in Jesus.[57] From scattered information it seems to be apparent that Rabinowitz tried to relieve the worst consequences for those who got into financial difficulties after their fellow-Jews broke off relations with them because of their contacts with Rabinowitz. But the clergyman E.H. Leitner, who told about this in 1887, stresses that Rabinowitz "cannot provide permanent means of subsistence for his followers". But just as the early church in Jerusalem was given assistance from outside through collections, this must be the case for "the first modern Hebrew Christian community," says Leitner. He also expresses the hope that Hebrew Christians all over the world will send yearly contributions to the "poor saints of Kischineff".[58]

Thus, right from the beginning, Rabinowitz did not hold out to anyone the prospect of its being a paying proposition to join up with him. But this did not prevent him from trying to set up a fund to help impoverished Jews, as touched upon already. Even if he exceptionally helped out with material goods, most of the money was not spent on this. This is particularly remarkable because in his *Thirteen Theses* of 1883 he stressed so strongly the financial and social advantages which a Jewish reception of Jesus would entail (see Chapter 4). Compared to the funds which, for instance, Faltin spent on social work, Rabinowitz's resources were indeed small. Thus he did not aim to set up a hostel for proselytes, as was so common. Nor did he start an agricultural colony, as Faltin did with Lhotzky's help - and doubtless inspired by Rabinowitz (see Chapter 10). If Faltin with such a project could be accused of enticing socially deprived Jews to convert to Christianity, this charge could not be laid against Rabinowitz. But he did not escape accusations of a personal kind for the way he spent the money he received from abroad.

It is of course hard to decide whether the accusations made against Rabinowitz in this matter had any substance. It can only be confirmed that the London Council never asked questions about his private consumption, nor did it lay down any stipulations for the receiving of assistance. It is certain that Rabinowitz did not suffer any material hardship after he began to receive money from abroad. There is nothing to suggest that he had a pietistic view of money and material goods. Finally it may be said in general that anyone who is given money collected for mission use, which also includes private consumption, is vulnerable on this point.

Particularly after Faltin's public attack on Rabinowitz, feelings began to run high. In 1888 at least, Venetianer, who completely backed Rabinowitz, indicates an atmosphere of rancour. He asserts that the following are the *ipsissima verba* [own words] of Faltin's henchmen:

> Rabinowitz is deceiving you! He is getting money from London for you, but it does not come here. Look, he was abroad, and he brought home with him a gold wrist-watch for his daughters, but he gives you nothing! Now, with the mission money, he has bought a house, but he does not pay your rent![59]

According to Venetianer, Rabinowitz was also criticized for not having, like Faltin, a farming-colony to which needy Jews could be sent. Although Rabinowitz passes as a Christian, ran the charge, he is the same as before, a pettifogger, only with this difference: that he now does better business with the British.[60] If Venetianer's description of the accusations is correct, they do seem to hit below the belt, in the light of what has been shown in this chapter.

There are hardly impartial sources which could be the final arbiters of Rabinowitz's private consumption. But if we look at the charges in the context of the imbroglio that had arisen after Faltin's public attack on Rabinowitz, we begin to suspect that they were exaggerated. We can say this without trying to present Rabinowitz as an ascetic. But we shall conclude by turning to a question more of principle: whether it would have benefited the movement to have been financially independent of foreign funds.

Was the taint of foreign money finally too strong?

Stefan Volf's claim that the missionary societies seized upon and enfolded
Rabinowitz does not correspond to the picture given in the primary sources.
For throughout his public ministry it was Rabinowitz who sought support
for his work. It is not in accord with the sources to say that Rabinowitz later
regretted this and withdrew from the relationship. But Volf - and Lhotzky
- do have a case. Volf asserts that it would have made a greater impression on
the Jews if Rabinowitz had stood without any connection to the missions.
"Then nobody could have said that he had a pecuniary advantage from
preaching Christ," argues Volf.[61]

Now Volf - along with Lhotzky and others - had arrived at a very
pessimistic view of the work of the missions to Israel. Obviously Volf could
not help causing a rumpus by writing: "...absolutely the greatest obstacle to
the conversion of Israel is the mission to Israel." He himself was employed
by the Danish Israel Mission, but he considered that the indirect form of
mission to Jews, in which efforts were made among Christians to create a
spiritual life that might attract Jews, was the only sound way of encountering
them. Also, he thought that it was largely correct that Jewish-born missionaries
to the Jews were either downright frauds or personal failures. He quotes with
approval "the old rabbi Lichtenstein in Leipzig", i.e. Rabinowitz's brother-
in-law, for the following: "It is true that the Christians do not know as much
Hebrew as Jews. But as missionaries to the Jews they have the great advantage
of not usually being frauds."[62]

It was in support of this case that Volf used - and abused - the name of
Rabinowitz. But that kind of argument could not win much of a hearing
from the contemporary missions to Israel, on whose payroll they had both
"Jewish-born" and "Gentile-born" missionaries.

Nevertheless Gustav Dalman, for instance, expressed regret that it
was necessary for Rabinowitz to accept funds from English supporters. He
did this in an article in 1889, in which he tried to be fair to both sides in the
conflict between Faltin and Rabinowitz - with a verdict rather in Rabinowitz's
favour. Dalman was of the opinion that since Rabinowitz had chosen to
remain within Israel, it would have been better if he had stayed financially
independent. If he had done this, the root cause of suspicion from both Jews
and Christians would have been removed.[63]

However, this argument does not sound particularly convincing if it
is looked at in a wider setting. If Rabinowitz had chosen to work under the
auspices of the Lutheran church and received his salary through Faltin, this
would hardly have silenced those who spread the rumour about the financial
benefits that Rabinowitz was supposed to obtain from preaching Christ. At
least it would not have stopped the accusations made by Jews. Nor is there
anything to suggest that Rabinowitz lived more extravagantly than Faltin,
for instance. But it is conceivable that his social position was better than that

of "ordinary" missionaries to the Jews. Viewed favourably, Dalman's assessment can, of course, be taken as an expression of a well thought-out mission strategy: a Hebrew Christian congregation must learn to manage on its own and stand on its own feet financially as well. But it does have a hollow ring when other Hebrew Christians received support if they but remained under the superintending eye of the respective missionary societies. In principle Rabinowitz did desire financial self-sufficiency. Dalman's remark, however right in principle, perhaps reveals some disappointment that the movement had become predominantly an English cause. We may here allude to Delitzsch's pragmatic attitude. In principle along with everyone else he might say that the Messianic movement ought to be self-supporting, but in practice he was then realistic enough to recommend financial support from the London Council for Rabinowitz. For Delitzsch was no doubt convinced that he - and the Germans - had a better theology; but the British were the best people at raising money for missions.[64]

But all this has not finally answered the question whether the movement did not, after all, suffer from the taint of foreign money. It may be noted that the accusations that were made were themselves tainted with personal intrigues or expressed attitudes which were not consistently applied to other similar circum- stances. With hindsight, it may be asserted that in certain areas people acted too hastily; and that a smaller building than that known as Somerville Hall would have been perfectly adequate. But if all church buildings and adjacent parsonages were to be assessed on the same criteria, Rabinowitz's buildings would hardly prove unique.

It might also be seen as an expression of vision and expectation.

But the important thing was that the money that was sent to Rabinowitz through the London Council was not hedged about with any demand - or any right - to interfere in his Christian views or the internal affairs of the movement. Rabinowitz did not merely receive money from abroad, he asked for it himself. The money made him financially independent, so that he could devote himself entirely to his cause: Jesus and Israel. If he had received the money through other channels, it is hardly probable that Jewish suspicion of him would have been any less. This is not because Jews could not recognize 'professional' men who lived by their religious activities. The wonder-rabbis and rebbes of that time with their courts prove this. The Jewish opposition to Rabinowitz was not so much caused by the question of money as by the message he proclaimed: that Jesus was the Messiah and brother of the Jews.

There he struck a tender spot. He also told a very pointed story about that matter (see Chapter 21).

Chapter 14

RABINOWITZ'S JOURNEYS ABROAD

Rabinowitz's travels abroad form a chapter for themselves. After his journey to Germany in 1885, during which he was baptized, England and Scotland came to be the main destinations. But his itineraries were planned so that he could visit other places on the way there and back. Although some information about his travels has already been incorporated in other chapters, we shall here take an overall look at Rabinowitz's foreign journeys. Since, through the London Council for Rabinowitz, he was receiving copious support for his work from friends in England and Scotland, it is understandable that the link with these countries had to be cultivated. So the main purpose of the journeys was to foster these contacts and increase people's knowledge of the work in Kishinev. However, we discover other details too, when we start looking into his journeys abroad.

First trip to England and Scotland in 1886-1887

As early as the autumn of 1884 John Wilkinson of the Mildmay Mission was devising plans for getting Rabinowitz to London to hold some meetings there. But nothing came of it just then (see Chapter 7). At the close of 1886 Rabinowitz wrote to Wilkinson that he wished to go to London to consult Wilkinson and Adolph Saphir. The letter was sent on to Saphir, who took the view, however, that a visit just then would be undesirable. Wilkinson concurred and informed Rabinowitz, enclosing Saphir's letter.[1] Although no reason is given for not welcoming Rabinowitz's plan, it probably had nothing to do with church politics; perhaps Saphir's poor health made the visit undesirable.[2] Nevertheless Rabinowitz stuck to his plan, a sign of his purposeful and indeed independent attitude to his English friends.

He arrived in London on 26 December 1886 - though where did he keep Christmas Eve? It is unlikely that he kept it on 5 January, as his programme in London was to be much too crowded. James Adler, whom he knew from the negotiations in Germany in 1885, met him at the station; he knew Yiddish and acted as Rabinowitz's interpreter.[3] That evening Rabinowitz attended a service held by the Mildmay Mission at which two Jews were among those baptized - and given a few words of exhortation by Rabinowitz.[4]

In the weeks to follow Rabinowitz took part in various meetings.[5] In this connection it is of interest that, although he was the guest of the Mildmay Mission, they did not monopolize him. Rather, everything was done to introduce him to as many different people and church leaders as possible. Special meetings were also arranged with Rabinowitz as speaker, at which he had opportunity to tell Christians about his work, and preach to Jews.

As regards the former, the British Society gives a favourable description of a meeting held on 18 January 1887 in a private setting in the home of the society's treasurer F.Y. Edwards. It may be noted that this time no disapproving comments were heard about Rabinowitz's presence in England (see Chapter 7). The secretary, J. Dunlop, kept a record of the meeting.[6]

The meetings for Jews turned out pretty stormy. Two major events were held, on 8 and 15 January. On both occasions Rabinowitz preached. At one meeting the Jewish listeners grew so furious with him that, in the ensuing conversation, they flung in his face or tore up the New Testaments that had just been handed out.[7]

According to Wilkinson's account, feelings reached boiling-point at the event on 8 January. The meeting had gathered 182 Jews, and Rabinowitz spoke on Gen. 49:10, a verse which, with the Hebrew *Shilo*, of many meanings, is also interpreted messianically in Jewish tradition. After the address, a Jew vehemently expostulated with Rabinowitz, and the company dissolved into small groups. The leaders of the mission split up among the groups endeavouring to answer the questions being asked. "It seemed a reproduction of apostolic times," wrote J. Wilkinson.[8] In another account of the same event Wilkinson says that Rabinowitz had to be accompanied away from the premises under police protection. "The Jews were told some very plain and unpalatable truths," he writes.[9]

During his stay in London Rabinowitz received an invitation to visit Scotland. Wilkinson goes to great pains to say that the Free Church of Scotland had the "first claim" to Rabinowitz, as it was from there £50 had been sent while Rabinowitz was still in London. Together with Adler, who interpreted for him from Yiddish, he held three or four meetings in both Edinburgh and Glasgow at the beginning of February 1887.[10] These meetings were well attended and made a deep impression, says an annual report of the Free Church of Scotland.[11] They resulted in the formation of committees to support Rabinowitz's work. The Scottish Free Church workers on the Continent had already once before been drawn into the plans of the Messianic movement. Through Professor Delitzsch, one of the mission staff in Prague, K.J. Gottlieb, had in 1885 been offered the post as head of the school which Rabinowitz wished to set up in Kishinev (see Chapter 15).[12] In the same report of May 1886 one could read that it would "be something for the Free Church Jewish Mission Committee to congratulate itself upon, that one of its labourers has been chosen to go there," as the Revd James Pirie put it from Prague. Since Adolph Saphir had close links with the Free Church of Scotland, this also helped to channel Scottish money through the London Council for Rabinowitz, the most concrete result of the first trip to Britain.

On 11 February Rabinowitz left London after another couple of days there.[13] A month later, on 15 March 1887, the London Council for Rabinowitz was formed. The Mildmay Mission's efforts to make Rabinowitz known were thus crowned with success. A. Saphir became the chairman of the Council, which otherwise consisted of individuals who worked in or supported the organisations of the various English missions to Israel. Among the nine council members was John Wilkinson.[14] The Council, which saw it as its main task to support Rabinowitz with advice and the requisite funds, did not however wish to interfere in his other arrangements (see Chapter 13). The formation of this council also hindered the movement around Rabinowitz from becoming the cause of only one organisation, although some organisations did write more often about Rabinowitz than others. This particular applies to the Mildmay Mission. It is much to Wilkinson's credit that he did not - as there was a tendency for the British Society to do (see Chapter 7) - monopolize Rabinowitz, but made the cause of Rabinowitz into a matter of common interest.

On the return journey from London, Rabinowitz arrived in Leipzig on 13 February 1887.[15] That evening a meeting was arranged for members of the Institutum Judaicum, at which Rabinowitz, among other things, told the story of his conversion (see Chapter 2). On 11 January he had dealt with the same theme in London.[16] The records do not mention whether his brother-in-law Herschensohn/ Lichtenstein was also present in Leipzig.

On 1 March Rabinowitz wrote to Saphir from Kishinev. All the Jewish newspapers in Russia had mentioned his journey, he says. Before his return to Kishinev, he had been in St Petersburg. He intimates that he had still not been granted permission to form an actual church, but he was looking forward to this happening when "the right moment arrives". He went on to say that in Leipzig he had met with Delitzsch three times to chat about the work in Kishinev.[17] As far as can be deduced, this was the last time the two of them met. Delitzsch died in 1890 and on his second journey to England Rabinowitz seems not to have travelled via Leipzig. Nevertheless Delitzsch made his voice heard in favour of Rabinowitz after their last personal meeting. This also happened in the conflict between Faltin and Rabinowitz, when Delitzsch both made his opinion known through Faber and spoke out publicly himself (see Chapter 10).

The second journey to England and Scotland in 1889

Rabinowitz was once more in England and Scotland in the autumn of 1889.[18] Relations with the London Council were strengthened. This time too he held meetings, for instance on 14 October 1889 in the Conference Hall of the Mildmay Mission, with C.A. Schönberger interpreting. He did not return home empty-handed from this visit either. The London Council was set up after the first journey; after his second journey he had a promise from Scottish mission-supporters that they would raise £500 to finance the building of a new place of worship.[19] The foundation stone of this hall, known as Somerville Memorial Hall, was laid in May 1890, no more than some six months after Rabinowitz's return (see Church 11). The well-known Scottish church leader A.N. Somerville, who had received an exceedingly favourable impression of Rabinowitz's work during his visit to Kishinev in the spring of 1888,[20] had died on 18 September 1889, shortly before Rabinowitz's visit to Scotland.

Rabinowitz travelled back from England and Scotland via Paris, where for the first time he personally met G.A. Krüger, who had backed him so strongly, both in his book of 1885 and through intelligence in the French periodical Le Réveil d'Israël. On 22 November a couple of meetings were held in Paris, one for his supporters in the afternoon, in Russian interpreted into French, and in the evening for Jews, when he spoke in Yiddish.[21]

It is possible that his daughter Rachel accompanied him on this journey and was left behind in Scotland. If not, she soon after set off on a journey. For in November 1891 James A. Mathieson of the London Council for Rabinowitz was able to say that in Edinburgh Rachel had joined in evangelisation work among Jewish women for "the past two years".[22] She did accompany him on several journeys and was also on Mrs Rabinowitz's baptismal journey, as we now shall see.

In Budapest in 1891: "Mama gerettet"

On her return from Scotland, Rachel went with her father and mother to Budapest at the beginning of October 1891.[23] After the family's three daughters had been baptized in Rohrbach in 1887 and the two sons in Odessa in October 1888, the only close member of the family left unbaptized was Mrs Rabinowitz. By E.H. Leitner, a clergyman in Constantinople, she is described after his visit to Kishinev in 1887 as a former fanatical Jewess who now loves Jesus and with Magdalene calls him "Rabboni", i.e. Jesus "my Master".[24]

Andrew Moody, pastor of the Free Church of Scotland's work in Budapest, told in his annual report about the most interesting baptism of the year in his church, when Rabinowitz's wife was baptized on 5 October 1891. It is related that she had wept that her husband had "bowed the knee to the despised Jesus of Nazareth", but she could now with joy confess faith in him as her saviour. After the baptismal service, relates Moody, Rabinowitz telegraphed home: "Mama gerettet" (mother saved). The following evening Rabinowitz spoke to a large gathering in the school building of the mission.[25]

On 7 October Rabbi Lichtenstein (his first name was Isak, and he is not to be confused with Yechiel Zvi Lichtenstein (or Herschensohn), who was Rabinowitz's brother-in-law) came to Budapest from Tapio-Szele, where he lived.[26] Rabbi Lichtenstein was another much talked-about Jew who believed in Jesus. But whereas Rabinowitz had taken the step and got baptized - and now his wife had become the last of his immediate family to be baptized - Rabbi Lichtenstein never took that step, at least not as an offical and public act. For that reason he could be buried in a Jewish burial ground, in 1908, even though his 'apostasy' was known to the Jews. According to some sources, however, he had baptized himself in a Sabbath *mikve*, immersing himself in the name of Jesus.[27]

Moody merely writes that Rabinowitz had a very interesting conversation with Lichtenstein, but goes into no details.[28] In a letter to H. Müller of 18/30 October 1891 Rabinowitz says, however, that they had met at Moody's house on two occasions, and he conveys that he was critical about Lichtenstein's view of Christianity. Strange though it is to see them used by Rabinowitz himself, he here uses similar expressions in his criticism of Lichtenstein to those others might use against himself. Through his conversations and by reading Lichtenstein's booklet *Judaism and Christianity* he reached the conclusion that Lichtenstein had not taken the crucial step away from Judaism or realized that one cannot put a patch onto an old garment. In his letter to H. Müller Rabinowitz expressed the hope that Lichtenstein might be granted "a living and pure faith in the only begotten Son, Jesus".[29] Already in a letter of 22 February (r?) 1889 Rabinowitz wrote to Moody that Moody was to greet Lichtenstein and remind him of what was written in John 12:23-24 and Romans 6:4. In the letter, which was published in the annual report of the Free Church of Scotland, Rabinowitz continued with some words clearly disapproving of Lichtenstein's failure to get baptized. "If Rabbi Lichtenstein verily loves his people Israel... let him be baptized." By getting baptized he will set a good example. "In general, the Jews are not standing in need of theology learning by their rabbis, but of good examples", Rabinowitz writes.[30]

We shall not here assess how great the gap actually was between Isak Lichtenstein and Rabinowitz. For his own part, Rabinowitz felt that there was a gap - and expressed this.

While Rabinowitz and his wife were satisfied with a three-day stay in Budapest, their daughter Rachel was left there to find out about the work of the Free Church of Scotland there. She returned to Kishinev at Christmas the same year.[31]

Third visit to England and Scotland 1893

After holding Christmastide services in Kishinev, Rabinowitz set out again for England and Scotland at the beginning of 1893.[32] His stay was of short duration, no more than two weeks, for in a letter of 13/25 January he reveals that he was then back in Kishinev.[33] Besides negotiating with the London Council, he spoke at meetings in Scotland. The report of these says that this time Rabinowitz spoke without an interpreter, i.e. in English.[34] This may be taken as a consequence of personal obstinacy, of which Lhotzky gives a brilliant description. Once he wanted to help Rabinowitz with an English letter. But "with a superior smile the Jew looked at me. 'Believe me, I shall finish the letter all by myself. I will read and understand any letter, when it interests me. I only need a little time!'"[35] But not everyone was as enthusiastic about Rabinowitz's proficiency in English. His speaking in English in Scotland in 1896 is described as a failure in the magazine of the Free Church.[36] In his address he often stumbled over the words, and finally he handed the manuscript over to S. Wilkinson, who read out the last part of the address. However, the very brief visit in January 1893 was only part of his travels abroad that year. Later he made a journey to America.

The American journey

In the summer of 1893 Rabinowitz spent 35 days in America.[37] The comparatively brief comments about the journey in the European mission magazines, say that the purpose of the journey was to preach to Jews at the World Exposition in Chicago.[38] The London Council was said to have booked Rabinowitz for this, partly at the invitation of the well-known evangelist Dwight L. Moody.[39] Rabinowitz preached for instance to 400 Jews at the Jewish mission of the Methodist clergyman Gaebelein in New York.[40] In September 1895 Gaebelein visited Kishinev (see Chapter 17). In America Rabinowitz composed a letter in Hebrew, which was translated into English and issued in Chicago and New York.[41]

Oddly enough Rabinowitz dissociated himself from the view that he went to America with the intention of preaching to his brethren there. He did this in a letter written to J. Wilkinson in autumn 1893.[42] In this he wrote that just as he had regarded it at one time as his duty to go to Palestine (1882), so he now also considered it his duty to go to America; he wished to see how his brethren were faring, since it was a grievous fact that so many had had to leave Russia to seek a new life in foreign parts. The picture he draws of the Jews' situation in America, is exceedingly unfavourable. Some have admitted that for instance they lose their influence over their children in the new country. And others have said: "It was much better to be persecuted as true Jews in Europe than to live without God in America."

Particularly remarkable is his criticism of those Jews who do indeed gather in the mission halls on the Sabbath, but who have no true faith. He makes a strong assault on the mission organisations and their reports boasting of 1000 Jews coming along every Sabbath, but without satisfactory proclamation. He writes:

> I did not meet one among thousands who through Moses and the prophets knew that Christ had to suffer and afterwards enter into glory, or that Jesus Christ died for our sins according to the Scriptures, or that he was buried and rose again on the third day according to the Scriptures.

In 1882 Rabinowitz had been disappointed in his Zionist expectations; now he returned from America disappointed in 1893. If we take his words at face value, it was not enough to gather thousands of Jews into Christian mission halls, if the proclamation of Jesus did not spring from the Scriptures and if the central point was not the forgiveness of sins through Jesus' death and resurrection. His criticism of other Hebrew Christians had also found expression when he met Isak Lichtenstein in Budapest in 1891 (see above).

On the other hand the Rev. A.J. Gordon was encouraged by his - chance - meeting with Rabinowitz in Chicago. When Rabinowitz expounded the Psalms at the morning and evening devotions, he showed that he was imbued with both the letter and spirit of the Hebrew Scriptures; one could imagine that he was Isaiah or one of the prophets of the old covenant, wrote Gordon. In an exposition of Zechariah 12:10 he played with the Hebrew letters in a Kabbalistic manner - a sign that Rabinowitz had not completely left such things behind. Gordon got Rabinowitz to give his opinion of the inspiration of the Bible, for instance. It is God's Word, he said, adding that when he preached he said to people: "Listen in silence to what the Lord will say." Compared with Homer and Shakespeare the inspiration of the Bible is not merely "a matter of degree, but of kind".[43]

Fourth journey to England 1893

The trip to America presumably started from England, so that he probably paid a short visit there on the way out and on the way back. At least he calls his visit to England in 1896 his fifth visit.[44] If that is correct, then the visit en route to America must be his fourth visit to England.

Cancellation of a trip to Germany in 1895

On 6-8 June 1895 a conference was held at the Institutum Judaicum Delitzschianum in Leipzig with many key persons in the Jewish missions of the time participating.[45] Rabinowitz had been invited to give an address on the right attitude of Christian Jews to the Law. Rabinowitz declined on the grounds that his health was not up to it.[46] But from Kishinev came Faltin, who had been invited to speak about whether the setting-up of Hebrew Christian congregations should be the aim of the mission. In his address it would seem that Faltin managed to avoid mentioning Rabinowitz's name! That this was no co-incidence may be seen from the fact that a number of other people who were the fruit of Faltin's work in Kishinev did get a mention. In the debate which followed A. Wiegand's lecture on the topic intended for Rabinowitz, G. Dalman stepped forward and read out a couple of sections of a work which Rabinowitz had written and sent to Dalman, i.e. the booklet: "What is an Israelite of the New Covenant?" In this, Rabinowitz lays down in strong terms that there is no difference between the "believing Jew and Gentile", i.e between a Hebrew Christian and a Gentile Christian. Any Jew who believes in Jesus Christ is completely free as regards the Law, "free from the heavy slave service according to the old essence of the letter" (see further Chapter 8).

It was a pity for the debate at this international conference that Rabinowitz could not take part. Rabbi Isak Lichtenstein was there, Dean Faltin from Kishinev was there. One can hardly help wondering whether health was the sole reason for Rabinowitz declining to attend. Although not present, his voice was heard - but not through Faltin, as far as we can judge.

Fifth and last journey to England and Scotland 1896

If he kept to his itinerary, Rabinowitz arrived in London on 18 May 1896, but immediately travelled on to Scotland with his daughter Rachel, who accompanied him on this journey.[47] He spoke at the General Assembly of the Free Church of Scotland on 22 May. In that connection, a sum of money was voted for his important work in Kishinev (see Chapter 13).[48] But he also spoke to the General Assembly of the Church of Scotland on 23 May.[49] As on his third journey in 1893, he spoke in English (see third journey).

At the beginning of June 1896 Rabinowitz was back in London, where he spent the rest of the month. Under the auspices of the Mildmay Mission he spoke at various events. When mentioning this visit, the magazine of the Mildmay Mission says that funds had declined.[50]

The journey home was via Berlin, where Rabinowitz and his daughter Rachel stopped off to see the Berlin exhibition.[51] This was also offering products from the new Jewish colonies in Palestine. In a letter Rabinowitz waxes ironical that Jewish products are there, when German anti-Semites and Berlin atheists wish to see the Jewish nation altogether rooted out. Likewise he cannot suppress his contempt that the stand with goods from Palestine was placed in the Cairo section.[52]

When he saw a cake of soap bearing the word "Yerushelaim" in Hebrew characters, he quoted aloud from Jer.2:22: "Though thou take thee much soap, yet thine iniquity is marked before me." When people heard this, they wanted to know who he was. He took the chance to witness about Jesus.

Before going back to Kishinev, he broke his journey in Warsaw, where he also had opportunity to witness to a grocer's family. Although Rabinowitz did not in general hold 'open-air meetings' in Kishinev or go to the market places to preach the gospel, these glimpses do reveal that on occasion he did such things. But no generalisations should be made. The usual thing in Kishinev was that he invited others in to services in his hall.

The last journey to Meran in the Tyrol in 1899

On 6 March Rabinowitz wrote to Samuel Wilkinson that he had been ill and was still very weak.[53] Three doctors had recommended him to recuperate for a while at Meran in the Tyrol, where he was going to set off the following day. He returned from the Tyrol on 22 April, shortly before Passover. His illness grew worse, and he was taken to Odessa, where he died at a sanatorium on 17 May 1899.[54] The following day his coffin was taken to Kishinev, where he was buried (see also Chapter 18).

Chapter 15

METHODS AND MAIN TASKS IN KISHINEV

Rabinowitz's ministry took place in Kishinev, although its effects were felt far and wide. It is therefore disingenuous to say that "Rabinowitz traveled in Eastern Europe and Russia",[1] the implication being that this was to preach. In the last couple of years of his life he was devising plans for building an evangelisation train. If this project had got off the ground, it would have taken him far around Russia (see on this Chapter 17).

When visiting England in autumn 1889 he described his own position. On the basis of some information which Lhotzky gave at the end of 1890 about Rabinowitz's procedure, as well as scattered notices elsewhere, we can reach conclusions about the character and methods of his work.

For the sake of clarity it may be useful first to summarize what Lhotzky brings out in 1890.

Lhotzky about Rabinowitz's methods of work

Lhotzky directs attention to Rabinowitz's methods and points out that they are not merely different from those of ordinary missionaries to Jews, but in contrast to them. As Rabinowitz has no permission from the authorities to administer baptism, he has no other possibilities than to preach about Christ. He invites Jews to his prayer-house, where he preaches the Word, but does not give baptismal instruction. But he makes no use of any "assertively outreaching, missionizing" method, and mentions four points about this:

- Rabinowitz does not go into tea houses and public premises to preach the gospel;

- he does not go on preaching-trips to other places, nor does he send out colporteurs;

- letters received which contain other matters that do not concern questions of salvation are not answered, at best a New Testament may be sent;

- he does not write annual reports or public articles.[2]

An objective assessment of these claims of Lhotzky's must however be balanced with information found in primary sources. We may also ask whether Rabinowitz's methods were not to some extent conditioned by the restrictions of the authorities rather than his principles of work. The limits that were set must also be seen in the light of the personal priorities and limited capacity to which anyone is subject. Finally we must ask whether

Rabinowitz did not compensate in another way for what he did not do, and whether parts of his ministry in the 1890s do not contradict Lhotzky's assertions. If so, there may have been a development in his principles.

Lhotzky's assertion that Rabinowitz did not seek out Jews in public premises but invited them to come to services, is largely correct, as also is his assertion that Rabinowitz did not go on preaching-trips or send out colporteurs. Actually there are examples of Rabinowitz taking advantage of public places to testify when this was possible, as in Berlin (see Chapter 14). In 1894, for instance, Rabinowitz with his son John visited some poor Jews who came to his services. When the news spread that Rabinowitz was visiting, a flock of Jews from the neighbourhood soon gathered, and he took the opportunity to preach the gospel. In the summer of 1894 he travelled with his sons Peter and John to Kerson, Kiev, and Kremenchuk "to speak about Jesus Christ and distribute sermons and tracts to his brethren", as Le Réveil d'Israël says.[3] This information had been culled from the 1894 annual report of the London Council for Rabinowitz; but it was evidently rebutted by a Russian newspaper, which alleged that it was not a journey of evangelization but a holiday trip. To this Krüger riposted that the two purposes might well be combined.[4] In this context it is not without interest that in a letter to Krüger Rabinowitz thanks him for the consolation he found in this particular article in Le Réveil d'Israël.[5] It is beyond dispute that Rabinowitz desired to spread his work out to other places than Kishinev. An attempt was made at the start of the 1890s, when Feinsilber was sent off to Odessa to commence a work there.[6] But it does not seem that the permission of the authorities was obtained to hold public meetings (see below).

The plans for an evangelization train prove that at the end of the 1890s Rabinowitz had no objection in principle to "preaching-trips", but indeed wanted them. To S. Wilkinson he had stressed that he wanted to get started on a more "aggressive testimony" in Russia than the regular preaching in Kishinev (see further Chapter 17).[7] Nevertheless Lhotzky's main contention remains correct that Rabinowitz's activity primarily took place in Kishinev and in his prayer-hall. Rabinowitz asked people to come in rather than going out to them himself. In 1896 P. Wolff wrote from Kishinev that Rabinowitz lacked the strength to go to the Jews in their homes, because of his crippled leg.[8] But that is hardly the full explanation, for it did not stop him going on a number of journeys! Perhaps Wolff comes closer to the true explanation when he says that Rabinowitz had been given a great gift for preaching, "but he does not particularly have the gift of conversing with the Jews."[9]

In some periods Rabinowitz received many letters (see below). The fact that he did not reply to them all but sorted them out after assessing their contents, shows that he tried to give a higher priority to other sides of his work. We shall summarize below what Rabinowitz himself had to say about the content of the letters received up to 1889.

Lhotzky's assertion that Rabinowitz did not write annual reports or public articles is not particularly illuminating. It gives an erroneous picture of Rabinowitz's expansive force as regards publicity around his work. From his visit to Kishinev in 1887 E.H. Leitner tells that Rabinowitz did not want to concern himself much with literary work or with reports, which would divert him from the work which required his full attention.[10] But there was time for some written work (see below). In various ways he compensated for not writing reports. Partly he fed others, e.g. the London Council for Rabinowitz, with information which the Council pieced together into a report. Partly he wrote letters to overseas missionary organisations and to individuals. The contrast which Lhotzky tries to make between the reports of missionaries to the Jews and Rabinowitz's lack of these is therefore a figment. His letters are filled with information about his activities, which for a large part fulfil the same function as the reports and news from the missionaries. But he did as a rule refuse to give details of people's conversion experiences, but there were exceptions. He also refrained from putting exact numbers on how many had been converted through his work.

Unlike 'missionaries', he was unable to enter any numbers under the heading "number baptized". But in his letters he was able to give detailed information about his view of his opponents, e.g. Faltin. There is nothing to suggest that he objected to the publication of such details. It may also be added that his co-workers, e.g. R.F. Feinsilber, were in 1890-1891 assigned the task of informing foreign mission-leaders about Rabinowitz's work.[11] There can be no question that Rabinowitz wanted this PR activity. And finally, through other people's reports Rabinowitz had achieved a fame which far outdid that which missionaries to the Jews enjoyed.

Lhotzky is partly right in saying that Rabinowitz did not write public articles. But on this point no contrast can be drawn with ordinary Jewish missionaries. And the whole matter needs careful assessment. In foreign mission magazines a number of his letters performed the role of public articles; as also did reports of his addresses and translated sermons or extracts from them which were printed abroad. In 1896 for instance he promised the Mildmay Mission that he would occasionally supply their magazine with articles.[12] This promise was kept only to a slight extent, although in the last years of his life there are a few examples of his writing articles specially intended for foreign readers.[13] In Russia his tracts and printed sermons made up for the lack of public articles, although there were some of these. When occasion offered, he spoke up in various ways: in 1888 for instance he sent his congratulations to the Russian Church on the celebration of the ninth centenary of the introduction of Christianity. An extract from this was published in English.[14] In 1893 he gave an interview to Lerner (see Chapter 12); in 1898 he gave information about a project for train evangelization to a reporter from one of the leading Russian newspapers.[15] And in the mid

1890s he had an item published in a monthly called Bratskoe Pomosh when his work was being discussed in it, and so on.[16]

So Lhotzky's assertion has to be modified on a number of counts. It is correct that Rabinowitz's usual method was to invite people to listen to and read what he had to proclaim. In general he did not reach out to Jews where they were in order to preach to them there, as did a number of missionaries to Jews. Although Lhotzky indicates Rabinowitz's general practice correctly, we must query the way he suggests a profound contrast between Rabinowitz and missionaries to the Jews in general. Already in 1889 Rabinowitz was saying in London that he would rejoice if, in "God's way and time", Kishinev should become the central place from which the gospel might go forth to districts with Jews not yet reached with the gospel.[17] In other words it was not his principles of work as such which hindered a more outgoing work than that done in Kishinev. Thus the train evangelisation project was not a completely new departure in Rabinowitz's working-principles in the mid 1890s. It was rather an expression of a realisation that the work in Kishinev did not, as it did before, require all his energy - perhaps too an expression of disappointment that progress was so slow (see below).

It may be noted that Rabinowitz did not wish to be regarded as a 'missionary'.[18] That smacked too much of Gentile Christianity. But whatever the methods to which he particularly gave priority, he acknowledged the justification of other people's methods. In 1897 he asserted to S. Wilkinson that no particular mission was perfect, although he found there was good in the methods of each. "When the sun's rays pass through a prism," he said, "the light is resolved into its seven colors. Each color is beautiful in itself but perfection is only found in the blending of the whole."[19] In this connection it is also of significance that it was on Rabinowitz's recommendation that his son-in-law Joseph Axelrud was employed by the Mildmay Mission to distribute tracts and Bible portions, first in Odessa (1892); later he travelled around south-western Russia. But his employment did not last long, as he died of cholera in October 1893.[20] Shortly before, he had edited a book of sermons by and articles about the work of his father-in-law. It was published in Russian (Gabe states that he read it in Yiddish).[21]

After assessing Lhotzky's main thesis, we shall now see how Rabinowitz described his own position when he was in London in 1889. It was on this occasion he told the story about the castaways - standing on the rock Jesus - to whom he "signalled" the gospel (see Introduction).

Rabinowitz about himself in 1889

In addresses in London Rabinowitz took stock of his work in the period between his first and second visits to England (1886/1887-1889).[22] He emphasized that his task was to preach at the place in Kishinev where he held services, and to distribute the printed sermons and tracts. In this way he was obeying the command given by the prophet: "Cry aloud, spare not, lift up thy voice like a trumpet, and shew my people their transgression, and the house of Jacob their sins" (Is. 58:1).

He admitted that it was difficult to answer all the many letters he received, although he did his best. As regards the contents, he mentioned a couple of examples. Some related that they had followed his example and begun to witness in other towns. Others wrote about their sufferings for Christ's sake and asked whether he was able to help them. Others again, who were now "99% dead" expressed the wish to spend the rest of their lives among believing brethren. Many letters came from young men who believed; their parents were preventing them from professing Christ, and they asked Rabinowitz to come and take them away with him. There were also many - particularly teachers - who asked for New Testaments and sermons in order "to learn about Jesus Christ and teach others." Baptized Jews enquired how they could join his movement and become one with it. Others who had come to faith asked whether he had permission to baptize them, or which church they should go to. To this Rabinowitz would reply that he could only act like someone who saw a house on fire. He would shout, "Save yourselves, save yourselves." Then Rabinowitz quoted the words of Peter, "Save yourselves from this untoward generation" (Acts 2:40). For "there is none other name under heaven given among men, whereby we can be saved" (Acts 4:12).

Rabinowitz also touched upon the way other people regarded him and his work, mentioning three points of view. Some looked upon his as a fool for believing in the Messiah. Others adopted a neutral position, regarding him as a reformer doing useful work among his brethren. And others again saw him as wanting to start a new church. The first group wrote absurd tales about him in the newspapers; the second gave him advice as to various reforms; and the third group had showed him some interest, but concluded that his attempt would fail and the new church soon disappear.

For his part Rabinowitz had the following comments to make about these three views:

The Jews were discovering that he was not a fool. He claimed that prominent Jewish rabbis confided in him in a way they would not do if he were a fool.

Those who regarded him as "a mere reformer" had realized that he looked to the Bible alone for support, from Genesis to Revelation. He would not put reason in first place, but put his complete trust in God's Word.

Finally, those who thought he wished to form a new church had come to realize "that the Jews who come and hear me preach the Gospel, and who accept the Gospel of Christ, remain Jews still as much as they were formerly."

Rabinowitz also claimed that Jews and Christians no longer looked upon the Messianic movement as just a curiosity to be placed in some museum. "They have found out that the Jew may receive Christ and remain a Jew still, even as the Englishman, Frenchman, or German receives Christ and remains an Englishman, Frenchman, or German as before."

Finally Rabinowitz expressed his opinion of the cause of the Jews not seeking the Lord. Their "self-glory" had found expression in three points. Firstly, they claimed they were God's children and had Abraham as father, which John the Baptist and Jesus rebutted. Secondly, since the destruction of Jerusalem they had gloried in being wise men, and in the Talmud, the Mishna, and the Torah. "Who can keep the Sabbath like us? Who will fast like us?" Recently this glorying had been replaced by glory in being foremost in commerce, industry, banking, and science, which is the third error of their self-glory. But Israel's true glory must be Jesus "the Fulfiller of the law, the Son of David, the Son of Abraham, and the Son of God."

Although in 1889 Rabinowitz was striking an optimistic note in his addresses about the views of those around on his work, in other contexts he expressed the view that the work was not proceeding as rapidly as he might wish.[23] Not only did he say this to a visitor in 1888, but in 1892 two Norwegians were asked to greet those at home and say that the work was going "slowly, slowly" (see Chapter 11).

A discussion of Rabinowitz's methods leads on to the question of whether he succeeded in attaching fellow-labourers to the work in Kishinev.

Rabinowitz's co-workers

Apparently only for one single - brief - period was it possible to attach a regular co-worker to Rabinowitz's ministry. The reasons for this are hardly to be sought in Rabinowitz alone, but in the outward political circumstances and the peculiar status of the Messianic movement. At any rate there is evidence that Rabinowitz had the will to attach fellow-labourers to his work.

He consulted Professor Delitzsch about setting up a congregational school in March 1885.[24] Through Delitzsch, Karl Joseph Gottlieb, who was on the staff of the Scottish Free Church's work in Prague, was asked to serve as a teacher,[25] which he declared himself willing to do.[26] The school was to be housed on the ground floor of the house in which Rabinowitz held his first services. In Pentecost week 1885 Lhotzky reported that it was expected to be possible to open the school that summer.[27] But it remained on the drawing-board; the permission of the authorities was not forthcoming.

While on a visit to St Petersburg in early 1887, Rabinowitz found a man who could assist him. "He is about fifty years of age, and was brought to Christ through the movement in Russia. He is known to Prof. Delitzsch, speaks Hebrew and Russian, and is familiar with the Talmud and the Kabbalah," wrote Rabinowitz.[28] But it would seem that this unnamed person did not join the work.

The man who did join the work was R.F. Feinsilber, a Jew who had come to faith through Rabinowitz's work.[29] From the spring of 1890 and into 1891 he wrote for instance on Rabinowitz's behalf about the work in Kishinev (see above). It is possible that the optimism around the building of Somerville Memorial Hall was also a factor in this appointment. In autumn 1890 the London Council for Rabinowitz concurred in the employment of Feinsilber.[30] He was also included in the council's budget in 1891.[31] Later that year he was sent to Odessa to take up the movement's work there (see above). He was later linked with The Hebrew Christian Testimony to Israel.[32] In 1903 he figured in this society's deliberations about sending him to Kishinev to resume Rabinowitz's work (see further Chapter 19).

In various ways Rabinowitz was assisted by his children, particularly his youngest daughter Rachel (see Chapter 14) and by his eldest son Vladimir (see Chapter 17). Most probably he also received help from the group around him in e.g. operating the little printing-press which, in connection with the inauguration of Somerville Hall, was presented by the Free Church in Edinburgh - a press which did work, unlike the one sent from England in 1887, which Rabinowitz returned, partly because the authorities demanded duty on it, partly because he was advised that such a machine could not work in the warm climate of Bessarabia.[33] The machine he got from Edinburgh did work. Besides tracts probably also the pewsheets that were issued at the services, giving the Scripture passages, were printed on it. The Christmas and New Year cards he sent were doubtless also produced on it.

Neither in 1897, when S. Wilkinson brought up the subject of a successor, nor in his will was Rabinowitz able to point to a successor (see further Chapter 18).

Rabinowitz's writings

Already in 1887 Rabinowitz had come to terms with the fact that the work of forming a Messianic movement did not make possible a literary production of any size. He aimed at getting some of his sermons printed, and some small tracts and leaflets. In 1885 Delitzsch advised him not to have too many different sermons printed. The fewer and choicer they were, the better![34] Some booklets were also written. In his final years he was also engaged as a Bible-translator (see Chapter 17).

Brief mentions of the most important works have been made in the narrative and will not be repeated here. The bibliography at the end of the book gives an impression of the total literary production. As far as tracts and published sermons are concerned, the production is greater than is listed in the bibliography.

In its report for 1890, the London Council for Rabinowitz says that around 27,000 copies of Rabinowitz's sermons and tracts had been printed and distributed in Hebrew and Yiddish[35] - and perhaps Russian should be added.[36] When visiting London in 1889 he was given a promise by the Religious Tract Society that they would in future support him by publishing sermons.[37]

Rabinowitz's writings were not primarily intended for Gentile Christian readers. They could of course use the works translated into English, German etc. to orient themselves, but these translations were mainly intended for Jews who might understand these languages best. There is definite evidence that some people were marked for life by reading these writings (see Chapter 19). Others found their ideas, which were similar to Rabinowitz's, confirmed by them, for instance Jakob Zebi Scheinmann in Siberia, who corresponded with Rabinowitz.[38] The works were also read aloud in circles outside Kishinev, where groups regarding themselves as Israelites of the New Covenant had been established. For instance, a reader of Berith Am - Dalman's periodical in Yiddish - mentions that one Christmas Day he had read aloud Rabinowitz's sermon of 24 December 1895.[39] A sermon preached on 16 June (r) 1890, which was published in German, even found its way onto the shelves of the library of the Jewish congregation in Berlin, as is revealed by the stamp-mark in the copy now in the National Library in Jerusalem.

To sum up

Rabinowitz's writing-activity was largely an outflow of his preaching-activity. He invested time in getting his sermons printed and distributed, which he regarded as one of his main tasks. Also, the New Testament in Hebrew, Yiddish, and Russian was channelled through his work. By those who heard his sermons and were favourably disposed to them he was sought out as a counsellor, and for some periods at least Bible-readings were held. At Pentecost 1885 for instance, Lhotzky wrote from Kishinev that Rabinowitz was holding Bible-readings and was occupied with personal conversations with those who called upon him.[40] At the beginning of 1888 Rabinowitz wrote that since the onset of winter he had been running a Bible-class in his house attended by both men and women desiring to be taught out of the New Testament about the way of salvation.[41] In 1891 he recounted that Bible-readings were being held every Tuesday.[42]

From those who read his writings, he received letters which he tried to answer as far as possible. Also, he carried on an extensive correspondence with foreign missionary organisations and individuals. After setting out his theological principles in 1884, he spent considerable energy on applications to and negotiations with the authorities, on the conflict with Faltin, and on initiating the building of Somerville Memorial Hall (1890). In the last years of his life he spent a couple of hours each day revising the Yiddish New Testament.

Throughout the years, however, his work was first and foremost marked by his being a preacher who each Sabbath as well as at Christian and Jewish festivals preached sermons in Kishinev - interrupted only by his journeys abroad.

Chapter 16

ONE OF RABINOWITZ'S SERMONS

All Christian observers expressed themselves favourably about Rabinowitz's abilities as a preacher. This was true even of those whose general attitude was critical of his Jewish theology, his distinctive views, and his efforts to form an independent Messianic congregation. We have noted such testimonies as our narrative proceeded.

Choosing to present just one sermon instead of making a minute analysis of the whole corpus of sermons, means that we are not able to cover all aspects of Rabinowitz the preacher. But this Good Friday sermon, preached in April 1891, may give some impression of the content of his sermons, and also of his heart's yearning to communicate with his "brethren". Professor Strack translated it from Russian into German; it was later translated into Norwegian.[1]

Sermon on Good Friday 1891

Psalm 69:7: "Because for thy sake I have borne reproach; shame hath covered my face."

Matt. 27:29: "... and they bowed the knee before him, and mocked him, saying, Hail, King of the Jews!"

Dearly beloved children of Israel! Let us together magnify the eternal God of Israel, who changes times and seasons, and let us in thankful prayer draw nigh unto Him who according to His goodness has ordained the changing of the times. Through many centuries the Jews have in this week, the week before the holy Passover, lived in great disquiet. For they were afraid through a word or an act of attracting the anger of the Christians, whose hostility was particularly easy to arouse at this season, because the fathers of the Jews had before Passover handed Jesus Christ over to be scourged and crucified.

This anger from the Christians cost the Jews much blood, and it is not surprising that the Jews on their part also showed their resentment when this week approached, indeed even at the slightest reminder of the bloodstained story of Jesus of Nazareth, whom the whole Christian world regards as Christ, the Son of the living God.

To the Jews it was painful to think that this story had become a perpetual heritage to almost the whole world, to all peoples. In this way this important week was equally difficult for both parties. But thanks be to God, He has now by his goodness and love given us, the children of Israel, leave to come together in our sanctuary in this great week, on the day which reminds us of the crucifixion of Jesus Christ. And like all true Christians we can through His holy name and the books of the Old and New Covenants come to know this eternal, divine drama, this fearful undeserved death, which the Redeemer of the world took upon himself in love and humility.

Yea in truth, boundless is our gratitude towards the heavenly Father who gave us all, Jews and other peoples, the opportunity for us now, when human intellect is making rapid progress, and when a fresh flowering of science and art is taking place, to recognize and see in the mocked and crucified Jesus the same as the devout and righteous Simeon saw in Him when he saw the child on his mother's lap, i.e. the salvation which God had prepared before the face of all people, a light to lighten the Gentiles, and the glory of His people Israel (Luke 2:31-32).

That which the righteous Simeon's old eye viewed in the power of the Holy Spirit, neither the proud Jews, nor the ignorant and bold Romans were capable of seeing. For the head of the Jewish people, the high priest Caiaphas, it was easy to decide upon Jesus' death, when he said, "... it is expedient for us, that one man should die for the people, and that the whole nation perish not." (John 11:50). It could not occur to him that this very same Jesus was the only person to show himself as Redeemer not only for the sins of the Jewish people, but for those of all humanity. About this the prophet foretold, "he bare the sin of many" (Is. 53:12). For the head of the Gentiles, the proconsul Pilate in Jerusalem, it was not difficult either to wax merry over Jesus and hand him over to the Jews with these words: "Behold the man!" (John 19:5). He could have no inkling that men only become men in the full sense of the word, when the picture of the God-Man Jesus is perpetually before their eyes and they follow unswervingly in his footsteps.

Not until later did the regenerate of the Gentiles enter more fully into the words: "Behold the man!" - words which were uttered by their former head. And many of the children of Israel also began to listen to the words, "it is expedient for us that one man should die for the people, and that the whole nation perish not."

Today, the day which reminds us of the sufferings and the death which Jesus Christ has taken upon himself but which are due to the sins of Jews and Gentiles, we must unite with all men who sincerely believe that the precious and holy blood of the Son of God Jesus cleanses all of us who are sinners, Jews and Gentiles. On our knees we must pray to God the Father:

- that he may open our eyes more and more so we may see in Jesus Christ the salvation he has prepared for all peoples, the redemption which cleanses every believer from sins.

- that he may pour out his Holy Spirit upon us all and enable us, Jews and Gentiles, to understand that Jesus Christ has not come into the world as a man to sow strife and hatred among men, and also enable us to acknowledge the holy words of the apostle Paul: "For he is our peace, who hath made both one, and hath broken down the middle wall of partition between us" (Eph. 2:14)

- and that he may help us all to put off the old man with its sins and death and become a completely new man by true faith in Jesus, about whom the Holy Spirit spoke through the lips of Pilate: "Behold the man!"

With amazement and awe we stand silent before the deep and boundless faith which the holy evangelists Matthew, Mark, Luke and John have in Jesus Christ as the Messiah, the Son of David, the King of the Jews. We must bear in mind that all four Gospels were written during the first century after the birth, earthly life, death, and resurrection of the Redeemer. It was then that folk in the higher classes of society looked with contempt upon such four small books telling about some crucified Jew Jesus. It was when people were called insane and were mocked if they openly ventured to own to their faith in Jesus, the Son of the living God, who rose from the dead and ascended to heaven as an eternal king over the house of Jacob. In such circumstances one might imagine that the evangelists would have rather concerned themselves with the parables and the teaching which distinguished the life of Christ before He was delivered into the hands of the Jews. But we see that they pay more attention and give more space to his sufferings, and that they take pains to give posterity a full description of the mockery to which He was exposed before the crucifixion and while He was nailed to the cross.

If for a moment we go along with the Talmudists' idea that the evangelists were base deceivers who through various fables endeavoured to make an impression on the simple-minded masses in order to win them over, then of necessity the question presents itself: why did they not keep quiet about the ignominious death and instead glory in accounts of the courageous and heroic ending to His life? The purpose of the evangelists was evidently quite different.

In their depiction of the passion of Jesus they did not lay the colours on thick so as to bring tears to the eyes and compassion to the hearts. They did not pour out their grief in tear-stained lamentations, as Jeremiah had done at the destruction of the temple in Jerusalem. We hear neither groaning nor sighs from them occasioned by the Redeemer's death. They very well knew his wish that people should not weep over him (Luke 23:28). No, they wrote their Gospels about the abasement and sufferings of Jesus with a divine, sublime, heavenly smile on their faces, with the laughter which the psalmist speaks of: "He that sitteth in the heavens shall laugh" (Ps. 2:4). Their intention was that men's ignorance, wretchedness, and blindness should emerge the clearer, so men might have a sense that their power and willing meant nothing, and that God's will is brought about without their recognition, and that they only serve as instruments in His hand, and that they only carry out what He has foreordained, even though they think they are acting according to their own will.

The evangelists narrate in detail how Jesus was mocked and put to shame. At the same time they give a full account of the great work which it has pleased God to accomplish through them and with those who reproached him as channels.

As we now after 1800 years read about the ignominy to which the Redeemer was exposed, we will put to the sons of the nineteenth century the question: Who was it who most quickly understood the great mission of Jesus of Nazareth? Was it the thousands of Jews, Pharisees and Scribes, Sadducees and Roman soldiers who made merry about Him and shouted: "Crucify him!"? Or was it the simple-minded, ordinary fisherfolk who in truth believed in Jesus that He - the Son of the living God, the Saviour of the world, and the eternal Son of David - that He was the King of the Jews? Did not the crown of thorns that covered his head in mockery become the most precious of all the world's crowns? Is it not true that his enemies' scornful bowing of the knee has been turned into millions of people devoutly bowing the knee to him?

The time has also come to be convinced that the mocking words of Christ's enemies: "Hail, king of the Jews!" in reality may easily be fulfilled. For the Jews may even yet arise and in accordance with God's will - like other peoples - become a living nation; this will be when they come to faith in the Messiah of their people and all peoples, Jesus of Nazareth - the King of the Jews.

What a warm and mighty faith, what a living and mighty trust filled the hearts of the evangelists, so that they were able to write down all the sufferings and insults which their Messiah had been exposed to by his contemporaries! From where, one may ask, did the disciples of Jesus get such faith and deep conviction that the mocked and crucified Jesus really was the Lord and King of the world? I am not speaking of the way in which the confidence of some simple-minded, pious Jews was fulfilled. But I am asking: from where did they themselves obtain this confidence? It is vain to seek the answer in historical or scholarly data. We find the answer in the evangelist himself, in Luke 24:25-30. He recounts that after His resurrection from the dead He called two of his disciples slow of heart for not understanding from all the holy scriptures of the prophets that this had been foretold of Him, and that Christ had to suffer and then enter into His glory.

So, the Holy Scriptures - they are the source of their faith! The persevering reading of these books inspired by God opened their eyes and helped them to see in all Christ's sufferings His infinite and unfading glory. These books, of which Jesus said that not one jot of them should pass away, also gave them the faith which convinced and shall convince the whole world.

Dearly beloved brethren! I believe firmly and fully that you too, on the basis of Psalm 69, which we have read and which the Redeemer undoubtedly read to his disciples, are capable of arriving at the conviction that the scorned and crucified Jesus is the Christ, the glorified King of the Jews, who sits at His Father's right hand, until everything - in heaven and on earth - is subjected to Him and through Him reconciled to God the Father.

So pray to our heavenly Father that He will help you to understand the words with which the holy psalmist was imbued by the Spirit: "... They that hate me without a cause are more than the hairs of mine head: I am become a stranger unto my brethren ... the reproaches of them that reproached thee are fallen upon me ... I looked for some to take pity, but there was none ... They gave me also gall for my meat; and in my thirst they gave me vinegar to drink ... But I am poor and sorrowful: let thy salvation, O God, set me up on high ...For God will save Zion."

You must impress upon your memories these significant words, "God will save Zion," and you must understand that all the sufferings of Jesus had this intent that "your heart shall live that seek God". A new heaven and a new earth will be created - "Let the heaven and earth praise him" - and the three concepts: God, salvation, and Zion, will be transformed into an indissoluble whole.

Jesus showed that it was according to the Father's will that He bore the reproach. But the heavenly Father also showed that He fulfilled His Son's prayer: "Let not those that seek thee be confounded for my sake, O God of Israel" (Ps. 69:6). Be not ashamed of the crucified Jesus! Believe that by God He has been given power to see the founding of the new Jerusalem, and that the promise will be fulfilled: "They that love his name shall dwell therein" (Ps. 69:36). Amen.

Chapter 17

PROJECTS OF THE FINAL YEARS

During the last years of his life Rabinowitz was involved in various projects. We shall here pick out four of them. Each of them in its own way refutes Lhotzky's picture of Rabinowitz as a man who with a cunning smile pocketed money from foreign missions merely paying them back with some good mission stories for the societies' magazines (see Chapter 13). Right until his death Rabinowitz was occupied with work for Jesus and Israel - whether the projects were carried out or not. The reports also contradict Sh.L. Tsitron's assertion that in the time before his death Rabinowitz had fallen into a bitter darkness and profound depression and that he walked like a shadow,[1] and Steven J. Zipperstein's similar picture of Rabinowitz as "a largely forgotten and isolated figure who had fallen into a deep depression in the last years of his life".[2]

The first project we shall mention was completed. There is an interesting story behind it which has doubtless not been told before.

Rabinowitz and a prize assignment

At the large international conference on Jewish missions held in Leipzig in 1895, Rabinowitz had been invited to be a speaker, but had to decline (see Chapter 14).[3] The invitation itself implied a recognition of Rabinowitz's efforts. At the conference, one of the speakers was G. Dalman, who delivered an interesting lecture on the kind of literature that was wanted in the work of the Jewish missions.[4] He did not pull his punches in criticizing the existing literature, and many good proposals were made in the subsequent debate. The missionary M. Löwen of the Berlin Society gave a precise example of the sort of thing he wanted when he called for a book about the life of Jesus in Yiddish and German.[5] At the close, Professor Strack promised the assembly that he would announce a competition on this very subject.[6]

This promise was kept. At the beginning of 1896 the Institutum Judaicum in Berlin announced a competition with a prize for the best book in Yiddish dealing with the life and work of Jesus. When announcing the assignment, H.L. Strack mentioned that the following would be asked to adjudicate: A. Bernstein of London, Joseph Rabinowitz of Kishinev, and G. Dalman of Leipzig. If it should emerge that any of these three was unwilling to take on the job, possibly because he wanted to compete himself, then a substitute would be found, it was said.[7]

That Rabinowitz was asked to join the panel of adjudicators was in itself a recognition of his expertise in the area of Yiddish, the language in which he preached in Kishinev. But when the result of the competition was published, it turned out that only Bernstein and Dalman had adjudicated, and that Strack had made the final decision. So Rabinowitz was not on the judging committee.

Of the four who sent in entries, the winner was M. Löwen of the Berlin Society, interestingly enough the very person who had put forward the idea originally! His entry did indeed exceed the limit laid down of 2 or 4 printed sheets. The names of the three other competitors are not given. Each of their entries contained meritorious things, though Strack had to point out that they did not really meet the terms of the assignment.[8]

There may have been many and interesting reasons for Rabinowitz's refusal to be an adjudicator. But it is most probable that he declined so that he might enter for the competition himself! This is not just a wild surmise, but is demonstrably likely.

As far as can be deduced, Rabinowitz's entry for the competition was in all essentials identical with the book which A.C. Gaebelein published in English translation at the end of the 1890s, translated from Yiddish - as the title page says - and entitled: Jesus of Nazareth, the King of the Jews,[9] not "Jesus the Christian, King of the Jews," as Zipperstein gives the title, and hardly with "Yeshu" as name in the Yiddish version.[10] The title page of the English version also reveals that this had been "Abridged and Revised by A.C.G[aebelein]". It is of 32 small pages. It would only be possible to judge how much Gaebelein may have abridged it if we could compare it with the edition in Yiddish. Krüger mentions in his magazine that the Yiddish edition ran to 80 pages.[11] Here we must make do with looking at the contents of the English edition. It is not difficult to fit the contents of the book with the description of what the competition entry had to contain.

Besides an outline of the sources and the historical circumstances of his time, the entry had also to deal with the teaching of Jesus, and his attitude to the Old Testament was to be clearly shown. No exhaustive treatment of the miracles and miraculous birth of Jesus was wanted. The readers of the entry were to be given an impression of the adult Jesus through his teaching and ministry.

If we now compare this description of the contents of the competition assignment with Rabinowitz's book Jesus of Nazareth, the King of the Jews, it is not hard to see a connection. From page 3 Rabinowitz recounts the history of Israel focusing on Abraham, Moses, and David (see his story about the four wheels, Chapter 5). These "children of God" had always in their hearts and mouths the words of the great prophet Isaiah, "that a rod would spring out of the stem of Jesse, on whom the Spirit of the Lord would rest, the Spirit of wisdom and understanding, the Spirit of council [counsel?] and might, and that He would slay the wicked one with the breath of His mouth" (Is. 11:1-2).

Under the changing occupation powers, the Pharisees and Sadducees cultivated their own interests and had lost their faith in God's eternal promise to Abraham that his children would one day become a great nation. But, says Rabinowitz, at the time when Palestine was a province of the Roman Empire, God gave his people "two children". First John the Baptist, of the tribe of Levi and the house of Aaron, i.e. of priestly lineage, and then Jesus, of the tribe of Judah and the house of King David. "These two children have wrought a great change in human history."

From page 12 of the book there is an account of these "two children". Only briefly is the miraculous birth of Jesus narrated, reference being made to the account in John. One comment is made: "To describe the wonderful birth of the second child is as impossible for a man of blood and flesh as it is to describe the origin of the light, which Almighty God made to shine on the first day of the seven days of creation."

The childhood of Jesus is briefly mentioned, introduced with the words: "Over the childhood of Jesus, His youth and the greater part of His life rests Jehovah's cloud." From page 16 on some main points are brought out from the three and a half years of Jesus' teaching and miracles recounted in the Gospels, e.g. the raising of Lazarus.

The story of Jesus' life is told very traditionally and, judging by the English version, without the characteristic stories which Rabinowitz was usually renowned for spicing his sermons with. The focus is on the events in the life of Jesus like his baptism, temptation in the wilderness, the address in the synagogue in Nazareth, Peter's confession at Caesarea Philippi, the transfiguration, and the last week in Jerusalem.

Rabinowitz maintains that at first Jesus was taken by his contemporaries to be a "divine teacher", but rapidly the number of those "who loved Him with heart and soul" dwindled. The religious leaders are put in the dock for their attitude to Jesus. Two points sum up what Jesus taught on his last visit to Jerusalem: "(1) That Jehovah is to be in and through Him, Jesus of Nazareth, the King over all the earth, and (2) how He would draw all men unto Himself."

After referring to the death and resurrection of Jesus, the book goes on to mention that the Holy Spirit is given to anyone, "whether he is a Jew or a Gentile". In conclusion, there is a look forward to the day when Jesus will come again, not as a lowly servant, but in great power and glory. On that happy day when "God has gathered His Israel" and they shall look upon Him whom they have pierced, all will rejoice. "May the Holy One of Israel come soon again! Even so come, Lord Jesus. Amen! and Amen!"

Not only is the book exceedingly traditional, but the distinctive ideas linked to Rabinowitz's name find little expression in it. If we are going to award points to the adjudicators, it cannot surprise us that they did not find that the terms of the assignment had been met by this account.

To sum up, we must maintain that it is more than a vague hypothesis that Rabinowitz went in for the competition in 1896. But it is also very characteristic of Rabinowitz that he did not merely take note in the summer of 1897 that his entry was not regarded as adequate. He had his entry published, first in Yiddish, then in an English translation. International bibliographies make do with giving the year of publication of the English version as "189?".[12] Zipperstein says about this and the pamphlet "What Is an Israelite of the New Covenant?" that they were written "either in the late 1880s or early 1890s".[13] But the year of publication of "Jesus of Nazareth" and the Yiddish edition can be fixed more precisely.

We have not found the exact Yiddish title anywhere. In 1904 Lhotzky mentions Rabinowitz's "last work", written "in Jewish-German in Hebrew square characters". In size it is like a Gospel or a little smaller, and "it is a brief treatment for Jews of the life of the Messiah Jesus."[14] He is certainly talking about the same book. Lhotzky had been sent the Yiddish version by Rabinowitz, and its existence is mentioned by Krüger in the February 1898 issue of his magazine.[15] But back in November 1897 S. Wilkinson was writing in connection with a notice about his visit to Kishinev earlier the same year, that the latest booklet had the title given above, and that it had been his privilege to translate it from Yiddish into English.[16] Whatever the explanation may be, Gaebelein, who also had a good relationship with Rabinowitz, got in first. Gaebelein had visited Kishinev in September 1895.[17]

It fits in very well that Rabinowitz received the adjudicators' "grading" in the summer of 1897 and had the Yiddish version printed and ready some months later.

As regards the English version, the Mildmay Mission magazine for June 1898 mentions it among books that had come in - though Rabinowitz's name is not directly mentioned.[18] In all probability this version appeared in the spring of 1898. Finally, we can add that the Mildmay Mission magazine in 1900 mentions receiving a reprint of Rabinowitz's *Yeshua Hanotzri*. I have not had opportunity to decide whether this is the Yiddish edition or a completely different work. The publisher was Asher Publishing Co., St. Paul, Minn., USA.[19]

About the same time as the competition was announced, Rabinowitz made known that he was considering moving his work to Palestine.

The Palestine Project

In 1896 Rabinowitz's ideas about moving his work to Jerusalem were made public. He wrote about it in a couple of American magazines in January and June,[20] and it was quoted in the periodicals of the European missions to Israel.[21] In his address to the General Assembly of the Free Church of Scotland in May 1896 he also touched upon this theme.[22]

His plan was to set up a school or centre for young men in Jerusalem, and to establish this as a place to train young men "who have, through my preaching, become convinced of the Divinity of Christ and of His glorious appearing."[23] To his Scottish friends, he links his plan with the continuation of his work after his death. Moses handed on the leadership to Joshua before he died. In the same way he himself must take steps regarding the future.

He did not tell this assembly that he himself was going to leave Kishinev and Somerville Memorial Hall. But he did this in one of his articles.[24] Four years earlier, doubtless in 1892, when he was in London, he had broached to some friends the plan "to go to Palestine and make Jerusalem the centre of my activity". For he did not think that there was a place for Jewish believers in the existing churches in Europe. Nor are they given sufficient nurture in these. He finds that in many churches the message of Christ's return is ignored - as also is the belief in the salvation of the Jewish nation.

The aim of the school would be to equip Messianic Jews so that they could bring the Jews as a nation to faith in Jesus. The school was not to be under the influence of any existing churches and denominations. The best place would be Palestine, "which is only for a certain time in the possession of Turkey". Here, the students would escape influence from current dogma. And they could study their own ancient history in close contact with the land where Jesus Christ accomplished his expiatory service. They were to be trained in the spirit of faith, hope, and love to Jehovah and his nation Israel. After completing their studies, these Hebrew Christians would preach Christ and his glorious return throughout the world wherever their brethren according to the flesh were scattered, wrote Rabinowitz.

I have not had opportunity to trace how the plans were received in the USA. But it does not seem that Rabinowitz gained much of a hearing for his ideas in Europe. Krüger for instance asked the question what was then to become of the work in Kishinev.[25] And de le Roi was confirmed in his view that Rabinowitz had gone astray in claiming that Hebrew Christians were not finding the necessary nurture in the existing churches.[26]

Perhaps because of this lack of support from Rabinowitz's backers, perhaps because of his involvement in the next project to be mentioned, the Palestine project was shelved.

Rabinowitz as a Bible-translator

Rabinowitz made his expertise in Yiddish available when the Mildmay Mission felt a need for a revision of the New Testament in Yiddish. The revision in view was to take especial account of the form of Yiddish used by the Russian Jews. During the final years of his life Rabinowitz was involved in this project.

The project was decided upon in 1896. At a conference under the auspices of the Mildmay Mission it was determined that W. Nelom, the

Mildmay missionary in Berditschev, was to prepare a trial translation into the dialect of Yiddish that was spoken in Lithuania. (From mid 1899 he worked in Vilna, also in Lithuania.) Rabinowitz was then to modify this translation on the basis of the dialect spoken in Bessarabia. A council consisting of Jewish missionaries was to later scrutinize the revision.[27]

The sources do not give an unambiguous picture of how the work was done. At one point Lerner in Odessa was also involved in the work of revision.[28] In the spring of 1899, when Trusting and Toiling, the Mildmay magazine, brought news of Rabinowitz's illness, it had not yet been clarified whether his part just had to wait or would be passed on to someone else.[29] The many notices in the magazine would suggest that Rabinowitz's share of the work had not become any smaller than first envisaged.

In November 1898 the work was in full swing. The Mildmay Mission gave it high priority.[30] Although they were in agreement with the evangelization train project - the fourth project - they had no objection to it being shunted into a siding for a while, so that Rabinowitz and his colleagues could complete the revision work. In Rabinowitz's letter of 6 March 1899, in which he made known that he was ill, he also explained that the work of revision was almost complete and ready for printing. He had reached chapter 2 of Hebrews.[31] After recuperating at Meran in the Tyrol for a time, he returned to Kishinev in April 1899, but his illness grew worse, and he went into a convalescent home in Odessa.

His daughter Rachel wrote in a letter of 22 May 1899 - five days after her father's death - that he had intended to finish the translation in Odessa.[32] So he had taken the necessary books with him. Shortly after his father's death, his son John made known that during the last year Rabinowitz spent a couple of hours each day on the translation work.[33]

It is hardly possible to decide from these comments whether during the course of the revision work Rabinowitz assumed main responsibility for it. But it may be remarked that in Trusting and Toiling the revision is called "the new Rabinowitz translation".[34] It is a moot point whether this was because he had the main responsibility or because it was the best PR for the new translation.

Before the work of revision was finished, Marcus S. Bergmann's new translation of the New Testament into Yiddish appeared in the spring of 1899. Before then the Mildmay Mission had had parts of this translation printed. But the existence of this translation brought about a new situation. S. Wilkinson discussed the matter in an article. He asked the question whether this translation by Bergmann would have an effect upon the work of Rabinowitz and the two others - and make their revision superfluous. The answer was a definite no. But it was admitted that the acute need for it had been diminished by Bergmann's translation. But the Mildmay Mission did not agree with Bergmann's claim that his translation would meet all needs.

Without disparaging the new translation, which is described as an invaluable work that would also be used in the mission's work in Russia, they felt that the situation in Russia did require a Testament in Yiddish (jargon) which could meet the special needs peculiar to Russian Jews. The work of revision now being prepared by "eminent jargonists in Russia" would, according to S. Wilkinson, undoubtedly be the best for an attempt to reach "the most ignorant" Jews in Russia. It had been adapted to the three main dialects spoken in Lithuania, Bessarabia, and Galicia. So they were praying for a rapid completion of the revision and thankful for the funds which had already come in. There was still need of £5000 before the order could be given for the printing of 100,000 copies.[35]

These statements, which were published in the issue of Trusting and Toiling that appeared two days before Rabinowitz's death, can be supplemented by a notice in the October issue. This expressed the hope that the Yiddish Testament for Russia would be completed at the end of the year or the beginning of the new year, 1900.[36]

But another year was to pass before it was printed and ready. On 30 January 1901 the Mildmay Mission was presented with the first copy produced by the British and Foreign Bible Society. A total of 100,000 were printed. The issue for February 1901 says that the first 9,000 copies would soon be in Russia for "careful distribution". The Bible Society had obtained permission from the Russian censors for this.[37]

I would not venture an opinion about the quality of the revision. But excerpts from letters sent to the Mildmay Mission show that it was appreciated by many, not least because it was not 'pure', but was the particular form of Yiddish that was best understood in a number of Jewish centres in Russia.[38] And indeed in other places to which Jews from these parts had emigrated. For instance, 5,000 copies were sent to Chicago.[39] The Mildmay Mission had to regret, however, that the revision was printed sooner than they had been expecting. So not all the errors they had spotted had been corrected, nor had the desired improvements been made. That this was a serious mistake is shown by the fact that the Bible Society took back 25,000 copies![40]

Thus the name of Rabinowitz must also be included in the table of Bible translators!

Rabinowitz and railway evangelization

Concurrently with the revision work on the Yiddish New Testament, Rabinowitz was working on a project which, had it been carried out, would have taken him far and wide in Russia.

In November 1897 Samuel Wilkinson gave a fairly detailed account of Rabinowitz's plans for railway evangelization.[41] The plan was that a railway coach should be built with three compartments: one sleeping-compartment for him and his helpers, one compartment for Bibles and tracts, and one as a meeting-room; the last two might possibly be turned into one compartment. The plan was that permission should be sought from the authorities to travel around Russia, run the coach into a siding at stations, and hold meetings and distribute New Testaments at places where the gospel was not otherwise being preached to Jews.

Wilkinson fell in with the idea. But he had to admit to his readers that the plan might seem strange to English ears, but unlike an English railway station, a Russian station was a place where people could freely cross the track; there was usually quite a concourse of people there. Also, the breweries did in fact already use this method, selling beer in this way. It was also claimed that there were school trains visiting remote places with no public school. Rabinowitz was quoted as having asked the question why the railway, which was already being used for spreading strong drink, should not also be used in the service of Jesus.

The same words (Acts 2:36, see Ch. 11) were to be written on the train as outside the building in Kishinev. This, together with Rabinowitz's name, would draw great crowds of Jews, thought Wilkinson. And as there was a *gendarmerie* at each station, they would keep things in order.

In February 1898 Wilkinson mentioned that the first budget for the railway coach of £200 was too low.[42] About £500 had to be collected, of which £20-£30 had come in. It was added that friends in America had told that American Baptists had three such evangelization trains and were building a fourth.

By the beginning of October 1898 the train fund had grown to £130. In a letter of 30 October 1898 Rabinowitz revealed that the expenditure was now estimated at £540. Along with his eldest son - the engineer - he had negotiated with manufacturers of railway coaches, and he enclosed a drawing. But before the money was gathered in, he would go to St Petersburg to apply to the authorities for permission to preach to Jews at railway stations.[43] The leadership of the Mildmay Mission did not wish to be hasty. The November issue of the magazine says that perhaps the Lord had delayed the matter a little so that Rabinowitz and the other translators might first be able to complete the revision of the Yiddish Testament. When that had been done, they looked forward to the train project being realized.[44]

In January 1899 the Mildmay Mission made known that there had recently been an item in one of the leading Russian newspapers about Rabinowitz's plans for travelling around south-western Russia, an area which had a large Jewish population.[45] As the reporter had been in Kishinev, it must be assumed that his source was Rabinowitz himself.

On 6 March 1899 Rabinowitz wrote in a letter to Wilkinson that he was ill and that, as recommended by the doctors, he was going to Meran. He added that it was therefore not the time to talk about the train project.[46]

After Rabinowitz's death in May 1899, it was announced that a decision as to what the funds were to be used for would await S. Wilkinson's return from his trip to Russia.[47] The August issue of the magazine said that the fund for the evangelization train stood at over £227.[48] Now that Rabinowitz had gone, the possibility of carrying out the project was not envisaged. The money that was specifically earmarked would be spent on the purposes desired.

But most of the money had not been earmarked, so the donors would be able to have it returned or converted to another purpose. If the donors did not respond before the end of September, then the leadership of the Mildmay Mission would conclude that they supported the Mission's proposal; that the money be given to Rabinowitz's widow and children. Wilkinson promises in the next issue of Trusting and Toiling to give news of how the money had been dealt with. He seems to have forgotten to do this.

The projects we have mentioned show with all clarity that Rabinowitz did not, as some people alleged, shamelessly pocket money from overseas supporters. Particularly the work of revising the Yiddish New Testament shows that until his death he was doing something for his money. The train project shows that he had not lost heart, despite having through the years had his applications to the authorities turned down. On the contrary, he had kept some visions about reaching out with the gospel.

A story of visions

In May 1897 Rabinowitz crossed the frontier and met up with P. Gordon and David Baron in Jassy in Rumania. The former repeated then an episode (which somewhat inaccurately is claimed to have occurred 15 years before) with which Rabinowitz had entertained them:

Fifteen years ago, when he was seeing the head of the Russian church in St Petersburg to get permission to form a Hebrew Christian congregation - which as we know was successful - the latter asked him how many members he had already. Rabinowitz replied by asking him how many passengers the Czar had for the Siberian railway that was going to be built. The answer was: "The passengers will come when the work is finished."

"In the same way," answered Rabinowitz, "I shall act in the Lord's work and ring the station bell of the gospel and show my Jewish brethren the way to complete salvation, Jesus Christ, the crucified and risen one, who leads sinners to God. And I know that my poor brethren will make use of this way; for there is not given unto men any other way, any other name, by which they can be saved."[49]

Until his death Rabinowitz kept the vision that it was worthwhile doing something for his "poor brethren". And such stories do not seem to have been quite forgotten even as late as the 1930s (see Chapter 20).

Chapter 18

RABINOWITZ'S DEATH IN 1899

On the 6 March 1899 Rabinowitz wrote S. Wilkinson a letter which was to prove to be his last. In it he says that he is ill and that, at the urging of three doctors, he is going to Meran in the Tyrol on the following day. He asks Wilkinson to understand that the time is not opportune for talking about the train project. He also says that the work of revising the Yiddish Testament is almost complete. When he fell seriously ill, he had stopped at the last verse of the second chapter of Hebrews, which he quotes: "For in that He Himself hath suffered being tempted, He is able to succour them that are tempted."[1]

Later, his son John and daughter Rachel gave foreign missionaries an account of how their father's last days had passed. We shall give a brief summary here.

Rabinowitz's illness and death

In autumn 1898 Rabinowitz was attacked by malaria, which debilitated him increasingly. On 23 January (r) 1899 he held his last service in Somerville Hall.[2] He was accompanied on his journey of convalescence by his daughter Sara[3] and perhaps by his son Peter.[4] The change of air in Meran brought an improvement, and Rabinowitz returned to Kishinev on 22 April hoping to be able to hold Passover services. On 29 April Rachel writes that her father is much better, but that he must have another month of quiet in order to regain his health.[5] John Rabinowitz later writes: "But the return to malaria-filled Kishinev was a fatal mistake."[6] The illness increased, and accompanied by Sara and Peter, Rabinowitz went to Odessa, where he was admitted to a sanatorium. He took with him the books required for completing the revision work.[7] "But it was already too late," writes John.[8] A telegram sent by Rachel came in to the London Council for Rabinowitz saying "Father passed away peacefully, May 17, one o'clock morning. Pray for family."[9]

At the sanatorium Rabinowitz had opportunity to witness to a Jewish doctor among others, John relates.[10] It had also made a great impression upon Rachel that on his departure for Meran her father had gathered his family around him, read the whole of Isaiah 53, and then asked the Lord to give him another 15 years, if it should please him. Finally he had blessed them with the Aaronic blessing in Hebrew. On the same occasion he had told them where they could find his will. It was, writes Rachel, as if he was thinking that he would never return home.[11]

Early on the morning of 18 May Rabinowitz's body was taken from Odessa to Kishinev, accompanied by Pastor Kornmann of the Reformed Church in Odessa and others. Brief prayers were held at the station, and then the coffin was taken to Somerville Hall and placed near the pulpit. The funeral oration was delivered by Kornmann. As mentioned, Faltin was away, and even if he had been in Kishinev, it is unlikely that he would have been asked to conduct the funeral (see Chapter 10).

At the burial ground of the Israelites of the New Covenant, the family tomb had already been built in Rabinowitz's lifetime. It contained eight chambers, and Rabinowitz's coffin was placed in the first one, as he had himself ordained in his will. He had placed there an open New Testament, which the family found after reading about it in the will. S. Wilkinson, who relates this, visited the place shortly afterwards and made a sketch of the tomb (see the beginning of this book).[12] A photograph was taken in 1935 (see the beginning of this book). Rabinowitz was the first - and indeed maybe the last - person to be buried in the burial ground of the Israelites of the New Covenant (see Chapter 19). Sh.L. Tsitron writes, in 1923, that at Rabinowitz's death, "it was said" that he had expressed the wish to be buried in the Jewish burial ground, a request which had been turned down by the Jewish burial authorities as well as the police.[13] Certainly this is no more than a rumour.

The inscription on the tomb was to be: "An Israelite who believed in Jehovah and in his anointed, Jesus of Nazareth, the King of the Jews. Joseph, son of David, Rabinowitz." This too Rabinowitz had stipulated in his will.

In his will Rabinowitz had also spoken his mind on the question of a possible successor. Other people had of course also had thoughts about this.

The question of a successor

In the obituary written by S. Wilkinson, he says directly that there is no successor in view to take up Rabinowitz's labours. When he had brought up this subject during his visit to Kishinev in October 1897, Rabinowitz had admitted that he did not have anyone in mind himself (see Chapter 15). Wilkinson says in the obituary that it is hard to see how the work can continue, as Rabinowitz's "personality as well as work was unique."[14] During his visit in June 1899 Wilkinson had long discussions with the bereaved family about this matter, without anything definite being decided on that occasion.[15] The London Council for Rabinowitz was wound up in the winter of 1899-1900. In the last booklet which the Council published the hope was expressed that in some way the work might be continued.[16] Great efforts were indeed made - not least by the Mildmay Mission - to do this, which will be described more fully in the next chapter.

Shortly after his father's death John Rabinowitz wrote that sadly it was impossible at that time to point to a successor. But they had not lost heart. "Our opinion about this is the same as was expressed by our dear father in his will: 'Concerning the holy cause which my Lord Jesus entrusted to me to carry out among my brethren the Jews, in this matter I have no private will of my own. All interests in this matter are in the hands of "the Holy One of Israel", Jesus Christ, and the Holy Spirit'." John Rabinowitz expresses his conviction that the Lord will call new people from the midst of the Jewish nation. "According to the Holy Scriptures, the salvation of the Jews shall be brought about, so new sowers must be found," he writes.[17]

P.L. Anacker, mission secretary of the German Central Agency, who reproduces this, goes on: "But this hope also gives us the right, indeed makes it our duty, to pray the Lord that he will raise up a man of Israel who can continue the work commenced..."

Anacker's obituary does not contain any hints of criticism, and nor do those in the magazines of the Mildmay Mission[18] and the British Society.[19] These obituaries were reprinted in for instance the magazines of the Swedish Israel Mission[20] and the Norwegian Israel Mission.[21] In The Christian an observer is quoted as saying the following, which gives a correct impression of many people's view of the scene after Rabinowitz's death: "What a loss to the Jewish Mission! There is no one to replace Rabinowitz." The same obituary speaks of "Somerville Hall and its prophet ..."![22] Le Réveil d'Israël writes: "The ways of the Lord are unsearchable; for who is to replace Mr Rabinowitz in Kishinev?"[23]

There are hints of criticism in the London Society's obituary. It is admitted that by his preaching activity Rabinowitz had "a fair amount of success". Nor can there be any doubt of his zeal. But his principles and methods might be subject to criticism, for he allowed his adherents to hold on to many peculiarly Jewish practices, "a course which seem hardly consistent with a full acceptance of the Gospel".[24] It also quotes a paragraph from the obituary in The Jewish Chronicle which maintains, for instance, of Rabinowitz: "In Russia, the reformation attracted little attention"[25] (see also Chapter 12). As we have already seen, Dean Faltin declared that Rabinowitz was Ebionite in his view, and that he was isolated at his death (see Chapter 10). When he wrote this in the autumn of 1899, Somerville Hall was not being used.

Despite stubborn efforts, no successor for Rabinowitz was found. So services could not be held, and the circle around Rabinowitz crumbled away. Before we take a closer look at the efforts to get a new work started in Somerville Hall, it may be appropriate to sum up - and assess - the various explanations that were later given for the dispersal of the group.

Why did the group around Rabinowitz fade away?

The material we have examined has surprisingly little to tell about how the group around Rabinowitz fared after his death. This is no doubt bound up with the fact that no services were held. But it must be assumed that some of Rabinowitz's followers sought fellowship elsewhere. One notice hints that after Rabinowitz's death some went to Odessa and joined up with R.H. Gurland's work there. After the Kishinev pogrom in 1903 too, large numbers moved from Kishinev to Gurland, who in 1900 had been appointed by the Mildmay Mission as bishop over the Mission's missionaries in Russia.[26] As Gurland preserved an intimate friendship with Faltin, it must be presumed that this influenced his relationship with Rabinowitz during the latter's lifetime. It must remain uncertain whether some from Rabinowitz's group also joined the Lutheran Church in Kishinev.

Even though the sources are remarkably silent on this matter, various explanations have been put forward for the failure of the movement to continue after Rabinowitz's death.

Some Jewish sources explain it by the small support, i.e. that there was no movement to be carried on after 1899 (see Chapter 12).[27] On the other hand, the Jewish scholar B.Z. Sobel points to Rabinowitz's basic theological views, when he says: "He eschewed all denominational affiliation, insisting that his belief was a Jewish belief, thus isolating himself and condemning his work to an inevitable demise."[28] The Norwegian C. Ihlen comes close to this view by speaking of the "untenability of his stance" as the reason that support for Rabinowitz steadily diminished.[29] Faltin was another who thought that Rabinowitz had isolated himself in his peculiar theological views.[30] While Rabinowitz lived, Faltin had pointed out defects in his personality (see Chapter 10). I. Fauerholdt took this point up in 1914 saying that one was saddened if 'today' one asked in Kishinev how the movement had developed after Rabinowitz's death. "Everything seems as if it were a dream; Rabinowitz is not spoken of any more. Is this bound up with a defect in himself?" Fauerholdt concludes that it did not work in favour of Rabinowitz and his movement that even in his lifetime he was compared in fulsome terms to an apostle and prophet[31] (that still in the second decade of the twentieth century people were talking about Rabinowitz will be shown in the next chapter). Following Louis Meyer, David A. Rausch is of the view that the peculiar character of the place and the work can explain the impossibility of finding a successor to Rabinowitz.[32]

In connection with the fact that the movement began to fade out after Rabinowitz's death, Jacob Jocz points out that the terrible pogrom in Kishinev on Passover day 1903 must have contributed appreciably to destroying Rabinowitz's work.[33] Axel Torm follows the same line in trying to explain that the congregation "unfortunately faded away after Rabinowitz's death." He says: "It was not due to spiritual declension, but to a pogrom," adding, "If it [the congregation] arose without Christian help, it was wiped out with 'Christian' help".[34]

This last explanation for the non-continuance of the movement after Rabinowitz's death cannot be a main cause. For the group had disbanded long before the pogrom of 1903 came along. In some of the other explanations there are undoubtedly elements which are worth noting in drawing overall conclusions. Although it may be maintained that it shows a weak side of Rabinowitz's personality that he had not provided for a successor, it must not be overlooked that he had worked on the matter (see Chapter 15).

F. Torm says directly, "There was nobody to continue his ministry."[35] It cannot of course be taken for granted that a successor would have received the government's permission to continue the work. Rabinowitz had a special permission for his work.[36]

In drawing overall conclusions as to why Rabinowitz's group faded away, we can scarcely overstress the structure of the "congregation". As the authorities never gave Rabinowitz permission to form a proper congregation, with administration of the sacraments, it had to fade away. Any 'good' successor would, under the same conditions and with the same structure, only have delayed its demise.

Seen in this light, no conclusions may be drawn about the "untenability of his stance" as a factor in the rapid dispersal of the group around Rabinowitz.

The memory of Rabinowitz lived on,[37] and great efforts were made to continue his work, as we shall now see.

Chapter 19

WHAT BECAME OF THE MESSIANIC MOVEMENT IN KISHINEV?

As we hinted in the last chapter, the memories of Rabinowitz lived on after his death. The Somerville Memorial Hall still stood. What was it to be used for? Later accounts do not deal with this question and so give the impression that the thought of continuing Rabinowitz's work died with him. But the sources show that stubborn efforts were made to continue the work in Somerville Hall. It is of particular interest that at the close of the 1920s an independent Hebrew Christian congregation was formed in Kishinev. In it, the memories at least of Rabinowitz lived on.

We shall first give a brief outline of how Rabinowitz's bereaved family fared. It may be imagined that the lives of others of the Israelites of the New Covenant took a similar course to that of the Rabinowitz family. So if we bear that in mind, the question is not unimportant. And are there, I wonder, any Hebrew Christians alive today, who can trace their descent back to Joseph Rabinowitz?

What became of Rabinowitz's family?

At his death, Joseph Rabinowitz left a wife and three sons and three daughters. All had been baptized. At his father's death in 1899, the eldest son Vladimir - or Haim Zeev - was living with his family in a small town by the frontier with Rumania, probably Unghem, where for instance the Norwegian Blom visited him in 1892.[1] He was then an engineer with the railways. He had assisted his father in various ways, for instance with his engineering knowledge (see Chapter 17). He died in April 1913. B. Schapiro, a Swedish-supported Russian missionary to Jews who was stationed in Odessa, was in Kishinev when the news came in that Vladimir's funeral was to be held there.[2] Unfortunately he does not relate whether Vladimir Rabinowitz was buried beside his father in the burial ground belonging to the Israelites of the New Covenant. In the same context we learn that Joseph Rabinowitz's widow was then still alive. In 1913 she must have been 73 or 74. Although we may have overlooked a notice of her death, it does not seem that any lengthy obituary was written about her in e.g. the Mildmay Mission magazine. In 1911 a photograph was taken of her sitting by the living-quarters built adjacent to Somerville Hall (see the beginning of the book).[3]

The two youngest children, the sons David (also called John/Johan) and Nathan (also called Peter) who were born in 1874 and 1876, were studying at the University of Moscow in 1899.[4] Six days after their father's death, Rachel writes that her brother John was intending to write a book in Russian entitled "Joseph Rabinowitz and his Work". He had already begun to look through and study the enormous amount of material left by his father, she writes.[5] This project can hardly have been completed. And, sadly, the material mentioned must, I suppose, be regarded as lost. But John Rabinowitz did succeed in writing something. In the Mildmay Mission magazine of 1903 there is an interesting item of information. It mentions that John Rabinowitz had published an article in Russian.[6] In it he addressed the Zionists reminding them of his father's words: "The key to Palestine lies in the hands of Jesus Christ." Whether it was he or the editor who wrote "Jesus Christ" instead of "our brother Jesus" cannot be decided here (see Chapter 9). The editor of the Mildmay Mission magazine appends the following comment on John Rabinowitz's article:

> He seems, however, rather to aim at a national and nominal recognition of Christ than at personal conversion. He asks us to publish the essay in English and Jargon.

The editor's wording infers that the Mildmay Mission was not intending to pay for a translation. Nor has any trace been found that the article was translated.

In the summer of 1903 Peter Rabinowitz travelled to London to negotiate with the Mildmay Mission about whether Somerville Hall could be brought into use again. At the same juncture, S.H. Wilkinson was in Kishinev.[7] He had brought money to aid victims of the pogrom in April. A sum of money was given to one of Rabinowitz's daughters, called Bertha - whichever of the three daughters this may have been (see further below).[8]

In 1899 the three daughters, Sara, Rebecca, and Rachel, were living with their mother in the dwelling attached to Somerville Hall.[9] From the Mildmay Mission they - presumably - received financial help immediately after Rabinowitz's death. Sara's husband, Joseph Axelrud, had died of cholera in the epidemic of autumn 1893. At that time he was in the employ of the Mildmay Mission. In 1911 Sara was living with her mother and sister Rachel in the living-quarters at Somerville Hall.[10]

In 1911 Rachel is called "Mrs Kinna".[11] Everything indicates that she was unmarried at the time of her father's death. Her husband had presumably died before 1911. In the preserved photograph she is shown with her son, a smallish child, probably somewhat younger than ten. While Joseph Rabinowitz was alive, Rachel accompanied her father on some of his journeys abroad and corresponded with English and Scottish friends. In 1914 she was still in contact by letter with the Mildmay Mission. In autumn 1914 there is a mention that Mrs Kinna had written from Reval about the danger from a German fleet; but she was otherwise in good heart, as the editor expresses it.[12] No explanation is given for her being in Reval, the capital of the government of Estonia. But this was not the end of Rachel Kinna's geographically chequered life. In December 1919 there was a brief item in the Mildmay Mission magazine:

> Mrs. Kenna (the daughter of the late Joseph Rabinowitch) and her son have arrived in London from Vladivostock, where they were held up for some time as war refugees. They remain for the present the guests of the Mildmay Mission.[13]

The circumstances around their stay in Vladivostock - in eastern Siberia - are not mentioned. But in May 1920 the Mildmay Mission was trying to find a suitable paid employment for her, the Mission magazine describing her as "the surviving daughter of the late well-known Joseph Rabinowitz of Kischineff."[14] She was unable to take hard work, but she was a well-qualified teacher of Russian, who regarded herself as able to make herself useful in "a Christian home". As the 'advert' was not repeated, it must be thought probable that she obtained employment in England and also died there. Whether her son, who on their arrival in England must have been in his late teens, carried on his grandfather's faith, must here remain a question.

A glimpse of how Rabinowitz's sons David (John) and Nathan (Peter) and his daughter Sara fared was given by B. Schapiro, the Swedish-supported missionary to the Jews.[15] On a missionary journey to Moscow in 1928 - financed by the Hebrew Christian group there - Schapiro heard that Rabinowitz's children were living in the city. Though he does not name them, Rabinowitz's "sons" are mentioned, which can only mean the two just mentioned. Rabinowitz's daughter is also mentioned, who must be Sara. For Schapiro recounts - rather imprecisely, for Sara's husband, J. Axelrud, died in 1893 - that he had met her and her husband 34 years before in Kishinev. Around that time Sara was the only one of Rabinowitz's three daughters who was married. Along with other Hebrew Christians Schapiro sought out the "children". After general remarks that many Jews in Moscow did not wish to know of Judaism and in fact did not enquire about any religion at all, and after mentioning that there was however a group "of living Jewish witnesses to Christ and his gospel" with whom seeking Jews made contact, Schapiro writes about his conversation with Rabinowitz's sons:

> Rabinowitz's sons told me with tears in their eyes that their father's work is being carried on and kept alive. But they themselves had been very far away from true Christianity and had not been interested in religious questions, but perhaps the time has now come for a change in that respect. The Hebrew Christian group in Moscow is not in contact with them.

It was different with Rabinowitz's daughter, relates Schapiro. For a long while she had not had opportunity to meet with believing Christians. But now she rejoiced at being able to meet with God's children, and therefore she could die happy, she said. For she had been very afraid of having to die without having congregational fellowship and without being able to partake of the Lord's holy communion, but now the Lord had heard her prayers and given her this fellowship. On the Sunday after Passover the whole Hebrew Christian group did celebrate communion together, and Rabinowitz's daughter was also there.

One can scarcely draw any conclusions about the viability of the Messianic movement from the later history of the family. The material is too sporadic for that. But it does seem that, in the first years after 1899, all the members of Rabinowitz's bereaved family did want Somerville Hall to be brought into use again. The efforts to get the Hall 're-opened' are a story in themselves. It has almost certainly not been pieced together before.

What became of Somerville Memorial Hall?

In his annual report for 1898-1899 Faltin touched upon Rabinowitz's death. In that connection he mentioned Somerville Hall and says: "Now it is unused. God knows what it will later be used for."[16]

Earlier accounts of Rabinowitz do not take up this question, merely mentioning that the activity was suddenly broken off by Rabinowitz's death. The impression is thus easily given that the history of Somerville Hall ended with Rabinowitz's death. We shall now show that this was not the case. There are indeed some missing pieces in the jigsaw puzzle. But there are sufficient to enable us to form some kind of picture.

For the sake of clarity it may be useful to summarize what S.H. Wilkinson wrote about it in 1925. At that time Kishinev had become a Rumanian possession, and the Mildmay Mission was proceeding with a new work under the leadership of missionary L. Averbuch. In his short article Wilkinson mentions that after the massacres of Jews in Kishinev in 1903 and 1905 some changes occurred. Despite sincere and repeated attempts, it was impossible for it to be maintained as a place for proclaiming the gospel, he says. And he continues:

> It became a Greek military church - became later a cinema. Once only, and for a brief while, did we manage to rent it, cleanse it as far as possible of everything discordant with the Gospel and proclaim the Saviour within its walls. That was in the war period; but the war was working further changes and the hall was sold over our heads and is now converted into a private residence.[17]

Wilkinson's claim that the Mildmay Mission used Somerville Hall for a brief period during the war, must be due to a lapse of memory, if the First World War is meant. The so-called 're-opening' of Somerville Hall took place in autumn 1912 (see below). Wilkinson likewise passes over the fact that the hall was used for periods by other Christian groups and in the service of the gospel. But the sources give clear indication that the Mildmay Mission made stubborn efforts to get a work off the ground.

As soon as the news of Rabinowitz's death came in to the Mildmay Mission, they did not try to hide the difficulty of continuing the work.

Rabinowitz's ministry was regarded as unique, and it was realized that he had the Russian government's specific permission to preach in Somerville Hall.[18] S.H. Wilkinson, who came to Kishinev shortly after Rabinowitz's death, was however intended to investigate the possibility of the house continuing to be used in the cause of the gospel for the Jews. The question was then discussed with Rabinowitz's surviving family. But nothing definite was arranged in that connection, says Wilkinson.[19] In November 1899 the Mildmay Mission requested its friends to pray for light upon Somerville Hall and the continued work there.[20]

In April 1903 a violent pogrom broke out in Kishinev. 'Christians' turned upon the Jews, plundering, smashing, molesting, and killing. A few days after this massacre, S.H. Wilkinson arrived in Kishinev with the Swedish-supported missionary P. Wolff. After informing themselves of the scope of the massacre, they went to Rabinowitz's tomb. Wilkinson says of Somerville Hall that it lay unused and silent. In the forecourt trees and scrub were growing wild, but on the facade of the house there was still the Hebrew message of peace for Israel in the name of Jesus the Messiah (see Chapter 11). But against the background of the massacre by 'Christians' of the Jews, Wilkinson asks how the Jews were supposed to differentiate between true and false.[21]

The living-quarters at Somerville Hall had remained untouched, though they had been threatened. During conversation with Rabinowitz's widow and one of the daughters Wolff envisaged that he would return to Kishinev and, if possible, carry on the work at Somerville Hall. Whether this happened is doubtful, at least nothing has been found to confirm it.

Wolff himself does not mention this in his description of the visit. But there is no reason to doubt that he, who was stationed in Odessa, may have expressed such thoughts. In a PS to his description of the visit, he confirms that Somerville "is closed, and there is no one to take up the work there. What must this mean? That is what I ask myself and the Christians."[22]

Wolff writes that the disaster began on the very first Easter day, when joy that Christ truly had risen was at its height. The so-called 'Orthodox' who took part in the massacre he calls wild beasts: "To imagine that these wild beasts, as they killed men and women and flung little children down from the second and third storeys, were shouting: 'Christ is risen indeed.' What a mockery of the Lord and his cause among Israel!"

The Jews seldom met true Christians, says Wolff. And continues: "How difficult it feels for a missionary under such circumstances! One would rather hide and keep silent."

In connection with the pogrom in 1903 the Mildmay Mission entered into a large-scale relief work. On 2 July S.H. Wilkinson again travelled from London to Kishinev with £550 to be distributed to those who had suffered in the pogrom.[23] Also in connection with the pogroms which ravaged south-western Russian in 1905 the mission tried to assist the victims.[24] In this period a large proportion of the mission's financial resources were used for social work. Concurrently the missionary work was being carried on from the station in Odessa, but it is difficult to say anything definite about the effects of the pogroms on the efforts to start up the work in Somerville Hall. But in 1903 serious plans were being made to re-launch work based on the Hall.

It was while Wilkinson was in Kishinev in the summer of 1903 that Peter Rabinowitz came to London to negotiate about Somerville Hall.[25] In August the Mildmay Mission intimated that they would take the initiative in holding a conference about the 're-opening' with representatives of other missions interested in the matter.[26] For other circles too were working on plans for helping in Kishinev. The movement Hebrew Christian Testimony to Israel, which had backed Rabinowitz earlier, had plans for sending R. Feinsilber to Kishinev for a time.[27] Feinsilber, who at that time was a missionary in Budapest,[28] had himself come to faith in Jesus through Rabinowitz's preaching - and for a while had been Rabinowitz's co-worker in Kishinev (see Chapter 15). But that plan seems not to have come to fruition, either.

While money was coming in for the Mildmay Mission's relief work among victims of the massacre in Kishinev, earmarked money was also coming in to defray expenses in connection with - as it was called - 'the re-opening of Somerville Hall'.[29]

In October 1903 the Mildmay Mission made known that between £150 and £200 was needed once for all, and £200 annually for the next three years to cover running expenses.[30] In November it was announced that the "present trustees of the building" - the name of Rabinowitz's family is not expressly mentioned, although they are meant - were willing to make over the building to the Mildmay Mission on the proviso that the site be purchased and the hall used in accord with the aim which the mission itself had laid down for it. £600 was needed; for the purchase (£250), repairs (£100), and running costs the first year (£250).[31] These figures show that the schemes for setting up a new mission station in Kishinev under the Mildmay Mission were quite serious. It is mentioned in the same context that Somerville had been unused for five years. But yet more years were to pass before the hall could be 're-opened'.

In November 1910 S.H. Wilkinson mentions in a brief notice that, after a number of years, there was now again a possibility of purchasing Somerville Hall for use in preaching the gospel to "the 80,000 Jews in this city of tragedy". He cannot go into details, but asks for his supporters' prayers and also grace to follow the Lord's leading in this matter.[32] But a number of details emerged after his journey to Russia in 1911.

During his visit to Kishinev in April 1911, Wilkinson negotiated with the pastor of the British Society, George Friedmann, about the matter. Using Somerville Hall would not hamper Friedmann's work but would rather strengthen it. Both parties shared this view. Setting aside the emotions linked to Somerville Hall in the past, Wilkinson wished to look at the present and practical side of the matter. Somerville Hall was standing empty, and at small cost it would be possible to set it in such order that it could be used for preaching the gospel to the Jews of Kishinev. In the same connection Wilkinson mentioned that Somerville Hall had been used as a Greek military church. Likewise it seems that there had at least been plans to turn the hall into a kind of cinema.

Wilkinson admitted to his readers that there were difficulties. First, permission had to be obtained from the Russian government for the building to be used. The attempts which were made during his visit to Kishinev were not successful, but the mission was involved in negotiation about the matter. The next difficulty was to find a suitable man for "a work which demands unusual gifts and grace". And finally the financial aspect of the matter was mentioned.

Otherwise, it may be noted that Somerville Hall was still in the Rabinowitz family's possession. Wilkinson met Rabinowitz's widow and two daughters, who were living in the house on the same site (see the beginning of the book). At this time there was no suggestion by the Mildmay Mission of purchasing Somerville Hall; it was to be rented. In that connection Wilkinson writes about the family: "The renting of the building and the using of it for God's work would not only assist them in their modest needs, but delight their hearts, to feel that their beloved one's life witness was being perpetuated."[33]

In his New Year greeting of 1912 S.H. Wilkinson put the matter to his readers. Somerville Hall was described as "this beautiful building, erected with the gifts of God's children for Gospel ministry".[34] Maybe it is going too far to read a certain mortification in these words, that rent had to be paid for the building which was erected with funds collected abroad. It is true that six months previously Wilkinson had argued that a rental of Somerville Hall would relieve the strained finances of Rabinowitz's family. But collated with the other notices on this subject in the columns of the Mildmay Mission magazine over the years, this interpretation does find some support. We can at least detect that Wilkinson often avoided mentioning the Rabinowitz family by name when the rental of Somerville was being discussed, so that one might be led to believe that Somerville Hall had passed into other hands. That this was not so in 1911-1912 is shown clearly by Wilkinson's report in connection with his visit to Kishinev in April 1911.

What is more important, however, is that Wilkinson could write at the same time that the difficulties due to the government had "quite recently" been removed. Again the financial issue is commented upon. The repair expenditure would come to between £65 and £100, and the premises had to be furnished with new benches, which must mean that the former benches either had been removed or grown too old. The rental expenditure was set at 600 roubles = £65, and expenditure on the coming missionary and his living-quarters was estimated at £120 at least. He finally points out that during 1911 "one or two small sums came in for this object", which he sees as a sign from the Lord to continue the efforts.

At a conference for staff of the Mildmay Mission in eastern Europe which was held from 17 to 22 May 1912 in Odessa, the matter was put on the agenda. But Wilkinson minuted that the matter had been deferred once more. This step had been taken even though the government's permission was to hand, and although one of the mission's missionaries could be transferred to the work in Kishinev, and although £70 had come in for the project. The reason is given for the further postponement of the matter. It was that the worker in question could not be moved immediately, and that the expenses for the first year were estimated at £250, and since not so much money had come in, this was taken as a sign from God to defer the matter.[35]

Although it is hard for the historian to uncover whether there were other motives for this postponement, when a "faith mission" writes and acts like this, there can be no doubt that S.H. Wilkinson had personally worked hard for Somerville Hall to be brought into use by the Mildmay Mission.

Despite what was decided at the conference in May 1912, the November issue of the Mildmay magazine announced that Somerville Hall was now to be re-opened, the hall which for so long had been "in disuse or in use for other than evangelistic purposes". S.H. Wilkinson, who was once more in Russia to negotiate about greater freedom for the mission's work, wrote on 28 October 1912 from St Petersburg that he had laid the application personally before the interior minister. Although he was received not "uncordially", and although the British ambassador had given the application his "cordial backing", the interior minister had been unable to foresee a favourable reply, which Wilkinson admitted he found it hard to accept as the final answer.[36]

This application for extended freedom for the work of the Mildmay Mission in Russia seems not to have influenced the permission to use Somerville Hall. At any rate not at first. At least, in the letter mentioned, written in St Petersburg on 28 October, Wilkinson relates the following: "Somerville Hall, Kischineff, is now repaired, cleaned, and furnished (and the bill met), and will, I trust, be opened this week for Gospel testimony, after standing unused for the truth for so many years."[37]

Wilkinson proved right. Arriving home from Russia in December 1912, he was able to express his great joy that the efforts for a re-opening of

Somerville Hall had finally been crowned with success. Fresh problems were indeed soon encountered. But he expressed his joy at what had happened in the following words, summing up events of 1912: "It [the year] has also seen, after many months of waiting on God and much exercise of patience, the re-opening of Somerville Hall, Kischenew, for Gospel witness. My joy at recently seeing this building packed to overflow with eager Jewish faces, listening to the message of God's grace, was almost too deep for words."[38]

The Re-Opening of Somerville Hall in 1912

The re-opening of Somerville Hall took place on Saturday 2 November 1912. In its report of it, the Mildmay Mission says that the authorities had not placed any obstacles in the way of the resounding proclamation of the gospel "and soul-saving truth", even though discussion, singing, and prayer were regarded as "inadvisable". It also mentions that after the first meetings, a suspension of activities had been necessary in order to obtain a lasting permit for the work. "This is, we trust, but temporary," says S.H. Wilkinson. This permit had not been received before this was published in February 1913.[39] Indeed, on 16 February, there came a notification from the Russian authorities that the activity of the Mildmay Mission based on Somerville Hall had to be halted.[40]

But first let us look at the so-called 're-opening'. The event held at Somerville Hall on 2 November 1912 received press coverage both before and after. In its advance notice, a Jewish-edited Kishinev newspaper said that Leon Rosenberg was going to deliver an address in German on the topic "Jesus and the Jews". Of Rabinowitz the newspaper wrote that he used all his strength in spreading the Christian faith among Jews, "but he had no success whatever, and the gatherings he attracted, as we well remember, consisted of only about eight or ten people, all of whom were in some way dependent upon him." The newspaper's view was that Mr Rosenberg - "a miniature of Rabinowitz" - would not have anything new to say. The paper also stated that "this theme" had been discussed enough in Kishinev.

Press coverage after the meeting shows that there was a full house of Jews at Rosenberg's address, predominantly young people. In his address Rosenberg attempted to show that the Messiah of the Jews had come in and with Jesus. He refused to enter into the answering of questions, but invited to a meeting the following week. It was announced that it was the mission's plan to hold regular meetings for about a year, although Rosenberg would only occasionally come from Odessa to Kishinev - Rosenberg led the Mildmay Mission's work in Odessa.

Another newspaper confirms that Somerville Hall was crowded out. "The audience sought enlightenment on the moral and social and political conditions under which they and others live. But they went out with no information thereon," it says.[41]

In his comment on the Jewish newspapers' treatment of the re-opening, S.H. Wilkinson says that they could not be expected to show sympathy for a proclamation of Christian truth. Nevertheless he calls for love and asks his readers to heed the views that were expressed and the way they were put. He concludes by asking for prayer for the work in Kishinev so that the external obstacles to continuing the work may be removed.

After the re-opening, two more meetings were held in Somerville Hall at the end of 1912. Wilkinson's evidence shows that he personally was present at one of them.[42] The joy was great after all the efforts that had previously been made. Wilkinson's memory is actually at fault when he says that Somerville Hall was brought into use after not being used in the cause of the gospel for the Jews of Kishinev for 17 years.[43] It was 'only' 13 years. But the joy at the 're-opening' and the other two events was to be short-lived.

In the very next issue of the Mildmay magazine, for March 1913, S.H. Wilkinson had to reveal that the work based on Somerville Hall had "suddenly been banned and the hall closed by the police." He admits that, after all the efforts made in connection with the re-opening, and after the hall being packed with Jews at the three meetings held, it would come as a "shock" to many to hear this. Without elaborating on the authorities' reasons for this decision, he does say that the causes given by the police were inadequate. He considers that there must be other grounds, but has to confess that "the great adversary of God's work is triumphing at the moment." The only thing to be done now was to await a sign from God concerning the future work. "It is HIS work and His problem; let us not be in any sort of despair."[44]

The Russian authorities' grounds for closing Somerville Hall may have been "inadequate", as Wilkinson argues, but the facts given by the Mildmay Mission about the use of Somerville Hall immediately after the closure merit the same description. If we relied on the Mildmay magazine alone, we might be led to believe that Somerville Hall was not used at all in the cause of the gospel after this re-opening. But another source shows that for a short period after the so-called re-opening it was used by other evangelical Christians.

Somerville Hall, the Stundists, and B. Schapiro

B. Schapiro was a Russian Hebrew Christian who was employed by the Swedish Israel Mission as a colporteur and missionary and stationed in Odessa. He had, as it was put, "through reading of the New Testament and Rabinowitz's writings found his Saviour and Messiah."[45] In a letter dated 15 November 1913 he tells of an evangelization trip which also took him to Kishinev. He writes among other things:

> I visited Rabinowitz's family and rejoiced that the chapel in which he preached has been rented to the Russian evangelical brethren. As a result, I had opportunity myself to preach there. I asked the evangelical

brethren to invite the Jews to the meeting. It was what is known as the 'Great Sabbath'...[46]

The "Great Sabbath" mentioned is the Saturday before the Jewish Passover, which in 1913 fell on 19 April, thus only about two months after the Russian government's refusal for the Mildmay Mission to use Somerville Hall had arrived in London.

Because of bad weather, the meeting was not well attended by Jews, says Schapiro. As he had himself been baptized by those known as "Stundists",[47] it must be regarded as certain that the "Russian evangelical brethren" mentioned were in fact the Stundo-Baptists, an evangelical Russian movement that can be traced back to the 1860s, but was not granted freedom of assembly until the Edict of Tolerance in 1905. This Russian revival movement - and kindred movements - made considerable advances in the first decades of the twentieth century, and Rabinowitz had himself had contact with one of the prominent leaders, V. Paschkov, to whom he wrote a letter in March 1887.[48] Scattered items in the Mildmay magazine from the year 1906 onwards indicate that the mission's workers had contact with the Stundists. For instance, in May 1909 L. Rosenberg recounts that more than 300 Stundists had been arrested, also noting that there were "Christian Jews" among them.[49] From a missionary journey in autumn 1909 Rosenberg relates that in one place "the Russian brethren" had invited Jews to the meeting, although none came that evening.[50] He also spoke at the first congress of the Russian Baptists, which was held for the first time with government permission in 1909.[51]

It may also be commented that at least from April 1913 (perhaps earlier) the Stundists - or whatever version of their name is used - had taken over the rental of Somerville Hall. Their activity was not primarily aimed at Jews, although they gladly made the hall available to a missionary to Jews. At least Schapiro writes about the result of his visit to Kishinev that the Jews were now more open-minded than when Rabinowitz was active, so that they no longer mocked Christ when someone sought to speak to them about him. And he adds:

> And in Kishinev it is lawful to preach the gospel in the same chapel where Rabinowitz once preached. They asked me to visit Kishinev once a month and stay there for four or five days. I hope that this will be possible, when the Lord has given his "yea" to it.[52]

But it does not seem that Schapiro was able to carry out his wish to visit Kishinev once a month, even though he was stationed in Odessa. After the First World War broke out, he did make a missionary journey at the turn of year 1914-15, a journey which ended with his imprisonment and internment. Others of the evangelical missionaries were also interned.[53] But before that happened, Schapiro visited Kishinev. He had hoped that Kishinev would be the "ark" where Noah would reach out his hand and keep him for seven days:

> But no, Kishinev was not the ark for me. I could remain there only
> a few days. The Russian evangelical hall which belonged to Joseph
> Rabinowitz was sealed up, and they were trying to eradicate every-
> thing that was not Greek Orthodox. But I worked there [in the town]
> as much as I could.[54]

Later on the same journey Schapiro returned to Kishinev in an attempt to
be closer to his family, who lived in Odessa. As several of the evangelical
preachers in Odessa had been interned and sent to Siberia; he would not go
to Odessa. But he could not remain in Kishinev either, and soon afterwards
he was taken prisoner.[55]

In other words: for a short period up to the outbreak of the First
World War, Somerville Hall had been rented to the Stundists. But the
Russian authorities' sanctions against the Stundists and against other activity
of evangelical missionaries meant that the Stundists could only rent the hall
for a short while. After the First World War Somerville Hall was once more
used in gospel service. The Stundists and the Mildmay missionary Averbuch
worked together in this connection. A number of scattered mentions of this
are to be found in the Mildmay magazine. But one searches in vain for any
indications that the Stundists used Somerville Hall immediately after the
authorities had excluded the Mildmay Mission. Was this due to an oversight
by Mildmay, or did they want to spare their supporters this information...?

In his retrospect on the year 1913, S.H. Wilkinson was still expressing
the hope for an "afterwards" for the work based on Somerville Hall:

> We are still also holding in expectation of an "afterward" to the story
> of Somerville Hall, Kischineff, recovered for the work of God by
> many steps of prayer and guidance, and then, when re-opened,
> summarily closed by the police![56]

The war and the political upheavals also played their part in obliging the
Mildmay Mission to accept the sad facts. All the same, not all hope had been
abandoned that a new situation might alter this state of affairs. There is an
interesting little item in the mission's magazine in May 1917. It says that a
telegram had recently been received from Rosenberg in Odessa; he reported
that Somerville Hall was for sale.[57] That this means that Rabinowitz's widow
had now died, and that her estate was being settled up, is a possibility, but
only a guess. But the notice does reveal that the Mildmay Mission might
possibly be interested. Yet Somerville Hall was not sold straight away. And
an "afterward" did come when it was again used as a place for preaching the
gospel. And by a tortuous route the Mildmay Mission was also involved.

For after the First World War new frontiers were drawn. These new
frontiers made it possible for a fresh work to be started from Somerville Hall.
It was also to be the final period in the hall's history as a place for preaching
the gospel, as we shall now relate.

Somerville Hall in Chisinau, Rumania

After the end of the First World War, with the Peace of Versailles, the frontier was redrawn so that in 1918 Kishinev passed into Rumanian hands. In the newly set-up Greater Rumania, the city came to be called Chisinau, spelt differently in Rumanian but pronounced the same as formerly in Russian (we shall here go on calling the city Kishinev, except for direct quotations in which the form Chisinau is used). The city was in Rumanian hands from 1918 until the end of July 1940, when it again became Russian.

Later the Mildmay Mission regarded 1918 as the year of the mission's new work in Kishinev. Thus in 1928 they celebrated the tenth anniversary of this work. At the beginning Somerville Hall also played a part. It was not least the 'chance' holiday in Kishinev of L. Averbuch, the Mildmay missionary, in the summer of 1918 that brought the new work into being.

It is true that S.H. Wilkinson interprets the events differently in 1925. In an article in which he gives a brief outline of the history of the work in Kishinev and has to state with sorrow that Somerville Hall "was sold over our heads" - that happened in 1921 - he continues:

> The war is over. We are led to send Mr. L. Averbuch of the M.M.J. [Mildmay Mission to the Jews] to the town. It is a new beginning. The name is changed (at least in orthography). It is now Chisinau. The Somerville Hall is definitely beyond reach. There is no living community of believers. Thus five years ago his [Averbuch's] work began...[58]

Whatever may be thought of 'guidance', there are a number of factors to indicate that Averbuch was not directly sent to Kishinev by the Mildmay Mission in order to commence a new work there.

Averbuch, who was a Hebrew Christian himself, had since autumn 1913 been attached to the Mildmay Mission's work in Odessa. In the lists of mission staff there, his name figures from October 1913. From the January 1918 issue of Trusting and Toiling he figures as a missionary in Moscow. Not until the March 1919 issue does his name occur under the heading "Chisinau". The Mildmay Mission had evidently not planned that Averbuch should take up a work in Kishinev. Therefore it is slightly misleading when E.S. Gabe says that Averbuch was Rabinowitz's successor.[59] It was not due to an oversight that Averbuch was not listed under "Chisinau" earlier. Some external events were influencing developments. We know these from a Norwegian source whose reliability can scarcely be impugned.

The Norwegian missionaries Sister Margit Berg and Sister Olga Olaussen, who were stationed in Galatz, visited Kishinev in November 1921. On the day of their return home - 1 December - they wrote about the work in Kishinev.[60] Concerning Averbuch, whom they had met, they say that in the summer of 1918 he went to Kishinev with his wife to spend a holiday with some friends there. During his stay there, the frontier with Russia was sealed off. The Norwegian missionaries continue:

...and they had to stay where they were. They have been of great blessing to many in that city. They have joined up with the Baptists; along with them they have rented a hall, Rabinowitz's prayer-house, which may be remembered by the oldest friends of Israel missions at home. They helped each other at the meetings, had a combined choir and a little orchestra in which flute, mandolin, and guitar were played.

Of Hebrew Christians the two Norwegian missionaries met four men and a young girl, who had been baptized, and several others had come to faith, but were not yet baptized. It is expressly said of one man that he had been baptized by Averbuch. About activities for Jews, they mention that a prayer meeting was held on Saturday morning. On Saturday evenings there was a meeting for Jews in general, at which the languages used were Yiddish and Russian. And they continue:

On Sunday morning we were at the Protestant church, where the preaching was in German, and then in Rabinowitz's prayer-house, where a Sunday School was held. At six o'clock there was again a full house for the evening meeting, believers of all nationalities, Russians from the most varied parts, Bulgarians, Rumanians, a couple of Serbs, and an American missionary couple, ready to travel to Russia as soon as they could get in.

So in 1921 Somerville Hall was still in use. Averbuch and the 'Baptists' were working there together. This is also confirmed by notices in the Mildmay magazine, although the mission did not, as far as can be judged, explain directly how Averbuch ended up in Kishinev.

Without further comment, the February 1919 issue of the Mildmay magazine says that Averbuch was stationed in Kishinev.[61] In August S.H. Wilkinson expresses the wish to visit Kishinev, which was prevented by political circumstances.[62] He did not go to Rumania until 1922 and then did not visit Kishinev, which disappointed Averbuch.[63] On 8 July 1919 Averbuch wrote from Bucharest that he and his wife had been in Kishinev for ten months. He states that the "Russian Baptist Brethren" had rented Somerville Hall, and that without any form of restriction they had made it available to them so that he could arrange special meetings for Jews. He goes on to say that on one occasion he had spoken the Word in a synagogue. And of 50,000 tracts which the Mildmay Mission had paid to have printed, half had already been distributed.[64] In October 1919 he reports that he preached in Somerville Hall together with the "Russian brethren". He was also in close contact with the London Society's envoy in Bucharest, J.H. Adeney, and helped him occasionally in Bucharest, e.g. at the Jewish festivals.[65]

Although in 1919 the Mildmay Mission's policy seems to have been to wait and see, money was sent for Averbuch's work.[66] In 1920 Averbuch was able to say that there was liberty for the work in Kishinev.[67] And the November issue of the magazine reports that he had baptized two Jews.[68] At

. the beginning of 1921 the mission intimates that Averbuch was freely able to use Somerville Hall, which "is now in the hands of Russian Baptists".[69] But other information shows that they had not bought, merely rented the hall. In June 1921 the Mildmay Mission indicates that Rabinowitz's efforts and influence had, through Averbuch's work, achieved a fruitful "afterward".[70]

But soon after, in September 1921, the mission had to break the news to its supporters that Somerville Hall had been sold. It is said expressly that Rabinowitz's family had arranged the sale. But it is stressed that it would not directly affect the Mildmay work amongst the Jews, although it had been a personal disappointment to Averbuch. It is said of Averbuch that he had become the leader of "a congregation of Russian believers" who gathered in Somerville Hall, and this had a beneficial "indirect influence" on the activity among the Jews. Then the possibility of hiring another hall is mentioned. Even though Averbuch had one to hand, the mission would rather run the risk of losing it than - as it is put - "go before the Lord". Before this matter was arranged, Averbuch could take advantage of the authorisation he had received with Adeney's help to evangelize the whole of Bessarabia.[71]

Although the Mildmay Mission was able to bring news of the sale of Somerville Hall in September, it would seem that meetings were still being held in the hall in November, as the two Norwegian sisters relate. So it must be assumed that the tenancy continued for some months after the sale, after which Somerville Hall was turned into a private residence.

In sum, it can be asserted that Somerville Hall also had a history as a place for preaching the gospel after Rabinowitz's death. It is true that the hall was used only for brief periods up until 1921. But this was not due to lack of effort, but to the political conditions and the resulting restrictions on Protestant activity. Fauerholdt's remark in 1914 that Rabinowitz was no longer spoken about in Kishinev, has thus also been corrected (see Chapter 18). But the question has not yet been answered whether the activity based on Somerville Hall ought in fact to be related in some way to Rabinowitz's earlier work. There is definite evidence that the Mildmay Mission itself understood its efforts as a continuation of Rabinowitz's work. Shortly before Somerville Hall was sold for a private dwelling in 1921, the point was being made, as we have already shown, that Averbuch's labours were a continuation of Rabinowitz's work. On the other hand the work which the Stundists ran had nothing directly to do with Rabinowitz, although the Stundists willingly made the hall available to the missionaries to the Jews.

But in spite of this, it would not seem that Averbuch followed any of Rabinowitz's distinctive principles. As far as can be judged, the Jews he baptized became members of a particular denomination. But an attempt was made to maintain some form of Jewish identity, of which a few glimpses will now be given.

Chapter 20

THE WORK IN KISHINEV 'AFTER'
SOMERVILLE HALL (1922-1945)

In 1921, shortly before Somerville Hall ceased to be the gathering-place for the work of the Baptists and Averbuch, the number of baptized Jews was reckoned to be five. In addition, in the group around Averbuch there were some Jewish believers who had not yet been baptized. Without going into too many details, we shall now show how the work developed and expanded. It is of particular interest in this context that an independent Hebrew Christian congregation saw the light of day in 1928. Although it is a question difficult to answer, it has to be asked whether any lines of connection can be traced between the formation of this congregation and the work of Rabinowitz. There are at least instances of the memory of Rabinowitz living on in various ways in Hebrew Christian contexts in Kishinev in the 1930s.

Averbuch's work in Kishinev 1922-1928

The sale by the Rabinowitz family of Somerville Hall in 1921 did not have a negative effect on the work amongst Jews. On the contrary, the work of the Mildmay Mission expanded under the leadership of Averbuch. On 15 October 1922 "Bethel" was inaugurated, and later an organ was acquired.[1] In 1927 a new tenancy was taken up of other premises. These were also called Bethel and could seat 400 people.[2] Averbuch's reports show that at special events - often in connection with Christmas and the Jewish festivals - they even had to turn people away because the hall was packed out.[3] Meetings with lantern-slide lectures also aroused interest.[4]

There is no reason to doubt the accuracy of Averbuch's information that special events attracted large crowds of Jews. It is quite certain that a great deal of activity was based on Bethel. Each day of the week had its particular activity, either choir or orchestra rehearsals, on which the musical Averbuch laid considerable stress, or prayer meetings or meetings to edify the believers, or meetings for gospel outreach.[5] Along with the distribution of Bibles and tracts, the periodical Hambaseir Toiv was published - in Yiddish, Rumanian, and Russian (and one issue appeared in English, produced by E.S. Gabe, who later worked with Averbuch for some years).[6] There was also time for social relief work among needy Jews. In the work Averbuch had the assistance of the Hebrew Christians N. Feigin and M. Tarlew, so that there was also manpower for a school ministry for Jewish children.[7] It is scarcely surprising that Averbuch, who also made gospel-preaching journeys out from Kishinev, not only could feel overburdened, but sometimes had to go away to recuperate.[8]

Indeed, the Mildmay Mission was able to claim in 1925 that Averbuch's work in Kishinev was the place where most blessing was being experienced, compared with all the mission's other fields of work.[9] And in 1926 his work was described as "completely *sui generis*", i.e. without parallel.[10]

The collaboration between the Russian Baptists and Averbuch was continued even after the 'loss' of Somerville Hall. Although the 'Baptists' did get their own premises and their own pastor, Averbuch also functioned in this context as the "guiding hand and head", as S.H. Wilkinson expressed it in 1925. Although the work that was based on the Mildmay Mission's hall, Bethel, was primarily - but not exclusively - aimed at Jews, the two centres were viewed by the leaders of the Mildmay Mission as a unit, because of Averbuch's leading position in both places. Members of the Baptist congregation attended events in Bethel and assisted with singing and music. And the "newly-saved Jewish souls", who had been won through the work of Bethel, came to the Baptists' hall. And among the Baptists these Hebrew Christians found - in S.H. Wilkinson's words - "Christian fellowship at a high mark of sincerity, and learn in practice that in Christ Jesus there is neither Jew nor Gentile."[11] This last avowal does not signal any change of view by the Mildmay Mission. But it may be remarked that we search in vain for such expressions in regard to the same mission's support for Rabinowitz's work. If Rabinowitz had gone along with similar statements, the conflict between him and Faltin would hardly have arisen.

However, in 1925 the Mildmay Mission was saying that the growth in the Baptist congregation and in the specific work amongst Jews at Bethel were among "the happiest experiences in the history of the Mission".[12] It is certain that, owing to their connection with Averbuch, the Baptists were actively involved in the work of bringing the gospel to the ears of Jews. Not only in Kishinev, but elsewhere in Bessarabia too, the Russian Baptists were distributing the magazine that Averbuch edited.[13]

In the 1920s there was nothing to suggest that Averbuch wished to break off the connection with the Baptists. On the contrary, it was with regret that he had to accept that in autumn 1925 the Rumanian authorities banned him from acting as a Baptist preacher.

The ministry wrote to him that in future he had to confine himself within the framework of the Mildmay Mission, which was all that the government authorisation entitled him to do. As a Russian by nationality, Averbuch had been under Rumanian government scrutiny. But hitherto the London Society's envoy in Bucharest, J.H. Adeney, had used his influence to ensure that Averbuch could work in Kishinev. Concerning the government's ban on his working as a Baptist preacher, Averbuch wrote on 8 October 1925:

> The Government's prohibition of preaching at the Baptists' has halved my work, as it had all the time been developing there in close connection with the Mission to the Jews; for Jews attend the Baptists' meetings, and become members of the congregation when converted.[14]

This prohibition did not have any major effect on the collaboration between the two centres, either because Averbuch directly breached it, or because it was only a ban on his acting as an official preacher. At any rate, we discover that in his report for the year 1925 Averbuch does not touch upon it at all, but relates that Russian Baptists elsewhere in Bessarabia had invited him to come and preach to the Jews living there.[15] In connection with meetings at Christmas and New Year in 1925-1926 the two groups continued to attend each other's gatherings, and on 3 January 1926 he preached at the Baptists' chapel.[16] And in his report for 1926 he says that he "often" preached in the Baptists' chapel on Sundays and Thursdays.[17]

In the summer of 1927 the new - and larger - Bethel was brought into use, coinciding with the beginning of Averbuch's visit to America.[18] S. Ostrovsky, a member of the Mildmay Mission's London staff, had arrived in Kishinev in mid May 1927 so that the work, which had been prospering in an "atmosphere of revival", should not suffer during Averbuch's furlough.[19] Averbuch was back in Kishinev in March 1928.[20] And, without further explanation, the Mildmay prayer list for April 1928 calls for prayer that "various difficulties which the work in Chisinau, Bessarabia, is facing, may be resolved now that Mr and Mrs Averbuch have returned."[21]

These difficulties may have had something to do with the formation of the new Hebrew Christian congregation, to which we shall refer in the next section. But it is more likely that they concern the government restrictions on the Mildmay Mission's work, which were however removed later in the year.[22]

To sum up, we can say that in the period 1922-1928 the work in Kishinev under Averbuch's leadership was in a period of growth. Although the large numbers of Jews mentioned as attending special meetings do not give an accurate picture of how many of them came to faith and were baptized, they do indicate an openness to the gospel. It is beyond any doubt that the Hebrew Christian group was growing in this period. Averbuch's communications show that the annual number of baptisms fluctuated between one and five.[23] Although the collaboration between Averbuch and the Russian Baptists was excellent, some of the Hebrew Christians will have felt a greater need to manifest their Jewish identity, although they did hold separate meetings during this period. At any rate, a Hebrew Christian congregation was set up in 1928. Unfortunately the sources do not give answers to all the questions one would like to ask. But we can say something about it.

A Hebrew Christian congregation is formed in Kishinev in 1928

In 1928 a proper Hebrew Christian congregation was formed in Kishinev. Unfortunately the sources that have been available do not give a full description of the distinctives of this congregation. So on the one hand we must be cautious in postulating that Rabinowitz's ideas were now - at last - bearing fruit. On the other hand, it cannot be ruled out that Rabinowitz's earlier work may have been a source of inspiration. The memory of him was still alive in various ways in Kishinev in the 1930s (see below). E.S. Gabe says that what made his "relationship with the Kishineff Community so easy and pleasant was they were not extremists". And he continues:

> While having services on the Sabbath, that did not displace Sunday services. While commemorating Jewish festivals, that did not exclude Christmas or Easter. While believing in the sanctifying work of the Holy Spirit, that did not include senseless behaviour.

For this reason the Hebrew Christian Community of Kishineff was able to attract and influence people of every walk of life.[24] The sources consulted give no exact date for the formation of the Hebrew Christian congregation. There is also obscurity about who provided the decisive impetus. But it may be confirmed that the number of Hebrew Christians won through the work of Averbuch was now sufficient to warrant contemplating this possibility. It can also be confirmed that Averbuch came to head up the Hebrew Christian congregation, but this does not necessarily mean that it was he who had advocated the new departure. He may have received impulses during his visit to America, from which he returned to Kishinev in March 1928.[25] But it is equally conceivable that the need for an independent Hebrew Christian congregation had been felt for some time, and had grown in step with the influx of new Hebrew Christians, who through their baptism became members of the Russian Baptist congregation.

It would appear that the Hebrew Christians' breach with their former church setting had occurred before S.H. Wilkinson's visit to Kishinev in October 1928, when the tenth anniversary of Mildmay's new work in Kishinev was celebrated.[26] It is possible that the final decision to set up an independent Hebrew Christian congregation should be related to the conference of the International Hebrew Christian Alliance in Hamburg in July 1928. This was attended by the Hebrew Christian N. Feigin from Kishinev, who made a strong impression with his great love for Christ, according to a report.[27]

Sir Leon Levison, the president of the Alliance, mentioned Rabinowitz's name in his address at the Hamburg conference. Dealing with the countries in which the Alliance had branches, he says of Rumania:

> In Rumania we have as yet no Hebrew Christian branch, notwith-
> standing that since the days of Rabinowitz there have been many
> Hebrew Christians. Our friend Feigin's fervent faith and love for our
> people guarantee that such a branch will soon be set up.[28]

Even though we cannot without more ado attribute the formation of the
Hebrew Christian congregation in Kishinev to the desire to set up a branch
of the World Alliance, it is conceivable that Feigin, by his attendance at the
conference, found inspiration and boldness to fight for the formation of the
Hebrew Christian congregation in Kishinev.

The Hebrew Christians' breach with their former congregation did
not occur quite smoothly. The Norwegian missionary Sister Olga Olaussen,
who was stationed in Galatz, visited Kishinev at the end of October 1928 -
after S.H. Wilkinson had been there. She writes that, whereas in 1921 when
she first visited the town there were only four or five Jewish believers, i.e.
Hebrew Christians, the flock had now grown, and she refers to a photograph
taken during Wilkinson's visit. She says that the Hebrew Christians had
formerly belonged to the Baptist congregation, although the Hebrew
Christians did have their special meetings as well as gospel meetings for Jews.
"But now they have withdrawn from the Baptist congregation and formed
the Hebrew Christian congregation in Kishinev." She adds that it came as a
blow to the Baptist congregation to lose so many members at once, as
relations had always been excellent. For that reason the Baptists could not
understand the Hebrew Christians' urge to form an independent congregation.
However, the parties had succeeded in "settling this in peace, without the
bond of brotherhood suffering thereby," she says.[29]

Although in this matter Olga Olaussen may be regarded as a fairly
neutral source, it would seem that matters were only settled in peace on the
surface. At any rate, it may be noted that the prayer lists in the Mildmay
magazine in 1930-1931 betray that there was still a painful aftermath to the
Hebrew Christian breach with the Russian Baptists.[30] Averbuch's annual
reports after the breach also show that it had affected relations between the
activity based on Bethel and the work at the Baptist premises. They were no
longer visiting and helping each other as they did before.[31] In his report for
1933, however, he was able to say that he sent his magazine to Baptist
congregations, who at their places distributed it to Jews.[32] In connection with
a Christmas gathering in 1934, Baptist believers - again - came to Bethel, and
in 1935 the situation seems to have been normalized.[33] At Passover 1935 the
Russian Baptists celebrated their 25th anniversary. The Hebrew Christians
and also a number of Jews from Bethel came to this celebration, and
Averbuch was among those asked to speak. The following day the Hebrew
Christian congregation arranged a meeting in the premises of the German
Lutheran congregation. Averbuch spoke at this, and the Russian Baptists
also attended this event.[34] In connection with the Christmas and New Year

meetings in 1935-1936 the picture is the same: the various groups attended each other's gatherings, so that the situation was now comparable to that in the period 1922-1928 - before the breach and the formation of the Hebrew Christian congregation.[35]

To return to the situation in 1928: without overmuch enthusiasm, the Mildmay Mission accepted the Hebrew Christians' wish to form an independent congregation. The magazine issue for January 1929 evinces some sympathy, but without venturing to predict the congregation's possibilities and development.[36] But the same issue prints a letter about the new congregation. The man behind it was L. Averbuch, who is described as the leader of the congregation; members of the council are given as N. Feigin, T. Trachtman, and M. Dreitschman, with M. Tarlew as the secretary. The last four of these were closely linked to the work of the Mildmay Mission.[37] Apart from Dreitschman, they had all been on the payroll of the mission at times.

In the letter the leadership of the new congregation express thanks for being hitherto housed in the Mildmay premises, and say that it was through the mission they had come to faith in Christ. They add that they feel a deep need for a place "where the Hebrew Christian community and its growing children could gather for Christian worship as well as for performing other Christian rites according to our convictions". Finally a collection is mentioned among the Hebrew Christians for the building of a Hebrew Christian "tabernacle". The building is estimated to cost £400-£500. "We are weak for such a great work, but we believe that the Lord is with us in this matter."

As far as can be judged, the new Hebrew Christian congregation did not succeed in building a tabernacle. But they did get their own premises, probably rented. In the summer of 1933 Averbuch took the children who came to Bethel on an outing, and they went to the large garden which the Hebrew Christian congregation had at their disposal.[38] In the autumn of 1936 the congregation got new premises, called The Tabernacle or Mishkan.[39] It is not clear whether this was rented or purchased.

Although Averbuch headed up both the work carried out under the auspices of Mildmay and the new Hebrew Christian congregation, his references in his bulletins to the latter work are exceedingly sporadic. It must be assumed that even though the Hebrew Christian congregation obtained its own meeting-place, its members continued to attend Bethel. It also has to be presumed that the Jewish element in their meetings was stronger than could be the case at Bethel. The "other Christian rites" mentioned in the above letter from the new congregation might conceivably be circumcision, for instance, though it would be an unusual way of referring to it. In the winter of 1930-1931 the Hebrew Christians in Bessarabia organized themselves and affiliated to the International Hebrew Christian Alliance, yet another sign that they wanted to protect their Jewish identity.[40]

At a Hebrew Christian gathering arranged by the Norwegian missionaries in Galatz at Passover 1931, about 40 travelling visitors attended. More than half, i.e. 22, came from Kishinev, led by Averbuch, 12 came from Bucharest, headed by Adeney, and the other few came from other towns.[41]

Although it is not possible to give any clear picture of the distinctive character of the new Hebrew Christian congregation, it is possible to say that it grew in the 1930s. For instance, in his 1936 annual report Averbuch mentions that in the summer he had had the privilege of baptizing three Jews "in the baptistry of the Jewish Christian community, which is in a garden". In the same connection, Averbuch mentions that the work "is now carried forward on two fronts, so to speak", from Mildmay's Bethel, and from "The Tabernacle", the "property" of the Hebrew Christian congregation.[42]

As the sources do not, unfortunately, say any more about the distinctive features of the new congregation, and as the two works are viewed from the same angle because of the overlap of personnel, we shall conclude by glancing at the work which was based on Bethel in the 1930s and giving a few instances to prove that the memory of Rabinowitz lived on.

The memory of Rabinowitz in Kishinev

As we have mentioned, Somerville Hall was in use from 1918 to 1921, after Kishinev had passed into Rumanian hands. The Bible which had lain on the "altar" while Rabinowitz was alive, and which was inscribed *Kitvei ha-Kodesh* in some way came into Averbuch's possession. It can, at least, be noted that it was spoken of a couple of times in the 1930s.

In the early summer of 1931 S.H. Wilkinson visited Kishinev. At the same time the Russian Professor Marzinkowsky was in the town, where he worked in conjunction with Averbuch in Bethel. At a meeting in Bethel, both of them read "from the Hebrew Bible which had been in Rabbi Rabinowitch's possession."[43]

The same Bible recurs in 1936 in a description of an outreach in connection with meetings held in Bethel in the days after Yom Kippur. At the meeting Averbuch described that *Simchat Torah* - the joy feast of the Law - was not actually a day in the calendar, but a lasting experience to the Jew who believes in Jesus. A large flock of children walked singing through the hall accompanied with music and holding flags in their hands resembling the flags which Jewish children had at the *Simchat-Torah* festival. But with the difference, writes Averbuch, that the name "Jesus" was written on these flags. And he continues:

> At the head of the procession a little boy, called Moses, was carrying the beautifully bound Bible of the late Joseph Rabinowitch on which the words Kisvè Hakodesh [Kitvei ha-Kodesh] (Holy Scriptures) were displayed in large metal letters.[44]

Although Rabinowitz's name figures little in the accounts of and from Kishinev in the period onward from 1918, it may be noted that towards the close of Mildmay activity in Kishinev, the Rabinowitz Bible was at least incorporated into special occasions. The work closed down in 1937 (see below).

Another example that the memory of Rabinowitz was alive in the Kishinev of the 1930s is given by N. Rosef, the national secretary of the Norwegian Israel Mission in 1934-1937. On a journey in Rumania in spring 1935 he also visited Kishinev. He describes Averbuch, by whom he was entertained, as "one of the most energetic missionaries in Jewish mission".[45] He writes:

> The mission is flourishing here, with a Hebrew Christian congrega-
> tion and even their own Hebrew Christian cemetery. We went there
> straight away, and among others visited the tomb of Joseph Rabinowitz,
> the world-renowned Hebrew Christian and missionary. (Here tombs
> are often whole chambers in the ground, with a stairway down and
> the coffins placed in individual chambers in the walls).

Rosef continues with some words which, in part, he borrowed from P. Gordon:

> We felt we were standing on holy ground at this man's grave. He
> sowed so much that has borne fruit for eternity among God's own
> covenant people. He resembled a volcano, it has been said, when his
> love of Jesus was to be expressed in words. And his love for Israel was
> the other and practical side of his love for Jesus. Through his great
> intellect and brilliance Rabinowitz acquired something of an apos-
> tolic power and authority about him. And he was animated by an
> unshakable confidence in God's promises to Israel...[46]

After this, Rosef repeats the story which P. Gordon told about Rabinowitz in 1897 (see Chapter 17). Would it not be very plausible to imagine that just such stories were current in the circles which in the 1930s were working for and in a Hebrew Christian congregation in Kishinev?

The day after the visit to Rabinowitz's grave, Rosef visited the Jewish cemetery. After standing by a communal Jewish grave, he has to write: "Here lies the dust of about 200 of Jesus' brethren according to the flesh, killed by 'Christian' hands, in Christ's name."[47]

Averbuch also showed E.S. Gabe the tomb of Rabinowitz when Gabe visited Kishinev at Easter 1936. Gabe mentions that he heard about Rabinonowitz a few months after he had himself become a believer in Jesus. It was Averbuch who told him about Rabinowitz during a Christmas celebration in Bucharest in 1935.[48] According to Gabe Averbuch had retrieved the vineyard and burial ground for the Hebrew Christian community; they had been lost after Rabinowitz's death. Gabe calls

Rabinowitz's grave an "impressive tomb".[49] In 1936 it was a large garden and still the property of the Hebrew Christian community.[50]

The close

Against the background of Averbuch's activity and the character of the work in Kishinev through the 1930s, it comes as a surprise that the Mildmay Mission closed the work down in 1937. As late as June 1937, a brief notice written by Averbuch says that four Jews were awaiting baptism, and that one of them had come to faith during Averbuch's illness - and in his sickroom.[51] The July issue of the magazine contains this brief notice: "We regret to say that we have lost the services of Mr. Leon Awerbuch, after some twenty years' connection."[52]

There is no amplification of this. If Averbuch's illness was the sole reason, one might expect this to have been mentioned. The August issue of the magazine says: "The loss to the Mission of Mr. L. Averbuch, and its consequences, have rendered it wisest to close the Mission's work in Chisinau - at least for a while."[53] It is John H. Wilkinson who announces this, and says in the same connection that his father - S.H. Wilkinson - had made this decision, judging that the work might perhaps be resumed later.

In the survey of the work of 1937, Kishinev and Averbuch are not named at all by the Mildmay Mission. In this context we had probably better refrain from probing into the actual reason for the sudden closure of the work. Averbuch died in London in 1941, as is mentioned in a notice in 1946 in connection with the news of Mrs Averbuch's death.[54]

The war came and with it the bestial atrocities against the Jews, including many Hebrew Christians. At the end of June 1940 Russia laid claim to the return of Bessarabia, the area that had passed into Rumanian hands in 1918 with the Peace of Versailles. In August 1940 the Rumanian Jews were deprived of civil rights, and many Jews who were living elsewhere in Rumania, but had been born in Bessarabia, returned there. But the German and Rumanian forces advanced eastwards and made the area "*judenrein*" either by deporting them further east or murdering them.[55]

This horrific story is not one to be told here. We shall merely note that after the end of the Second World War there was said to be only one surviving Hebrew Christian in Kishinev. Owing to the new political circumstances, the work in Kishinev was never resumed.[56]

While all British citizens had left Rumania in February 1941, the envoy of the Norwegian Israel Mission, Magne Solheim, remained with his wife Cilgia in Rumania.[57] After the war a number of the Hebrew Christians with whom Solheim had contact emigrated to Israel, and a new work was established there. In that connection it may be mentioned that one Hebrew Christian - "Aunt Klara" - with whom the Norwegian Mission had contact, survived the Second World War. She was a Hebrew Christian, had grown up in Kishinev, and was one of the first to move into Ebenezer Old People's Home in Haifa in 1976.[58]

In conclusion we shall give one example to show that, for Hebrew Christians, Jewish identity was more than just a high-sounding phrase in Kishinev during the Second World War. In her diary Marie Antonia Aniksdal, one of the envoys of the Norwegian Israel Mission in Galatz on 10 October 1942, writes:

> Saturday. Milan [Haimovici] today returned from his labour service at the hospital in Kishinev. He recounts that the town has been completely destroyed, all the houses burnt. Only a number of cottages on the outskirts are left. Our Hebrew Christian friends there have gone. Only Moise Dreitschman, married to Olga who served us for the first couple of years we were here, has been left. During the Russian time, suddenly all who lived in the Mission's property were arrested and sent to Siberia. The Dreitschmans had managed to hide - and later they had remained hidden until the Rumanians came. Two of the Hebrew Christians had been working with a number of other Jews at a petrol depot. This caught fire - and as they could not find the culprit, it was decided that every fifth man should be shot. Oddly enough, both the believers were among them. The officer was told they were Christians. He said that they could step aside and two others were to be found. But they said that, since the lot had fallen on them, they would rather die, and so they were shot.[59]

Olga Dreitschman died in 1946. Moise Dreitschman settled with his new wife Sara in Israel in 1967. In their old age they also moved into the Ebenezer home in Haifa.[60]

Chapter 21

RELEVANCE

Before Theodor Herzl emerged as the spokesman of modern Zionism, there had been other Jews who had expressed similar ideas. Before the "Herzl of Hebrew Christianity", Joseph ben David Rabinowitz, emerged, other Hebrew Christians had broached some of the problem areas which came to mark Rabinowitz's life. Herzl and Rabinowitz each had his forerunners. Herzl was not the first Zionist, and Rabinowitz was not the first Hebrew Christian to wish to retain his Jewish identity as a believer in Jesus. But through their activity, the causes which Herzl and Rabinowitz stood for gained a serious hearing in wide circles. Herzl succeeded in getting Zionism on the agenda. Rabinowitz succeeded in getting the question of the continued Jewish identity of Hebrew Christians on the agenda. In their time both found themselves encountering understanding, but also contempt.

After Rabinowitz had put his faith in Jesus as the Messiah on a firm footing, he fought a stubborn battle against the general assumption that a Jewish believer in Jesus should live like a Gentile (viz. a Gentile Christian) when he had come to faith in the Jew Jesus.

We may refer to the last chapters of this book to support our assertion that Herzl's visions were realized to a far greater extent than Rabinowitz's. But we cannot conclude from this that Rabinowitz's ideas were irrelevant to his own time, nor that they are irrelevant today.

As early as 1885 A. Saphir was saying that the importance of the Messianic movement in Kishinev should not be assessed on its numerical strength, but on its intrinsic value (see Chapter 12). If one will, one can see this as hedging one's bets. But it meant something else to Saphir. He maintains that in missionary activity among Jews it has not been adequately stressed that Jesus does not come to them *ab extra*, from outside. He emphasizes that the question, "Is Jesus the Messiah and Lord?" is not so much a question between the Christian church and the Jews, but is first and foremost a Jewish question. The predominant feeling amongst the Jews is, says Saphir, that becoming a Christian is the same as becoming a Gentile, whereby they are broken off their own tree and grafted onto another tree.[1]

Even de le Roi, who had a critical attitude to Rabinowitz's distinctive causes, argues that Rabinowitz brought Jesus from the periphery and into the actual centre of Jewish life.[2]

Rabinowitz made the question of Jesus into a Jewish matter and thereby riled the Jewish world, not only orthodox but also Enlightenment Judaism. He also complicated matters for Hebrew Christians, both for those who saw in Christianity the sole chance of escaping their Jewish identity, and for those who had come to faith out of honest conviction but who by the Gentile Christians around them were not allowed much scope for retaining a Jewish identity. But Rabinowitz also succeeded in capturing and holding Gentile Christians in the kind of problems he regarded as important to Hebrew Christians. F. Delitzsch in particular is to be commended for so strongly supporting and defending Rabinowitz, even though Delitzsch in principle considered that Rabinowitz went too far in his retention of e.g. the Sabbath and circumcision.[3]

With few exceptions, prior to Rabinowitz it was a general conception bordering upon the obvious that a Jew who went over to Christianity ceased to be a Jew. Rabinowitz decisively brought this attitude into question. Likewise he protested against the idea that 'legalism' was an automatic consequence of his desire to retain national Jewish customs. This label was - and is - the easiest way of dismissing Rabinowitz. But it is too facile without further ado to pin this label on Hebrew Christians, for evangelical Christianity also has its written and unwritten laws, so that 'legalism' is not merely a danger for Jewish Christianity but a common danger to all.

Although there are great problems of a theological nature in Rabinowitz's basic positions, it must be seen as a simplification when Gisle Johnson presents the matter in the following way:

1) Jewish-style Jewish Christianity in Jewish surroundings gives the result: Judaism.

2) Jewish-style Jewish Christianity in Christian surroundings gives the result: neither Judaism nor Christianity.

3) Definitely Christian-style Jewish Christianity, whether lived in Jewish or Christian surroundings, gives the result: the Jewish character is deleted as something inessential, as it becomes a hindrance to living a full and whole Christian life.[4]

It was also a simplification when in 1960 a Danish editor passed judgement on the Messianic Jews of the day in Israel with the following summing-up: "But much suggests that the 'Messianic Jews' like Rabinowitz's 'Christian synagogue' are premature babes who are not viable."[5]

And it simply pre-empts any serious theological assessment of the matter to say, as was declared at a consultation in Løgumkloster, Denmark, in 1964 under the auspices of the Lutheran World Federation that with a designation like 'Jewish Christian' or similar, an unbiblical splitting-up of the church is brought about.[6]

The lasting significance of Rabinowitz's activity lies first and foremost in his stubborn insistence that his faith in Jesus had not made him an ex-Jew, and that his Jewish identity had not been drowned in baptism, and that a Hebrew Christian has liberty to live in a Jewish manner. Because his faith was rooted in a New Testament doctrine of justification by faith and in a biblically oriented Christology - a conviction at which he had arrived during a thorough study of the New Testament after his journey to Palestine - he helped to make it possible to re-assess the matter on a serious basis. Hereby Gentile Christians were obliged to weigh up why they would not give Jews a liberty corresponding to that Paul had won for Gentiles, as regards the relationship to the law. For his own part, Rabinowitz desired this liberty, but without denouncing other Hebrew Christians who chose to be assimilated in a Christian church. On the other hand, his attitude to Isak Lichtenstein, another of the well-known Jesus-believing Jews of the time, who would not get baptized, was strongly critical (see Chapter 14). It was not Rabinowitz's fault that he did not achieve a true Hebrew Christian congregation with administration of the sacraments, as he desired. Through his baptism he showed that he regarded it as necessary and important to become part of Christ's universal church without becoming a member of a particular Gentile Christian denomination and without abandoning his Jewish identity.

Of course, on a number of points Rabinowitz was conditioned by his time, but his main views are still challenging, both to Gentile Christians and to Hebrew Christians of today. Whereas it was previously possible for Gentile Christians to maintain that a Hebrew Christian church was neither desirable nor feasible, because the Jews did not have their own country,[7] this argument no longer applies, at least not in Israel. We shall not elaborate on this question here, but merely note that an amazing resemblance can be shown between the problems which Messianic Jews in Israel - and for that matter also Hebrew Christians in the USA - contend with today, and the problems about which Rabinowitz attempted to reach conclusions a hundred years ago.[8] On the one side there is at this very time a Hebrew Christian theology growing up in which the theological problems are subjected to serious debate.[9] This debate can be followed e.g in the journal Mishkan, A forum on the Gospel and the Jewish People. On the other side Hebrew Christian leaders can complain of a mystical, anti-intellectual and irrational Jesus-faith among Messianic Jews, which is due to a deficient grounding in the Scriptures.[10]

Both these parties would doubtless gain from a closer acquaintance with Rabinowitz. It is regrettable that few, as far as we can judge, have had close contact with his writings. For it may be said in general that people have been very sparing in the questions they have asked and the answers they have been given. A reasonable insight into Rabinowitz's theology and the way he argued and into his struggle to retain his Jewish identity as a Christian believer is sought in vain. His conversion story has always been good copy for popular books about Hebrew Christian personalities, but with few exceptions people have rested content with that. Conversion stories do have their value, but they give no real insight into the later activity of the person in question. We discover that Gartenhaus, for instance, when dealing with the complicated questions of Rabinowitz's baptism, his relations with the Lutheran Pastor Faltin, and his decisions on Gentile Christian denominational allegiance, merely has the following to say:

> Rabinowitz was baptized in Berlin by Professor Mead of Andover, Massachusetts, on March 22 [read March 24] 1885, and he was asked by the pastor of the Lutheran church at Kischeneff to join the church. He declined, however, for neither he nor his followers, who had separated from the synagogue, could worship in a church where there was a crucifix. For yet stronger reasons he could not join the Russian church, though he was asked to do so by the highest authorities.[11]

Even in the case of the esteemed Hebrew Christian scholar J. Jocz it is plainly apparent that he has not been in close contact with Rabinowitz's own writings.[12] A reliable survey is given, but no deeper insight into how Rabinowitz argued his cause. Nor is it particularly apt to describe Rabinowitz, as Jocz does, as "a great organizer", whose merit it was to become the "founder of the first modern Hebrew-Christian community without any outside assistance", and that he is "the finest example of a Hebrew-Christian missionary".[13] Such a summing-up is imprecise in both content and choice of words.

D. Juster, an American Messianic Jew, who has attempted to give a basis for Messianic Jewish theology, admits that "Messianic Judaism is a babe: immature, babbling and learning to walk."[14] If this is correct, then Rabinowitz undoubtedly has something to teach them. In their efforts to make the link back to the first believing Jews, they ought not to sidestep Rabinowitz too quickly. He wanted the same thing that they want, and he was capable of reflecting theologically upon the issues. His love for Israel and his Jewish brethren had as its reference point his love for and faith in Jesus the Messiah. With this as his reference point he adopted a critical stance towards the Jews of his time, avoided any romantic Israel-theology, while at the same time his love for his brethren and his people remained intact, and the hope of Israel's salvation did not waver.

Although one might wish that even more than was the case Rabinowitz had devoted himself to theological preoccupations and the clarification of his ideas, he did show - particularly at the beginning of his public ministry - that enthusiasm and theological preoccupation are not mutually exclusive. On that point too he has something to say to Hebrew Christians of our time.

Through his activity and his preaching he struck home to his Jewish brethren at a tender spot. He told an apt story about that. It is found in slightly variant versions and can be traced back to 1884-1885. It goes under the designation "Joseph's Misfortune".[15]

Joseph's Misfortune

The misfortune of my people has always been on my heart. I have also tried various remedies to relieve it, but all has been in vain.

When a doctor comes to a patient, he first has to question the patient closely before he can prescribe a remedy for the disease. He feels the pulse, presses here and there, asking all the time, "Does it hurt here?" "Is there pressure there?" "Have you pain here?" But not until the doctor touches the tender spot, does a really clear answer come from the patient. The pain squeezes the words from him, "Don't press so hard, it hurts!"

That was my experience when I concerned myself with my people's sufferings. I have in vain pressed various places. As I was not striking the tender spot, there was hardly any answer.

If I said, "The Talmud and all the rabbinical extraneous matter do not come, as is claimed, from Sinai, but they are human matters full of wisdom and unwisdom," then these words made little impression upon my people.

If I said, "Nor does the Tanakh (the Old Testament) contain anything other than human words, unproven stories, and unbelievable miracles," then all the time I remained the respected Rabinowitz; that did not cause my people any pain either.

My people remained calm when I placed Moses on an equal footing with the conjurors of our day; it did not hurt them when I called the same Moses an impostor. Indeed, I might even deny God without my people uttering a single sound of pain.

But when I returned from the Holy Land with the glad news: Jesus is our brother, then I struck the tender spot. A scream of pain could be heard and resounded from all sides, "Do not press, do not touch that, it hurts!" Well, it does hurt: But you must know, my people, that that is indeed your illness; you lack nothing but your brother Jesus. Your illness consists precisely in your not having him. Receive him and you will be healed of all your sufferings.

TECHNICAL DETAILS

1 Dates

In Russia up to 1917, they used the Julian calendar (old style) unlike many other countries which had introduced the Gregorian calendar (new style).

When the text gives two dates, e.g. 24 December/5 January, the first date is in accord with the Julian calendar, i.e. the dating that was used in Russia, the last is identical with the West European mode of dating. In the sources it is sometimes uncertain which calendar the dating refers to.

A date followed by (r) indicates that the Russian, i.e. the Julian, calendar has been has been followed; a (r?) means that there is some doubt as to which calendar has been used.

In other words: Add 12 days to the Russian/Julian dating to arrive at our Gregorian dating.

2 Names

a) Rabinowitz's name: In the sources, the name of Rabinowitz is spelled in many different ways. I have chosen the spelling which, for example, can be seen on the autographed photo at the beginning of the book.

b) Transcription of names: Russian names are usually given in the form they have in the sources I am quoting from, no matter which system of transcription these sources apply. Concerning Hebrew names, my primary concern has been to make them easy to read rather than to observe a particular system of transcription consistently.

3 Full names of missionary organisations

Most of the names mentioned in the book are self-evident. The following are less obvious:

Berlin Society	Die Gesellschaft zur Beförderung des Christentums unter den Juden
German Central Agency	Der evangelisch-lutherische Centralverein für die Mission unter Israel
British Society	The British Society for the Propagation of the Gospel among the Jews
London Society	The London Society for Promoting Christianity amongst the Jews
Mildmay Mission	The Mildmay Mission to the Jews

CHAPTER REFERENCES

Introduction (p.ix)
1 Schonfield 1936:223.
2 Kjær-Hansen & Kvarme 1983, Kjær-Hansen 1986.
3 JH 1888:142, Smith 1890:362.
4 JH 1890:11-12.

Chapter 1 (p.1)
1 MTI 1894:28, MBI 1894:45.
2 Sch. 4/1884:VI.
3 MBI 1885:75, cf. CW 1888:376.
4 JH 1884:117.
5 Gredsted 1886:5.
6 Poulsen 1886:65-66.
7 Poulsen 1889:11.
8 MBI 1885:4.
9 Sch. 4/1884:III-VI.
10 SaH 1885:165-172.
11 Sch. 16/1887:X.
12 SaH 1885:171.
13 JH 1884:56, 59, 117, The Daily News 3/3 1884, Ch. 6/3 1884:18, MTI 1885:28.
14 JH 1884:117.
15 SK 1889:219-220.
16 Saphir 1888:3.
17 JH 1889:199.
18 MBI 1890:14.
19 TT 1897:166.
20 MTI 1896:66.
21 MTI 1898:15.
22 SaH 1899:178.
23 Venetianer 1888:28, cf. RdI 1889:12.
24 RdI 1894:99.
25 JH 1890:11-14.
26 SaH 1889:49, RdI 1889:26.
27 StPES 1888:42, Deutsche-Evangelische Kirchenzeitung 1888:215, SaH 1889:45.
28 RdI 1889:61 n.l.
29 SaH 1889:49.
30 WW 1885:156.
31 TT 1896:46.
32 JH 1887:24.
33 de le Roi 1899:346.
34 Lhotzky 1904:123, 125.
35 e.g. SaH 1885:172-182.
36 Wilkinson 1908:221.
37 MBI 1885:139.
38 TT 1896:134.
39 JH 1899:22-23.
40 e.g. Ch.31/10 1890:26, RdI 1891:89, 1895:24-26,56, 1899:25.
41 Rausch 1982:92-99.
42 MB 1906:137-140, 150-152, 155-158, cf. 177-179.
43 Tsitron 1923.
44 Rejzen 1929.
45 Ginsburg 1946.
46 JH 1887:78-80.
47 Zipperstein 1987:226.
48 MBI 1885:14-16.
49 Wagner 1978:163 n.192.
50 JH 1885:17.

Chapter 2 (p.11)
1 Sch.44-46/1896:10-11, MBI 1895:116.
2 Adler 1884:10, Wilkinson 1908:209, MTI 1884:185.
3 Letter to Wilkinson, translated into English from MTI 1894:28, MBI 1894:45.
4 FCSP 1896:30.
5 Goldberg 1934: 13ff., Rengstorf & Kortzfleisch 1970:652.
6 Goldberg 1934:26,40.
7 Lambroza 1982:25-29.
8 Enc. Jud. XII, 1972:1037-1041, Goldberg 1934:54.
9 Goldberg 1934:53-54.
10 Goldberg 1934:51.
11 RdI 1887:85, MBI 1887:172.
12 Nath. 1885/86:151, TT 1899:86, MTI 1899:133, MBI 1899:109.
13 Tsitron 1923:121.
14 HM 19/1882:376-378.
15 HM 30/1882:608.
16 Tsitron 1923:126.
17 RdI 1887:85.
18 Tsitron 1923:121.
19 HM 22/1882:433, cf. Nath. 1895:81.

20 HM 30/1882:608.

21 I am indebted to Rabbi Chaim Pearlman, Jerusalem, for his translation into English of Rabinowitz's article in HM 30/1882:608.

22 HM 21/1882:414-418, 22/1882:431-434.

23 Zipperstein 1991:228 n.30.

24 HM 19/1882:377, RdI 1887:85-87.

25 Jew. Enc. IX, 1925:393-394, New Standard Jew. Enc. X, 1975:1470, JI 1890:155.

26 HM 21/1882:414-418, 22/1882:431-433.

27 RdI 1887:86.

28 SaH 1884:239-244, Gidney 1908:453-454.

29 Venetianer 1888:13.

30 Sch. 16/1887:III.

31 SK 1887:40.

32 Ch. 3/3 1887:1-2, cf. JH 1887:78-80.

33 RdI 1887:84-87.

34 MBI 1887:173, MTI 1888:53-55, RdI 1887:87.

35 e.g. TT 1899:86, Ch. 25/5 1899:22, Wilkinson 1905:77, Schonfield 1936:224, Rausch 1982:94.

36 TT 1899:86.

37 Torm 1909:71.

38 Torm 1984:306.

39 JH 1886:33.

40 MTI 1887:17, Korff:1a-b, Dunlop 1894:447.

41 Lhotzky 1904:118.

42 FüI 1888:9-10, MTI 1888:58.

43 TT 1898:171.

44 SK 1885:137.

45 MTI 1886:64, Kahle 1964:176.

46 JH 1887:23-24, MBI 1887:31.

Chapter 3 (p.23)

1 Sch. 16/1887:III.

2 See Survey III,1 at the back of this book.

3 Sch. 16/1887:54.

4 Lippe 1881:643.

5 HM 21/1882:414.

6 HM 6/1884:81-82, cf. Sch. 5/1885:9-12.

7 Sch. 16/1887:11, RdI 1887:84.

8 cf. Mahler 1916:590-591.

9 Adler 1885:7.

10 HBO 1879:1069-1072, 1131-1141, cf. HM 10/1879:201-203.

11 HM 9/1880:171-173, 10/1880:194-195, 11/1880:214-216.

12 Tsitron 1923:116-127.

13 Rejzen 1929:32-34.

14 Ginsburg 1946:80-81.

15 HM 11/1880:216.

16 HM 19/1882:379, 22/1882:433.

17 JC 265 1899:13.

18 See Bibliography: Rabinowitz J.: Selected Hebrew correspondent articles.

19 Jew. Enc. X, 1925:303-304.

20 Laskov 1982:268-272, cf. Zipperstein 1987:228 n.27.

21 Zipperstein 1987:225.

22 Zipperstein 1987:208.

23 Lhotzky 1904:111.

24 SK 1884:254, Adler 1884:4.

25 Sch. 5/1885:29, cf. MTI 1886:93-94, 1888:55.

26 FCSM 1888:137, TT 1897:167.

27 RDI 1895:85-86, JH 1895:92, TT 1896:134.

28 FCSM October 1889.

29 TT 1897:167.

30 Acc. to Lerner in Axelrud 1893:69-91, excerpts in MTI 1895:89.

31 FCSR 1886:29; Draitschmann 1971:15 cf. JH 1884:117.

32 Zipperstein 1987:211.

33 Ch. 33 1887:1.

34 FCSM 1896:159.

35 Ch. 17/6 1887:11, 1/11 1889:16.

36 Smith 1890:361.

37 Nath. 1885/86:150-151.

38 HM 22/1882:433.

39 Enc. Jud. VII, 1972:787-789.

40 Priluker 1895:22-28, Enc. Jud. XII, 1972:1026-1027, de le Roi 1899:345-346.

41 New Standard Jew. Enc. X, 1975:1592-1593.

42 New Standard Jew. Enc. X, 1975:1456.

43 Enc. Jud. XIII, 1972:1473.

44 SaH 1885:243-245 (Novorossiiskii Telegraf No 3138, 22/8 1885), SaH 1886:100-102 (Narodnie Noving No 2, 1886).

45 FCSR 1885:10.

46 de le Roi 1899:345.

47 Zipperstein 1987:216.
48 Nath. 1895:129-135 (German extract).
49 Sch. 16/1887:III.
50 Poulsen 1886:37.
51 Sch. 4/1884:V.
52 Saphir 1885:22-23.
53 Wilkinson 1908:208.
54 Ch. 33 1887:1, cf. 201 1887:11.
55 Dunlop 1894:445.
56 Jüdische Presse 6/11 1884, acc. to JC
28/11 1884:12.
57 JI 1899:102, Gidney 1908:542.
58 StPES 1885:26.
59 Kahle 1964:150.
60 StPES 1885:26, Harder 1952/53:167.
61 de le Roi 1899:173, MTI 1912:65.
62 Tsitron 1925:109, Zipperstein 1987:213.
63 Tsitron 1925:116-117.
64 MTI 1912:65, cf. 1912:313, de le Roi
1899:173.
65 SaH 1868/69:189.
66 de le Roi 1899:173, SaH 1912:54.
67 Zipperstein 1987:213.
68 MTI 1912:66, de le Roi 1899:173.
69 Gordon 1890:87, MTI 1912:313, cf.
Dobert 1971:40.
70 Wilkinson 1908:214.
71 Sch. 4/1884:IV-V.
72 Nath. 1911:108.
73 RdI 1887:87.
74 Korff:33-34.
75 StPES 1885:26.
76 MBI 1887:7-8.
77 SaH 1888:46.
78 Krüger 1885:9.
79 SK 1884:273-274.
80 SK June 1885 (back page) and p. 137.
81 MTI 1885:180, MBI 1886:1, JEra
1893:201.
82 TT 1899:85.
83 TT 1899:100, 107.
84 Ch. 33 1887:1, JH 1887:79, 1899:117,
Dunlop 1894:446, Fauerholdt 1914
(Introduction) etc.
85 MTI 1899:126, Ussing 1908:509.
86 e.g. Gartenhaus 1979:147.
87 Lhotzky 1904:110, Poulsen 1886:35.
88 Poulsen 1886:35.
89 MBI 1885:76.
90 Wilkinson 1908:220, Smith 1890:359.

Chapter 4 (p.41)
1 HM 6/1884:81-82.
2 Cf. Sch. 5/1885:16.
3 MBI 1885: 76.
4 StPES 1885:26.
5 Wilkinson 1908:215.
6 Kahle 1964.
7 Gurland 1908.
8 Sch. 4/1884:VI.
9 Ihlen 1947:106-107.
10 Gidney 1908:442-443.
11 Stenberg 1925:45.
12 StPES 1885:29.
13 MBI 1885:74, Ihlen 1947:259.
14 Sch. 4/1884:V.
15 MBI 1883:177-183.
16 MBI 1884:89.
17 StPES 1885:26.
18 MBI 1885:71.
19 StPES 1885:26-27.
20 Korff: 33.
21 SaH 1884:106-110, StPES 1885:27.
22 MTI 1884:65-66.
23 Sch. 4/1884:1-5, Hebrew p.III-V.
24 SaH 1884:112.
25 Adler 1884:12-14, Krüger 1885:29-32,
see Survey III,1.
26 Kjær-Hansen 1982:251-259.
27 SaH 1884:107-108.
28 Gartenhaus 1979:149, cf. Torm
1984:306.
29 Zipperstein 1987:218.
30 Sch. 4/1884:43-44.
31 Sch. 4/1884:40-42, Hebrew p.XXII-
XXIII, StPES 1885:28, Adler 1884:36-38.
32 Zipperstein 1987:225.
33 Wilkinson 1908:216, Ch. 3/3 1887:2.
34 SaH 1885:31.

Chapter 5 (p.53)
1 Sch. 4/1884:VI, StPES 1885:27.
2 Poulsen 1886:42, CW 1887:269,
Fauerholdt 1914:15.
3 Nath. 1911:71, 107.
4 Nath. 1911:73.
5 Nath. 1911:107.
6 StPES 1885:28.
7 JH 1884:143, 1887:80, 1892:90, Dunlop
1894:445-446.

8 Zipperstein 1987:229 n.35.
9 MBI 1884:166-175, JH 1884:117-119,
129-132, 140-142, 1885:1-3, 17-20, 45-46, JI
1884:232-236, 251-256.
10 Nath. 1911:108.
11 JH 1884:118.
12 CMJ d. 50/10:3.
13 MBI 1884:174-175, JH 1884:118, JI
1884:235-236.
14 MBI 1884:167.
15 Nath. 1911:71.
16 Nath. 1911:108.
17 Nath. 1911:108-109.
18 Nath. 1911:109-110.
19 Nath. 1911:114-126, cf. 1911:111.
20 Nath. 1911:71.
21 Dunlop 1894:446-448, Nath. 1886:31-
32, JI 1890:96, Ch. 33 1887:2.
22 JI 1884:87.
23 JH 1884:56.
24 JH 1884:69.
25 Dunlop 1894:445, cf. JH 1884:56,
1885:17.
26 WW 1884:668.
27 Hefter for Hefker acc. to JC 129
1884:6.
28 Odesski Listok No 199, 2/14
September 1884; Tserkovno-
Obshchestvennyi Vestnik; Novorossiiskii
Telegraf No 257.
29 Aug.1884, acc. to Sch.5/1884:11, 16.
29 HM 71/1884:1173, cf. Sch.5/1885:10-
12, JH 1885:17-18.
30 JC 28/11 1884:12, Jüdische Presse 6/11
1884.
31 Sch. 5/1885:12-15.
32 Sch. 5/1885:23, 12 n.l.
33 Poulsen 1886:46.
34 Sch. 4/1884:VI.
35 Sch. 5/1885:23.
36 SaH 1885:105.
37 Nath. 1911:108.
38 Sch. 5/1885:15.
39 SaH 1885:106; Hamagid Tishri 5646,
English translation SK 1885:256.
40 Sch. 5/1885:15-23, JH 1885:18-20.
41 Sch. 5/1885:29.
42 Sch. 5/1885:32.
43 Sch. 5/1885:24-26, cf. WW 1884:787.
44 Poulsen 1886:44.

45 StPES 1885:28-29, Sch. 5/1885:25.
46 WW 1884:787, Sch. 5/1885:39-40.
47 Sch. 16/1887:42-44.
48 Klier p. 41.
49 Klier p. 33-35.
50 StPES 1885:28.
51 Nath. 1885/86:153.
52 MBI 1885:13-14, Saphir 1885:24-25.
53 Nath. 1885/86:152-153.
54 WW 1885:156.
55 Sch. 16/1887:51.
56 SaH 1899:145-147.
57 MBI 1900:161-162, IM 1906:81-82.

Chapter 6 (p.67)

1 Crétien évangélique 1885:221 acc. to
Krüger 1885:19.
2 Enc. Jud. X, 1972:1063-1069, CW
1887:269.
3 Kahle 1964:150.
4 Enc. Jud. X, 1972:1065, Amishai-Maisels
1982:91.
5 Sch. 5/1885:25.
6 Sch. 4/1884:I.
7 SaH 1885:104, 165, 243, Sch. 16/1887:1.
8 Sch. 4/1884:VI.
9 SaH 1885:169.
10 StPES 1885:29, 1886:27.
11 MBI 1885:15, StPES 1885:28, 1887:50.
12 SaH 1885:104, 165, Sch. 4/1884:V,
Gredsted 1886:4.
13 Venetianer 1888:19.
14 SaH 1886:52.
15 Sch. 5/1885 on German title page.
16 JH 1885:47.
17 e.g. TT 1899:85, 89.
18 StPES 1900:314.
19 Torm 1984:306.
20 Sch. 5/1884:25, MTI 1884:185,
1891:158, MBI 1885:5, 12,
WW 1885:6.
21 Dalman 1893:40.
22 StPES 1900:314.
23 TT 1899:105.
24 HM 71/1884:1173.
25 Sch. 5/1885:10.
26 Kjær-Hansen & Kvarme 1979:14-17,
Kjær-Hansen 1982:9.
27 Sch. 4/1884:X, XI.
28 Sch. 4/1884:XI.

29 Sch. 4/1884:XII, XV.
30 Wechsler 1885:3.
31 Sch. 9/1885:5-6.
32 Rabinowitz 1885:15 (Ha-Davar...),
Rabinowitz 1897:175, 177 (Devarim
Nechumim...).
33 Sch. 16/1887:50.
34 Gabe 1987:87f.
35 MBI 1885:15-16.
36 MBI 1885:76.
37 MTI 1885:154.
38 Crétien évangélique 1885:221, acc. to
Krüger 1885:18-19, Poulsen 1886:49.
39 MBI 1885:76.
40 Nath. 1885/86:154.
41 Poulsen 1886:51.
42 JC 30/1 1885:9.
43 WW 1885:156, MBI 1885:31, 48.
44 Nath. 1885/86:154.
45 MBI 1885: 76.
46 WW 1885: 156
47 MBI 1885:75
48 WW 1885:156.
49 StPES 1885:28.
50 Nath. 1885/86:153-154.
51 Wechsler 1885:3-4, Sch. 9/1885:5-7.

Chapter 7 (p.75)

1 Nath. 1911:107.
2 Nath. 1911:108.
3 Sch. 5/1885:29.
4 Sch. 5/1885:34.
5 Wilkinson 1908.
6 Nath. 1911:121.
7 Nath. 1911:123.
8 WW 1884:668, Adler 1884 (Preface).
9 SK 1884:222-223.
10 SK 1884:252-254, Wilkinson 1908:209-211.
11 WW 1884:668.
12 WW 1884:668, SK 1884:254.
13 WW 1884:668.
14 WW 1884:787.
15 WW 1884:787.
16 WW 1884:787.
17 JH 1884:142-143.
18 JH 1884:143.
19 JH 1885:4.
20 JH 1885:34.
21 SK 1884:273-274.
22 Nath. 1911:114-118.
23 MBI 1885:15.
24 SaH 1885:104.
25 Wilkinson 1908:211.
26 CMJ Minute-book, c. 29 item 961.
27 WW 1885:232.
28 MBI 1885:77.
29 SK 1885:84-85.
30 SK 1885:85.
31 SK 1885:61.
32 SK 1885:85.
33 Adler 1885:7-19, Wilkinson 1908:213-221.
34 Adler 1885:15-18.
35 Adler 1885:17-18.
36 Adler 1885:45.
37 Nath. 1885/86:155-156.
38 Nath. 1885/86:155.
39 CW 1887:270, Nath. 1885/86:156,
Poulsen 1886:55.
40 Rausch 1982:113 n.16, Meyer 1983:93.
41 Adler 1885:19-20, Wilkinson 1908:221.
42 Lhotzky 1904:121.
43 StPES 1888:108.
44 SaH 1885:169.
45 Nath. 1885/86:156.
46 Nath. 1885/86:156.
47 Nath. 1885/86:156.
48 MTI 1887:11 (Sch. 9/1885:6), MTI
1888:57 (FüI 1888:9).
49 Meyer 1983:93.
50 Adler 1885:44.
51 MBI 1885:97-98, StPES 1886:26-28.
52 MBI 1885:99.
53 MBI 1885:99-100.
54 SaH 1885:172-182.
55 SaH 1885:165 note.
56 SaH 1885:169.
57 Nath. 1911:119.
58 Lhotzky 1904:120.
59 SK 1885:61, WW 1885:156.
60 Lhotzky 1904:121.
61 Adler 1885:15, Wilkinson 1908:220.
62 Lhotzky 1904:121.
63 Adler 1885:40-41.
64 Adler 1885:42.
65 Adler 1885:43.
66 Lhotzky 1904:119.
67 Lhotzky 1904:121.
68 Adler 1885:18.
69 Nath. 1885/86:155.

70 Ch. 1887:11.
71 Draitschmann 1971:15.
72 Meisl 1930:347.
73 Tsitron 1923:127, Rejzen 1929:35, Ginsburg 1946:87.
74 Clausen 1923:134.
75 Zipperstein 1987:219.
76 Adler 1885:45.

Chapter 8 (p.91)
1 Poulsen 1886:57.
2 Adler 1885:28.
3 Krüger 1885:53-61.
4 Tsitron 1923:127.
5 Rejzen 1929:34.
6 Ginsburg 1946:82.
7 Sch. 4/1885:VI.
8 SaH 1899:177-179.
9 SaH 1899:180.
10 Adler 1885:20.
11 Se Wolf 1958:113-115, Schonfeld 1974:74-76.
12 JH 1884:118.
13 MBI 1884:174-175.
14 CMJ d. 50/10.
15 Krüger 1885:14.
16 Sch. 4/1884:VI.
17 Adler 1885:28-29. The words "He is One" are in §1 of the Hebrew original but not in Adler's translation.
18 Sch. 9/1885:29.
19 SaH 1885:105.
20 Krüger 1885:32.
21 Poulsen 1886:70.
22 Gidney 1908:152.
23 Adler 1885:24-28.
24 Zipperstein 1987:220.
25 Nath. 1911:107.
26 Adler 1885:10.
27 Adler 1885:46.
28 e.g. Sch. 91885:11, Good Friday 1888 (SaH 1889:53, An 1897:119).
29 Sch. 16/1887:VIII.
30 Zipperstein 1987:212.
31 Adler 1885:10-11.
32 JH 1884:130.
33 Sch. 4/1884:VI, HM 71/1884:1173, Krüger 1885:15-16, CW 1887:270, Fauerholdt 1914:15.
34 Sch. 5/1885:32-34.

35 Sch. 5/1885:34-36, cf. Faber in CW 1888:376.
36 Lhotzky 1904:140-143.
37 Sch. 16/1887:VII-VIII.
38 Lhotzky 1904:143.
39 SaH 1889:49-52.
40 WW 1885:6.
41 Sch. 4/1885:III-IV, cf. SaH 1884:106-110.
42 Sch. 5/1885:III.
43 SaH 1885:169.
44 Sch. 16/1887:VIII-IX.
45 SaH 1899:180.
46 Sch. 16/1887:V.
47 Sch. 4/1884:VI.
48 Sch. 5/1885:IV.
49 Nath. 1885/86:157.
50 SaH 1884:180-181.
51 de le Roi 1899:350.
52 Nath. 1896:53.
53 Nath. 1895:110-128.
54 Nath. 1896:41-56, 161-178.
55 Nath. 1897:34-35.
56 Hardeland 1895:363-368.
57 SaH 1896:84-102.
58 RdI 1887:133-135, MBI 1890:13-15.
59 Krüger 1885:79-132, SaH 1886:226-233.
60 Gartenhaus 1979:41, 178.
61 CMJ Minute-book c.30 item 1291.
62 CMJ Minute-book c.30 item 1445.
63 Zipperstein 1987:224.
64 Klier p. 48.
65 Klier p. 48-53 lists the following: Kievlianin no 20, 24/1(r) 1885 Novorossiiskii Telegraf no 2962, 12/1(r) 1885, Sanktpeterburgskie Vedomosti no 8, 8/1(r) 1885, Rukhovodstvo Dlia Selskikh Pastyrei no 16, 1885, Tserkovnyi Vestnik no 3, 19/1(r) 1885; no 2, 11/2(r) 1886, Rus no 24, 14/12(r) 1885, Tserkovno-Obshchestvennyi Vestnik no 7 16/1(r) 1885, Sovremennye Izvestiia no 43, 13/2(r) 1886; no 219, 11/8(r) 1886, Novoe Vremia no 4840, 20/8(r) 1889.
66 Novorossiiskii Telegraf no 2962, 12/1(r) 1885, Sanktpeterburgskie Vedomosti no 8, 8/1(r) 1885.
67 Rus no 24, 14/12(r) 1885.
68 Tserkovnyi Vestnik no 3, 19/1(r) 1885.
69 Tserkovnyi Vestnik no 2, 11/2(r) 1886.
70 Klier p. 42.

Chapter 9 (p.117)
1 Sch 4/1884:VI.
2 Kjær-Hansen 1982:152-208.
3 Kjær-Hansen 1992:30-34.
4 Sch. 20-21/1888:69-70.
5 Sch. 5/1885:37-38.
6 Sch. 5/1885:39-40.
7 Sch. 5/1885:23.
8 JEra 1893:200.
9 Rabinowitz 1897:29, 171.
10 SaH 1885:171.
11 SaH 1884:205-206.
12 SaH 1884:180-181.
13 Sch. 16/1887:45-49.
14 Sch. 16/1887:40.
15 Zipperstein 1987:218-219.
16 Venetianer 1888:13.
17 Ihlen 1947:106.
18 Sch. 4/1884:VI.
19 SaH 1885:44, Sch. 11/1887:40.
20 TT 1903:20.
21 SaH 1885:44.
22 Axelrud 1893, MTI 1895:90.
23 TT 1896:134-135.
24 Gordon 1895:12-13.
25 Lindhagen 1896:11.
26 Nath. 1898:9.
27 JEra 1897:107.
28 JH 1899:20-23.

Chapter 10 (p.127)
1 StPES 1886:26.
2 StPES 1887:50.
3 StPES 1888:35.
4 SaH 1885:181-2, MBI 1887:20-26, 36-38.
5 Adler 1885:11.
6 StPES 1887:50.
7 cf. Kahle 1964:176 n.32.
8 cf. Kahle 1964:176 n.34.
9 Nath. 1911:122.
10 MBI 1886:181.
11 MBI 1887:31-32.
12 StPES 1886:28.
13 MTI 1885:141.
14 Saphir 1888: 6-10.
15 Saphir 1888:10-21.
16 Venetianer 1888:10.
17 Venetianer 1888:10-11.
18 Venetianer 1888:11.
19 Ven. 1888:12-13, cf. Nath. 1895:134-135.

20 Venetianer 1888:13.
21 Saphir 1888:8, Venetianer 1888:23.
22 Sch. 16/1887:52-54.
23 JH 1888:69, 159-161, Saphir 1888:27-30.
24 JH 1888:159-160, Saphir 1888:29.
25 Saphir 1888:8.
26 Venetianer 1888:24.
27 JH 1888:161.
28 JH 1888:161, Saphir 1888:8, cf. RdI 1887:180-181.
29 Saphir 1888:29-30.
30 JH 1888:161.
31 Venetianer 1888:23-24.
32 Venetianer 1888:24-27.
33 Venetianer 1888:27.
34 RdI 1889:46.
35 Deutsche-Evangelische Kirchenzeitung 1888:215-216.
36 StPES 1888:42-44.
37 MBI 1885:15.
38 SaH 1889:46.
39 JH 1888:135-137.
40 JH 1888:32.
41 JH 1888:47.
42 JH 1888:135-136.
43 cf. Sch. 16/1887:53.
44 JH 1888:135.
45 JH 1888:137-138.
46 JH 1888:137.
47 SaH 1889:49.
48 Fül 1888:8-10, cf. also CW 1888:375-6.
49 StPES 1888:108.
50 Acc. to RdI 1888:161-162 in e.g. Rheinisch. Westf. Missionsblatt, 1888:61.
51 SaH 1889:40-49.
52 Smith 1890:361.
53 RdI 1889:12.
54 RdI 1889:27, cf. p. 25, Wilkinson 1906:35.
55 Zipperstein 1987:224.
56 RdI 1889:60.
57 StPES 1889:60, cf. 1888:319.
58 StPES 1894:90.
59 StPES 1900:314.
60 SaH 1885:171.

Chapter 11 (p.143)
1 Lhotzky 1904:115.
2 Kahle 1964:150.
3 JH 1899:23.

4 JI 1899:42, cf. TT 1896:135.

5 JH 1895:192.

6 RdI 1890:158.

7 JH 1888:140-142, SK 1889:220, Smith 1890:359-363.

8 FSCP 1896:31.

9 RdI 1895:86, MTI 1896:65, 87, cf. the title of Gordon's book from 1895 and Nath. 1891:187.

10 JH 1888:137.

11 RdI 1890:197.

12 Ch. 31/10 1890:26.

13 WW 1891:107.

14 RdI 1891:18, JH 1891:19.

15 RdI 1890:9.

16 RdI 1891:36-37, Nath. 1891:187.

17 TT 1897:165-166.

18 Nath. 1891:187.

19 Nath. 1891:187-189.

20 WW 1891:107, JH 1891:36, TT 1899:86-87.

21 Sch. 5/1885:25-26, JH 1885:45-46, cf. MBI 1885:9.

22 JC 231 1885.

23 SaH 1911:122.

24 Poulsen 1886:61-62.

25 Venetianer 1888:5-9.

26 Smith 1890:359-363.

27 MBI 1892:150-151.

28 Axelrud 1893:69-91, acc. to Nath. 1894:30-32, MTI 1895:84-91.

29 TT 1897:165-167.

30 RdI 1891:36-37, Nath. 1891:187-189.

31 Venetianer 1888:6.

32 RdI 1891:36.

33 Nath. 1891:187.

34 Smith 1890:359-360.

35 RdI 1891:37.

36 cf. Meyer 1983:93.

37 Nath. 1911:107.

38 MBI 1885:76.

39 Poulsen 1886:65.

40 Venetianer 1888:6-9.

41 Rabinowitz 1890a:6.

42 MBI 1885:76.

43 Smith 1890:360.

44 JH 1888:140-142.

45 Smith 1890:360.

46 JH 1889:198-199.

47 MBI 1892:150-151.

48 Axelrud 1893:69-91, Nath. 1894:30-32, MTI 1895:84-91.

49 TT 1897:165-167.

50 Nath. 1911:106-107.

51 SaH 1885:105, Baumgarten 1891:174.

52 Krüger 1885:71-77, Poulsen 1886:62-64.

53 Enc. Jud. XI, 1972:311, Wolf 1958:146-147.

54 Poulsen 1886:62.

55 Adler 1885:21.

56 Krüger 1885:71.

57 Sch. 4/1884:XVIII-XXII (Hebrew), p.29-39 (German).

Chapter 12 (p.155)

1 MBI 1885:76.

2 Zipperstein 1987:230 n.56.

3 Venetianer 1888:8, RdI 1891:18, 36f.

4 Tsitron 1923:128.

5 Wechsler 1885: 3-4, Sch. 9/1885:6, Nath. 1911:122, StPES 1886:27, SK 1885:136, 1889:220, JH 1885:34, 1889:199, MBI 1885:100, Ch. 21/9 1888:6.

6 Venetianer 1888:8-9.

7 Saphir 1888:21-27.

8 MTI 1887:76, cf. Ch. 17/6 1887:11, JH 1888:137.

9 CW 1888:376, MBI 1890:14.

10 Nath. 1891:186.

11 RdI 1891:20.

12 JH 1891:36.

13 MBI 1892:150.

14 Nath. 1894:31. MTI 1895:88.

15 WW 1891:107.

16 Nath. 1894:29.

17 RdI 1895:56, cf. p. 26.

18 RdI 1895:26.

19 CMJ 50/10:14.

20 Zipperstein 1987:230 n.56.

21 RdI 1895:56.

22 SK 1896:46.

23 RdI 1896:27.

24 JH 1895:192.

25 JH 1896:172.

26 MTI 1896:87.

27 TT 1896:84-85.

28 TT 1897:166.

29 TT 1896:135.

30 JI 1899:42, RdI 1899:25.

31 Zipperstein 1987:230 n.59.

32 WW 1885:6, Saphir 1888:4-6.
33 StPES 1886:27.
34 StPES 1893:52.
35 Priluker 1895:222.
36 MBI 1885:76.
37 Nath. 1911:122.
38 JC 1899:13.
39 TT 1913:29.
40 New Standard Jew. Enc. X, 1975:1456.

Chapter 13 (p.160)
1 MBI 1885:76, SaH 1885:170.
2 Sch. 16/1887:12-18.
3 Zipperstein 1987:209.
4 Zipperstein 1987:211.
5 Tsitron 1923:128.
6 Zipperstein 1987:217.
7 Sch. 5/1885:21-22.
8 MB 1906:140.
9 Lhotzky 1904: 117-119.
10 Sch. 5/1885:V, WW 1885:6.
11 JH 1885:17, RdI 1886:14.
12 WW 1885:156.
13 SK 1885:85.
14 Wilkinson 1908:211, SK 1885:93.
15 Wilkinson 1908:220.
16 MBI 1885:76.
17 SK 1885:136-137.
18 SK 1885:85.
19 SK 1885:108.
20 SK 1885:279.
21 Ihlen 1947:109.
22 MTI November 1885 (Cover), 1886:93-94, 1887:75-77, 1888:55.
23 JI 1886:72.
24 FCSP 1896:30.
25 SK 1887:60.
26 Saphir 1888:3-4.
27 Ch. 17/6 1887:11.
28 Saphir 1888:4.
29 SK 1887:60.
30 JH 1891:36.
31 CMJ d. 50/10:16.
32 Ch. 22/1 1889:23.
33 SK 1887:60.
34 JH 1888:140-142.
35 JH 1887:22.
36 MTI 1887:75-77.
37 Ch. 17/6 1887:11.

38 JH 1888:137.
39 MTI 1888:55.
40 RdI 1888:54.
41 RdI 1891:89, 1892:8, 1894:17 (Appendix), cf. RdI 1894:19.
42 FCSR 1897:15.
43 Zipperstein 1987:224.
44 CMJ d. 50/10:16.
45 Minute-book CMJ c.32 item 1547.
46 Zipperstein 1987:224-225.
47 Minute-book CMJ c.29 item 1001.
48 Minute-book CMJ c.29 item 1091.
49 Minute-book CMJ c.30 item 344.
50 CMJ d. 50/10:6.
51 Minute-book CMJ c.31 item 60.
52 Minute-book CMJ c.31 item 86.
53 CMJ d. 50/10:12.
54 TT 1899:194.
55 TT 1899:116.
56 Nath. 1885/86:154.
57 RdI 1886:14.
58 Saphir 1888:26.
59 Venetianer 1888:23.
60 Venetianer 1888:40.
61 MB 1906:140.
62 MB 1906:151.
63 SaH 1889:48, Dalman 1893:41.
64 Nath. 1911:123.

Chapter 14 (p.171)
1 SK 1887:37.
2 SK 1887:60.
3 SK 1887:37, 59.
4 SK 1887:60.
5 RdI 1887:19, SK 1887:39-40, 59-61, Ch. 3/3 1887:2.
6 JH 1887:22-24, Ch. 20/1 1887:11.
7 SK 1887:179.
8 SK 1887:40.
9 SK 1887:59.
10 SK 1887:60, Ch. 10/2 1887:22.
11 FCSR 1887:1.
12 FCSR 1886:29-30.
13 SK 1887:61.
14 SK 1889:219-220, RdI 1888:145.
15 RdI 1887:85-87.
16 SK 1887:40, Ch. 20/1 1887:11.
17 Ch. 24/3 1887:5.
18 Ch. 22/11 1887:23, JH 1890:11-14.
19 SK 1889:219-220.

20 JH 1888:140-142, RdI
1890:197.
21 RdI 1890:16-17.
22 RdI 1892:8, TT
1897:165.
23 RdI 1892:8.
24 Saphir 1888:23.
25 FCSR 1892:3-4.
26 Gartenhaus 1979:123-126
writes about Isak
Lichtenstein, but refers to
him as "Iechiel Lichtenstein".
The text to Zipperstein
1987:213 n. 21 is about Isak
Lichtenstein, whom
Zipperstein erroneously
takes for "Jehiel Zevi
Hirschensohn-Lichtenstein".
27 MBI 1908:175-176.
28 FCSR 1892:5.
29 SaH 1892:40-45.
30 FCSR 1889:24-25.
31 FCSR 1892:5.
32 RdI 1893:11, 42-44,
MTI 1893:32, FCSR
1893:1.
33 RdI 1893:42-44
34 FCSR 1893:1.
35 Lhotzky 1904:112-113.
36 FCSM 1896:159.
37 MTI 1894:30.
38 MTI 1893:172, RdI
1893:146-147.
39 RdI 1893:146-147.
40 RdI 1893:233-234.
41 MTI 1894:30.
42 MTI 1894:27-30, MBI
1894:45-47.
43 RdI 1894:99-100, MTI
1928:280-282.
44 TT 1896:134.
45 Sch. 44-46/1896.
46 Sch. 44-46/1896:17,
MBI 1895:122.
47 TT 1896:67.
48 FCSR 1897:1, 15.
49 RCS 1896:407.
50 TT 1896:84-85.
51 JH 1896:172.
52 TT 1896:134-135.

53 TT 1899:61.
54 TT 1899:88-89.

Chapter 15 (p.179)
1 Juster 1986:149.
2 Fül 1891:8-9.
3 RdI 1895:24-26.
4 RdI 1895:56.
5 RdI 1895:85.
6 Dalman 1893:92, MBI
1892:20-21.
7 TT 1897:167.
8 MTI 1896:65, 88.
9 MTI 1896:88.
10 Saphir 1888:24.
11 RdI 1890:95, 158-159,
1891:19-20, 36-38, 68.
12 TT 1896:134.
13 e.g. The Watchword
(Boston USA) acc. to Ch.
25/6 1896:23,
RdI 1896: 128-130, JH
1899:22-23.
14 Ch. 21/9 1888:6.
15 TT 1899:5.
16 FCSP 1896:32.
17 Ch. 22/11 1889:23.
18 JH 1890:11.
19 TT 1897:167.
20 TT 1897:165,
Wilkinson 1905:77.
21 Nath. 1894:29-32, Gabe
1987:87.
22 JH 1890:11-14, Ch. 22/
11 1889:23.
23 WW 1888:205.
24 Nath. 1885/86:156,
SaH 1885:170, 1899:180.
25 FCSR 1886:29.
26 FCSR 1886:31.
27 SaH 1885:174.
28 Ch. 24/3 1887:5.
29 MTI 1925:275.
30 Ch. 31/10 1890:26.
31 JH 1891:36.
32 MTI 1925:275.
33 FCSP 1896:31, RdI
1891:89, Gabe 1987:89.
34 SaH 1899:181.
35 RdI 1891:89.

36 Ch. 31/10 1890:26.
37 Ch. 20/12 1889:26.
38 SaH 1887:83-94.
39 MBI 1898:23.
40 SaH 1885:175.
41 JH 1888:47.
42 SaH 1891:154, JH
1891:36.

Chapter 16 (p.187)
1 See Bibliography,
Survey III,2.

Chapter 17 (p.192)
1 Tsitron 1923:129.
2 Zipperstein 1987:224.
3 Sch. 44-46/1895, Nath.
1895:97-128.
4 Sch. 44/1895:56-65.
5 Sch. 44/1895:11.
6 MBI 1895:109, Nath.
1895:103.
7 Nath. 1896:31-32.
8 Nath. 1897:124-125.
9 See Bibliography,
Survey III,1.
10 Zipperstein 1987:229
n.44.
11 RdI 1898:25.
12 The National Union
Catalog, Pre-1956
Imprints, 478, London
1976:225.
13 Zipperstein 1987:229
n.44.
14 Lhotzky 1904:143.
15 RdI 1898:2.
16 TT 1897:166.
17 RdI 1895:169, Rausch
1982:96.
18 TT 1898:96.
19 TT 1900:46.
20 Our Hope, January
1896, acc. to RdI 1896:60;
The Watchword, June
1896.
21 Ch. 25/6 1896:23, RdI
1896:60, 128-30.
22 FCSP 1896:31.
23 FCSP 1896:31.

24 Ch. 25/6 1896:23.
25 RdI 1896:60.
26 Nath. 1897:34.
27 TT 1896:67.
28 TT 1899:75.
29 TT 1899:56.
30 TT 1898:164.
31 TT 1899:61.
32 TT 1899:88-89.
33 SaH 1899:142-144, MBI 1899:175.
34 TT 1899:75.
35 TT 1899:75.
36 TT 1899:153.
37 TT 1901:20.
38 TT 1901:45.
39 TT 1901:106.
40 TT 1901:51.
41 TT 1897:167.
42 TT 1898:23.
43 TT 1898:171.
44 TT 1898:164.
45 TT 1899:5.
46 TT 1899:61.
47 TT 1899:83.
48 TT 1899:116.
49 MTI 1898:15, MBI 1898:58, cf. MBI 1935:138-140.

Chapter 18 (p.201)
1 TT 1899:61.
2 SaH 1899:142.
3 TT 1899:77.
4 SaH 1899:142.
5 TT 1899:77.
6 SaH 1899:143.
7 TT 1899:88-89.
8 SaH 1899:143.
9 TT 1899:85.
10 SaH 1899:143, TT 1899:90.
11 TT 1899:89.
12 TT 1899:105.
13 Tsitron 1923:129.
14 TT 1899:88.
15 TT 1899:107.
16 TT 1899:194.
17 SaH 1899:144.
18 TT 1899:85-88.

19 JH 1899:114-118.
20 MTI 1899:123-132.
21 MBI 1899:108-117.
22 Ch. 25/5 1899:22.
23 RdI 1899:108-109.
24 JI 1899:102-103.
25 JC 26/5 1899:13.
26 Gurland 1908:403-405.
27 JC 26/5 1899:22.
28 Sobel 1974:207 n.8.
29 Ihlen 1947:109.
30 StPES 1900:314.
31 Fauerholdt 1914:31-32.
32 Meyer 1983:44, Rausch 1982:97.
33 Jocz 1949:237.
34 Torm 1984:310.
35 Torm 1951:74.
36 TT 1899:83.
37 Schonfield 1936:226.

Chapter 19 (p.206)
1 MBI 1892:152.
2 MTI 1914:15-17.
3 TT 1911:90.
4 TT 1899:99.
5 TT 1899:89.
6 TT 1903:20.
7 TT 1903:124.
8 TT 1903:123.
9 TT 1899:99.
10 TT 1911:90.
11 TT 1911:90.
12 TT 1914:141.
13 TT 1919:103.
14 TT 1920:39.
15 MTI 1928:153-156.
16 StPES 1900:314.
17 TT 1925:96.
18 TT 1899:83, 88.
19 TT 1899:107.
20 TT 1899:176.
21 TT 1903:90-92.
22 MTI 1903:152-157.
23 TT 1903:122.
24 Wilkinson 1906.
25 TT 1903:124.
26 TT 1903:117.
27 TT 1898:158, 1903:124.
28 MTI 1925:275.

29 TT 1903:138.
30 TT 1903:149.
31 TT 1903:171.
32 TT 1910:165.
33 TT 1911:88-90.
34 TT 1912:3.
35 TT 1912:88.
36 TT 1912:164-165.
37 TT 1912:166.
38 TT 1912:178.
39 TT 1913:28-30.
40 TT 1913:35.
41 TT 1913:29-30.
42 TT 1913:3, 35.
43 TT 1913:28.
44 TT 1913:35-36.
45 MTI 1915:162, Stenberg 1925:113.
46 MTI 1914:15-17.
47 MTI 1915:162.
48 RGG VI, 1962:437-438, cf. V, 1961:1247-1248, Gabe 1987:88f.
49 TT 1909:85.
50 TT 1910:21.
51 TT 1910:25.
52 MTI 1914:16-17.
53 Stenberg 1925:120-121.
54 MTI 1918:32.
55 MTI 1918:35.
56 TT 1913:178.
57 TT 1917:39.
58 TT 1925:96.
59 Gabe 1987:40.
60 MBI 1921: 260-263.
61 TT 1919:11.
62 TT 1919:59.
63 TT 1922:28.
64 TT 1919:62.
65 TT 1919:86.
66 TT 1919:79.
67 TT 1920:67.
68 TT 1920:119.
69 TT 1921:19.
70 TT 1921:70.
71 TT 1921:110.

Chapter 20 (p.221)
1 TT 1922:103, 135, 1923:158.

2 TT 1927:110, 1929:11.
3 TT 1925:64, 1926:21-22, 1929:11.
4 TT 1924:127.
5 TT 1927:10.
6 TT 1924:32, Gabe 1987:88.
7 TT 1925:72, 1926:10.
8 TT 1927:110.
9 TT 1925:130.
10 TT 1926:19.
11 TT 1925:96, 130.
12 TT 1925:130.
13 TT 1925:9.
14 TT 1925:134-135.
15 TT 1926:9-10.
16 TT 1926:21-22.
17 TT 1927:10.
18 TT 1927:110.
19 TT 1927:79.
20 TT 1928:32.
21 TT 1928:50 cf. p. 38.
22 TT 1928:95, 115, 119, 131-132.
23 TT 1920:119, 1924:19, 1926:33, 1928:7-8.
24 Gabe 1991:50.
25 TT 1928:51.
26 TT 1929:11.
27 MTI 1928:205.
28 MTI 1928:208.
29 MBI 1929:29.
30 TT 1930:111, 1931:67, 114.
31 TT 1929:7-8, 1930:7-8, 1931:8-9,
1932:7.
32 TT 1934:7.
33 TT 1935:21-22.
34 TT 1935:69.
35 TT 1936:22-23.
36 TT 1929:3.
37 TT 1929:12.
38 TT 1934:7.
39 TT 1936:132, Gabe 1989:48.
40 MBI 1931:115, cf. Schonfield
1936:226.
41 MBI 1931:113-114.
42 TT 1937:8.
43 TT 1931:82.
44 TT 1936:132.
45 MBI 1935:138.
46 MBI 1935:139, MTI 1898:15, MBI
1898:58.
47 MBI 1935:140.
48 Gabe 1987:40.

49 Gabe 1989:51.
50 Gabe 1988:91.
51 TT 1937:75, cf. p. 69-70.
52 TT 1937:86.
53 TT 1937:90-91.
54 TT 1946:181-182.
55 Solheim 1981:114-118, Enc. Jud. X,
1972:1068.
56 TT 1945:166, Solheim 1981:161.
57 Solheim 1981:122.
58 Solheim 1981:132, MBI 1931:115.
59 Aniksdal, non-published diary
10.10.1942.
60 Haddal 1982:104-107.

Chapter 21 (p.231)

1 WW 1885:6, Saphir 1888:4-5.
2 de le Roi 1899:350.
3 Dalman 1893:42-43.
4 Acc. to Torm 1949:42-43.
5 OoI 1960:63.
6 Meyer 1964:339, Jocz 1981:143-144.
7 JI 1902:69.
8 Kjær-Hansen & Kvarme 1983, Kjær-
Hansen 1986.
9 e.g. Juster 1985 and 1986 and Mish. 2/
1985.
10 Maoz 1987:6.
11 Gartenhaus 1979:l50.
12 Jocz 1949:235-237.
13 Jocz 1949:254.
14 Juster 1986:IX.
15 Sch. 9/1885:31-32, SaH 1886:100-102,
Gredsted 1886:31-32.

BIBLIOGRAPHY AND SURVEYS

The Bibliography and Surveys include some writings by Rabinowitz which I have not been able to consult personally. Such writings are marked with an *. The original titles of a few writings are uncertain. The title is sometimes given in agreement with the relevant source where the title in question has been translated.

The Bibliography and Surveys are not exhaustive. E.g. articles in periodicals *about* Rabinowitz are not listed.

Abbreviations in Bibliography and Surveys: Apart from those used about the periodicals: D = Danish, E = English, F = French, G = German, H = Hebrew, N = Norwegian, NL = Dutch, R = Russian, S = Swedish, Y = Yiddish/jargon.

An = Anthology of Sermons = Rabinowitz 1897; Ax = Axelrud 1893; FD = Franz Delitzsch; Ha-Davar = Rabinowitz 1885.

I Periodicals consulted, and their Abbreviations

CaS	Church and Synagogue, London 1897.
Ch.	The Christian, A Weekly Record of Christian Life, Christian Testimony and Christian Work, London 1884ff.
CW	Die christliche Welt, Marburg 1887f.
FCSM	The Free Church of Scotland Monthly, Edinburgh 1887ff.
FCSP	Free Church of Scotland. Proceedings and Debates of the General Assembly, Edinburgh 1896.
FCSR	Free Church of Scotland. Report on the Conversion of the Jews, Edinburgh 1882ff.
FüI	Friede über Israel. Nachrichten aus dem Institutum Judaicum zu Leipzig, Leipzig 1888-1893.
HBO	Haboker Or, Warsaw 1879.
HM	Hamelitz. Wochenblatt für Politik und Literatur in hebraischer Sprache, St. Petersburg, 1870ff.
IM	Israelsmissionen, Horsens, Denmark 1906.
JEra	The Jewish Era. A Christian Quarterly. Published by The Chicago Hebrew Mission, 1893ff.
JC	The Jewish Chronicle, London 1884ff.
JH	The Jewish Herald and Record of Christian Work among the Jews, London 1883ff.
JI	The Jewish Intelligence: A Monthly Register of the London Society for promoting Christianity amongst the Jews, London 1884ff (from 1893: Jewish Missionary Intelligence).
MB	Missionsbudet, Copenhagen 1906.
MBI	Missions-Blad for Israel, Kristiania/Oslo 1882ff.
Mish.	Mishkan, Jerusalem 1984ff.
MTI	Missionstidning för Israel, Stockholm 1884ff.
Nath.	Nathanael, Zeitschrift für die Arbeit der evangelischen Kirche an Israel, Berlin 1885/86ff.
OoI	Ordet og Israel, Skjern, Denmark 1960.

RCS	Report by the Committee for the Conversion of the Jews to the General Assembly of the Church of Scotland, Edinburgh 1893ff.
RdI	Le Réveil d'Israël, Gaubert par Orgeres (Eure et Loire) 1886ff.
SaH	Saat auf Hoffnung, Erlangen/Leipzig 1882ff.
SC	The Scottish Congregationalist, Edinburgh 1885ff.
Sch.	Schriften des Institutum Judaicum in Leipzig, Leipzig 1884ff.
SK	Service for the King, London 1882ff.
StPES	St. Petersburgisches Evangelisches Sonntagsblatt, St. Petersburg 1882ff (from 1896: St. Petersburger...).
TT	Trusting and Toiling on Israel's Behalf, London 1895ff.
WW	Word and Work, London 1884ff.

II General Bibliography

Adler, J. (ed.) 1884	*The First-ripe Fig*, The remarkable Religious Movement amongst the Jews in South Russia...Edited by Professor Delitsch of Leipsig; Translated into English by Mr James Adler. And here prefaced by a letter in Hebrew and in English, received by Revd J. Wilkinson from Mr Rabinowitch, London (1884).
Adler, J 1885	A New and Enlarged Edition of *The First-ripe Fig*. Articles, Creed and Form of Worship of Joseph Rabinowitch and the Sons of the New Covenant. Translated from the Hebrew by Mr James Adler. Together with Mr Wilkinson's Account of his Personal Interview with Rabinowitch in Berlin and in Leipsig, London (1885).
Amishai-Maisels, Z. 1982	*The Jewish Jesus* - Journal of Jewish Art, IX, 1982:84-104.
Aniksdal, M.A., not publ.	*Dagbok for Den norske Israelsmisjon i Galatz.* 1/1 1940 - 4/9 1946. This non-published diary is in the possession of the Norwegian Israel Mission (= Norwegian Church Ministry to Israel).
Axelrud, J.R. (ed.) 1893*	German translation of Russian title: *Die Bewegung zum Christentum unter den Juden in Kischinew. Reden des Oberhaupts dieser Bewegung J.D. Rabinowitz*, acc. to Nath. 1894:29; acc. to Gabe 1987:87 also published in Yiddisch (?), Kischinew 1893.
Baumgarten, M. 1891	*Ein aus 45 jähriger Erfahrung geschorfter Beitrag zur Kirchenfrage*, in: H.H. Studt (ed.) II, Kiel 1891.
Book of Com. Prayer 1841	*Seder ha-Tefila* (Hebrew version), London 1841.
Clausen, E. 1923	*Jøde og Kristen*, Copenhagen 1923.
CMJ	*Archives of The Church's Ministry among the Jews* [The London Society], Bodleian Library, Oxford.
Dalman, G.H. (ed.) 1893	*Kurzgefasstes Handbuch der Mission unter Israel* (Schriften des Institutum Judaicum in Berlin Nr. 18), Berlin 1893.
de le Roi, J.F.A. 1884	*Die evangelische Christenheit und die Juden...Von der Reformation bis zur Mitte des 18. Jahrhunderts*, Karlsruhe und Leipzig 1884.
de le Roi, J.F.A. 1899	*Geschichte der evangelischen Judenmission seit Entstehung des neueren Judentums*, II, Leipzig 1899.

BIBLIOGRAPHY & SURVEYS   251

Delitzsch, F. (ed.), Sch. 4/
1884
Documente der national-jüdischen christgläubigen Bewegung in Südrussland. Im Original und deutscher Uebersetzung mitgetheilt von Franz Delitzsch (= Sch. 4/1884), Erlangen 1884.

Delitzsch, F., Sch. 5/1885
Fortgesetzte Documente der national-jüdischen christgläubigen Bewegung in Südrussland. Mitgeteilt von Franz Delitzsch (= Sch. 5/1885), Erlangen 1885.

Delitzsch, F., Sch. 9/1885
Zwei Predigten in dem Gotteshause Bethlehem in Kischinew gehalten von Joseph Rabinowitsch (= Sch. 9/1885), Leipzig 1885.

Delitzsch, F., Sch. 16/1887
Neue Documente der südrussischen Christentumsbewegung. Selbstbiographie und Predigten von Joseph Rabinowitsch. Herausgegeben von Franz Delitzsch (=Sch. 16/1887), Leipzig 1887.

Dobert, R. (ed.) 1971
Zeugnis für Zion. Festschrift zur 100-Jahrfeier des Evang.-Luth. Zentralvereins für Mission unter Israel e.V., Erlangen 1971.

Draitschmann, I. 1971
Von Kischinew nach Haifa, Schweiz 1971.

Dunlop, J. 1894
Memories of Gospel Triumphs among the Jews during the Victorian Era, London 1894.

Enc. Jud. 1972
Encyclopaedia Judaica, C. Roth & G. Wigoder (eds.), VII, XI, XII, XIII, Jerusalem 1972.

Fauerholdt, I. 1914
Joseph Rabinowitsch. Eine prophetische Gestalt aus dem neueren Judentum, (Kleine Schriften zur Judenmission), Leipzig 1914.

Gabe, E.S. 1987
The Hebrew Christian Movement in Kishineff. Articles in 16 parts in The Hebrew Christian 1987-1991.

Gartenhaus, J. 1979
Famous Hebrew Christians, Grand Rapids 1979.

Gidney, W.T. 1908
The History of the London Society for promoting Christianity amongst the Jews, from 1809 to 1908, London 1908.

Ginsburg, S.M. 1946
Meshumodim in tsarishn Russland, New York 1946.

Goldberg, M. 1934
Die Jahre 1881-1882 in der Geschichte der russischen Juden, Berlin 1934.

Gordon, Ph. 1890
Judarne i Helg och Söcken, Stockholm 1890.

Gordon, Ph. 1895
Betlehem. Josef Rabinowitz och kristendomsrörelsen bland judarne i södra Russland, Stockholm 1895.

Gredsted. Fr. 1886
To Prædikener, holdte i Gudshuset Bethlehem i Kischinew af Joseph Rabinowitsch..., Copenhagen 1886.

Gurland, R.H. 1908
In zwei Welten. Ein Lebensbild..., Gütersloh 1908.

Haddal, I. 1982
Jøder som fant hjem, Oslo 1982.

Hardeland, O. 1895
Geschichte der lutherischen Mission nach den Vorträgen des Prof. D. Plitt..., Leipzig 1895.

Harder, G. 1952/53
Christen und Juden wahrend der letzten 150 Jahre, in: Evangelische Theologie 1952/53:161-186.

Ihlen, Chr. 1947
Den norske Israelsmisjons historie i hundre år 1844-1944, Oslo 1947.

Jew. Enc. 1925
The Jewish Encyclopedia, New edition, I. Singer, Projector and Managing Editor, IX- X, New York - London 1925.

Jocz, J. 1949
The Jewish People and Jesus Christ, London 1949.

Jocz, J. 1981
The Jewish People and Jesus Christ After Auschwitz, Grand Rapids 1981

Juster, D. 1985   *Growing to Maturity. A Messianic Jewish Guide*, Rockville 1985.

Juster, D. 1986   *Jewish Roots. A Foundation of Biblical Theology for Messianic Judaism*, Rockville 1986.

Kahle, W. 1964   *Der Probst Rudolf Faltin und seine Arbeit an Israel in Kischinev*, in: Friede über Israel, 5/1964:150-160, 6/1964:171-181.

Kjær-Hansen, K. 1982   *Studier i navnet Jesus*, Aarhus 1982.

Kjær-Hansen, K. 1986   *Jøde-kristne spændingsfelter*, Århus 1986.

Kjær-Hansen, K. 1992   *Yehoshua, Yeshua, Jesus and Yeshu. An Introduction to the Names*, in: Mishkan 17-18, 1992-93:23-38.

Kjær-Hansen, K. & Kvarme,O.C.M. 1983   *Messianische Juden: Judenchristen in Israel*, Erlangen 1983

Klier, J.D., not publ. ms.   *Prejudice into Policy: The Jewish Question in Counter-Reform Era Russia*, 1881-1894.

Korff, F.W.A. 188?/ 189?   *Joseph Rabinowitsch. De beweging onder de joden in Rusland, een merkwaardig teeken des tijds.* Uitgegeven door de Nederlandsche Vereeniging voor Israel, Nijmegen.

Krüger, G.A. 1885   *Une église judéo-chrétienne en Bessarabie..*, Lausanne 1885.

Krüger,G.A.1889* (ed.)   *Exposé de la foi de peuple d'Israel fils de la nouvelle alliance*, Versailles 1889.

Krüger,G.A.1890* (ed.)   *Les Souffrances du Messie, sermon par Joseph ben David Rabinowitsch*, Paris 1890.

Lambroza, S. 1982   *The Pogrom Movement in Tsarist Russia 1903-06*, Ann Arbor, Michigan 1982.

Laskov, Sh. 1982   *Documents on the History of Hibbat-Zion and the Settlement of Eretz Israel.* First Compiled and Edited by Alter Druyanow. New Revised Edition by Shulamit Laskov, Vol.I: 1870-1882, Tel-Aviv 1982.

Lhotzky, H. 1904   *Eine Judengeschichte aus unseren Tagen*, in: J. Müller (ed.) *Blätter zur Pflege persönlichen Lebens*, VII, 110-156), Leipzig 1904.

Lindhagen, T. 1896   *Föredrag öfver Josef Rabinowitz*, Stockholm 1896.

Lippe, Ch.D. 1881   *Lippe's Bibliographisches Lexicon der gesammten jüdischen Literatur der Gegenwart und Adress-Anzeiger*, Wien 1881.

Mahler, E. 1916   *Handbuch der jüdischen Chronologie*, Frankfurt a. Main 1916, Hildesheim 1967.

Maoz, B. 1987   *The Gospel Scene in Israel*, Chislehurst 1987.

Mathieson, J.E. 1899*   *Rabinowitsch and his Mission to Israel. A Retrospect*, London 1899.

Meisl, J. 1930   *Nowij Israel*, in: Jüdisches Lexikon, IV/2, 347-348, Berlin 1930.

Meyer, H. (ed.) 1964   *Die Kirche und das jüdische Volk. Bericht über eine Konsultation*, in: Lutherische Rundschau XIV, 1964.

Meyer, L. 1983   *Louis Meyer's Eminent Hebrew Christians of the Nineteenth Century. Brief Biographical Sketches.* Edited with an Introduction by David A. Rausch, New York and Toronto 1983.

New Standard Jew. Enc. 1975   *The New Standard Jewish Encyclopedia*, C. Roth & G. Wigoder, (eds.) New, revised edition, X, London 1975.

Nielsen, Fr. (ed.) 1887   *Josef Rabinowitschs Levned fortalt af ham selv*, Copenhagen 1887.

Poulsen, A.S. 1886   *Den jødekristelige Bevægelse i Syd-Rusland*, Copenhagen 1886.

Poulsen, A.S. 1889   *Israelsmissionen. Et udvidet Foredrag*, Copenhagen 1889.

Priluker, J. 1895   *Under the Czar and Queen Victoria. The Experiences of a Russian Reformer*, London (1895).

Rabinowitz, J.   **See the end of this section**

Rausch, D.A. 1982   *Messianic Judaism: Its History, Theology, and Polity*, New York 1982.

Rejzen, Z. 1929   *Leksikon fun der yidisher literatur, prese un filologie*, Vol.IV, Vilna 1929.

Rengstorf, K.H. & Kortzfleisch, S. von 1968, 1970   *Kirche und Synagoge. Handbuch zur Geschichte von Christen und Juden*. I, Stuttgart 1968, II, Stuttgart 1970.

RGG 1961, 1962   *Die Religion in Geschichte und Gegenwart*, V, Tübingen 1961, VI, Tübingen 1962.

Saphir, A. 1885   *The Everlasting Nation*, London 1885 (?).

Saphir, A. 1888 (ed.)   *Rabinowich and his Mission to Israel*, London (1888).

Schonfeld, S. (ed.) 1974   *The Standard Siddur-Prayer Book with an orthodox English Translation*, London 1974.

Schonfield, H.J. 1936   *The History of Jewish Christianity. From the First to the Twentieth Century*, London 1936.

Smith, G. 1890   *A modern Apostle. Alexander N. Somerville, D.D. 1813-1889*, London 1890.

Sobel, B.Z. 1974   *Hebrew Christianity: The Thirteenth Tribe*, New York 1974.

Solheim, M. 1981   *I skuggen av hakekross, hammar og sigd*, Oslo 1981.

Stenberg, H. 1925   *På Israels skördefält. Svenska Israelsmissionens arbete under femtio år*, Stockholm 1925.

Torm, A. 1949   *Kristne jøder i trange kår*, Copenhagen 1949.

Torm, A. 1984   *Er du Kristus? Jødisk syn over for kristen tro*, Copenhagen 1984.

Torm, F. 1909   *Fortællinger af Israelsmissionens Historie*, Copenhagen 1909.

Torm, F. 1951   *Israelsmissionens Historie*, Copenhagen 1951.

Tsitron, Sh.L. 1923, 1925   *Me-Achorei Ha-Pargod*, Vol.I, Vilna 1923, Vol.II, Vilna 1925.

Ussing, H. 1908   *Evangeliets Sejrsgang ud over Jorden*, Copenhagen 1908.

Venetianer, A. 1888   *In Kischinew. Bei Rabinowitsch I.II*, Wien 1888.

Wagner, S. 1978   *Franz Delitzsch. Leben und Werk*, München 1978.

Wechsler, J. (ed.) 1885   *Leku we-Neshuwa (Two Sermons by Joseph Rabinowitz)*, Leipzig 1885.

Wilkinson, S. 1905   *In the Land of the North. The Evangelization of the Jews in Russia*, London (1905).

Wilkinson, S.H. (ed.) 1906   *Ruin and Relief*, London 1906 (no name of the author).

Wilkinson, S.H. 1908   *The Life of John Wilkinson, The Jewish Missionary*, London 1908.

Wolff, P. 1891   *Den judekristna rörelsen i södra Ryssland (= A.S. Poulsen 1886)*, Söderhamn 1891.

Zipperstein, S.J. 1987   *Heresy, Apostasy and the Transformation of Joseph Rabinovich*, in Todd Endelman (ed.) Jewish Apostasy in the Modern World, pp. 206-231. New York/London 1987.

Rabinowitz J. - Selected Hebrew correspondent articles up to and including 1882

Ha-Tsefirah   2 June 1876 (acc. to Zipperstein 1987:227 n.6).
Haboker Or   1879:1069-1072, 1131-1141.
Hamelitz   1872:119-120, 1872:156, 1873:44-45, 1878:478-479, 514-515, 538-539,
                       1879:201-203, 1880:171-173, 194-195, 214-216, 1882:376-378, 1882:608.
Kol Mevasser   1870:61 (acc. to Rejzen 1929:33).

Rabinowitz, J. - Various Writings

1881   *Application to the Governor of Bessarabia*, 6/11 1881, R*, G Nath. 1885:150-
            151 with a translation of the first paragraph of the statutes for the agricultural
            colony, p. 151.

1885   *Ha-Davar Asher Darash. Joseph Rabinowitz be-Beit Elohim - Beit Lehem be-
            Kishinev...* (sermons 3/8(r) and 5/10(r) 1885), Kishinev 1885.

1885a   *Tefila* H* (see Survey III,1).

1886   *Sermon on Christmas Eve* 24/12 (r) 1885, title unknown, Y* bilingual H* and
            Y*, Kishinev 1886 (acc. to Sch. 16/1887:51).

1886a   *Gospel Harmony*, title unknown, H*, Kishinev 1886 (see Survey III,1).

1887   G* *Das Wort, welches I. Rabinowitsch hat gepredigt in Gotthaus "Beth Lechem"
            in Kischinew*, 17 October 1887 (acc. to the Voskhod 1888:45-46).

1890   *In was besteht der jüdischer Unglück*, German version of unknown title, Y*,
            Kishinev 1890 (see Survey III,1).

1890a   *Rede gehalten am 16. Juni 1890 im Bethause "Bethlehem" der Israeliten des
            Neuen Bundes in Kischinew von Joseph Rabinowitz*, Odessa 1890.

1892   *Tefila we-Ikarei Emuna le-Bnei Brit Chadasha*, Kishinev 1892.

1894   *Was ist a Isra'el ben b'rith chadascha*, Y*, Kishinev 1894.

1897   *Devarim Nechumim...Kishinev 1897* (Anthology of sermons).

1897a   *Jesus of Nazareth, the King of the Jews*, English version of unknown title, Y*,
            Kishinev 1897 (see Survey III,1).

Texts by Rabinowitz published by others

See Adler 1884 and 1885, Axelrud 1893, Delitzsch (Sch. 1884-1887), Gredsted 1886,
Nielsen 1887, Korff, Krüger 1885, 1889, 1890, Wechsler 1885 and Wolff 1891. Cf. Surveys
below.

Rabinowitz, J. - not published

1884   *Sinai und Horeb oder Priester und König*, H*, German version of title in Hebrew
            ms (acc. to Sch. 5/1885:32-36, Sch. 16/1887:VII, Lhotzky 1904:140).

Rabinowitz, J. - Selected Poetry

1884	*Mi uM'i*, H Sch. 4/1884 (verso of title page).
1884	*Prosa-Uebersetzung eines hebräischen Gedichts von J.R.*, G Sch. 5/ 1885:37-38.
21/12 (r) 1884	*Lied auf die Geburt Jeschuas des Maschiach*, Y* (Appendix in Siddur/ Order of Service, acc. to SaH 1899:144), G SaH 1899:145-147, N MBI 1900:161-162 (in part), D IM 1906:81-82 (in part).
1885	*Das Kischinewer Lied*, Y Sch. 20-21/1888: 69-70.
1885	*Brüder, bnei Jisroel*, Y* Appendix in Sermon 9/11(r) 1885, acc. to FD Sch. 16/1887:51.
1886	*Jeschua, du bist mein Goël, mein Retter, was horch ich meine Son'im [Hasser] die Spötter?* Y* in Christmas sermon 1886, see Rabinowitz 1886:14 (Sermon on Christmas Eve, bi-lingual ed.) acc. to FD Sch. 16/1887:51.
1886	*Verlassen wärst du? Nein mit nichten!* H* in Sermon 2/8 (r) 1886, acc. to Sch. 16/1887:51.
1886	*Neie Motiven für den jüdischen Volk von a jüdischen Bruder*, Y*. First booklet, Kishinev 1886, acc. to FD Sch. 16/1887:51.

III Surveys

1 Publication of Rabinowitz's theological documents, tracts, pamphlets, articles etc.

The Thirteen Theses 1883	H* Kishinev (acc. to Rejzen 1923:34), H Sch. 4/1884:III-V, G Sch. 4/1884:1-5 + SaH 1884:108-110 + StPES 1885:27, E Adler 1884:12-14, F Krüger 1885:29-32, NL Korff:13-16.
The Twelve Articles of Faith 1884	H CMJ d.50/10, E JH 1884:118-119, N MBI 1884:174-175.
The Ten Articles of Faith 1884	H Sch.4/1884:VI-IX, G: 6-13, E Adler 1884:14-18, F Krüger 1885:32-38.
An Exposition of the Ten Articles of Faith 1884	H Sch. 4/1884:X-XVII, G:14-28, E JH 1884:129-132, 141-142 (Roeder), E Adler 1884:18-29, F Krüger 1885:38-53, N MBI 1884:168-173 (Part 1).
Easter Haggada 1884	H Sch. 4/1884:XVIII-XXII, G 29-39, E JH 1885:1-3 (Roeder), E Adler 1884:29-36, F Krüger 1885:63-71.
Kol Kore 17/11 (r?) 1884	H* Y* R* (planned acc. to Sch. 5/1885:37), E WW 1884:787, G Sch. 5/1884:37-38, S Gordon 1895:14-15.
Order of Service (1884-85)	H* 1884-85 (acc. to SaH 1885:105). H Tefila 1892:3-13, G* 1884-85 (acc. to Baumgarten 1891:174). E Adler 1885:21-23 (only Morning Service), F Krüger 1885:71-77 (only Morning Service).
The Twenty-Four Articles of Faith (1884-85)	H* 1884-85 (acc. to Krüger 1885:56-59), H Tefila 1892:17-28, E Adler 1885:24-28 (with 25 Articles), G* (acc. to Krüger 1885:56 translated by FD), F Krüger 1885:53-61.

The Seven Articles of   H* 1885 (?), H Tefila 1892:14-16, G Sch. 9/1885:29-30, E
Faith/Credo/Symbol   Adler 1885:28-29, D Gredsted 1886:29-30, D Poulsen 1886:56-
1884-85   57, F Krüger 1885:62-63, S Gordon 1895:20-21.

Article/Reader's Letter   R* Odesski Listok 20/1 (r) 1885, G Nath. 1885:153-154, F
19/1 1885   Krüger 1885:143-144.

Gospel Harmony 1886   H* Kischinew 1886 (probably referred to as Buch von
irdischen Leben und der wahrhaftigen Lehre des Herrn
Jesu Christi, acc. to FD Sch.16/1887:51. 12§§ including
Jesus in the Temple).

Autobiography 1887   G Sch.16/1887:1-33, D Nielsen 1887:6-26, E JH 1887:78-
80 (abridged), E SC 1890:178-182 (abridged), E CaS 1897:49-
59 (abridged), F RdI 1888:4, 26-27, 109-112, 145-147
(paraphrased), N MBI 1887:153-157, 164-170 (abridged), S
MTI 1888:9-15 (abridged).

In was besteht der jüdischer   Y* 1890 (acc. to Nath. 1891:186), R* Ax. 1893 (acc. to
Unglück 1890   Nath. 1894:30).

Tefila 1892   H (with a prayer for the Czar in R - presumably a reprint
of an ed. from 1884-85, contents: worship liturgy with
Symbol and the Twenty-Four Articles of Faith and Is. 53),
Kishinev 1892.

Appeal to Jews in North   H An 1897:166-173 (written before the journey to America
America 1893   in the summer of 1893).

Was ist a Isra'el ben b'rith   Y* Kischinew 1894, G Nath. 1895:129-135, (the end), E*
chadascha 1894   London 1895: What is an Israelite of the New Covenant?
(acc. to TT 1895:190).

Article before May 1896   R* Bratskoe Pomosh, E* (hardly publ., acc. to FCSP
1896:32).

Jesus of Nazareth, the King   Y* [1897?] (cf. above Ch. 17; title perhaps: Jeschua Hanotzri,
of Jews 1897   reprint 1900), E (revised and abridged by A.C. Gaebelein),
New York [1898?].

(NT in Yiddish 1896-99)   Co-worker on a revision of NT in Yiddish, published
London 1901 (cf. above Chap.17).

2 Publication of some of Rabinowitz's sermons and speeches

(Unless otherwise stated, the dating follows the Russian calendar.)

8/6 1885   Num. 19:1-14, John 5: H Wechsler 1885:3-10, H An 1897:142-154, G
Sch. 9/1885:5-18, D Gredsted 1886:7-19.

29/6 1885   Num. 35:9-34, Matt. 5:1-27: H Wechsler 1885:11-16, H An 1897:155-
165, G Sch. 9/1885:18-28, N MBI 1885:161-168, D Gredsted 1886:19-
28, NL Korff: 38ff.

3/8 1885   Deut. 17:4-20, 1 Sam. 16, Luke 22:24-39: Ha-Davar 1885:3-13, H An
1897:5-23.

5/10 1885   Gen. 12:1-9, Is. 45:25, John 8,51-59: H Ha-Davar 1885:17-27, H An
1897:24-39.

17/8 1885   Deut. 28, Matt. 25:31-46: Hebrew Ms. in FD's possession (acc. to Sch.
16/1887:50).

12/10 1885   Gen. 18:1-15, Is. 40,27, Rom. 15:1-15: H* in book, Kishinev 1885 (acc.
to FD Sch. 16/1887:50-51), H An 1897:40-50 (An gives the year 1886
for this and the next two sermons).

19/10 1885	Gen. 23, Mark 12:18-27: H* (like the previous sermon), H An 1897:51-65.
9/11 1885	Gen. 32-33, Jer. 17:6-8, Matt. 7:21-29: H* (like the previous sermon), H An 1897:66-94).
24/12 1885	Christmas gospel: Y* Kishinev 1886, H* Y* Kishinev 1886.
11/4 1885	Good Friday, Zech. 12:10-13,1: R* in a Russian paper (acc. to JI 1886:142), H* Ms. in FD's possession (acc. to Sch. 16/1887:51), E JI 1886:120-121.
22/4 1886	Is. 46:5, John 19:7: H An 1897:113-121.
1/6 1886	Pentecost sermon, R* leaflet (acc. to FD Sch. 16/1887:51), G Sch. 16/1887:27-33, R* Ax 1893.
5/7 1886	(Num. 27:12ff, John 10,11): R* leaflet (acc. to FD Sch. 16/1887:51), R* Ax 1893, G Sch. 16/1887:34-41, N MBI 1888:3-5.
12/7 1886	Speech on receiving permission from the authorities to aquire a burial ground: R* (acc. to Faltin MBI 1886:136), R* Ax 1893, G Sch. 16/1887:42-44, N MBI 1888:3-5.
2/8 1886	Deut. 3:23-26, Is. 29:1-5, Luke 11,1-14: H* leaflet (acc. to FD Sch. 16/1887:51), H An 1897:95-112.
22/4 1888	Good Friday: H* (acc. to Nath. 1891:186), H An 1897:113-121, G Venetianer 1888:30-31 (excerpt), G SaH 1889:52-54 (partial).
7/4 1889	Good Friday, Is. 53, Luke 23:27-44: H* (acc. to Nath. 1891:186), H An 1897:122-141, G* Gordon 1895:26, S Gordon 1895:25-34.
16/6 1890	Num. 21:4-9, John 3:14f: Y* (acc. to Nath. 1891:186), G in Rabinowitz 1890a, R* Ax 1893.
19/4 1891	Good Friday, Ps. 69:8, Matt. 27:9: R* Ax 1893, G Nath. 1894:22-29, N MBI 1894:33-37.
24/12 1895	Christmas sermon Y* (or H*), (acc. to MBI 1898:23).
22/5 1896 (r = 10/5)	Speech from English manuscript at the general assembly of the Free Church of Scotland, FCSP 1896:29-32.

3 Extract of Rabinowitz's correspondence

The main part of the letters below (or excerpts of these) were written in Hebrew. They are listed according to the languages to which they were translated and in which they were published. (r) after a date indicates certainty that the Russian/Julian calendar was used. A date without (r) indicates doubt as to which calendar system was used when the letters were published.

English
W.E. Blackstone 18/9 1894: JEra 1894:19. 25/9 1897: JE 1897:106-107.
A.C. Gaebelein 1894-95: Our Hope,I, February 1895 (acc. to Rausch 1982:113 n.14).
London Society 8/5 (r) 1886: JI 1886:142.
Andrew Moody 22/2 1889: FCSR 1889:24-25.
Nahum Nürnberg 29/3 1886: JI 1886:72-73.
The 900th Anniversary of the Russian Church: Ch. 21/9 1888:6.
A. Saphir 1/3 1887: Ch. 24/3 1887:5. 17/5 1887: Ch. 17/6 1887:11. Aug./Sept. 1888: Ch. 21/9 1888:6.

C.A. Schönberger 28/7 1887: Saphir 1888:27-30. 30/1 1888: JH 1888:47,
   (NL Korff:51-53). 2/4 1888: JH 1888:135-136. 14/5 1888: JH 1888:137.
John Wilkinson 30/8 (r) 1884: SK 1884:252-254, Adler 1884:9-11, Wilkinson 1908:209-
   211, (N MBI 1884:185-186, S MTI 1885:5-6). 8/10 1884: WW 1884:668. Nov. 1884: WW
   1884:787. Jan. 1885: WW 1885:156. 6/2 1885: WW 1885:156. 15/2 (r) 1885:WW
   1885:156, SK 1885:84-85. 3/3 1885: SK 1885:85. 6/4 1885: Adler 1885:44-46. 30/4 1885:
   Adler 1885:49-50, SK 1885:136. Oct. 1885: SK 1885:278-279. Late summer 1893: SK 1893
   E* (presumably), (S MTI 1894:27-30, N MBI 1894:45-47).
Samuel Wilkinson 16/8 (r) 1896: TT 1896:134-135. 15/1 1898: TT 1898:23. 30/10 1898:
   TT 1898:171. 22/2 (r) 1899: TT 1899:61.
J.H. Wilson 12/3 1888: FCSM 1888:137-138.

French

G.A. Krüger 26/10 1888: RdI 1889:23-27. 27/12 1889: RdI 1890:24-25. 6/9 1892: RdI
   1892:192-193. 13/1 (r) 1893: RdI 1893:42-44. 28/3 (r) 1895: RdI 1895:85-86.
E.H. Leitner beginning of 1889: RdI 1889:60-62.

Hebrew

J. Wilkinson 30/8 (r) 1884: Adler 1884:8-4 (see English).

Yiddish

V. Pashkov 18/3 (r) 1887: Hambaseir Toiv 193?, The Hebrew Christian 1987:89.

Swedish

The Swedish Israel Mission 7/5 1886: MTI 1886:93-94. 26/4 1887: MTI 1887:75-76. New
   Year 1888: MTI 1888:55. Summer 1891: MTI 1891:158.

German

Anonymous American kinsman and fellow-believer June 1885: Sch. 16/1887:45-49, (D
   ed. Nielsen 1887:29-32).
G. Dalman 4/3 (r) 1888: SaH 1889:46. 23/4 1891: Nath. 1891:187-189.
F. Delitzsch 15/6 (r) 1884: Sch. 5/1885:30. 9/7 (r) 1884: Sch. 1884:30-32, (E JH 1884:46).
   4/9 (r) 1884: Sch. 1884:32-34. 8/8 (r) 1888: SaH 1889:49, (F RdI 1889:65).
W. Faber 1/6 (r) 1884: Sch. 5/1885:29. 16/10 (r) 1884: Sch. 5/1885:15-23, (E JH 1885:18-
   20, E Adler 1885:34-39, N MBI 1885:7-9, S MTI 1885:121-122).
J. Müller beg. of 1891: SaH 1891:153-154, (F RdI 1891:140-141, N MBI 1891:110-111).
   18/10 (r) 1891: SaH 1892:40-45.
A. Saphir turn of the year 1890/1891: (G SaH 1891:152-153).
C.A. Schönberger 25/7 (r) 1888: SaH 1889:49-52, (F RdI 1889:62-65).
H.L. Strack 27/3 (r) 1885: Nath. 1885/86:156.

INDEX OF PERSONAL NAMES

INDEX OF SCRIPTURE REFERENCES